LEADERSHIP
IN THE
MODERN
PRESIDENCY

Edited by Fred I. Greenstein

Harvard University Press
Cambridge, Massachusetts
and London, England

Library of Congress Cataloging-in-Publication Data

Leadership in the modern presidency / edited by Fred I. Greenstein.
   p.   cm.
   Bibliography: p.
   Includes index.

   ISBN 0-674-51855-1 (paper)
   1. Presidents—United States—History—20th century.   2. Political
leadership—United States—History—20th century.   3. United States—
Politics and government—20th century.   I. Greenstein, Fred I.
E176.1.L33 1988   87-27801
973.9'092'2—dc19   CIP

To the memory of
Wilbur J. Cohen
president watcher and aide to presidents
June 10, 1913–May 18, 1987

CONTENTS

Leadership in the Modern Presidency

INTRODUCTION

Toward a Modern Presidency

Fred I. Greenstein

Two premises underlie the following accounts of the leadership of the nine presidents who held office during the fifty-six years from Franklin D. Roosevelt's inauguration in 1933 through Ronald Reagan's second term. The first is that American presidents strongly influence public policy. The second is that the impact of the president is almost invariably a function of the personal leadership qualities he brings to and displays in office, as well as of the political context of his presidency.

Neither premise is likely to be surprising to most Americans; it is not difficult to pinpoint specific administrations as the sources of quite literally life-and-death importance. For example, Americans' quality of life is significantly influenced by welfare policies such as Social Security and Medicare that had their roots in the leadership of Presidents Franklin D. Roosevelt and Lyndon B. Johnson. The deadly significance of the president's responsibility to exercise the final word in deployment of nuclear weapons is well known. The ominous significance of this aspect of presidential power was documented in the 1962 Cuban missile crisis. President Kennedy was to observe that the odds of a nuclear exchange between the United States and the Soviet Union in that episode had been "between one out of three and even" and that in such an exchange 100 million Americans, 100 million Soviet citizens, and millions in other nations would have perished.[1]

It *is* surprising that scholars have not previously acted on a major implication of the two premises. If the potentialities and limitations of the presidency are a function of its incumbents' performance, it follows that understanding of the presidency as an institution of government must be rooted in an understanding of how individual presidents have carried out their responsibilities. The following accounts of the leadership of modern presidents should therefore be understood both as analyses of the performance of individual presidents and as parts of an effort to assess the presidency itself.

The impact of modern presidents on public policy need not be apocalyptic to be important. During the years covered by this analysis there have been massive increments to the *Statutes at Large*. It is difficult to think of any American laws of consequence passed since Roosevelt took office that were not in some way influenced by presidents. Furthermore, as the bulging pages of the *Federal Register* testify, much of contemporary public policy is made directly by executive order.

To say that presidents put their imprint on policy is by no means to say that they are omnipotent policymakers. Presidents rarely achieve their aims without compromise and periodically have been stalemated, sometimes to the point of becoming politically impotent. Indeed, four of the nine presidents under consideration here—Johnson, Nixon, Ford, and Carter—left office for want of support: Johnson announcing he would not run again in the wake of massive disenchantment with his "success" at committing the nation to a land war in Southeast Asia, Nixon resigning lest he be impeached and convicted, Ford and Carter defeated at the polls.

The seeds of both successful and failed presidential leadership can be found in the complex, contradictory role requirements of the presidency itself. Some of these persist from the period of the framing of the Constitution. Some result from incremental changes in expectations during the nineteenth century and the first third of the twentieth about the role of presidents in the policy-making process, and some result from the transformation in the 1930s of the traditional presidency into the modern variant that is the concern of this volume.

Since its invention in the Philadelphia convention of 1787, the presidency has been sometimes strengthened and sometimes weakened by being part of a system of separated powers. Separation of powers ensures the stability of the chief executive by enabling him to stay in office despite congressional opposition to policies. But the separation of powers also limits the president's ability to attain his goals by not making the executive and legislature parts of a unified team. The open-endedness of the characterization in Article 2 of the president's responsibilities leaves him much latitude for initiative in national affairs but also exposes him to punishment by Congress and other political entities for allegedly illegitimate use of his powers. The condensation of head of state and chief politician in a single presidency also produces a role strain. As head of state the president needs to be a national unifier, much like a constitutional monarch; yet as politician he must also be responsive to the intrinsically divisive demands made of prime ministers in other democracies. This conjunction can enhance the president's influence by reinforcing policy appeals with patriotic emotions, but it can also have the reverse effect of holding presidents to unrealistically idealized standards of comportment and performance.

Periodically, the presidency has changed, either temporarily or for good. One kind of change has been simple variation from president to president in will and skill to make effective use of the persisting components of the presidential role and to avoid their perils. A number of changes in single aspects of the president caught on. There were shifts early in the nineteenth century to popular election and to increasing acceptance of the veto as a normal presidential power rather than as an exceptional procedure to be used only if the president doubts the constitutionality of congressional enactments. The activist presidents of the early twentieth century, Theodore Roosevelt and Woodrow Wilson, established a precedent by appealing directly to the public, in contrast to the eighteenth- and nineteenth-century practice of directing persuasive communications mainly to Congress.[2]

During Franklin Roosevelt's administration, in response to presidential leadership and such social and political conditions as the Great Depression, World War II, and the availability of network radio, the presidency began to change in at least four major ways. These added up to so thorough a transformation that a modifier such as "modern" is needed to characterize the post-1932 manifestations of the institution that had evolved from the far more circumscribed traditional presidency.[3]

Like such persisting characteristics of the presidency as its embeddedness in the separation of powers and the hybrid requirement that the president be both head of state and political leader, the new attributes of the chief executive's role are double-edged. Compared with traditional presidents:

1. Modern presidents have far greater formal and informal power to make decisions on their own initiative, but the continuing pluralism of American institutions and society and the potential for backlash in response to the president's actions create the danger that a president's use of command power will weaken rather than enhance his leadership.

2. Modern presidents have come to be the chief agenda setters in federal-level policy-making, but the advent of official presidential programs that are the centerpiece of Washington politics has also led presidents inevitably to create expectations that they can rarely fulfill.

3. Modern presidents have been provided with a major staff and advisory capacity, but a presidential bureaucracy can be a liability as well as a strength: aides can not only help their boss but can also abuse power in the president's name, distort the information he receives, and contribute to other organizational pathologies.

4. Modern presidents have become by far the most visible actors in the political system, overshadowing even the most influential legislators, but the political leverage deriving from this visibility is offset by the danger of becoming the scapegoat for national woes.[4]

The delicate balance between success and failure built into the job of the modern president is made more precarious by the intractability of many of the national and international problems arising from the social and political changes of the past century, as well as from a political system that remains remarkably true to its founders' intentions in its capacity to restrain the chief executive. Indeed, President Reagan's frequent difficulty in achieving his ends after the dazzlingly successful first year of his first term, as well as the inability of his four predecessors to succeed in serving two full terms, has led to characterizations of the presidency as a "no-win" office.

Clearly, if presidents and their administrations simply were doomed to political failure, there would be little need to attend to their leadership. There are, however, two broad reasons why presidents can and do succeed in making an impact and therefore why close scrutiny of the properties of each president and his associates is essential.

1. The job of the president is extraordinarily ill defined and ambiguous. This is illustrated by the wide diversity of presidential

operating practices, extending to such personal variants as Roosevelt's tendency to foster palace politics, Eisenhower's attention to team building and staff work, Kennedy's stress on collegial informality, and Carter's style of solitary work and personal synthesis of information and advice. On a continuum from ambiguity to structured constraint, the presidency is as close to the former as repetitive assembly-line work is to the latter. And the more ambiguous the definition of a role, the more it will of necessity be shaped by the personal makeup of the individual who fills it.

2. Even though the presidency and its circumstances can hamstring the incumbent, presidents can also take actions that have significant and occasionally momentous impact. The most vivid example is the president's capacity to deploy strategic nuclear weapons. Less dramatic illustrations abound. Thus, President Ford, at a time when he had little support on Capitol Hill or from the general public, was nevertheless able to use the veto often and with great effect. And the greater the actor's potential impact on historical outcomes, the more important the actor's makeup, even if the actor's role itself is quite *unambiguous*.[5]

In Chapters 1 through 9, authorities on each of the modern presidents from Roosevelt to Reagan dip into their continuing research to discuss the elements that they consider central to the leadership of the presidents they study. In Chapter 10, I present a synthesis. As samplings of the work in progress of nine investigators with varying intellectual sensitivities and disparate protagonists, the chapters on the individual presidents inevitably differ in emphasis.

In assessing Roosevelt, a president whose influence some scholars seek to diminish, William Leuchtenburg asks and answers affirmatively the counterfactual question, "If Roosevelt had not been president, would it have made a difference?" In his effort to decipher the "little man" who followed FDR and whose angry impulsiveness on small matters contrasted with his measured decisiveness on large ones, Alonzo Hamby explores how Truman coped with largely surmounted personal insecurities. My account of Eisenhower delineates a dispassionately analytic side of the supreme commander-turned-president that was not publicly known in the 1950s, asking whether Eisenhower's propensity to think strategically about politics helped him keep simultaneous events—such as the 1954 hearings on Senator McCarthy and decisions about whether to intervene in Indochina—from colliding and undermining his leadership.

Carl Brauer finds the salient features of Kennedy's leadership to be his inspirational qualities and his capacity to make the mass media and journalists his "spear carriers." Johnson, Larry Berman concludes, was incapacitated in his efforts as president to deal with Vietnam by the very capacities that had made him a brilliant Senate leader. Joan Hoff-Wilson finds Nixon's administrative style more instructive than the aspects of his personality that have made him the object of numerous psychobiographers.

Roger Porter demonstrates the potential for flexibility in a president's advisory consultations with his associates; he shows that Gerald Ford employed different modes of White House organizations to address different policy areas, the modes varying with the president's interest in the policies, his expertise, and his assessment of their current importance. Jimmy Carter's failure to adhere to the norms of Washington politics, Erwin Hargrove suggests, was rooted in his conviction that problems of public policy demand comprehensive solutions and that he could ignore "special interests" and advance such policies, because he would be supported by a wider public. Finally, underlying "the rhetorical presidency" of Ronald Reagan, William Muir finds Reagan's deeply held convictions and his determination to transform the nation's political ethos.

The fact that the modern presidency has been able to accommodate incumbents with extraordinarily diverse political styles is both consequential and instructive: consequential for explaining both the public policies of the modern era and the continuing evolution of the modern presidency; instructive as the most reliable source of evidence about the leadership capacity of the modern presidency.

1

FRANKLIN D. ROOSEVELT

The First Modern President

William E. Leuchtenburg

By almost all accounts, the presidency as we know it today begins with Franklin Delano Roosevelt. To be sure, many of the rudiments of the executive office date from the earliest years of the republic, and, in the nineteenth century, figures such as Andrew Jackson demonstrated how the president could serve as tribune of the people. In this century, too, both Theodore Roosevelt and Woodrow Wilson showed that the White House could radiate power. Yet, as Fred I. Greenstein has observed, "With Franklin Roosevelt's administration . . . the presidency began to undergo not a shift but rather a metamorphosis."[1] Indeed, so powerful an impression did FDR leave on the office that in the most recent survey of historians he was ranked as the second greatest president in our history, surpassed only by the legendary Abraham Lincoln.[2]

This very high rating would have appalled many of the contemporaries of "that megalomaniac cripple in the White House."[3] In the spring of 1937 an American who had been traveling extensively in the Caribbean confided, "During all the time I was gone, if anybody asked me if I wanted any news, my reply was always—'there is only one bit of news I want to hear and that is the death of Franklin D. Roosevelt. If he is not dead you don't need to tell me anything else.' "[4] One of FDR's Hudson Valley neighbors exiled himself to the Bahamas until Roosevelt was no longer in the White House; and the radio manufacturer Atwater Kent retired because he would not do business while "That Man" was president.[5] It has been said that "J. P. Morgan's family kept newspapers with pictures of Roosevelt out of his sight, and in one Connecticut country club . . . mention of his name was forbidden as a health measure against apoplexy."[6] In Kansas, a man went down into his cyclone cellar and announced he would not emerge until Roosevelt was out of office. (While he was there, his wife ran off with a traveling salesman.)[7]

Roosevelt, his critics maintained, had shown himself to be a man without principles. Herbert Hoover called him a "chameleon on plaid,"[8] while H. L. Mencken declared, "If he became convinced tomorrow that coming out for cannibalism would get him the votes he so sorely needs, he would begin fattening a missionary in the White House backyard come Wednesday."[9]

This reputation derived in good part from the fact that Roosevelt had campaigned in 1932 on a promise to balance the budget but subsequently asked Congress to appropriate vast sums for relief of the unemployed. Especially embarrassing was the memory of his 1932 address at Forbes Field, home of the Pittsburgh Pirates, in which he denounced Hoover as a profligate spender. Sam Rosenman recalls:

> Just before the start of the campaign of 1936, he said to me:
> "I'm going to make the first major campaign speech in Pittsburgh at the ball park in exactly the same spot I made that 1932 Pittsburgh speech; and in the speech I want to explain my 1932 statement. See whether you can prepare a draft giving a good and convincing explanation of it" . . .
> That evening I went in to see the President in his study and said that as long as he insisted on referring to the speech, I had found the only kind of explanation that could be made. He turned to me rather hopefully and, I think, with a little surprise, and said, "Fine, what sort of an explanation would you make?"
> I replied "Mr. President . . . deny categorically that you ever made [that 1932 speech]."[10]

A good number of historians have also found fault with FDR. New Left writers have chided him for offering a "profoundly conservative" response to a situation that had the potential for revolutionary change,[11] while commentators of no particular persuasion have criticized him for failing to bring the country out of the depression short of war, for maneuvering America into World War II (or for not taking the nation to war soon enough), for permitting Jews to perish in Hitler's death camps, and for sanctioning the internment of Japanese-Americans.

Roosevelt has been castigated especially for his failure to develop any grand design. Most great leaders have had an idea they wanted to impose, noted a contemporary critic, "whereas Roosevelt, if he has one, has successfully concealed it."[12] Similarly, the political scientist C. Herman Pritchett claimed that the New Deal never produced "any consistent social and economic philosophy to give meaning and purpose to its various action programs." He added, "Priding itself on its experimental approach, guided by a man who thought of himself as a quarter-back trying first one play and then another and judging their success by immediate pragmatic tests— the New Deal, along with all its great positive contributions to American life, may well be charged with contributing to the delinquency of American liberalism."[13] Even harsher disapproval has come from a man who in many ways admired FDR, Rexford Tugwell. "The Roosevelt measures were really pitiful patches on agencies he ought to have abandoned forthwith when leadership was conferred on him in such unstinted measure," the former Brain Truster maintained. "He could have emerged from the orthodox progressive chrysalis and led us into a new world." Instead, he busied himself "planting protective shrubbery on the slopes of a volcano."[14]

Given all of this often very bitter censure, both at the time and since, how can one account for FDR's ranking as the second greatest president ever? In raising that question, we may readily acknowledge that such polls often say more about the ideological predisposition of scholars than about the nature of presidential performance, and that historians have been scandalously vague about establishing criteria for "greatness." Yet there are in fact significant reasons for Roosevelt's rating, some of them substantial enough to be acknowledged even by skeptics.

One may begin with the most obvious: he has been regarded as one of the greatest of our presidents because he was in the White House longer than anyone else. Alone of American presidents, he broke the taboo against a third term and served part of a fourth term too. Shortly after his death the country adopted a constitutional amendment limiting a president to two terms. Motivated in no small part by the desire to deliver a posthumous rebuke to Roosevelt, this amendment has had the ironic consequence of assuring that Franklin Roosevelt will be, so far as we can foresee, the only chief executive ever to have served more than two terms.[15]

Roosevelt's high place rests also on his role in leading the nation to accept the far-ranging responsibilities of a world power. When he took office the United States was firmly committed to isolationism; it had refused to join either the League of Nations or the World

Court. Denied by Congress the discretionary authority he sought, Roosevelt made full use of his executive power in recognizing the USSR, crafting the Good Neighbor Policy, and, late in his second term, providing aid to the Allies and leading the nation into active involvement in World War II. So far had America come by the end of the Roosevelt era that Henry Stimson was to say that the United States could never again "be an island to herself. No private program and no public policy, in any sector of our national life, can now escape from the compelling fact that if it is not framed with reference to the world, it is framed with perfect futility."[16]

As a wartime president, FDR was able to demonstrate his executive leadership still more widely by guiding the country through a victorious struggle against the fascist powers. Never before had a president been given the opportunity to lead his people to a triumph of these global dimensions, and it seems improbable, given the nature of nuclear weapons, that such a circumstance will ever arise again. As commander in chief, a position he was said to prefer to all others, Roosevelt not only supervised the mobilization of men and resources against the Axis but also made a significant contribution to fashioning a postwar settlement and creating the structure of the United Nations. "He overcame both his own and the nation's isolationist inclination to bring a united America into the coalition that saved the world from the danger of totalitarian conquest," Robert Divine has concluded. "His role in insuring the downfall of Adolf Hitler is alone enough to earn him a respected place in history."[17]

Whatever his flaws, Roosevelt came to be perceived by antifascists everywhere as the leader of the forces of freedom and of hope. A decade after the president's death, Isaiah Berlin wrote:

> When I say that some men occupy one's imagination for many years, this is literally true of Mr. Roosevelt's effect on the young men of my own generation in England, and probably in many parts of Europe, and indeed the entire world. If one was young in the thirties and lived in a democracy, then, whatever one's politics, if one had human feelings at all, or the faintest spark of social idealism, or any love of life, one must have felt very much as young men in Continental Europe probably felt after the defeat of Napoleon during the years of the Restoration: that all was dark and quiet, a great reaction was abroad, and little stirred, and nothing resisted.

In these "dark and leaden thirties," Professor Berlin continued, "the only light in the darkness was the administration of Mr. Roosevelt and the New Deal in the United States."[18]

Similarly, in *Christ Stopped at Eboli*, Carlo Levi noted the impression the American leader made on a remote Calabrian village:

> What never failed to strike me most of all—and by now I had been in almost every house—were the eyes of two inseparable guardian angels that looked at me from the wall over the bed. On one side was the black, scowling face, with its large, inhuman eyes, of the Madonna of Viggiano; on the other a colored print of the sparkling eyes, behind gleaming glasses, and the hearty grin of President Roosevelt. I never saw other pictures or images than these: not the King nor the Duce, nor even Garibaldi; no famous Italian of any kind, nor any one of the appropriate saints; only Roosevelt and the Madonna of Viggiano never failed to be present. To see them there, one facing the other, in cheap prints, they seemed the two faces of the power that has divided the universe between them. But here their roles were, quite rightly, reversed. The Madonna appeared to be a fierce, pitiless, mysterious ancient earth goddess, the Saturnian mistress of this world; the President a sort of all-powerful Zeus, the benevolent and smiling master of a higher sphere.[19]

For good or ill, also, the United States first became a major military power during Roosevelt's presidency. As late as 1939 the American army ranked eighteenth in the world, behind the forces of Greece and Bulgaria; its soldiers trained with pieces of cardboard labeled "TANK." Under FDR, Congress established peacetime conscription and after Pearl Harbor put millions of men and women into uniform. His long tenure also saw the birth of the Pentagon, the military-industrial complex, and the atomic bomb. By April 1945, one historian has noted, "A Navy superior to the combined fleets of the rest of the world dominated the seven seas; the Air Force commanded greater striking power than that of any other country; and American overseas bases in the . . . Atlantic, the Mediterranean, and the Pacific rimmed the Eurasian continent."[20]

But there is one explanation more important than any of these in accounting for FDR's high ranking: his role in enlarging the presidential office and expanding the domain of the state while leading the American people through the Great Depression.

Roosevelt came to office at a desperate time, in the fourth year of a worldwide depression that raised the gravest doubts about the future of the Western world. "The year 1931 was distinguished from previous years . . . by one outstanding feature," commented the British historian Arnold Toynbee. "In 1931, men and women all over the world were seriously contemplating and frankly discussing the possibility that the Western system of Society might break down and cease to work."[21] On New Year's Eve 1931 in the United States, an American diplomat noted in his diary, "The last day of a very unhappy year for so many people the world around. Prices at the bottom and failures the rule of the day. A black picture!"[22] And in the summer of 1932, John Maynard Keynes, asked by a journalist whether there had ever been anything before like the Great Depression, replied: "Yes, it was called the Dark Ages, and it lasted four hundred years."[23]

By the time Roosevelt was sworn in, national income had been cut in half and more than 15 million Americans were unemployed. Every state had closed its banks or severely restricted their operations, and on the very morning of his inauguration the New York Stock Exchange had shut down. For many, hope had gone. "Now is the winter of our discontent the chilliest," wrote the editor of *Nation's Business*. "Fear, bordering on panic, loss of faith in everything, our fellowman, our institutions, private and government. Worst of all, no faith in ourselves, or the future. Almost everyone ready to scuttle the ship, and not even women and children first."[24]

Only a few weeks after Roosevelt took office, the spirit of the country seemed markedly changed. Gone was the torpor of the Hoover years; gone, too, the political paralysis. "The people aren't sure . . . just where they are going," noted one business journal, "but anywhere seems better than where they have been. In the homes, on the streets, in the offices, there is a feeling of hope reborn."[25] Again and again observers resorted to the imagery of darkness and light to characterize the transformation from the Stygian gloom of Hoover's final winter to the bright springtime of the First Hundred Days. Overnight, one eyewitness later remembered, Washington seemed like Cambridge on the morning of the Harvard–Yale game: "All the shops were on display, everyone was joyous, crowds moved excitedly. There was something in the air that had not been there before, and in the New Deal that continued throughout. It was not just for the day as it was in Cambridge."[26] On the New York Curb Exchange, where trading resumed on March 15, the stock ticker ended the day with the merry message: "GOODNITE . . . HAPPY DAYS ARE HERE AGAIN."[27]

It was altogether fitting to choose the words of FDR's theme song, for people of every political persuasion gave full credit for the revival of confidence to one man: the new president. In March a Hoover appointee from the Oyster Bay branch of the Roosevelt family wrote his mother, "I have followed with much interest and enthusiasm Franklin's start. I think he has done amazingly well, and I am really very pleased. One feels that he has what poor Hoover lacked, and what the country so much needs—leadership."[28] A month later the Republican senator from California, Hiram Johnson, acknowledged: "The admirable trait in Roosevelt is that he has the guts to try . . . He does it all with the rarest good nature . . . We have exchanged for a frown in the White House a smile. Where there were hesitation and vacillation, weighing always the personal political consequences, feebleness, timidity, and duplicity, there are now courage and bold-ness and real action."[29] On the editorial page of *Forum*, Henry God-dard Leach summed up the nation's nearly unanimous verdict: "We have a leader."[30]

The new president had created this impression by a series of ac-tions—delivering his compelling inaugural address, summoning Congress into emergency session, resolving the financial crisis—but even more by his manner. Supremely confident in his own powers, he could imbue others with a similar confidence. He felt altogether comfortable in the world into which he was born and raised, and with good reason. As his aunt said, "Il a été élevé dans un beau cadre" (He was brought up in a beautiful frame).[31] Like George Wash-ington, as David Potter suggested, "he was a 'code man' who had fixed himself upon a model (perhaps of Groton, Harvard, and Hudson River society), and who found small place for personal introspection in such a role."[32] Moreover, he had acquired an admirable political education: state senator, junior cabinet officer, his party's vice-pres-idential nominee, two-term governor of the largest state in the Union.

Roosevelt faced formidable challenges as president, but he never doubted that he would cope with them, for he believed that he belonged in the White House. He had sat on Grover Cleveland's knee, cast his first vote for Uncle Teddy, and seen Woodrow Wilson at close range; but the office seemed peculiarly his almost as a birthright. As Richard Neustadt has observed: "Roosevelt, almost alone among our Presidents, had no conception of the office to live up to; he was it. His image of the office was himself-in-office."[33] He loved the majesty of the position, relished its powers, and rejoiced in the opportunity it offered for achievement. "The essence of Roosevelt's Presidency," Clinton Rossiter has written, "was his airy eagerness to meet the age head on. Thanks to his flair for drama, he acted as if never in all history had there been times like our own."[34]

FDR's view of himself and of his world freed him from anxieties that other men would have found intolerable. Not even the weightiest responsibilities seemed to disturb his serenity. One of his associates said, "He must have been psychoanalyzed by God."[35] A Washington reporter noted in 1933: "No signs of care are visible to his main visitors or at the press conferences. He is amiable, urbane and apparently untroubled. He appears to have a singularly fortunate faculty for not becoming flustered. Those who talk with him informally in the evenings report that he busies himself with his stamp collection, discussing in an illuminating fashion the affairs of state while he waves his shears in the air."[36] Even after Roosevelt had gone through the trials of two terms of office, *Time* reported: "He has one priceless attribute: a knack of locking up his and the world's worries in some secret mental compartment, and then enjoying himself to the top of his bent. This quality of survival, of physical toughness, of champagne ebullience is one key to the big man. Another key is this: no one has ever heard him admit that he cannot walk."[37]

Roosevelt's sangfroid was matched with an experimental temperament. Like his father, he always had his eye out for something new. As Frank Freidel wrote: "James was a plunger in business, Franklin in politics."[38] FDR had twice actually gone on treasure-hunting expeditions. "The innovating spirit . . . was his most striking characteristic as a politician," Henry Fairlie has commented. "The man who took to the radio like a duck to water was the same man who, in his first campaign for the New York Senate in 1910, hired . . . a two-cylinder red Maxwell, with no windshield or top, to dash through (of all places) Dutchess County; and it was the same man who broke all precedents twenty-two years later when he hired a little plane to take him to Chicago to make his acceptance speech . . . The willingness to try everything was how Roosevelt governed."[39]

Serenity and venturesomeness were precisely the qualities needed in a national leader in the crisis of the depression, and the country drew reassurance from his buoyant view of the world. Frances Perkins remarked: "Overshadowing them all was his feeling that nothing in human judgment is final. One may courageously take the step that seems right today because it can be modified tomorrow if it does not work well . . . Since it is a normal human reaction, most people felt as he did and gladly followed when he said, 'We can do it. At least let's try.' "[40]

Roosevelt scoffed at the idea that the nation was the passive victim of economic laws. He believed that the country could lift itself out of the depression by sheer will power. In one of his fireside chats the president said: "When Andrew Jackson, 'Old Hickory,' died, someone asked, 'Will he go to Heaven?' and the answer was, 'He will if he wants to.' If I am asked whether the American people will pull themselves out of this depression, I answer, 'They will if they want to' . . . I have no sympathy with the professional economists who insist that things must run their course and that human agencies can have no influence on economic ills."[41]

FDR's self-command, gusto, and bonhomie created an extraordinary bond between himself and the American people. Rex Tugwell wrote of him: "No monarch . . . unless it may have been Elizabeth or her magnificent Tudor father, or maybe Alexander or Augustus Caesar, can have given quite that sense of serene presiding, of gathering up unto himself, of really representing, a whole people."[42] Millions of Americans came to view the president as one who was intimately concerned with their welfare. In the 1936 campaign he heard people cry out, "He saved my home," "He gave me a job."[43] At Bridgeport, Connecticut, he rode past signs saying "Thank God for Roosevelt,"[44] and in the Denver freight yards a message scrawled in chalk on the side of a boxcar read "Roosevelt Is My Friend."[45]

In November 1934 Martha Gellhorn reported to Harry Hopkins from the Carolinas:

Every house I visited—mill worker or unemployed—had a picture of the President. These ranged from newspaper clippings (in destitute homes) to large coloured prints, framed in gilt cardboard . . . And the feeling of these people for the President is one of the most remarkable phenomena I have ever met. He is at once God and their intimate friend; he knows them all by name, knows their little town and mill, their little lives and problems. And though everything else fails, he is there, and will not let them down.[46]

FDR nurtured this relationship by making the most of the advantage his position offered to instruct the citizenry. Shortly after his first election he declared:

> The Presidency is not merely an administrative office. That is the least of it. It is pre-eminently a place of moral leadership.
>
> All of our great Presidents were leaders of thought at times when certain historic ideas in the life of the nation had to be clarified. Washington personified the idea of Federal Union. Jefferson practically originated the party system as we now know it by opposing the democratic theory to the republicanism of Hamilton. This theory was reaffirmed by Jackson.
>
> Two great principles of our government were forever put beyond question by Lincoln. Cleveland, coming into office following an era of great political corruption, typified rugged honesty. Theodore Roosevelt and Wilson were both moral leaders, each in his own way and for his own time, who used the Presidency as a pulpit.
>
> That is what the office is—a superb opportunity for reapplying, applying to new conditions, the simple rules of human conduct to which we always go back. Without leadership alert and sensitive to change, we . . . lose our way.[47]

To acquaint the country with new moral imperatives and with his departures in public policy, Roosevelt made conscious use of the media almost from the moment he entered the White House, with his press conferences serving to educate newspaper writers and, through them, the nation on the complex, novel measures he was advocating. He was fond of calling the press meeting room in the White House his "schoolroom," and he often resorted to terms such as *seminar* or the budget *textbook*.[48] When in January 1934 the president invited thirty-five Washington correspondents to his study, he explained his budget message to them "like a football coach going through skull practice with his squad."[49]

According to Leo Rosten, FDR's performance at his first press conference as president, on March 8, 1933, became "something of a legend in newspaper circles":

> Mr. Roosevelt was introduced to each correspondent. Many of them he already knew and greeted by name—first name. For each he had a handshake and the Roosevelt smile. When the questioning began, the full virtuosity of the new Chief Exec-

utive was demonstrated. Cigarette-holder in mouth at a jaunty angle, he met the reporters on their own grounds. His answers were swift, positive, illuminating. He had exact information at his fingertips. He showed an impressive understanding of public problems and administrative methods. He was lavish in his confidences and "background information." He was informal, communicative, gay. When he evaded a question it was done frankly. He was thoroughly at ease. He made no effort to conceal his pleasure in the give and take of the situation.[50]

Jubilant reporters could scarcely believe the transformation in the White House. So hostile had their relations become with Roosevelt's predecessor that Hoover, who was accused of employing the Secret Service to stop leaks and of launching a campaign of "terrorism" to get publishers to fire certain newspapermen, finally discontinued press conferences altogether.[51] Furthermore, Hoover, like Harding and Coolidge before him, had insisted on written questions submitted in advance. Roosevelt, to the delight of the Washington press corps, immediately abolished that requirement and said that questions could be fired at him without warning. At the end of the first conference, reporters did something they had never done before— gave the man they were covering a spontaneous round of applause. One veteran, and often sardonic, journalist described it as "the most amazing performance the White House has ever seen." He added: "The press barely restrained its whoopees . . . Here was news—action—drama! Here was a new attitude to the press! . . . The reportorial affection and admiration for the President [are] unprecedented. He has definitely captivated an unusually cynical battalion of correspondents."[52]

The initial euphoria persisted long afterward. Roosevelt could sometimes be testy—he told one reporter to go off to a corner and put on a dunce cap—but, for the most part, especially in the New Deal years, he was jovial and even chummy, in no small part because he regarded himself as a longtime newspaperman, having been "president"—that is, editor-in-chief—of the Harvard *Crimson*.[53] He showed his lively interest in the field by appointing the first official press secretary, Stephen Early. He also saw to it that every nervous newcomer on his first White House assignment was introduced to him for a handshake, and he made clear that members of the Fourth Estate were socially respectable by throwing a spring garden party for them at the White House.

Above all, FDR proved an inexhaustible source of news. Jack Bell, who covered the White House for the Associated Press, observed: "He talked in headline phrases. He acted, he emoted; he was angry, he was smiling. He was persuasive, he was demanding; he was philosophical, he was elemental. He was sensible, he was unreasonable; he was benevolent, he was malicious. He was satirical, he was soothing; he was funny, he was gloomy. He was exciting. He was human. He was copy."[54] Another correspondent later said, "We never covered Washington in the twenties. We covered the Senate. You wasted your time downtown."[55] But under FDR, "downtown"—the White House—became the best beat in the land.

Reporters came to view their encounters with Roosevelt as the greatest show around. One columnist wrote afterward: "The doubters among us—and I was one of them—predicted that the free and open conference would last a few weeks and then would be abandoned."[56] But twice a week, with rare exceptions, year after year, the president submitted to the crossfire of interrogation. After observing one of these conferences, John Dos Passos noted that Roosevelt replied to questions "simply and unhurriedly as if he were sitting at a table talking to an old friend"; "his voice is fatherly-friendly, without strain, like the voice of the principal of a first-rate boy's school."[57] He greeted reporters by first name, spanked them verbally on occasion, teased them, and joked with them. Sometimes he would remark: "If I were writing your stories to-day, I should say . . ."[58] At the end, the words "Thank you, Mr. President" were the signal for a pell-mell scramble for the telephones in the White House press room. Reporters had never seen anything like it. He left independent-minded newspapermen such as Raymond Clapper with the conviction that "the administration from President Roosevelt down has little to conceal and is willing to do business with the doors open." If reporters were 60 percent for the New Deal, Clapper reckoned, they were 90 percent for Roosevelt personally.[59]

Some observers have seen in the FDR press conference a quasi-constitutional institution like the question hour in the House of Commons.[60] To a degree, it was. But the fact remains that the president had complete control over what he would discuss and what could be published. He intended the press conference not as an instrumentality to accommodate his critics but as a public relations device he could manipulate to his own advantage. In particular, the press conferences gave Roosevelt a way of circumventing the hostility of right-wing publishers to his program and of stealing the scene from his opponents in the other branches of government. In his extraordinary "horse-and-buggy" monologue following the *Schechter* decision, Roosevelt used the press conference as a forum for what amounted to a dissenting opinion delivered to the nation, with correspondents reduced to the role of scribes.[61]

Franklin Roosevelt was the first chief executive, too, to take full advantage of the capacity of the radio to project a president's ideas and personality directly into American homes. When FDR got before a microphone, he appeared, said one critic, to be "talking and toasting marshmallows at the same time."[62] In his first days in office, he gave a radio address that was denominated a "fireside chat" because his intimate, informal delivery made every American think the president was talking directly to him or her. As David Halberstam has pointed out,

> He was the first great American radio voice. For most Americans of this generation, their first memory of politics would be sitting by a radio and hearing *that* voice, strong, confident, totally at ease. If he was going to speak, the idea of doing something else was unthinkable. If they did not yet have a radio, they walked the requisite several hundred yards to the home of a more fortunate neighbor who did. It was in the most direct sense the government reaching out and touching the citizen, bringing Americans into the political process and focusing their attention on the presidency as the source of good ... Most Americans in the previously 160 years had never even seen a President; now almost all of them were hearing him, *in their own homes*. It was literally and figuratively electrifying.[63]

By quickening interest in government, Roosevelt became the country's foremost civic educator. Charles A. Beard, often a vehement critic, went so far as to say that Franklin Roosevelt discussed "more fundamental problems of American life and society than all the other Presidents combined."[64] FDR's rousing inaugural address drew 460,000 letters; in contrast, President Taft had received only 200 letters a week. Whereas one man had been able to handle all of Hoover's mail, a staff of fifty had to be hired to take care of Franklin Roosevelt's incoming correspondence, which averaged 5,000 letters a day, and on birthdays an astonishing 150,000. "The mail started coming in by the truckload," a former White House aide said. "They couldn't even get the envelopes open."[65] His chief of mails recalled: "When he advised millions of listeners in one of his fireside chats to 'tell me your troubles,' most of them believed implicitly that he was speaking to them personally and immediately wrote him a letter. It was months before we managed to swim out of *that* flood of mail."[66]

Not only by fireside chats and public addresses but also by his openness to ideas and to people not previously welcomed in Washington, Roosevelt greatly broadened the political agenda and encouraged outsiders to enter the civic arena. One scholar has observed:

> Franklin Roosevelt changed the nature of political contests in this country by drawing new groups into active political participation. Compare the political role of labor under the self-imposed handicap of Samuel Gompers' narrow vision with labor's political activism during and since the Roosevelt years. The long-run results were striking: Roosevelt succeeded in activating people who previously had lacked power; national politics achieved a healthier balance of contending interests; and public policy henceforth was written to meet the needs of those who previously had gone unheard.[67]

Roosevelt and his headline-making New Deal especially served to arouse the interest of young people. From 1926 to 1936, government was the Harvard department that chalked up the biggest single rise in majors,[68] and Roosevelt attracted any number of young men, and not a few young women, into public service. When Lyndon Johnson learned of FDR's death, he said, "I don't know that I'd ever have come to Congress if it hadn't been for him. But I do know that I got my first desire for public office because of him—and so did thousands of other men all over this country."[69] "Of course you have fallen into some errors—that is human," a former Supreme Court justice wrote the president in 1937, "but you have put a new face upon the social and political life of our country."[70]

FDR's role as civic educator frequently took a decidedly partisan turn, for he proved to be an especially effective party leader. In 1932, in an election that unraveled traditional party ties, he became the first Democrat elected to the White House with a popular majority since Franklin Pierce eighty years before. Yet this heady triumph, reflecting resentment of Hoover more than approval of FDR and the Democrats, might have been short-lived if Roosevelt had not built a coalition of lower-income ethnic voters in the great cities tenuously aligned with white voters in the Solid South. The 1936 returns confirmed the emergence of the Democrats as the new majority party in the Fifth American Party System in an election that showed a sharp cleavage along class lines. FDR won only 42 percent of the upper-income share of the two-party vote, but 80 percent of union members and 84 percent of relief recipients. In tripling the vote received by the Democratic presidential nominee in 1920, Roosevelt carried 98.6 percent of South Carolina at the very time that blacks were abandoning the party of the Great Emancipator to join the FDR coalition.[71]

Although Roosevelt has been scolded for failing to bring about a full-fledged party realignment, no president has ever done so much to redraw the contours of party conflict. He brought into his administration former Republicans such as Henry Wallace and Harold Ickes; enticed hundreds of thousands of Socialists, such as the future California congressman Jerry Voorhis, to join the Democrats; worked with anti-Tammany leaders such as Fiorello LaGuardia in New York; backed the Independent candidate George Norris against the Democrats' official nominee in Nebraska; and forged alliances with third parties such as the American Labor party.[72] In 1938 he dared attempt, largely unsuccessfully, to "purge" conservative Democrats from the party, and in World War II he may even have sought to unite liberal Republicans of the Wendell Willkie sort with liberal Democrats in a new party, although the details of that putative arrangement are obscure.

Roosevelt won such a huge following both for himself and for his party by putting together the most ambitious legislative program in the history of the country. Although he was not the first chief executive in this century to adopt the role of chief legislator, he developed its techniques to an unprecedented extent. He made wide use of the special message, and he accompanied these communications with draft bills. He wrote letters to committee chairmen or members of Congress to urge passage of his proposals, summoned the congressional leadership to White House conferences on legislation, used agents such as Tommy Corcoran on Capitol Hill, and revived the practice of appearing in person before Congress. He made even the hitherto mundane business of bill signing an occasion for political theater; it was he who initiated the custom of giving a presidential pen to a congressional sponsor of legislation as a memento. In the First Hundred Days, Roosevelt adroitly dangled promises of patronage before congressmen, but without delivering on them until he had the legislation he wanted. The result, as one commentator put it, was that "his relations with Congress were to the very end of the session tinged with a shade of expectancy which is the best part of young love."[73]

To the dismay of the Republican leadership, Roosevelt showed himself to be a past master not only at coddling his supporters in Congress but also at disarming would-be opponents. The conservative congressman Joseph E. Martin, who sought to insulate his fellow Republicans in the House from FDR's charm, complained that the president, "laughing, talking, and poking the air with his long cigarette holder," was so magnetic that he "bamboozled" even members of the opposition. "As he turned on his radiance I could see the face of one of my men lighting up like the moon," Martin recorded resentfully. He had to step swiftly to rescue the man from the perilous "moon glow" and give him a dose of "dire warnings."[74] On another occasion a visitor outside the Oval Office observed Roosevelt just after he had deftly disposed of a mutinous congressional delegation. The president, uaware that he was being watched, slowly lit up a Camel in his ivory cigarette holder, and, as he settled back, "a smile of complete satisfaction spread over his face."[75]

To be sure, his success with Congress has often been exaggerated. The Congress of the First Hundred Days, it has been said, "did not so much debate the bills it passed . . . as salute them as they went sailing by";[76] but even in 1933 Roosevelt had to bend to the wishes of legislators more than once. In later years Congress passed the bonus bill over his veto; shelved his "Court-packing" plan; and, on neutrality policy, bound the president like Gulliver. After putting through the Fair Labor Standards Act in 1938, Roosevelt was unable to win congressional approval of any New Deal legislation. Moreover, some of the most important "New Deal" measures credited to Roosevelt—federal insurance of bank deposits, the Wagner Act, and public housing—originated in Congress as proposals that he either opposed outright or accepted only at the last moment. Judged by latterday standards, his operation on the Hill was almost primitive. He had no congressional liaison office, and he paid too little attention to rank-and-file members.

Still, Roosevelt's skill as chief legislator is undeniable. One historian concluded that "Franklin Roosevelt's party leadership as an effective instrument of legislation is unparalleled in our party history,"[77] and a political scientist has stated: "The most dramatic transformation in the relationship between the presidency and Congress occurred during the first two terms of Franklin D. Roosevelt. FDR changed the power ratio between Congress and the White House,

publicly taking it upon himself to act as the leader of Congress at
a time of deepening crisis in the nation. More than any other president, FDR established the model of the powerful legislative presidency on which the public's expectations still are anchored."[78]

Roosevelt achieved so much in good part because of his exquisite
sense of timing. No one has captured that trait so well as Erwin
Hargrove:

> In his leadership of public opinion FDR oscillated from the
> heroic to the cautious. With his sensitivity to public moods,
> he was forthright as a leader when crisis was high and public
> sentiment was ripe for heroic leadership. This was the case
> when he first entered office and embarked on the dramatic
> legislative leadership of the first hundred days. It was also the
> case in the 1936 campaign when he proclaimed the need for a
> new era of reform and in 1941 when the nation entered the
> war. At other times he was more cautious and gradually pre-
> pared the public for a new departure. For example, he held off
> on social security legislation in order to . . . educate people that
> it was not alien to the American tradition of self-reliance. He
> did this by blending press conferences, a message to Congress,
> two fireside chats, and a few speeches, in each of which he
> progressively unfolded the Americanness of the plan. It cul-
> minated in a State of the Union message . . . He did this kind
> of thing with artistry, and the artistry was an extension of his
> own empathy and ability to act to win others over.[79]

As one aspect of his function as chief legislator, Roosevelt broke
all records in making use of the veto power. By the end of his second
term, his vetoes already totaled more than 30 percent of all the
measures disallowed by presidents since 1792. Unlike the other famous veto president, Grover Cleveland, who limited his disapproval
primarily to pension legislation, Roosevelt expressed his will on a
range of subjects from homing pigeons to credit for beer whole-
salers.[80] Franklin Roosevelt was the first chief executive to read a
veto message personally to Congress, and he even defied the un-
written canon against vetoing a revenue measure when in 1944 he
turned down a tax bill on the grounds that it benefited the greedy
rather than the needy.[81] According to one credible tale, FDR used
to ask his aides to look out for a piece of legislation he could veto,
in order to remind Congress that it was being watched.[82]

So far did Roosevelt plumb the potentialities of the chief executive

as legislative leader that by the end of his first term the columnist
Raymond Clapper was writing, "It is scarcely an exaggeration to say
that the President, although not a member of Congress, has become
almost the equivalent of the prime minister of the British system,
because he is both executive and the guiding hand of the legislative
branch."[83] And by World War II FDR's leadership in the lawmaking
process was so accepted that a conservative Republican found fault
with the president for failing to submit to Congress a detailed list
of bills that he expected it to enact."[84]

Roosevelt rested his legislative program on the assumption that
government should actively seek social justice for all Americans,
not least those who are disadvantaged. In 1936 he said: "Governments can err, Presidents do make mistakes, but the immortal Dante
tells us that Divine Justice weighs the sins of the cold-blooded and
the sins of the warm-hearted in different scales. Better the occasional
faults of a Government that lives in a spirit of charity than the
consistent omissions of a Government frozen in the ice of its own
indifference."[85] Less than two years later, in his annual message to
Congress, Roosevelt made his views about the duty of the state still
more explicit: "Government has a final responsibility for the well-
being of its citizenship. If private co-operative endeavor fails to provide work for willing hands and relief for the unfortunate, those
suffering hardship from no fault of their own have a right to call
upon the Government for aid; and a government worthy of its name
must make fitting response."[86]

Starting in the electrifying First Hundred Days, Roosevelt brought
the welfare state to America, years after it had become a fixture in
other lands. Although European theorists had been talking about
der Staat for decades, the notion of the state got little attention in
America before FDR.[87] In the spring of 1933, however, that situation
began to change drastically. André Maurois has remarked:

> One cannot help calling to mind, as one writes the history of
> these crowded months, the Biblical account of the Creation.
> The first day, the Brain Trust put an embargo on gold; the
> second day, it peopled the forests; the third day, it created the
> three point two beer; the fourth day, it broke the bonds that
> tied the dollar to gold; the fifth day, it set the farmers free; the
> sixth day, it created General Johnson, and then, looking upon
> what it had made of America, it saw that it was good.
> But it could not rest on the seventh day.[88]

Before Roosevelt's tenure was over, the state's role had expanded further. For the first time the country enjoyed the benefits of a Social Security program of old-age pensions, unemployment compensation, aid to the handicapped and to dependent children, and work-relief projects financed by the greatest single peacetime appropriation in history. For the first time the national government became intimately involved in a large way with shelter—enabling millions of people to buy their own homes, others to move into public housing, and some to live in entirely new model communities. For the first time the national government deliberately sought to foster unionization. When Roosevelt took office, almost no factory worker in America belonged to a union; when he left, industrial unionism was firmly established, in part because the government broke precedent by entering factories to conduct elections in which workers could choose whether to join a union and which union to join. For the first time, under FDR's leadership, the national state extended its sphere in a great many other ways: building the much-admired regional experiment of the Tennessee Valley Authority, making documentary films, creating a corps of young people to work in the forests, serving hot lunches to schoolchildren, founding symphony orchestras, even running its own circus.

Roosevelt moved beyond the notion that "rights" embodied only guarantees against denial of freedom of expression to the conception that government also has an obligation to assure certain economic essentials. In his State of the Union message of January 1944 he declared:

> This Republic had its beginning, and grew to its present strength, under the protection of certain inalienable political rights— among them the right of free speech, free press, free worship, trial by jury, freedom from unreasonable searches and seizures . . .
>
> As our Nation has grown in size and stature, however—as our industrial economy expanded—these political rights proved inadequate to assure us equality in the pursuit of happiness.
>
> We have come to a clear realization of the fact that true individual freedom cannot exist without economic security and independence. "Necessitous men are not free men." People who are hungry and out of a job are the stuff of which dictatorships are made.
>
> In our day these economic truths have become accepted as

self-evident. We have accepted, so to speak, a second Bill of Rights under which a new basis of security and prosperity can be established for all—regardless of station, race, or creed.

Among these are:

The right to a useful and remunerative job in the industries or shops or farms or mines of the Nation;

The right to earn enough to provide adequate food and clothing and recreation;

The right of every farmer to raise and sell his products at a return which will give him and his family a decent living;

The right of every businessman, large or small, to trade in an atmosphere of freedom from unfair competition and domination by monopolies at home or abroad;

The right of every family to a decent home;

The right to adequate medical care and the opportunity to achieve and enjoy good health;

The right to adequate protection from the economic fears of old age, sickness, accident, and unemployment;

The right to a good education.[89]

In expanding the orbit of the state, Roosevelt demanded that business recognize the superior authority of the government in Washington. At the time, that was shocking doctrine. In the pre–New Deal period, government had often been the handmaiden of business, and many presidents had shared the values of businessmen. When FDR made clear that he did not hold the same system of values, he was denounced as a traitor to his class. But in one way Roosevelt was not of their class. He was a member of the landed gentry and the old mercantile class who could claim ancient lineage. Claes Martenzen van Rosenvelt, the first Roosevelt in the New World, had come to New Amsterdam in the seventeenth century. Both the Roosevelts and the Delanos were prosperous merchant families who had derived much of their fortunes from seafaring. As a landowner with a Hudson River estate, a man from a family that moved easily in the Edith Wharton universe of Knickerbocker society, Roosevelt approached economic problems with different preconceptions from those of the industrialist or the financier on the make.

With a country squire's contempt for the grasping businessman and a squire's conviction of *noblesse oblige,* FDR refused to accept the view that business and government were coequal sovereigns. Although the New Deal always operated within a capitalist framework, Roosevelt insisted that there was a national interest that it was the duty of the president to represent and, when the situation called for it, to impose. Consequently, the federal government in the 1930s came to supervise the stock market, establish a central banking system monitored from Washington, and regulate a range of business activities that had hitherto been regarded as private.

As a result of these many new measures Roosevelt was frequently referred to as "the great economic emancipator,"[90] but his real contributions, as James MacGregor Burns has said, were "far more important than any possible set 'solution'—a willingness to take charge, a faith in the people, and an acceptance of the responsibility of the federal government to act." Burns adds:

> While Roosevelt's symbolic leadership was related to definite, concrete acts of government, his interpretation of the situation, in the broadest sense, was more important than any specific program. For he established then and later that the federal government must and could be accountable for the nation's economic well being . . . Roosevelt accomplished a decisive interpretation of events: he dramatized the role of the federal government so that people would see it not as a remote and passive power but as a force that could salvage them and shape the nation's economy.[91]

After a historic confrontation with the Supreme Court, Roosevelt secured the legitimation of this enormous expansion of the state. In 1935 and 1936 the Court struck down more important national legislation than in any other comparable period in our history. Roosevelt responded in February 1937 with an audacious scheme to "pack" the Court with as many as six additional justices. Although he did not get his plan through, he was able to claim that he had lost the battle but won the war, for the Court never again struck down a New Deal law. In fact, as a consequence of "the Constitutional Revolution of 1937," the Supreme Court has never since invalidated any significant statute regulating the economy.[92]

Roosevelt quickly learned that enacting a program was an altogether different matter from getting it implemented and that he had to turn his thoughts to being not only chief legislator but also chief administrator. He once complained:

> The Treasury is so large and far-flung and ingrained in its practices that I find it almost impossible to get the action and results

I want—even with Henry [Morgenthau] there. But the Treasury is not to be compared with the State Department. You should go through the experience of trying to get any changes in the thinking, policy, and action of the career diplomats and then you'd know what a real problem was. But the Treasury and the State Department put together are nothing compared with the Na-a-vy. The admirals are really something to cope with—and I should know. To change something in the Na-a-vy is like punching a feather bed. You punch it with your right and you punch it with your left until you are finally exhausted, and then you find the damn bed just as it was before you started punching.[93]

To overcome resistance to his policies in the old-line departments, Roosevelt resorted to the creation of emergency agencies. "We have new and complex problems," he once said. "Why not establish a new agency to take over the new duty rather than saddle it on an old institution? . . . If it is not permanent, we don't get bad precedents."[94] This tactic often turned out wonderfully well, for those who engaged in freewheeling ventures such as the TVA had a sense of liberation and an élan missing in the encrusted bureaucracies. Still, as Arthur Schlesinger, Jr., the ablest defender of FDR as an administrator, has acknowledged, the president sometimes "acted as if a new agency were almost a new solution. His addiction to new organizations became a kind of nervous tic which disturbed even avid New Dealers."[95]

Roosevelt also departed from orthodoxy in another way. In flat defiance of the cardinal rule of public administration textbooks— that every administrator ought to appear on a chart with a clearly stated assignment—the president not only deliberately disarranged spheres of authority but also appointed men of clashing attitudes and temperaments. Although the squabbling of a Harry Hopkins with a Harold Ickes left the impression of a government in disarray, this procedure had the advantage of alerting Roosevelt to policy conflicts and permitting him to resolve them when they were ripe. Schlesinger has maintained: "His favorite technique was to keep grants of authority incomplete, jurisdictions uncertain, charters overlapping. The result of this competitive theory of administration was often confusion and exasperation on the operating level; but no other method could so reliably insure that in a large bureaucracy filled with ambitious men eager for power the decisions, and the power to make them, would remain with the President."[96]

To secure trustworthy information, Roosevelt relied on a congeries of informants and personal envoys. Though there were times when one man enjoyed his close confidence—Louis Howe early in the New Deal, Harry Hopkins in the war years—Roosevelt never had a chief of staff, and no individual was ever permitted to take the place of the "countless lieutenants and supporters" who served "virtually as roving ambassadors collecting intelligence through the Executive Branch," often unaware that more than one person had the same assignment.[97] "He would call you in, and he'd ask you to get the story on some complicated business," one of FDR's aides later said, "and you'd come back after a couple of days of hard labor and present the juicy morsel you'd uncovered under a stone somewhere, and *then* you'd find out he knew all about it, along with something else you *didn't* know. Where he got his information from he wouldn't mention, usually, but after he had done this to you once or twice you got damn careful about *your* information."[98]

So evident were the costs of FDR's competitive style—not only bruised feelings but also, at times, a want of coherence in policy— and so "harum-scarum"[99] did his methods seem, that it became commonplace to speak of Roosevelt as a poor administrator. Grant McConnell has stated bluntly: "Usually there is . . . something intensely personal, whether inborn or not, in the capacity to manage a complex organization. Obviously, the talent for administration may be cultivated and improved. Some presidents, Franklin Roosevelt for example, had neither talent nor taste in this direction."[100] And a British analyst has commented that although the "mishmash" Roosevelt put together was "inspired," it resulted not in a "true bureaucracy" but in "an ill-organized flock of agencies, with the sheep dogs in the White House snapping at their heels as the President whistled the signals."[101]

Roosevelt himself appeared to believe that these charges were not without foundation. Over cocktails at the White House in the fall of 1936 he mused, "You know, I just had a lovely thought. I've just been thinking what fun it would have been if I could have run against Roosevelt. I don't know whether I could have beaten him but I'd have given him a close race." He explained: "First off in the campaign I would have repudiated Hearst. Second, I would have repudiated the DuPonts etc. Then I'd have said 'we want Security, relief, etc. etc.' But here's the story: 'the Democrats can't be trusted with the administration of these fine ideals.' I'd have cited chapter and verse on WPA inefficiency (and there's plenty of it). You know the more I think about it the more I believe I could have licked myself."[102]

Not a few commentators, though, have concluded that Roosevelt was a superior administrator. They point out that he vastly improved staffing and that he broke new ground when he assigned Henry Wallace to chair a series of wartime agencies, for no vice-president had ever held administrative responsibilities before.[103] Granted, there was no end of friction between subordinates such as Hopkins and Ickes, or Cordell Hull and Sumner Welles, but Wallace once observed, in a rare witticism, that FDR "could keep all the balls in the air without losing his own."[104] In Abe Fortas's words: "Roosevelt was a master at controlling friction and making it constructive. He was a real Toscanini. He knew how to conduct an orchestra and when to favor the first fiddles and when to favor the trombones. He knew how to employ and manipulate people. As you go through life you see giants become men, but in the New Deal days men became giants."[105] Furthermore, his admirers maintain, if the test of a great administrator is whether he can inspire devotion in his subordinates, FDR passes with flying colors. Even Ickes, the most notorious grumbler of the Roosevelt circle, noted in his diary, "You go into Cabinet meetings tired and discouraged and out of sorts and the President puts new life into you. You come out like a fighting cock."[106]

An even better test of an administrator is whether he can recruit exceptional talent, and Roosevelt broke new ground by giving an unprecedented opportunity to a new corps of officials: the university-trained experts. Save for a brief period in World War I, professors had not had much of a place in Washington; but in his 1932 presidential campaign FDR enlisted several academic advisers, most of them from Morningside Heights, to offer their thoughts and to test his own ideas. The press called this group "the Brain Trust." During the First Hundred Days droves of professors, inspired by that example, descended on Washington to take part in the New Deal. So, too, did their students—young attorneys fresh out of law school and social scientists with recent graduate degrees who received an open-arms reception from the federal government that had never been extended before. Some were as young as twenty-one-year-old Wilbur Cohen.

This influx of New Dealers upset all the traditional assumptions

about who was supposed to be running the government. As Raymond
Moley recalled:

> We stood in the city of Washington on March 4th like a handful
> of marauders in hostile territory . . . The Republican party had
> close to a monopoly of skillful, experienced administrators. To
> make matters worse, the business managers, established law-
> yers, and engineers from whose ranks top-drawer governmental
> executives so often come were, by and large, so partisan in their
> opposition to Roosevelt that he could scarcely be expected to
> tap those sources to the customary degree.[107]

The sudden change of personnel discountenanced the president's
critics, not least H. L. Mencken, who wrote: "A few years ago all
the New Deal Isaiahs were obscure and impotent fellows who flushed
with pride when they got a nod from the cop at the corner; today
they have the secular rank of princes of the blood, and the ghostly
faculties of . . . archbishops." "You Brain Trusters," he complained,
"were hauled suddenly out of a bare, smelly classroom, wherein the
razzberries of sophomores had been your only music, and thrown
into a place of power and glory almost befitting Caligula, Napoleon
I, or J. Pierpont Morgan, with whole herds of Washington correspondents crowding up to take down your every wheeze."[108]

Roosevelt had such success in recruiting this new cadre of administrators because of his openness to groups who had long been
discriminated against. Before the New Deal, the government had
largely been the domain of white Anglo-Saxon Protestants. Under
FDR that situation altered perceptibly, with the change symbolized
by the most famous team of FDR's advisers: Tommy Corcoran and
Ben Cohen, the Irish Catholic and the Jew. Nor did ethnic diversity
end there. Although some patterns of racial discrimination persisted,
the president appointed enough blacks to high places in the government to permit the formation of what was called the "black cabinet."[109]

For the first time, also, women received more than token recognition. In appointing Frances Perkins secretary of labor, Roosevelt
named the first woman ever chosen for a cabinet post. He also selected the first female envoy and the first female judge of the U.S.
Circuit Court of Appeals. "At times, Washington seemed like a
perpetual convention of social workers as women from the Consumers League, the Women's Trade Union League, and other reform
groups came to Washington to take on government assignments,"

William H. Chafe has written. "Mary Anderson, director of the Women's Bureau, recalled that in earlier years women government officials had dined together in a small university club. 'Now,' she said, 'there are so many of them they would need a hall.' "[110] As First Lady, Mrs. Roosevelt, in particular, epitomized the impact that women could have on public affairs. According to Rex Tugwell, one of the original Brain Trusters, "No one who ever saw Eleanor Roosevelt sit down facing her husband, and holding his eyes firmly, say to him 'Franklin, I think you should' . . . or, 'Franklin surely you will not' . . . will ever forget the experience."[111] She became, as one columnist said, "Cabinet Minister without portfolio—the most influential woman of our times."[112]

In addition to attracting hitherto-neglected talent to government service, Roosevelt, his improvisational style notwithstanding, also made significant institutional changes. In November 1933 he established the National Emergency Council to coordinate the work of the New Deal field agencies, and his first term also saw the creation of a National Planning Board and its successors, the National Resources Board and the National Resources Committee. From the very outset he had a keen interest in reorganizing the government, and over time that concern developed from a desire to cut costs, which had been the traditional rationale, to a determination to strengthen the president's managerial capacity.[113]

Roosevelt took an initiative with important long-range consequences when he named three of the country's foremost scholars of public administration—Louis Brownlow (chairman), Charles E. Merriam, and Luther Gulick—to a President's Committee on Administrative Management, and in response to their report created the Executive Office of the President, which has become "the nerve center of the federal administrative system."[114] By an executive order of 1939 he moved several agencies, notably the Bureau of the Budget, under the wing of the White House and provided for a cadre of presidential assistants. This Executive Order 8248 has been called a "nearly unnoticed but none the less epoch-making event in the history of American institutions" and "perhaps the most important single step in the institutionalization of the Presidency."[115]

Harold Smith, who served in the prewar era and throughout the war years as FDR's budget director, later reflected:

When I worked with Roosevelt—for six years—I thought as did many others that he was a very erratic administrator. But now, when I look back, I can really begin to see the size of his programs. They were by far the largest and most complex programs that any President ever put through. People like me who had the responsibility of watching the pennies could only see the five or six or seven per cent of the programs that went wrong, through inefficient organization or direction. But now I can see in perspective the ninety-three or -four or -five percent that went right—including the winning of the biggest war in history—because of unbelievably skillful organization and direction. And if I were to write that article now, I think I'd say that Roosevelt must have been one of the greatest geniuses as an administrator that ever lived. What we couldn't appreciate at the time was the fact that he was a real *artist* in government.[116]

The amount of attention drawn by the New Deal intellectuals has, in some respects, served to diminish FDR's reputation, for commentators have implied that national programs owed less to the president than to those who wrote his speeches and drafted his bills. It has become commonplace, even among his admirers, to view the president as an intellectual lightweight. He read few books, and these not very seriously. According to one historian, "He was neither a philosopher, like Jefferson, nor a student of government, like Wilson, the two Presidents he most admired."[117] He had small talent for abstract reasoning, though perhaps no less than most men in public life. He loved brilliant people, commented one of his former aides, but not profound ones.[118] Raymond Moley has observed that the picture of Teddy Roosevelt "regaling a group of his friends with judgments on Goya, Flaubert, Dickens, and Jung, and discussions of Louis the Fat or the number of men at arms seasick in the fleet of Medina Sidonia—this could never be mistaken for one of Franklin Roosevelt. F.D.R.'s interests have always been more circumscribed. His moments of relaxation are given over exclusively to simpler pleasures—to the stamp album, to the Currier and Ives naval prints, to a movie or to good-humored horseplay."[119]

Roosevelt kept himself informed not by applied study but by observation and conversation, and his particular qualities of mind served him reasonably well in the 1930s. True, he was not well versed in economic theory, but had he accepted the greater part of what went for economic wisdom in 1932, he would have been badly misguided. Furthermore, contrary to the general notion, he knew far more about economic matters—utilities regulation, agriculture, banking, corporate structure, public finance—than was usually recognized.

He impressed almost everyone who worked with him with his knowledge of detail. The publisher J. David Stern recalls an occasion when the president recited the average price of ten commodities in 1933 and ten years before and was correct on nine of them.[120] Another observer, a sharp critic of FDR, reported on a 1936 conversation with him on judicial review: "As our talk went on, I was amazed by his reading on the subject and by the grip of his mind . . . For example, he quoted at length from Madison's *Journal* and Elliot's *Debates.*"[121] Similarly, in June 1940 *Time* reported:

> For three weeks he had discussed battlefield contours in military detail with U.S. experts; again and again they have whistled respectfully at his apparent knowledge of Flanders—hills, creeks, towns, bridges. The President's particular forte is islands; he is said to know every one in the world, its peoples, habits, population, geography, economic life. When a ship sank off Scotland several months ago, experts argued: had the ship hit a rock or had it been torpedoed? The President pondered latitude and longitude, said: "It hit a rock. They ought to have seen that rock." Naval Aide Daniel J. Callaghan recalled the rock, disagreed. "At high tide, Mr. President, that rock is submerged." No such thing, said the President, even at high tide that rock is 20 feet out of the water.[122]

Far more important, though, than his knowledge of particulars was his grasp of the interrelationship of the larger aspects of public policy. "Never, at least since Jefferson," a prominent jurist wrote to Justice Brandeis in 1937, "have we had a President of such constructive mind as Roosevelt."[123]

Indeed, so manifest has been FDR's mastery of the affairs of state and so palpable his impact on the office as chief administrator, chief legislator, and tribune of the people that in recent years a separate, and disturbing, line of inquiry has surfaced: Does the imperial presidency have its roots in the 1930s, and is FDR the godfather of Watergate? For four decades much of the controversy over the New Deal centered on the issue of whether Roosevelt had done enough. Abruptly, in the Watergate crisis, the obverse question was raised: Had he done too much? Had there been excessive aggrandizement of the executive office under FDR? In an address on Watergate, Senator Alan Cranston of California, a liberal Democrat, declared: "Those who tried to warn us back at the beginnings of the New Deal of the dangers of one-man rule that lay ahead on the path we were taking toward strong, centralized government may not have been so wrong."[124]

The notion that the origins of the Watergate scandal lie in the age of Roosevelt has a certain plausibility.[125] In the First Hundred Days of 1933 Roosevelt initiated an enormous expansion of the federal government, with proliferating alphabet agencies lodged under the executive wing. Vast powers were delegated to presidential appointees, with little or no congressional oversight. In foreign affairs, Roosevelt bent the law in order to speed aid to the Allies, and in World War II he cut a wide swath in exercising his prerogatives. FDR was the only president to break that barrier against election to a third term, and for good measure he won a fourth term too. Only death cut short his protracted reign.[126]

Those captivated by the historical antecedents of the Watergate era allege that Roosevelt showed no more concern for the sensitivity of Congress than did Nixon. When Roosevelt was asked in 1931 how much authority he expected from Congress if he became president, he snapped, "Plenty."[127] While in office he experienced so much conflict with Congress that on one occasion he said he would like to turn sixteen lions loose on the body. But, it was objected, the lions might make a mistake. "Not if they stayed there long enough," Roosevelt answered.[128]

Many have found Roosevelt's behavior on the eve of America's intervention in World War II especially reprehensible. Edward S. Corwin and Louis W. Koenig protested that, in the destroyer deal, "what President Roosevelt did was to take over for the nonce Congress's power to dispose of property of the United States . . . and to repeal at least two statutes,"[129] while Senator William Fulbright accused Roosevelt of having "usurped the treaty power of the Senate" and of having "circumvented the war powers of the Congress."[130] His detractors point out that six months before Pearl Harbor, on shaky statutory authority, the president used federal power to end strikes, most notably in sending troops to occupy the strikebound North American Aviation plant in California; and that in the same period he dispatched American forces to occupy Iceland and Greenland, provided convoys of vessels carrying arms to Britain, and ordered U.S. destroyers to shoot Nazi U-boats on sight, all acts that infringed Congress's warmaking authority.

After the United States entered the war, Roosevelt raised the ire

of his critics once more by his audacious Labor Day message of
September 7, 1942, "one of the strangest episodes in the history
of the presidency."[131] In a bold—many thought brazen—assertion
of inherent executive prerogative, the president demanded an effective price and wage control statute in the following terms:

> I ask the Congress to take . . . action by the first of October.
> Inaction on your part by that date will leave me with an ines-
> capable responsibility to the people of this country to see to it
> that the war effort is no longer imperiled by threat of economic
> chaos.
>
> In the event that the Congress should fail to act, and act
> adequately, I shall accept the responsibility, and I will act . . .
>
> The President has the powers, under the Constitution and
> under Congressional acts, to take measures necessary to avert
> a disaster which would interfere with the winning of the war . . .
>
> The American people can be sure that I will use my powers
> with a full sense of my responsibility to the Constitution and
> to my country. The American people can also be sure that I
> shall not hesitate to use every power vested in me to accomplish
> the defeat of our enemies in any part of the world where our
> own safety demands such a defeat.
>
> When the war is won, the powers under which I act auto-
> matically revert to the people—to whom they belong.[132]

Congress quickly fell into line, and Roosevelt never had to make
use of this threat, which has been likened to the "claim . . . advanced
by Locke in the seventeenth century on behalf of royal prerogative";[133] but the bad aftertaste lingered.

It has also been argued that Nixon's overweening privy councillors
wielded such power as a consequence of a reform implemented by
Roosevelt. The 1937 report of the President's Committee on Administrative Management called for staffing the Executive Office
with administrative assistants "possessed of . . . a passion for anonymity."[134] That job description sounded tailor-made for the faceless
men around Nixon, for Haldeman and Ehrlichman seemed so indistinguishable that they were likened to Rosencrantz and Guilden-
stern.

Yet the parallels between Roosevelt and Nixon have to be set
against the dissimilarities. "To Roosevelt, the communications of
a President had to be . . . lively, intimate, and open," Emmet Hughes
has observed. "He practiced an almost promiscuous curiosity."[135] In

marked contrast to the obsessionally reclusive Nixon regime, the New Deal government went out of its way to learn what the nation was thinking and to open itself to questioning. Each morning the president and other top officials found a digest of clippings from some 750 newspapers, many of them hostile, on their desks, and before Roosevelt retired for the night he went through a bedtime folder of letters from ordinary citizens. During the First Hundred Days he urged the press to offer criticism so that he might avoid missteps, and both then and later he solicited everyone from old friends to chance acquaintances outside the government to provide information that would serve as a check on what his White House lieutenants were telling him and that would give him points of view at variance with those in Washington officialdom.[136]

Roosevelt differed from Nixon, too, in creating a heterogeneous administration and in encouraging dissenting voices within the government. His cabinet included Republicans as well as Democrats; progressives and conservatives; Catholic, Protestant, and Jew. Whereas Nixon fired Wally Hickel and eased out George Romney, Roosevelt mollified cantankerous mavericks such as Harold Ickes when they threatened to leave. "What impresses me most vividly about the men around Roosevelt," wrote Clinton Rossiter, "is the number of flinty 'no-sayers' who served him, loyally but not obsequiously."[137]

Furthermore, even in the crisis of World War II, Roosevelt most often acted within constitutional bounds, and any transgressions must be placed in the context of the dire challenge raised by Hitler and his confederates. Despite his recognition that, after the fall of France, Britain stood alone, he did not conclude the destroyer deal until he had first consulted with the Republican presidential candidate, and his determination to undertake peacetime conscription was one of many that required congressional approval. Indeed, the biggest cache of discretionary power the president drew upon in the period before Pearl Harbor came from a decision freely taken by Congress in passing the Lend-Lease Act. Winston Churchill was to tell the House of Commons: "Of Roosevelt . . . it must be said that had he not acted when he did, in the way he did, had he not . . . resolved to give aid to Britain, and to Europe in the supreme crisis through which we have passed, a hideous fate might well have overwhelmed mankind and made its whole future for centuries sink into shame and ruin."[138]

Such defenses of Roosevelt, however impressive, fall short of being fully persuasive. As well-disposed a commentator as Schlesinger has said that FDR, "though his better instincts generally won out in the end, was a flawed, willful and, with time, increasingly arbitrary man."[139] Unhappily, of FDR's many legacies, one is a certain lack of appropriate restraint with respect to the exercise of executive power.

The historian confronts one final—and quite different—question: how much of an innovator was Roosevelt? Both admirers and detractors have questioned whether FDR's methods were so original as they have commonly been regarded. Grant McConnell has remarked: "His opponents claimed that he arrogated entirely new sources of power; even some of his supporters believed that this was true. In actuality, however, Roosevelt did no more than follow the examples of his predecessors"[140] Even FDR's reputation as a precedent-breaking Chief Legislator has been questioned. In focusing the special message on a single issue, Roosevelt has been said to have been merely the "apt pupil" of Woodrow Wilson, and in sending actual drafts of bills to Congress to have been "again the sedulous ape," imitating both Wilson and Teddy Roosevelt.[141] "While President Franklin D. Roosevelt's acomplishment as legislator has surpassed all previous records," Corwin wrote, "the story of it, so far as it is of interest to the student of constitutional practice, offers little of novelty . . .The pleasure afforded by its study is—to employ Henry James's classification—that of recognition rather than of surprise."[142]

Some skeptics have even asked: Would not all of the changes from 1933 to 1945 have happened if there had been no Roosevelt, if someone else had been president? Historians have long been wary of "the presidential synthesis" and of chronicles that assign larger importance to great men than to social forces. Certainly, secular trends toward the concentration of power in Washington, and more particularly in the White House, were in motion well before 1933. Furthermore, Roosevelt would not have had nearly so large a stage if he had been elected in 1928 before the crisis of the Great Depression.

FDR himself always refused to answer iffy questions, but this one invites a reply, for it came very close to being a reality. In February 1933, a few weeks before Roosevelt was to take office, he ended a fishing cruise by coming to Bay Front Park in Miami. That night an unemployed bricklayer, Giuseppe Zangara, fired a gun at him from point-blank range, but the wife of a Miami physician deflected the assassin's arm just enough that the bullets missed the president-elect and instead struck the mayor of Chicago, fatally wounding him.[143] Suppose he had not been jostled, and the bullets had found their mark. Would our history have been different if John Nance Garner rather than FDR had been president? No doubt some of the New Deal would have taken place anyway, as a response to the Great Depression. Yet it seems inconceivable that many of the more imaginative features of the Roosevelt years—such as the Federal Arts Project—would have come into being under Garner, or that the conduct of foreign affairs would have followed the same course, or that the institution of the presidency would have been so greatly affected. As Fred Greenstein has observed: "Crisis was a necessary but far from sufficient condition for the modern presidency that began to evolve under Roosevelt."[144]

That conclusion is one with which most scholars would agree—that Franklin Roosevelt was, to use Sidney Hook's terminology, an "event-making man" who was not only shaped by, but also shaped, his age.[145] He comprehended both what kind of opportunity the Great Depression offered to alter the direction of American politics and what kind of menace Hitler posed that the nation had to be mobilized to confront. As a consequence of both perceptions, America, and indeed the world, differed markedly in 1945 from what it had been in 1933, to no small degree because of FDR's actions.

Roosevelt is one of the few American presidents who looms large not just in the history of the United States but also in the history of the world. John Kenneth Galbraith has spoken of the "Bismarck–Lloyd George–Roosevelt Revolution," and Lloyd George himself called FDR "the greatest reforming statesman of the age."[146] To a character in a contemporary novel by an Australian writer, he was "the Daniel of our days."[147] But no one positioned him better in the history of his times than the Oxford don Herbert Nicholas, who in the spring of 1945 wrote:

> When Franklin Roosevelt died on April 12 he concluded a longer period of continuous office than any President of the United States or any British Minister since the Reform Bill. During these twelve crowded years, by political speech and ceremonial proclamation, by executive action and legislative direction, in his three roles of party leader, chief executive and titular head of state, he exercised a cumulative influence on the American public mind which for duration and intensity can hardly be paralleled in the history of modern democracies.[148]

Roosevelt, who affected so many of the institutions and attitudes in the United States, left an especially deep mark on the institution of the presidency. Nicholas has said that Roosevelt "discovered in his office possibilities of leadership which even Lincoln had ignored,"[149] and Joseph A. Califano, Jr., has written: "The foundations of the presidency for the final decades of the twentieth century were set more in terms of Franklin D. Roosevelt than in the terms of George Washington or any of his intervening successors . . . The combination of domestic crisis (depression) and global war focused ever-increasing power in the White House during his unprecedented four-term presidency. The presidency would never be the same again."[150] Not all would accept Rossiter's judgment that "the verdict of history will surely be that he left the Presidency a more splendid instrument of democracy than he found it."[151] Not a few analysts have expressed concern that Roosevelt may have come perilously close to creating a plebiscitary presidency and may have raised unrealistic expectations about what a chief executive can deliver.[152] But few would deny that Franklin Delano Roosevelt continues to provide the standard by which every successor has been and may well continue to be measured.

2

HARRY S. TRUMAN

Insecurity and Responsibility

The presidents made the highlights of American
history, and when you tell about them, you've got it.

—Harry S. Truman

Alonzo L. Hamby

Among scholars, probably no president has been the subject of more
controversy during the past twenty-five years than Harry S. Truman.
Academics have achieved a rough consensus—sometimes in agreement with the impressions of the broader public, sometimes not—
on most of our other twentieth-century chief executives. Herbert
Hoover, whom Truman personally respected but routinely denounced in political speeches, has been reevaluated and somewhat
rehabilitated. Theodore Roosevelt, Woodrow Wilson, and FDR seem
to hold solid positions among the greats or near-greats. Harding and
Coolidge repose among the mediocrities. Eisenhower appears to have
been elevated to at least a high-average estimate, John F. Kennedy
written down as at best a president whose potential was not realized,
Lyndon Johnson as above average on the basis of his domestic
achievements (his flawed foreign policy notwithstanding), and Richard Nixon as a talented man who failed because of inadequate personal resources. Ford, Carter, and Reagan await a scholarly consensus.
Those who study Truman have tended to see him either as a small,
shallow, visionless man attempting to function far beyond his capabilities or as a strong president who developed the power and
authority of his office, defended the accomplishments of his predecessors, and achieved great things in upholding America's international position.[1]

Scholars of the Truman presidency have, however, been struck by the widely perceived contrast between Truman and his awesome predecessor. As William Leuchtenburg has put it, no president labored so obviously and with so much difficulty in "the shadow of FDR." In general, Truman's detractors have considered the unfavorable contrast an accurate measure of Truman's ability and accomplishments. His defenders have seen it as mostly a matter of style, although none has been willing to place him on quite so high a pedestal as Roosevelt's. In large part, the argument stems from differing ideological preconceptions that scholarship is unlikely to surmount; but it is also a product of competing assumptions about the nature of presidential leadership.[2]

It is easier to talk about presidential leadership than to define it. A successful president must somehow lead the nation, the Congress, the executive branch, even the world, while containing actual or potential adversaries ranging from the opposition party to the judiciary to foreign enemies. These tasks call for diverse skills that are unlikely to be present all together in any human being. No one has handled them all flawlessly. Successful leadership has been a relative thing, resting on a mixture of individual charisma, managerial talent, solid judgment, manipulative skill, and a strong ego. In the age of the modern presidency, which has coincided with the age of electronic communications, the first of these attributes has become increasingly important, however irrelevant it may be to the task of day-to-day policy making and management.

Harry Truman possessed little or no charisma, struggled with an ego more fragile than most observers have understood, and had extreme distaste for the need to manipulate others. He was, however, a good manager and, on the important things, a person of sound judgment, not least because he understood his weaknesses. Often dismissed by contemporaries as a "little man" because his deficiencies were more apparent than his strengths, he actually was one of the more important and successful of twentieth-century presidents.

An obvious measurement of presidential greatness available to students of the modern presidency is the public approval rating routinely presented by opinion surveys. Most of us would dismiss such a standard as too narrow; still, it seems a truism that a president who enjoys the approval of less than a majority will have trouble achieving much over the long run. By this criterion Truman was, if not a failure, considerably less than a success as president: his public approval was lower than 50 percent for the larger part of his time in office, including the entire final three years of his second term.[3]

Another measure is the presidential scorecard: how many legislative accomplishments? how many international achievements? By this standard, Truman does not fare badly, largely because of his foreign policy record. Yet the scorecard is difficult as a universal measurement. It assumes the desirability of change and has to rest on criteria that may be debatable. Like almost all historical judgments, the debits and credits on the card are products of an often unconscious and necessarily subjective counterfactual analysis. For example, the high marks given to Franklin D. Roosevelt for his New Deal policies generally rest on the assumption that they provided a morally imperative welfare safety net, rightly curbed the power of big business, and promoted economic recovery. It is possible to argue with all these assumptions and by no means certain that future generations of scholars will accept any of them.

The length of the scorecard itself is largely a matter of opportunity. Some times call for change and activity, others do not; some political situations facilitate it, others make it all but impossible. Greatness, if measured by the scorecard, may be largely an accident of being in the White House at the right moment (if not the most comfortable one). And of course the scorecard cannot speak to the achievement of presidents who come to office with a felt belief that success means holding the line against change in one way or another. Nonetheless, it appears that the scorecard test and such closely related characteristics as "strength" or "activeness" have been most influential among students of the presidency.[4]

Perhaps the most intriguing and most useful of measurements involves an assessment of presidential personality. A simple and widely used character typology is David Reisman's distinction between inner-direction and other-direction. James David Barber has given us some good, if controversial, tools in his *Presidential Character* with its active-positive, active-negative, passive-positive, and passive-negative categories. These styles of characterization are relatively crude, but so are virtually all such gauges at this level of generalization; that such should be the case is not a bad thing.

Reisman and Barber have given us means of enduring value for understanding changes in American society as a whole and for analyzing the men who have held the American presidency. The goal of such an endeavor should not be one of clinical diagnosis; few scholars are equipped for such a task, and existing sources, invariably personal writings and secondhand reminiscences, rarely permit much confidence in the outcome. (There are few, if any, instances of an important historical figure meeting with a psychobiographer and surrendering confidences and anxieties as if he were talking to a therapist.) A scholarly examination of personality needs to be descriptive, suggestive, and, above all, without pretense of omniscience.

Such an approach has obvious limitations. Nonetheless, there can be few more constant truths about the American presidency than the exhausting, unceasing strain it places upon the individuals who occupy it. For this reason alone any assessment of the success or failure of presidential leadership must begin with an effort to understand the character and personality of the man in the White House.[5]

Barber clearly has some trouble categorizing Truman, concluding that he was an active-positive personality but conceding that he possessed tendencies toward the active-negative. My own work toward a full-scale biography of Truman leads me to conclude that the call is even closer than Barber believes. Truman spent most of his life struggling to achieve a positive self-image. He was only intermittently successful, and even during his presidency he had a way of emitting negative apprehensions about himself that consistently undermined his claims to authority. He was, I believe, a remarkably successful president, but his success rested less on a consistently active-positive personality than on a dogged determination to shoulder the burdens of responsibility and to achieve goals that he often felt were beyond his personal capabilities. To this he added an ability to make positive uses of his own sense of his limitations.

Harry Truman was sixty-one years old when he became president; by then his thought and character had been substantially formed. In order to understand the way he *felt* about the presidency and its obligations, in order to understand the way in which he tried to administer the office, we must look to his earlier life.[6]

Truman's boyhood experiences were not of the sort that create a positive self-image. Afflicted with myopia, he probably was close to being legally blind without eyeglasses. There is every indication that his visual disability—he used the word "deformity" years later—presented severe barriers to the development of a fully normal, confident personality during his childhood years in Jackson County, Missouri. It is necessary to remember that he grew to adulthood in a neofrontier society that valued aggressive masculinity. Jackson

Countians of Truman's childhood retained bitter and vivid memories of the way in which the Civil War had ravaged western Missouri; Quantrill's raiders held annual reunions; Frank James from time to time came into Independence to see to business and visit old friends. Partisan attachments were deeply felt allegiances, not simple preferences. Fistfights between adult men were common ways of settling disputes and frequent election-day events. No one in Truman's early life exemplified the ethos of this rough society more vividly than his aggressive, fiesty father, John Truman.

It is clear that young Harry did not fit in well. Assigned to household chores as a small child, he was a mamma's boy. The eyeglasses he wore from the time he started school at the age of eight made him a bit of a freak to other boys. The danger of broken glasses and the expense of replacing them led to strong injunctions from his parents against getting involved in rough games, and above all against fighting. In a society that told him to be aggressive, he devoted his psychic energy to the other-directed task of getting along with others. He became a conciliator among his peers whenever possible and ran away from fights when necessary. He learned early to discern the expectations of his teachers and always sought to please them. He studied the piano. He was scared of girls throughout his school years. He was, as he admitted years later, a "sissy."[7]

He was, nonetheless, the classic inner-directed nineteenth-century man in one respect. From his parents, especially his mother, he received a set of simple, traditional values, internalized them, and held steadfastly to them for ever after. Foremost among them were honesty, duty, loyalty, and Victorian moral behavior. It was in his dealings with others that he departed from the inner-directed profile. Avoidance of conflict in face-to-face encounters appears to have been not simply a manipulative tool but a compulsive need that led him to avoid the frank disagreement and angry words that had come so easily from his father. It was a personality characteristic that would stay with him almost to the end; the frustration it caused him would be channeled into the numerous angry letters and explosive outbursts that characterized his presidency.

If his mother doted on him, his father clearly preferred Harry's younger brother, the more conventional J. Vivian. While Harry was spending his spare time learning Mozart and Chopin, Vivian was virtually a junior partner in his father's livestock trading business. John Truman was seldom harsh with either son and never struck them; nonetheless, it is clear that Harry was not his favorite and nearly certain that the eldest son realized that he did not have a full measure of his father's respect and affection. His boyhood military ambitions, which included special tutoring for West Point entrance examinations, and his ostentatious interest in the sport of fencing strike one as manifestations of an effort to achieve a more masculine self-image. It was an attempt that culminated in young Harry's discovery that his eyes would make it impossible for him to be admitted to the Academy.

At some point in 1902 or 1903, John Truman lost his family's assets by speculating in grain futures. The adverse effects on Harry's life are obvious enough. He never attended a university, was forced to give up the piano, and had to drop out of a Kansas City business college he had attended for a summer and a semester. Other effects are less certain. It is clear, however, that the father's financial failure weighed heavily on his son, who for the rest of his life was acutely sensitive to observations that his father had been a failure.

Nevertheless, John Truman's bad luck did create a situation in which Harry must have increased his self-esteem. Working first as a construction crew timekeeper, then as a Kansas City bank clerk, he demonstrated that he could handle adult employment very well, became a substantial contributor to the family's income, developed a new circle of friends, and realized his military aspirations by joining the national guard. The construction crew experience involved living and associating with tough hobos; he got along, and his boss was pleased with his work. Surviving personnel records demonstrate that he was a valued employee at Commerce Bank right up until the time he moved to a position at Union National Bank with a substantial increase in salary. The jobs may not have amounted to much, although the bank positions held some promise of advancement. Most significantly, they had to make Truman feel better about himself.[8]

For that reason, it is hard to find any explanation, beyond family loyalty and a need to win his father's approval, for Truman's decision to help his father manage Grandmother Young's farm. At best, the eleven years he spent on the farm, most of them working under his father's supervision, could have added little to his self-confidence. He received considerable gratification from his father's approval and perhaps some satisfaction from his ability to handle hard farm work. It was during these years that he joined the Masons and other fraternal organizations, developing many new friends and winning the esteem of numerous older associates.

Yet he also functioned as an aging adolescent, living with his family, taking orders from his father, making a little money on his own, and failing to establish the sense of identity that he most coveted, that of an independent, successful adult. The central problem of his long courtship with Bess Wallace—his inability to achieve financial independence—must have gnawed away at whatever self-esteem he had developed. As late as November 1913, in a letter to her he described himself as "a guy with spectacles and a girl mouth."[9]

His first attempt to establish himself as an entrepreneur after his father's death must have further dampened whatever faith he had achieved in himself. A lead and zinc mine he purchased with two partners in northeastern Oklahoma developed into a financial fiasco. He lost about $5,000, some of it borrowed from (or possibly invested by) his uncle Harrison. A second business venture, in oil brokerage and exploration, produced more equivocal results. When Truman left for the army in mid-1917, it seemed possible that he was on the brink of riches. In the end, however, he no more than broke even.

In the meantime he had gone on to the most satisfying success of his life up to that time—perhaps the most satisfying ever—his experience as an artillery officer in World War I. In less than a year he made himself a leader of men. In training at Fort Sill, Oklahoma, he managed the only successful camp canteen and performed so well in field activities that he qualified for an elite advanced artillery school in France. Given a battery, he overcame his initial fear of command, displayed courage under fire, and won the respect of his troops. He returned home filled with confidence and determined to make a career as a successful businessman.

What occurred instead was a personal disaster. Almost everyone knows about the failure of the Truman & Jacobson haberdashery. Most, however, do not realize that the unfortunate partners failed far less because of bad luck and an unfavorable economic climate than because of their own poor business instincts. Undercapitalized, heavily dependent on debt, and up against stiff, well-established competition, Truman & Jacobson does not appear to have fared well in the few prosperous months it was open for business before a sharp economic recession hit the country in the last half of 1920. Even under good economic conditions, the odds would have been against its survival.

Truman also displayed considerable ineptitude as a petty real estate speculator. Receiving a substantial, if mortgage-laden, house in a posh neighborhood as compensation for his stake in the wartime oil enterprise, he swapped it for an interest in an apartment building, then traded that for 160 acres of grossly overvalued Kansas farmland just before the bottom fell out of rural land prices. The Kansas property was eventually signed over to a bank in an effort to settle a haberdashery loan. It did not do even that.

Truman's bad business judgment is of less interest than his explanation of his failure. He persuaded himself that he was the victim of an economic squeeze engineered by northeastern Republican financiers under the direction of Andrew Mellon, who he believed had precipitated an economic crisis by pursuing tight money policies as secretary of the treasury. This conviction was actually the rationalization of a man who had lost everything despite his hard, honest work; Truman bolstered his shaky ego by seeking external causes.

It was also easy and altogether natural for a regional small businessman with a populistic Democratic heritage to fall back on his political prejudices, and blame the financial establishment for his difficulty. (Actually, to the extent that monetary policy precipitated the recession, it was a result of Federal Reserve action during the last year and a half of the Wilson administration; under Harding and Mellon, interest rates declined.) Truman's fervent belief in easy money policies (rather paradoxically alongside fiscal restraint) would help precipitate conflict between the Treasury Department and the Federal Reserve Board during his second term as president.

What is perhaps most important about the saga of Truman & Jacobson, however, is the way in which Truman dealt with a hard blow. However discouraging his business career, he had inner resources and compensatory experiences that allowed him to maintain a balance between positive and negative images of himself. Truman literally lost all his assets; he voluntarily paid off numerous small creditors and dodged a couple of larger ones for years; he had one bank account garnisheed and two major court judgments rendered against him. Yet he seems hardly to have become discouraged.

His resilience stemmed largely from the success he enjoyed in other areas of his life. Active in the Kansas City area American Legion, he was for a time an influential figure in it. He did most of the work in establishing the local Reserve Officers Association. Almost daily, he enjoyed the company of men who had served under his command in the war and remained loyal to him. He rose rapidly in the Masonic order. In general, he had many friends and enjoyed the respect of numerous older and influential men. Throughout all his unsuccessful ventures, he appears to have had active encouragement and support from his mother and his wife. These positive experiences balanced the negative ones and paved the way for his successful move into politics.

Almost from the beginning, Truman established himself as the major Democratic figure in eastern Jackson County (that portion of the county outside the limits of Kansas City). The sensitivity to others that had been forced on him as a child served him well as a campaigner; he was a poor speaker, but his omnipresent smile and firm handshake were more important in a milieu of personal politics. His war service and reserve officer status broadened his appeal and added an important dimension to his network of friends, relatives, political organization allies, and fraternal contacts. His business experience and reputation for honesty were strong assets in a culture that still venerated the independent enterpriser. His demands for not simply honesty but also the use of modern budgetary techniques and greater efficiency in county government were attractive to an independent-minded, educated middle class drawn toward a newer technocratic managerial ethic.

More a follower than a leader during his single term (1923–1924) as eastern district judge, Truman dominated the county court during his two terms as presiding judge (1927–1934). He assured himself of control on most issues by handpicking the eastern district Democratic nominee and either coopted or overrode the western district incumbent. De facto eastern county leader after the death of Tom Pendergast's brother Mike in 1929, he used patronage effectively to consolidate his position. Yet he equally cemented his standing as an advocate of honesty and efficiency; he appointed a bipartisan team of professional engineers to design a modern county highway system and oversee its construction under a system of open and competitive bidding. He persuaded the voters to authorize bonds for the project by coordinating a shrewd public relations campaign, bringing around leading Republicans and independents, and arguing that the tax expenditures involved in bond financing for new roads would actually amount to less than would be required for annual rebuilding of the old crushed-rock and dirt roads.

During this period he also became involved with the Kansas City Public Service Institute (later the Civic Research Institute), a nonpartisan advocate of the managerial approach to local government and one of the early proponents of a bond issue for new roads. Truman and the institute favored a strong program of civic development—good roads, county sewer districts, zoning legislation, equitable tax valuation—all administered in as efficient and as politically neutral a fashion as possible.

Working with the institute, he developed proposals for streamlining county government that were introduced in the Missouri legislature. All involved a sharp reduction in the number of elective county offices, using the rationale that many such positions were primarily technical or administrative (such as highway engineer, county clerk) and thus beyond the possibility of an informed opinion by the electorate. All advocated a considerable increase in the power and authority of the presiding judge. Almost all failed to pass, but they serve as an indication that early on, Truman had adopted the idea of the strong executive as a practical working model for public leadership.[10]

There were other dimensions to this model. On at least one level, Truman during this period was a business manager who saw ordinary partisan politics as something of a regrettable necessity at the local level. Although a Democrat in politics, he was in many ways indistinguishable from the sort of petit bourgeois Republican whom Sinclair Lewis satirized as George F. Babbitt. Truman, like Babbitt, was a small businessman and civic booster, an individual who found emotional fulfillment in male camaraderie, an espouser of the idea that business methods were applicable to government.

To the greatest extent possible, he sought a reputation as a tight-fisted budget manager, not as a dispenser of social benefits. In 1924 he was capable of defending the county court's decision to terminate its charity payroll because it amounted to "paying people for being poor." His values were very much those of the business-minded middle classes. George F. Babbitt (if he were a Democrat) probably would have been a valued member of Truman's poker group, the Harpie Club. The future president's social consciousness would be largely an outgrowth of political experience yet to come.[11]

Privately, Truman chafed at the political compromise he had to make. A series of angry diary memoranda written on Pickwick Hotel stationery around 1930 and 1931 testify to the considerable discomfort he felt as a result of his association with the Pendergast machine. He had put "a lot of no-account sons of bitches" on the county payroll and had looked the other way at a few questionable transactions, he told himself. Perhaps he had squandered a million dollars (a grossly exaggerated figure) this way; but he had saved the county seven million. "Am I an administrator or not? Or am I just a crook?" He probably asked the questions in all seriousness.[12]

In fact he had done no more than what he had to do in order to win office and maintain himself there. He had made a Niebuhrian compromise akin to that of many politicians, then and now, accepting the imperfections of his world, working within them, and striving to improve an imperfect system. Nevertheless, the embarrassment persisted. Though a political asset, the Pendergast affiliation was a psychological liability. Truman managed it by reminding himself of his own honesty and modest financial circumstances, which constituted proof that he had preserved his honor. He assured himself that Tom Pendergast's associates rather than Tom himself were the real problem and ostentatiously cultivated what he considered a traditional virtue—reciprocal loyalty and support for the leader who had underwritten his political career. Despite this undercurrent of anxiety, he emerged from the local phase of his political career a stronger and more confident person, albeit one who would forever be defensive about his machine associations.

Truman's election to the U.S. Senate in 1934 represented in many ways a logical move for a maturing politician. During his years as presiding judge, he had learned to deal with city minority groups. As head of the state association of county judges, as a senior army reserve officer, and as a prominent Mason, he had made valuable contacts throughout Missouri. Still an awkward speaker, he nevertheless was a tireless and aggressive campaigner, at his best working the county fairs and local picnics that were the staples of rural Missouri political life in the 1930s.

But his victory does not appear to have increased his confidence. External circumstances and the delicate positive-negative balance he felt within himself conspired to deprive Truman of the steadily upward-trending "confidence curve" that success in county administration and victory in a statewide election might have delivered to other politicians. If anything, his first term seems to have subjected his self-image to its severest test since the haberdashery bankruptcy.[13]

For one thing, there was the manner of his election. Kansas City politics had grown increasingly violent, crime-ridden, and corrupt in the late 1920s and early 1930s. With a favorable state supreme court decision and the election of Democratic governor Guy B. Park in 1932, the Pendergast machine had taken control of the police force (hitherto controlled by a state-appointed board of commissioners) and made itself all but immune from law enforcement. In the violent municipal elections of March 1934, four persons were

killed and dozens injured. Truman himself won the August Democratic primary over two strong opponents only with massive support from the governor's office on down through the entire state
administration and with an estimated 40,000 ghost votes in Kansas
City. Well aware that he had been the beneficiary of massive fraud
and improper influence, he also understood that he had needed these
assists and could not afford to repudiate them.[14]

The move to Washington also created significant family strains.
The Trumans' tight finances made it impossible to buy a house and
at least difficult to consider any sort of year-round residential arrangements. Moreover, Bess Truman's attachment to her mother
dictated that she and daughter Margaret would spend at least six
months of the year in Independence, whatever the length of congressional sessions. Truman's extended separations from his family
throughout the remainder of the 1930s were a source of stress that
added to other pressures.[15]

First among these was establishing himself with his new peers.
His contemporary public comments and his memoirs document his
sense of insecurity, his feelings of inadequacy, and his resentment
at being typed a machine flunky. He was especially upset by the
ostentatiously self-righteous independent progressives, who seemed
to give him shortest shrift. It was a resentment he never abandoned;
during his presidency, it found such targets as Estes Kefauver, Herbert Lehman, and Helen Gahagan Douglas.

Characteristically, he told himself that he was a doer, not a talker
(as they were), and that he would prove himself by hard work and
solid performance. His attitude appealed to the Senate's professional
pols and party regulars. A good many were the products of machine
electioneering, and virtually all adhered to the Senate tradition that
new members should be diffident, quiet, and industrious. Adding
sociability to these virtues, Truman won over the senior Democrats
much in the way he had won over older men in the Masons. By the
end of his first term, he had many friends and supporters among his
colleagues.[16]

His relations with President Roosevelt were another matter. The
White House appears to have consulted him seldom on patronage
matters, preferring at first to deal with the powers in Kansas City
directly, then ignoring them and him altogether. Before 1941, lack
of presidential recognition was a constant, increasingly irritating
sore on Truman's psyche.

Most discouraging and stressful, however, was the overthrow of the Pendergast machine during the years 1937–1939. His home state power base disintegrating, his family frequently far away, Truman seems to have begun to experience prolonged periods of emotional exhaustion. In September 1937 he checked into the army-navy hospital at Hot Springs, Arkansas, complaining of nausea, severe headaches, and general debilitation. It was the first of at least three such visits over the next half-dozen years. Always, the doctors could find no serious physical problems and could recommend little more than rest and relaxation. Truman's successful renomination and reelection campaign in 1940, his subsequent stature as Missouri's leading Democrat, his increasing national prestige as head of the Truman committee, and his ability to dictate to the White House on patronage matters all did little to relieve the burdens he felt. Army records document stays at Hot Springs in 1941 and 1943.[17]

Throughout his life Truman appears to have wavered between positive and negative conceptions of himself. In politics, the American profession most productive of insecurity, this was a special burden. He was constantly aware that few voters would mark their ballots for him on the basis of who he was but rather that he must capture their support on the basis of what he did. Hard work and high achievement became in his mind the only way to secure public approval. Yet with each success, and especially with each move up the political ladder, the challenges seemed more formidable. The presiding judgeship of Jackson County was difficult but manageable; the Senate presented a far heavier burden on a new and daunting political turf; the presidency involved enormous responsibilities, a blinding spotlight of attention, and the additional handicap of following the most awesome chief executive of the twentieth century.

Few men thrust so suddenly into the White House could have felt altogether secure. Truman's confidence in himself ebbed and flowed during his presidency; perhaps its low point was in the fall of 1946, its high point in the months after his dramatic 1948 reelection. Most significant, however, is the persistence of his uneasiness with himself throughout his nearly eight years as chief executive. He had gotten ahead in life as most men do, possessed mixed feelings about himself that were relatively common, and was no more neurotic than most of us. Yet he found himself in progressively stressful situations guaranteed to magnify any intimations of insecurity. There is of course much more to a presidency than the personality of the

incumbent, but Truman's displays of an erratic personality powerfully affected public perceptions of his leadership.

His first attempts at putting together a staff were indicative of
the isolation and insecurity he felt upon taking office. He surrounded
himself with friends from his past. Some of them—Harry Vaughn
(military aide) and Jake Vardaman (naval aide)—were probably meant
primarily to be morale boosters. Others—John W. Snyder (Office of
War Mobilization and Reconversion) and Ed McKim (briefly Truman's chief administrative assistant) held genuinely important positions. Snyder quite probably has been over-criticized, but McKim,
one of Truman's Battery D men and a Reserve Officer Corps buddy,
was an unbelievable choice. An Omaha insurance executive, he had
no significant experience in politics at any level and held views that
would have placed him on the right wing of the Republican party.
It was fortunate for Truman and the country that he was on his way
back to Omaha in a matter of weeks. However, a few unsavory
characters, most notably John Maragon, hung on around the fringes
of the White House, and the image—never very accurate—of a presidency run by a host of unknown, second-rate characters persisted.[18]

Throughout Truman's life, he was a remarkably thin-skinned individual, quick to resent any criticism of himself, his family, or his
friends, however rough his own political rhetoric. From 1922 on, he
routinely characterized any campaign against him as the dirtiest
ever waged. The way in which he reacted to any criticism of members of his family is legendary. Dean Acheson has told how a Soviet
ambassador was almost expelled because of an alleged snub to Mrs.
Truman. The President's outrage at music critics who found little
merit in his daughter's voice is an oft-repeated story. While he physically threatened only Paul Hume—"I never met you, but if I do
you'll need a new nose and plenty of beefsteak and perhaps a supporter below"—he felt the same way about many. When friends and
associates came under attack, he tended to ignore the fact that they
usually were guilty of acts that were at least unseemly, at times
improper. He was especially prone to characterize the charges of
corruption in his administration as indirect attacks upon him rather
than as allegations worth investigating.[19]

Most remarkable of all in a president of the United States was an
incessant thirst for recognition that revealed a remarkably fragile
ego. It was a constant theme of his life, going back at least to 1914,
when he fretted about his family's lack of appreciation for his efforts
in managing a long and bitter legal action that finally cleared the

claims of Martha Truman and her brother Harrison Young to the family farm at Grandview. It may have been a natural enough attitude for a young man, but it seems astonishing to find it carried all the way to the Oval Office. In July 1949 Truman prepared, but did not send, a waspish letter to William Southern, the publisher and editor of the *Independence Examiner* (and the father-in-law of Bess's brother George), complaining about never being mentioned in its daily historical feature. Less than a year later he penned another, this one sent in abridged form, to the publisher and editor of the *Kansas City Star*, Roy Roberts, expressing indignation at the absence of his name in the *Star*'s centennial edition.[20]

Truman seems, in fact, to have been a man who carried around a lot of concealed, unfocused rage and hostility throughout his public career. From time to time, it boiled up within him and sought a target of opportunity, be it Westbrook Pegler, Drew Pearson, or Paul Hume. (The Hume letter is perhaps the classic example of Truman's tendency to channel his aggressions into situations that did not involve face-to-face contacts.) At other times it simmered just beneath the surface. Most newsmen, who thought they had a good personal relationship with the president they covered, would have been astonished at his private distrust of them.

The other-directed elements in his behavior most often controlled his working life, but they clashed with the inner-directed imperatives he had learned as a youth. Often frustrated at having to persuade people whom as chief executive he should have been able to command, he liked to believe that he had told off someone after engaging in the mildest of conversations with him. He even concocted after-the-fact accounts—which he no doubt came to believe as true—of key meetings with Secretary of State James F. Byrnes and General Douglas MacArthur. In both cases, he pictured himself as far more commanding and decisive than he actually was. The need to seem to be in charge led him to numerous verbal shots from the hip at press conferences and other public occasions. Inaccurate statements, undiplomatic comments, snappish exchanges with reporters—all were inconsistent with the image of the presidency that most Americans desired. All lowered Truman's standing with the public. Such were the psychological manifestations of a need to be in command that clashed with private doubts that one was actually capable of being so.[21]

At other times, faced with situations he could not control, he vented his anger on paper, drawing up a draft of a speech calling for the hanging of John L. Lewis or preparing a nuclear ultimatum to the USSR and China. Of course, he did not really intend to deliver the speech; nor did he have any actual expectation of nuking Moscow and Beijing. It was all simply a way of working off anger before he did what had to be done and probably was a good psychological therapy.[22]

A pattern of workaholism characterizes Truman's entire political career. From the time as eastern district judge he took his Dodge roadster out day after day to inspect back roads all over Jackson County through his years in the presidency, he found psychological vindication in hard work and mastery of detail, even when from time to time it brought him to the verge of physical collapse. He took pride in his detailed knowledge of the federal budget and carried armloads of work up to his private living quarters in the White House night after night. Admirers took it as an indication of his serenity that he had a way of falling asleep as soon as his head hit the pillow; more likely it was an indication of exhaustion. His tendency toward overwork, his difficulties with stress, and his tightly-wound psyche led his physician to counsel exercise, adequate rest, and relaxation. Regular morning walks, hours in the White House swimming pool, evening poker games, weekend yacht cruises, and Key West vacations all served a therapeutic purpose.

All too often Truman's prevailing public image was that of a man who was less than an admirable leader. Rather he was a "machine politician" surrounded by mediocre "cronies." He was a "little man" unable to handle his job, as demonstrated by such incidents as his mishandling of the Byrnes-Wallace dispute of 1946, his capitulation on meat price controls in the same year, his inability "to command" Congress (as FDR supposedly had been able to do), and his failure to bring the Korean War to a close. He too often appeared erratic and impulsive rather than decisive. The Pulitzer Prize cartoon of 1952 displayed an angry president telling a group of reporters: "Your editors ought to have more sense than to print what I say!"[23]

The image was deceiving in almost every respect. His critics notwithstanding, Truman put together a very solid White House staff after his hectic early months in office. If he was less imposing than FDR, sober analysts nonetheless must question whether FDR would have exercised any greater power over events. His temper was probably no worse than that of many other presidents, although almost all others were more adroit at keeping their outbursts private. (Eisenhower comes instantly to mind.)

Yet was the image, however deficient in its specifics, wholly inaccurate? Truman's defenders may blame the press, which was still the major means of presidential communication with the public and considerably more Republican than it is today. But whatever partisan exaggeration Truman endured cannot be taken as a major explanation. The fact was that in projecting an appearance of leadership, Truman was his own worst enemy; many aspects of his prevailing public persona accurately revealed his insecurities in his position and demonstrated how he often privately felt about himself.

Albeit he was in many respects a strong, important, and successful president despite his weak contemporary standing with the public. This success stemmed in part from his dogged determination to overcome his insecurities, in part from his ability to perceive some of his real deficiencies and to manage his presidency in ways that either circumvented them or occasionally turned them into strengths.

Truman's strengths were in general the obverse of his weaknesses. Most simply, if he tended to feel his shortcomings too keenly, he compensated intelligently for them by building a presidency that acknowledged his limitations as an individual while actually strengthening the office itself.

He came to a presidency that had grown in helter-skelter fashion during the dozen years before him. The proliferation of social programs during the New Deal and of foreign obligations during World War II had given the position enormous new burdens. These, along with FDR's brilliant use of the communications media, had made it a focus of public attention as never before. Franklin Roosevelt had of course responded to these developments by requesting executive reorganization. FDR had received six administrative assistants and had begun to make use of the Bureau of the Budget as a legislative clearinghouse. Nonetheless, he never came close to abandoning his penchant for improvisation and ad hoc arrangements. He continued to rely heavily upon outside advisers and established few clear lines of authority or issue-jurisdiction among his official staff.[24]

It probably was a corollary of Truman's limited confidence in himself that he made no effort to emulate his predecessor in juggling issues and personalities; it surely was a credit to his judgment. In general, his management of both immediate staff and the larger executive branch sacrificed few of the purported benefits of the Roosevelt model and displayed even fewer of its shortcomings. His first year or so was one of shakedown, characterized by some false starts, personality conflicts, and numerous comings and goings. In many respects this phase was to be expected in any sudden, unplanned transition resulting from the death of a president, but it was made immensely more complicated by the critical issues, diplomatic and political, that attended the end of World War II, the beginning of the Cold War, and domestic reconversion.

Truman fumbled initially on some appointments and had to grope for the right managerial techniques. His first director of the budget, Harold Smith, felt it necessary to lecture him on his mistaken efforts to use cabinet members as if they were working staff aides. But by mid-1946 something like a coherent staff system began to jell in the White House. The result might be called one of structured decentralization in which responsibilities were relatively clearly defined and access to the president was remarkably open. At no point did the Truman system contain a single chief of staff who was the only conduit to the president. In dealing with his administrative assistants, with whom he met daily, Truman functioned largely as his own chief of staff. Cabinet members appear to have been able to secure reasonable amounts of presidential time simply by requesting it.[25]

If any figure emerged from this arrangement as an informal assistant chief of staff, it was the president's special counsel, first Clark Clifford, then Charles Murphy. That the post became so important was less a matter of Truman's design than of Clifford's ambition, charm, and talent. Brought into the White House as aide to the naval aide, Clifford shrewdly analyzed the power vacuum around the president, made himself useful in numerous ways, established himself as the leader of a talented group of staffers, and won appointment as special counsel several months after Samuel Rosenman resigned from the position. He became the most impressive and best-known figure around Truman, wielding considerable influence upon the course of his presidency.

Yet it needs to be emphasized that Clifford's authority was never as great as that of Sherman Adams or Donald Regan. It is in fact hard to find a single instance in which his voice can be given sole or even preponderant credit for influencing a major presidential policy decision or political strategy. One need not gainsay Clifford's remarkable skill as an advocate, organizer, tactician, and speechwriter to observe that his advice to Truman generally consisted of reinforcement on major matters.

Truman for his part seems to have liked and respected his dynamic young aide. He not only tolerated Clifford's semiformal role as co-ordinator of the policy-oriented administrative assistants; he probably found it valuable. One suspects that he was uneasy about Clifford's high visibility and self-promotion with the press; however, he doubtless respected Clifford's ability and may well have understood that the Special Counsel's good public image was an asset to the administration. But he was equally protective of his need to receive inputs from other sources.[26]

Clifford's successor, Charles Murphy, an able staff man with extensive Capitol Hill experience, possessed much more of a "passion for anonymity" and hence made the position less visible. He was, however, at least as shrewd an adviser and was involved in almost every major issue of Truman's last three years in office. One suspects that the president valued him at least as much as he did Clifford and found his low-profile style considerably more agreeable.

Charles Ross, Truman's old friend and press secretary until his death in late 1950, always had his boss's ear on a wide range of issues. Among the adminstrative assistants, David K. Niles, the administration's contact with the northeastern Jewish liberal community, ostentatiously shunned Clifford and dealt directly with the president. John Steelman, always ready to remind visitors that his title was *the* assistant to the president, ran a separate office from which he handled a realm of administrative detail; he also wielded considerable influence in labor-management relations and Korean War economic mobilization.

Matthew J. Connelly, the appointments secretary, controlled access to the Oval Office, but with the understanding that his job was to schedule appointments, not to deny them to anyone with a legitimate need to see the president. He was more significant as a liaison to the professional politicians and money men of the Democratic party. Along with Donald Dawson, administrative assistant in charge of personnel, he had a large voice in political patronage decisions. The director of the budget always seems to have enjoyed substantial input on the larger strategic matters of program planning. The chairman of the newly established Council of Economic Advisers appears to have had all the access he desired. (Edwin Nourse, however, made little of it, thanks largely to his remote, academic style; his politically-minded successor, Leon Keyserling, was better at reaching Truman and more astute at building alliances with other staffers.)

Admirals William Leahy and Sidney Souers were always able to provide their perspectives on various matters pertaining to diplomatic and strategic issues. Clifford injected himself into many foreign policy matters during his tenure. Murphy seems to have been less prone to do so, although he was involved in some major decisions, including the discussions that led to NSC-68. The reduced role of the special counsel stemmed in part from the appointment in July 1950 of W. Averell Harriman as administrative assistant to the president with special responsibility for foreign policy and national security issues. In many respects the first "national security adviser," Harriman served as White House foreign policy coordinator. His contact with Truman was frequent and highly influential.[27]

Harry Truman had matured in a society that venerated masculine strength and leadership. As a boy he had been a hero-worshiper of Andrew Jackson; throughout his life he admired strong presidents. His reading of the Constitution reinforced his belief that the presidency was a position of power. The example of his predecessor underscored all these lessons and left him with a determination to defend his office against all encroachments. (Throughout his presidency, the Bureau of the Budget bolstered this attitude in its recommendations on specific pieces of legislation that contained real or imagined inroads into presidential authority.) If at times he overreached himself, as in the steel seizure of 1952 he was largely successful in his objective of passing the presidency on to his successor unimpaired.

Truman appears from the beginning to have been concerned with the possibility that he might somehow have his options narrowed by being improperly excluded from preliminary discussions of significant issues. He reacted negatively when secretary of the navy James Forrestal floated the idea of a cabinet "secretariat," which Forrestal hoped to use in the cause of improved interagency coordination. Early on in the administration, Dean Acheson (then under secretary of state) told the president that periodic informal luncheons of the cabinet were becoming a regular institution at which policy discussions rather than socializing seemed to be the main business.

Forrestal may have seen such gatherings simply as a way of preparing for the president's meetings with the cabinet. To Acheson they were reminiscent of Robert Lansing's abortive attempt to bring some coherence to the government after Woodrow Wilson's stroke. Truman apparently regarded them as a threat that might take the decision-making process out of his hands. Gently but firmly, he ordered an end to them. Budget Director Smith (or possibly his successor, James Webb), perhaps defending his own office, perhaps expressing Truman's opinion, told Forrestal: "We are not interested in having you organize the president. The president will organize you."

The cabinet lunches may have been the first in a series of efforts to preserve the influence of the Department of the Navy against what Forrestal perceived as the imminent threat of the unification of the armed forces. For two years Forrestal pressed unsuccessfully for some sort of a national security coordinating council; the membership of such a body would be broader than the military departments, and presumably it would eliminate the need for unification. Yet a national security body, established by act of Congress, could present serious challenges to the authority of the presidency.

What eventually developed, of course, was for Forrestal the worst of both worlds—a Department of Defense that embodied at least the pro forma concept of unification and a National Security Council (NSC) without the wide-ranging semiautonomous mission he had desired. Both outcomes were the result of intensive White House lobbying. To underscore the point that the NSC was to be a creature of the presidency, the Bureau of the Budget insisted on locating its offices in the Old State Department building next to the White House. In case any doubt remained, Truman declared at the NSC's first meeting "that he regarded it as *his* council." Periodically over the next two years he was annoyed by the efforts of Forrestal, whom he made secretary of defense, and Forrestal's successor, Louis Johnson, to make the NSC an "operating super-cabinet on the British model" with authority to enforce its presidentially approved decisions.

Administered by Sidney Souers and James Lay, the NSC served essentially as an information-gathering and policy-coordinating agency for the president during the first three years of its existence. Until the outbreak of the Korean War, Truman attended only twelve of its fifty-seven meetings. That did not prevent it from grappling with important questions. From the beginning, it was used as a mechanism for authorizing covert operations by the Central Intelligence Agency (CIA). In late 1949 it formulated what was to become its most famous document, NSC-68, a plan for a major American military buildup in response to the Soviet development of the atomic bomb.

Yet it was hardly an important body. Souers enjoyed Truman's confidence but does not appear to have considered himself a policymaker. Lay was a career civil servant. Neither man possessed significant White House clout or an independent power base. Some other way, no doubt, could have been found to authorize early CIA shadow activities. Truman approved NSC-68 in early 1950 but virtually ignored it until Korea gave it urgency. In his well-founded desire to protect the presidency, he failed to make maximum use of the council until war in Asia made it seem necessary.

The ejection of the obstreperous Louis Johnson from the cabinet in 1950 made it easier for the NSC to work together. Thereafter, largely because it provided a convenient mechanism for interdepartmental teamwork, it steadily grew in significance; nonetheless its purpose remained one of coordination among existing entities, not independent policy making. In 1952 candidate Dwight Eisenhower berated the Truman administration for failing to utilize the NSC properly; in 1953 President Eisenhower discovered that few changes were required to achieve the model he had in mind.[28]

Numerous students of the presidency have remarked that Truman institutionalized the office in its modern shape. This surely is a valid observation, but the White House structure under Truman strikes one as a model that may deserve attention for other reasons. The president actively involved himself with many issues and had multiple sources of advice. The members of his immediate staff all had relatively clearly defined functions. He thereby managed to achieve order and clarity without sacrificing control.

Moreover, while his staff was no freer than any other from ordinary tendencies toward turf battles, personality conflicts, and backbiting, such episodes were minimal. FDR had encouraged and apparently delighted in them. Truman, perhaps because he was less comfortable with the presidency and because he felt the weight of numerous other conflict-driven pressures, loathed them and made his feelings clear to his staff. However forced the cordiality may have been between some persons, they all maintained in it their dealings with each other—or found themselves leaving.

What Truman did with the organization of the White House he attempted to do for the executive branch as a whole. As soon as he took office he was anxious to phase out the special World War II agencies and return authority to the regular executive departments. Clearly, he considered the creation of the Department of Defense and the Central Intelligence Agency among his important accomplishments. The results "unified" neither the armed forces nor intelligence gathering but imparted more coherence to both. Although the Hoover Commission was forced on him by a conservative Congress, he made good faith use of it in an effort to consolidate and rationalize the entire executive branch. Here also the results were limited, but, because of the way in which Truman handled it, one unexpected by-product of the first Hoover Commission's work was to institutionalize numerous New Deal programs by converting the debate about them to the issue of efficiency rather than desirability.

However much Truman wanted neatness and clear lines of responsibility, he also wanted power. If the inner-directed side of his personality led him from time to time into unseemly displays of aggressiveness, it also told him that only the president was responsible for large policies, that only the president could make the major decisions, and that the preservation of his authority and discretion was paramount. To this impulse he added experience as a county administrator that had solidified his belief in a strong executive. His reading of history and his understanding of the Constitution had left him with a reverence for the presidency and a determination to maintain it undiminished.

No doubt his emotions were not as clearly sorted out as he implied when he declared that he sought respect only for the office, not for himself, but a bit of unconscious ego involvement was not a bad thing for the office. Subordinates who did not display that respect or who tried to preempt the president's decision making generally found themselves isolated and eventually outside the administration, even if their reputations were as formidable as those of James Byrnes or Douglas MacArthur.

It is a commonplace of civics textbooks that a president has numerous roles other than that of chief administrator. Most of them are in fact both more visible and ultimately more important.[29] Among them are chief diplomat, chief legislator, party leader, and, above all, leader of the public. No president in American history has come to the office well prepared for each and every of these functions. All are to some degree interconnected, but they equally have built-in conflicts with each other. Truman, like most presidents, juggled them with varying degrees of success. To a large extent he was a prisoner of circumstances. An accomplished politician, knowledgeable on social and economic issues, possessing influence on Capitol Hill, he nonetheless seemed to achieve little of his domestic program. Yet he carved out a record of strength and leadership in U.S. relations with the rest of the world that few would have predicted.

On issues about which he felt secure, Truman appears to have exercised a large measure of personal judgment. In areas where his intellectual ground was less firm, he frequently made rash statements but never took rash actions. Foreign policy provides a near-perfect illustration.

When he became president Truman had no experience in diplomacy, little travel abroad, and no record of consistent engagement with diplomatic issues while in the Senate. His attitude toward European and Asian nations was that of the quintessential American provincial, at once fascinated by foreign cultures and determined to assert their inferiority. Like many Americans, he found it difficult to conceive of foreign issues and leaders in non-American terms; when he made an offhand remark that Joseph Stalin reminded him of Tom Pendergast, he was only the latest in a long line of U.S. statesmen who had arrived at similarly inadequate analogies.

As befitted a Democrat of his generation, he was a Wilsonian idealist who deeply believed in American international leadership: the duty of American foreign policy was to promote the betterment of mankind. He could speak with great eloquence of TVAs for remote parts of the world and of the progress yet to come in human affairs. He probably would have been at a loss in any attempt to discuss totalitarianism on a theoretical basis. But as a sincere libertarian, he understood its challenge, whether Nazi or Soviet, better than did many of his contemporaries.[30]

But he was often woefully deficient in his knowledge of specifics. Coming to the presidency with something close to a *tabula rasa* when it came to global issues, he could never make the time to undertake a comprehensive survey of the U.S. position in the world and to develop a thorough understanding of the many political cultures with which the nation was engaged. The result was a mental data bank composed of random bits of information, frequently distorted by a tendency to personalize complex situations.

As a child who was a bit of a bookworm especially drawn to history, Truman had tended to see human affairs as dominated by great personalities, not by ideas or impersonal forces. "I saw that it takes men to make history, or there would be no history," he wrote in his memoirs. "History does not make the man." The concept remained central to his thinking throughout his presidency. He once shook up his staff by writing to Greenville Clark that Soviet foreign policy had been determined by "the will of Peter the Great." The statement displayed an understanding of the historical, nonideological bases of Russian expansionism, but the document to which it referred was as spurious as the Protocols of the Elders of Zion. He seems to have interpreted the collapse of Nationalist China largely as a matter of the crookedness of Chiang Kai-shek's government. He became especially upset about Franco's Spain after learning that the Caudillo persecuted Baptists and Masons. His instincts were sound, but his information was inadequate.[31]

To his credit, he realized the need for sound advice. Unlike Roosevelt, he apparently never had the illusion that he could function without the distraction of a State Department. He wanted a first-class secretary of state and expected substantial guidance from the department. At the same time, he was determined to be the decision maker in foreign policy. His successive relationships with his four secretaries of state illustrate his quest.

Edward Stettinius, whom he had inherited from Roosevelt, was widely considered a figurehead. Truman had little confidence in him and soon eased him out in favor of James Byrnes. At first glance, the appointment seemed felicitous. Few men in American public life enjoyed greater stature. Byrnes had been one of the most respected of senators, briefly a justice of the Supreme Court, then director of the Office of War Mobilization. He even enjoyed an undeserved reputation as a foreign policy expert because Roosevelt had taken him to Yalta. Truman admired him, and most observers agreed that he was an appropriate individual to be next in line to succeed the president. Yet Byrnes soon lost Truman's confidence.

In part, Byrnes was a victim of the inevitable compromises and disappointments of the early Cold War, in part, of his own relative inexperience as a diplomat. What was decisive to Truman, however, was Byrnes's attitude toward the president. The turning point came during the secretary's long absence at the Moscow foreign ministers' conference in December 1945 as Truman became increasingly annoyed that Byrnes was dealing with him "like one partner in a business telling the other that his business trip was progressing well and not to worry." Byrnes made matters worse by initially scheduling a national radio address on the conference in advance of his report to the president.

The White House told Byrnes to reschedule his radio speech and meet with Truman on the presidential yacht. Truman himself wrote out a stiff reprimand that he allowed to be published in 1951 and claimed to have read to Byrnes. Actually, as was so often the case when Truman dealt with people face to face, the two men appear to have ironed out their differences on a relatively amicable basis, and almost certainly without Truman's delivering the angry message he had put on paper. Neither seems, however, to have been comfortable with the other after this point. By the beginning of 1947 Byrnes was on his way back to South Carolina.[32]

Truman revered Byrnes's successor, George C. Marshall, as he did no other man in public life. Marshall, for his part, organized an operation, built around an elite policy planning staff, that brought the department to the zenith of its influence and accomplishment in modern American history. Yet even Marshall was not immune from presidential reversal. On the one issue about which the president and his State Department clearly had different perspectives and interests, Palestine, the president prevailed—though not without a long struggle and a few episodes that would have been comic in less serious situations.

The substance of the Palestine question remains difficult to assess. One can argue compellingly that Truman sacrificed a long-term national interest by acting on considerations that were political and sentimental, but that judgment must be tempered by an awareness of the vividness with which so many liberal-minded people still recalled the Holocaust. Most relevant to an examination of presidential leadership is Truman's determination to dictate a policy that originated in the White House and to do so even when Marshall threatened to vote against him in the upcoming election. (Also, Truman was generally flexible enough to be persuaded that an idea was bad, as was the case when Marshall persuaded him to abort a plan to send Chief Justice Fred Vinson to Moscow as a special negotiator in October 1948.)[33]

It was with Dean Acheson that Truman forged his ideal relationship with a secretary of state. Acheson, as a matter of principle and at times possibly of manipulation, gave the president the deference he wanted while keeping a firm hand on American diplomacy. In most cases Truman would approve what was suggested to him and would give in on some sticky issues if presented with sufficient justification. On something that clearly captured the president's imagination—most notably the Point Four program—Acheson held his tongue. Their collaboration was a productive one.[34]

Ultimately, Truman's greatest resource as chief diplomat was his temperament. His determination to be a decision maker preserved the powers of his office at a time when the president was forced to make foreign policy to a degree almost without parallel in past practice. Moreover, he never authorized an important decision without extensive input from the national security apparatus that he did so much to construct and regularize, nor did he embark upon major courses unless he believed them to be in the national interest.

It would surely be fallacious to assert that political considerations had nothing to do with either the Palestine issue or the Vinson plan. It would be an equally fallacious interpretation of the workings of Truman's mind, however, to assume that his motivation consisted of nothing more than a cynical political calculus. If politics exerted a tug on some issues, it was that of requiring a rethinking and possibly a reconciliation of political and national interests, not a surrender of the latter.

Finally, Truman never confused impulsiveness with decisiveness when it came to important matters, even if his own recollections sometimes made it appear that he did. In later years he claimed that he made his decision instantly when Dean Acheson called to inform him of the North Korean invasion of South Korea. He replied, as he recalled it, "Dean, we've got to stop the sons of bitches no matter what." No one remotely familiar with the numerous wide-ranging policy meetings held in Washington over the next week can seriously credit Truman's reminiscence. He no doubt accurately recalled his initial impulse, but in actual practice he knew the difference between an impulse and a decision. Roy Jenkins better expresses the dynamics of the relationship between Truman and his subordinates during those fateful days in 1950: "They filled in some of the gaps in his knowledge and confirmed most of his instinctive judgments. He stiffened them with his resolution." How strange that a man who exercised leadership in so commendable a fashion was incapable of describing it![35]

Truman's relationship with Congress has been among the most debated of his presidential roles. Historians committed to liberal domestic programs have argued vehemently about Truman's lack of success in taking the nation much farther down the social welfare road; a good many have asserted implicitly or explicitly that a resurrected Franklin Roosevelt would have piled domestic achievement upon domestic achievement. As early as 1951, Samuel Lubell in *The Future of American Politics* concluded that Truman was a president "who bought time" for the Democratic party by following a policy of zigs and zags that reflected the party's internal contradictions.

The legislative corollary of this thesis was that Truman's fight for his Fair Deal was a sham, undertaken to appease northern liberal Democrats while offering no real threat to the southern conservatives. My own judgment is that this argument is at best incomplete and, as usually expressed, rather simple-minded.[36]

Any evaluation of Truman as chief legislator must rest on some assumptions about the limits of presidential power, the character of each Congress with which he dealt, and the larger political climate of his era. My own general assumptions run roughly as follows: Presidents rarely move Congresses with rhetoric and have very limited resources to trade for votes. Congresses by nature are independent; they have numerous built-in constitutional conflicts with any presidency, and their members are the creatures of local constituencies, not of a national political organization headed by the president. Presidents are most likely to achieve domestic legislative objectives for which there is a widely felt need among the public, a strong push spearheaded by dedicated activists, and relatively weak opposition. Until recent years, presidents have usually been able to claim a greater degree of congressional tolerance on foreign policy matters than on domestic ones.

As for the specific situation, Truman faced four moderate to conservative Congresses, each of them more or less accurately reflecting a widespread lack of public interest in extending the New Deal. Given the experience of Roosevelt after 1937, of Kennedy throughout his administration, and of Johnson after 1966, it is hard to see how Truman could have driven Congress in his direction. Moreover, like all presidents from FDR on, he had the additional handicap of a backdrop of foreign policy distractions that put heavy claims on his energy and resources while also making it difficult to focus public attention on new domestic causes.

Critics who have emphasized Truman's lack of oratorical prowess and his frequent clumsiness in using the communications media have been quite accurate. Additionally, his generally weak standing in the polls gave him little leverage on Capitol Hill. Still, one must question their assumption that these deficiencies, hardly shared by FDR or JFK, were at all decisive. It is my contention that a close look at the ways in which Truman dealt with Congress demonstrates considerable political sophistication and that an equally close observation of the legislative scoreboard yields a greater total than many historians imagine.

At the time Truman became president, congressional liaison was a small-scale, rather informal White House function handled by the president in regular meetings with his party leaders in Congress and by a few political operatives who had other duties as well, among them the press secretary, the postmaster-general (who was likely to be the Democratic national chairman), and cabinet members or presidential assistants interested in specific pieces of legislation. The Truman administration largely continued this pattern. It never developed a legislative liaison operation in the modern sense, although a couple of nose counters were added to the staff in the later years of the administration. By contrast with the large, sophisticated operations that came after 1952, it seems primitive. By contrast with what came before, it was more of the same.

In part, this low-key operation may have resulted from Truman's respect for the institutional independence of the Congress. During most of his ten years in the Senate, he was surrounded by growing resentment against FDR's arm-twisting tactics and was highly sensitive to it when he became president. The White House staff as a rule attempted to stay out of the legislation-drafting business, and Truman usually deferred to congressional prerogatives as he understood them.[37]

Yet this attitude did not foreclose conflict with the legislative branch. In 1946 Truman instigated a successful primary purge of a Missouri congressman (Roger Slaughter) who had obstructed his program. He wielded the veto as readily as any other strong president in American history, dragged one Congress across thousands of miles of railroad track behind his campaign train to win reelection in 1948, did not hesitate to impound appropriated funds, and invoked the doctrine of executive privilege against congressional inquiries that he considered improper.

Nor did Truman's attitude foreclose concerted efforts at persuasion on behalf of high-priority legislation, much of it undertaken by the president himself, attempting to utilize the many friendships he had acquired during his years in the Senate. Given the atmosphere of resentment against Roosevelt's efforts to dominate Congress, and given the special assets of Truman's own congressional experience, the establishment of a lavishly staffed liaison office probably would not have been a productive step during the Truman years. In 1953, when the Republicans returned to power, led by a new president with a very different career pattern, a large-scale lobbying operation working out of the White House would seem logical and proper.[38]

What seems most compelling about Truman's relations with Congress are the limits one must put on any generalizations about the subject. Truman dealt rather differently with each of the four Congresses he faced, reflecting shifting priorities and political environments, at times engaging in remarkably adroit footwork.

His record with the Seventy-ninth Congress displayed an initial overoptimism about his ability to retain his influence and popularity on the Hill and about the manageability of the difficult problems of reconversion. Consequently, he faced this Congress with the most accommodative attitude. The results, of course, were politically disastrous, whether because of White House efforts to be deferential or not. The lesson appears to have been learned.[39]

The relationship between Truman and the Eightieth Congress remains famous primarily as an example of executive-legislative conflict. On the domestic side, it was a successful exercise in rebuilding the Roosevelt coalition. The president demanded legislation he knew he would not get (and in one or two cases did not want), used the veto to make points with selected constituencies, and abandoned virtually any pretense of real legislative leadership or coordination. He even ceased his weekly meetings with his party's congressional chieftains. It was a shrewd strategy, based on the surely accurate premise that Truman had no possibilities of reaching an accommodation with a hostile Congress.[40]

Yet it was with this same Congress that Truman worked out some of the most important steps in the history of American diplomacy. Even as he vocally attacked its domestic proclivities, he and State Department officials worked with some of its Republican leaders to construct a bipartisan foreign policy based on a policy of aid to Western Europe and the containment of Soviet expansion. It was a dazzling achievement, difficult to explain against the backdrop of mortal combat over domestic issues. Among the factors that allowed for this success, were: the political appeal of anticommunism and anti-Sovietism by 1947 and 1948; the persuasive power and prestige of men such as George Marshall, Dean Acheson, and Robert Lovett; and the administration's success in devising policies that put it squarely in the middle of the political spectrum (attacks only from the extreme left and the extreme right were a powerful coalescing force for the broad center among both Republicans and Democrats).

The Eighty-first Congress, the most studied of all the Truman Congresses, seems at first glance simply a persuasive example of Truman's inability to muster sustained support. With the exception of the Housing Act of 1949, he was unable to secure passage of his most publicized Fair Deal objective. His bipartisan foreign policy coalition began to unravel under such pressures as the fall of China, the Soviet atomic bomb, the rise of Joe McCarthy, and the Korean War. Yet, despite the public mood, the Eighty-first Congress approved a surprising amount of secondary New Deal–Fair Deal legislation, virtually all of it designed to update existing programs. Perhaps the most important such enactment was the Social Security Act of 1950, a major overhaul of the system that Arthur Altmeyer has described as almost as important as the original act itself. There was considerable support for such enterprises from a public that in the last analysis had elected Truman in 1948 because it wanted to preserve the political economy of the New Deal rather than to extend the frontiers of American liberalism.[41]

The Eighty-second Congress represented yet another shift of emphasis. Facing a stalemated conflict in Korea and a legislative branch in which Republican gains eliminated even slim hopes of domestic policy breakthroughs, Truman moved successfully to retain control of foreign policy. He largely united the Democratic party behind him to face the crises occasioned by the MacArthur dismissal, rampant McCarthyism, resurgent Republican isolationism, and mounting public frustration with the war. In order to win support from Democratic conservatives, he put the Fair Deal on the shelf so far as any serious legislation was concerned, bringing it out only for symbolic campaign and party purposes.[42]

From no Congress did Truman get everything he wanted. After an initial shakedown with the Seventy-ninth Congress, however, he does appear to have been shrewd and generally successful at the art of the possible. He assessed situations intelligently, defined priorities accordingly, and at times used defeats (such as the Taft-Hartley Act and his civil rights program) to consolidate his electoral coalition. It may be tempting to depict him as a futile little man flailing away at indifferent Congresses, and it would be fatuous to deny his failures. Nevertheless, a careful assessment reveals a strong president who achieved important objectives, almost always defined the terms of political debate, and tenaciously retained control of the main lines of domestic and foreign policy.

Clearly, Truman subordinated his role as legislative leader to broader considerations—first and foremost to the national interest as he understood it, then to electoral politics and party leadership. Both of the latter were rooted in his conception of American politics, which combined the dualistic folklore of the Democratic party with the instinctive pluralism of the centrist democratic politician.

Reared by vehemently partisan parents in an ethos of neofrontier democracy, an admirer of Bryan, then of Wilson, Truman as a young man naturally enough accepted all the myths of the Democratic party. It was or should be the party of the people against that of the interests, of the believers in liberty against that of the authoritarians, of the Jeffersonian heritage (interpreted in the light of twentieth-century needs) against that of Hamilton. The vision was an appealing one, reinforced by most of the popular and scholarly history of the 1920s and 1930s. Truman's sense of his party's traditions and mission stayed with him throughout his life, giving him his sense of the general welfare and bolstering his resolve in such critical episodes as the uphill 1948 campaign and the veto of the McCarran Internal Security Act of 1950.

Yet like all successful politicians, including Wilson and FDR before him, Truman operated as a pluralist at the practical level. He began his political career in a relatively homogeneous ethnic and religious setting; in private he spoke the standard language of the provincial bigot. Yet he was a fundamentally tolerant and open man who had mixed easily with other types during his days as a bank clerk in Kansas City and had won the affection of the predominantly Catholic artillery battery he had commanded in World War I. If at the beginning of his political career he was a somewhat narrowly focused business progressive, he soon learned that the key to wider political success was the construction of coalitions of diverse groups. Collectively these groups might be considered the ordinary people, but they tended to define themselves and their interests more narrowly.

Although he came close to joining the Ku Klux Klan for political reasons in 1922, Truman worked easily with Catholic politicians from the beginning. At about the same time, he had a warm relationship with a Jewish partner in his most famous business venture. At the local level, he learned to deal with Kansas City's substantial black population. He seems quickly to have accepted labor unions as legitimate political actors. In statewide politics, he dealt shrewdly with a multitude of forces: urban and rural organization politicians, farmers, unions, small businessmen, blacks, Jews.

As president he continued the same practice and outlook. In 1947 and 1948 he used the Eightieth Congress to rebuild a coalition. A close study of his rhetoric in the 1948 campaign yields alongside the generalized "people versus interests" oratory a consistent pattern of appeals to specific interests at one whistle stop or auditorium after another, the issue varying with the special constituency he was addressing—water projects and regional development for the West, price supports for the farmers, repeal of Taft-Hartley for labor, civil rights for blacks, anti-inflationary policies for consumers, housing for hard-pressed younger urbanites.[43]

At other times, as in the darker days of the Korean War, he could be even more inclusive. Building a coalition to sustain his foreign policy required an appeal to the party loyalty of the white South as well as to the principled internationalism of the northern liberals. Although his political instincts were on the left side of the political center, he consciously attempted to balance his administration with business-minded conservatives such as John Snyder and Charles Sawyer. He understood well that changing priorities meant changing coalitions, and he was devoted above all to the strength and growth of his party. He liked to tell people that there was room for everyone in the Democratic party no matter, how diverse their interests.

Remarkably, Truman left office in 1953 with his party probably more united than in 1945. Moreover, after twenty tumultuous years in power, the Democrats remained the party of choice of a solid plurality of the nation. The fact that the party enjoyed stronger support than did Truman himself may be taken by some as a demonstration of ineptness. However, it was more likely evidence of his strength that he had managed to institutionalize a political coalition that before 1945 had been in large measure built around a cult of personality.

His use of the presidency to set a national agenda preserved the fragile Roosevelt coalition. He had resolved no conflicts within it and had initiated no expulsions. Rather, he had pulled extremes of the right and the left back to it by demonstrating in 1948 that its solid core lay at its liberal center, that even an ordinary-looking politician whose name was not Roosevelt could rally enough of that support to win elections and thereby deprive mutinies of their potency. Historians may debate whether this was a positive achievement; a consideration of the likely alternatives suggests that it was.

How, then, did Truman fare in the trickiest of all presidential roles, that of national leader? Here, for all his accomplishments, he was, at least superficially, more often than not a failure. The Gallup and Roper polls tell a sad story: An 87 percent approval rating in June 1945 plunged to 42 percent in less than a year, bottomed out at 32 percent in the fall of 1946, and moved up sharply in the spring of 1947 all the way to 60 percent only to slide back down to 36 percent a year later. The story of his second term was even worse. Given a 69 percent approval rating in January 1949, he was below 50 percent a little more than a year later. During 1951 and 1952 the polls ranged between 37 and 23 percent.[44]

These numbers reveal almost no support based on personal allegiance. Yet survey results are not the sole measurement of leadership. Their fluctuations tended to conceal an ability to lead without personal magnetism. Millions of Americans had voted for Franklin Roosevelt because he was Franklin Roosevelt; few voted for Truman on the same basis. At times, Truman's support was based on sympathy (especially in the months after Roosevelt's death) or on a rally-around-the-flag impulse (the decision to defend South Korea), but more often it stemmed from the issues with which he identified himself.

Democratic electorates usually have a rational sense of their interests, but they also yearn for charisma in their leaders. The rise of electronic communications in the 1930s and 1940s stripped away barriers that had separated the people from direct contact with their president. The growth of the Washington press corps put more first-hand observations into the hands of newspaper readers across the country. Truman was terribly vulnerable to such developments. He endured nearly eight years of comparisons, implicit or explicit, to the master politician of the twentieth century; the effect on his public image was devastating.

The media spotlight tended to emphasize his uncomfortableness with the presidency, his apparent impulsiveness, his hot temper, his erratic character, his ineffective formal speechmaking. Opinion shapers who gained personal interviews with him generally came away unimpressed. His strength was based in a temperament that he was unable to exhibit in an attractive way. His weaknesses were on display day after day. Large segments of the public saw him as an "ordinary person," well-meaning perhaps but possessing the faults and limitations of ordinary people everywhere. To take such an image into political combat is to invite scorn.

Truman might have been more popular if he had accepted congressional government in 1945, presided over whatever the tide brought in for the next three years, and bowed out gracefully in 1948. It is doubtful that Harry Truman ever conceived of such an option. Instead he sought to do his duty as he conceived it, and he persevered at the expense of considerable psychic stress and discomfort. He had few illusions about his personal appeal, but possibly from time to time he consoled himself with the knowledge that no one ever *looked* more like a president than Warren G. Harding. Truman's own shortcomings as a national leader in what Theodore Roosevelt called the bully pulpit were considerable, but it is to his credit that he largely prevailed despite them. The results—the institutionalization of the New Deal at home and a lasting recognition of the country's interests abroad; the preservation of a Democratic party built around the Roosevelt coalition; and a powerful presidency resting on something more than the personal resources of its holder—were all the work of a strong chief executive who somehow managed to look weak.

3

DWIGHT D. EISENHOWER

Leadership Theorist in the White House

Fred I. Greenstein

For the eight years beginning with January 20, 1953, a career public servant for whom the theory and practice of leadership was a central concern occupied the presidency. Although Dwight D. Eisenhower has had no equals among post–Twenty-second Amendment presidents in his sustained ability to command the esteem of the American people, most scholars and other political commentators have treated his conduct of the presidency far less favorably. According to the conventional judgment, Eisenhower's presidency reflected the inertness and lack of skill and purpose of an aging hero who reigned more than he ruled. In this assessment, Eisenhower's professional background incapacitated him for the pull and haul of presidential leadership, because, unlike political leaders, generals can count on their orders' being obeyed.

Recently, however, what is often called "Eisenhower revisionism" has been a growth stock.[1] Some of the new interest in Eisenhower's leadership stems from nostalgia for the allegedly placid, uncomplicated 1950s. Other interest derives from post–Cold War, postliberal attraction to the kinds of policies Eisenhower espoused, such as curbs on defense spending, mildly incremental approaches to expanding welfare policies, and efforts to hold down inflation.

My own reassessment belongs to a different category, which might be called "instrumental revisionism": a reexamination of Eisenhower as a political practitioner. It is stimulated in part by the striking contrast between the political debacles of most of his successors and his own ability to maintain public support so effectively and so long. It is also spurred by the speculations of such journalists as Murray Kempton and Garry Wills, who reviewed what was known in the 1950s about Eisenhower's leadership and inferred that he was a gifted political operator.[2] His gift, in their views, rested on his ability to convey the impression that he was apolitical while he was in fact engaging in shrewd machinations.

Instrumental revisionism is no longer speculative. It is rooted in scholarship based on rich archival sources, many of which began to be declassified only in the mid-1970s. The resulting evidence shows Eisenhower to have been an engaged, serious political operator with a distinctive leadership style, including the characteristics Kempton and Wills deduced from his contemporary record. Although Eisenhower was not widely perceived during his presidency to be articulate, before, during, and after his years in the White House he produced volumes of instructive, and well-articulated private diary entries and correspondence, much of which he assiduously kept off the record by labeling it "personal and confidential." There are also detailed summaries or transcripts of his meetings, conversations, and even offhand comments to aides. A key supplement to his presidential (and postpresidential) papers is the rigorously edited *Papers of Dwight David Eisenhower*.[3] The volumes published thus far or scheduled for the near future contain his correspondence and certain other of his writings from the time shortly after Pearl Harbor, when he was moved into a major policy-planning position in the War Department, through his prepresidential career.

The very copiousness of this evidence casts doubt on the stereotype of an inert Eisenhower; the content of Eisenhower's papers causes any scholar who begins with the conventional impression of him to undergo a lasting transformation, as Theodore White did in covering Eisenhower as commander in chief of NATO: "I had made the mistake so many observers did of considering Ike a simple man, a good straightforward soldier. Yet Ike's mind was not flaccid; and gradually, reporting him as he performed, I found that his mind was tough, his manner deceptive; that the rosy public smile could give way, in private, to furious outbursts of temper; that the tangled, rambling rhetoric of his off-the-record remarks could, when he wished, be disciplined by his own pencil into clean, hard prose."[4] Likewise, a particularly attentive watcher of the White House Eisenhower, his vice-president, observed that Eisenhower "was a far more complex and devious man than most people realized, and in the best sense of those words. Not shackled to a one-track mind, he always applied two, three or four lines of reasoning to a single problem and he usually preferred the indirect approach where it would serve him better than a direct attack on a problem."[5]

The following evaluation of Eisenhower's presidential leadership is necessarily incomplete: Eisenhower's years as president still have not been definitively studied; much of his foreign policy record remains classified; and new challenges are being raised by "postrevisionist" scholars, who question whether his leadership was effective.[6] But there is enough evidence available to draw some conclusions about his leadership *style*. Future analyses will have to link Eisenhower's style with his qualities of mind, policies, and policy-making and judge whether his approach to leadership led to desirable results (by his or other standards), given the constraints and opportunities of his time.

Eisenhower's presidential leadership style was grounded, to an unusual degree for a public figure, in more or less self-conscious principles of how to conduct public affairs. He had a remarkably articulated view of the means (tactics, strategies, procedures) and ends (premises and goals) of his leadership. Though not a leadership theorist in any scholarly sense, compared with other American presidents he appears to have had a uniquely extensive operational code, one grounded in his long prepresidential experience in positions of authority. Because Eisenhower entered office with well-formed views about what his procedures, as well as his goals, should be, his papers reveal not only what he did in office but also how and why he did it, and why he rejected alternative courses of action.

As Kempton and Wills surmised, a covert preoccupation with getting political results while appearing publicly nonpolitical was central to Eisenhower's leadership style. Many elements of this mode are discernible in the practices of other modern presidents, but Eisenhower blended them into a distinctive ensemble of tactics that is in many ways the obverse of such classic depictions of forceful presidential leadership as Richard Neustadt's *Presidential Power*.[7]

Eisenhower's interest in leadership theory and practice stemmed less from his studies at West Point than from his close association in the early 1920s with the legendary military planner General Fox Connor and from his studies in the advanced service schools. His long experience in important staff positions in the military bureaucracy, with its explicit formal rules and almost as explicit informal procedural norms, further fostered his impulse to summarize principles of leadership in abstract form.

David Eisenhower has recently observed that his grandfather's presidential leadership needs to be understood in terms of how it was shaped by his military leadership.[8] As World War II European commander, postwar army chief of staff, and NATO chief, Dwight Eisenhower participated in making and executing important and intricate military strategies that required him to think about organization, propaganda, deception, maneuver, and other matters that apply to political as well as to military leadership. Moreover, in these and other posts, his military responsibilities made it necessary for him to work closely and become acquainted with the political leaders of his time.[9]

Perhaps most fundamentally, Eisenhower had a highly analytic cognitive style. He reasoned explicitly about the means and ends of any endeavor in which he was engaged, whether it was his bridge game, his medical regimen after his heart attack, or his presidency. And he was disposed to commit his thoughts to paper. On New Year's Day 1950, for example, when pressures were mounting for him to become a presidential candidate, he weighed his circumstances in a personal diary, observing that writing down his thoughts would "tend to clarify my mind to some degree and thus give me confidence that I am not straying away from what I believe to be principle in any of my statements, conversations or decisions affecting any part of this confusing problem."[10]

Eisenhower typically commented on principles of leadership in the interstices of his other discourse. To his statements about specific problems he often added what one editor of his papers describes as "throwaway lines"[11]—brief general explanations of the rationale for his views and actions. As president, Eisenhower frequently explained his actions by relating them to the prepresidential posts he had occupied, each of which, he noted, "had its own leadership requirements."[12] When he did not state general principles underlying his actions in so many words, his practice tended to be so consistent that it seems certain that he *could* have expressed them if the occasion arose. In some of the latter cases—for example, in his "passion for organization," discussed below—the occasion arose while he was writing his memoirs after he left office. The following themes are major in the theory and practice of Eisenhower's leadership.

Planning for Unplanned Contingencies

Eisenhower did not believe that military leadership procedures were mechanically transferable to the presidency. Indeed, even among military roles, he recognized that leadership must be adapted to the specific requirements of specific jobs, as in his 1943 remarks to General Marshall concerning the differences between generals gifted at consolidation and those—such as George Patton—gifted at attack.

> Many generals constantly think of battles in terms of, first, concentration, supply, maintenance, replacement, and, second, after all the above is arranged a *conservative* advance. This type of person is necessary because he prevents one from courting disaster. But occasions arise when one has to remember that under particular conditions, boldness is ten times as important as numbers. Patton's strength is that he thinks only in terms of attack as long as there is a single battalion that can keep advancing. Moreover, the man has a native shrewdness that operates in such a way that his troops always seem to have ammunition and sufficient food no matter where they are. Personally, I doubt that I would even consider Patton for an army group commander or for any higher position, but as an army commander under a man who is sound and solid, and who has enough sense to use Patton's good qualities without becoming blinded by his love of showmanship and histrionics, he should do as fine a job as he did in Sicily.[13]

Eisenhower's observation about Patton's personality suggests that he was also attentive to such contingencies as individual differences. As he noted in a 1953 letter to William Benton, "A factor of course that always affects organization is the personality of a responsible individual. One system will work for one man or group of men while for other personalities a somewhat different system is often better."[14]

Eisenhower's continuing sensitivity to the personality differences and other factors that make general principles contingent extended to a self-conscious assessment of his own strengths and weaknesses. For example, he had great confidence in his appraisal of international politics, and in most cases he felt comfortable dealing with political tasks that entailed broad conceptualization of the overall goals to be attained by a policy and the basic strategies for reaching those goals. Moreover, he was ordinarily disposed to invest only certain kinds of effort in policy-making. He was willing to engage, on the one hand, in enunciating general principles and, on the other, in behind-the-scenes planning and persuasion. But he emphatically did not want to be *visibly* engaged in political bargaining, and he especially avoided public involvement in what has come to be called confrontational politics.

Although, as we shall see, his long-standing "no personalities" policy had prudential justifications, it also arose from a self-assessment of a personal weakness, namely his fiery temper. Eisenhower had occasion to take stock of his own leadership in an August 1960 letter to Henry Luce. Commenting on a *Life Magazine* analysis of his presidency seven and a half years after he took office, he reported: "I adopted and used those methods and manners that seemed to be most effective. (I should add that one of my problems had been to control my temper—a temper that I have had to battle all my life!) . . . In war and in peace I've had no respect for the desk-pounder, and have despised the loud and slick talker. If my own ideas and practices in this matter have sprung from weakness, I do not know. But they were and are deliberate or, rather, natural to me. They are not accidental."[15]

In short, Eisenhower held what social scientists call an "interactionist" conception of leadership.[16] That is, he believed that leadership practices would—and should—vary with the situation and with the qualities of the leaders themselves. He held this belief as part of a world view that took contingencies for granted as a norm of the human condition, rather than viewing them as annoying perturbations to be ignored so that policies or principles of leadership can be applied consistently. Thus he once remarked in a draft letter to a liberal congressman who had suggested that he invite Chou Enlai to the United States, "As you know, I, currently, do not agree with you—but I do point out that I do not use the word 'never' in expressing my conviction. Circumstances could conceivably so alter as to change my feeling on this matter."[17]

On this conviction, as on other of Eisenhower's views, it is striking to see how early he had reached general conclusions about the practice of leadership. In 1943 he wrote his son John about the need to "plan" for unplanned contingencies. Referring to one of the most awkward civil-military controversies of his World War II leadership, the Darlan affair, he observed that "no situation is ever the same in war as was foreseen or anticipated. You must be able to think as the problem comes up. For example, what textbook or formal preparation could have gotten one ready to meet the political crisis involved in the Darlan matter? The only thing possible in practice is logical thinking, a clear conscience, and a determination to do your duty."[18]

A Passion for Organization

Numerous political commentators took it for granted that some of Eisenhower's most conspicuous presidential leadership practices were unthinking extensions of standard military procedure. In fact he quite consciously distinguished political from military leadership. At the same time, he was sure that he had gained insights that extended beyond the armed services in his previous professional incarnation as a military leader. And on taking office, he drew on his experiences with both military and civilian staffing, expanding on the formal organization of the White House and creating a more articulated presidential office than had hitherto existed.

Eisenhower's administrative arrangements reflected his preoccupation with organized leadership.[19] Most conspicuously, Eisenhower's White House staff had an official chief, Governor Sherman Adams, whose title "the assistant to the president" and listing at the head of White House Office staff in the *Government Organization Manual* added weight to his formal status. Adams was never officially called chief of staff. Military language was studiously eschewed in the public vocabulary of the Eisenhower presidency.[20] But observers inevitably concluded that Adams's job had been modeled on those of Eisenhower's military chiefs of staff—for example, General Walter Bedell Smith in World War II and General Alfred Gruenther at NATO headquarters.

Other newly established specialized positions and organizational arrangements in the Eisenhower White House included a legislative liaison staff, a cabinet secretary who prepared agendas before cabinet meetings and kept track of domestic policy implementation, and a White House secretariat that coordinated the flow of communications to the president. Moreover, under Eisenhower the National Security Council was more systematically organized than in the past. It acquired a principal staff aide (the special assistant for national security affairs) and two staffs, one assigned to systematize the information and options to be discussed in NSC meetings and the other to do this in planning the implementation of NSC decisions.

In his memoirs, written during the Kennedy presidency, Eisenhower set forth an abstract justification for systematizing the organizational skeleton of his presidency. His successor did away with what many political observers of the time viewed as Eisenhower's stultifyingly bureaucratized "staff system."[21]

Was it wrong for the Eisenhower White House to have had an explicitly articulated organizational structure? Characteristically, instead of taking the defensive by asking this question, Eisenhower "replied" by referring to unnamed critics of sound organizational procedures and explaining in general terms the reasons for employing systematized formal procedures:

> Organization cannot make a genius out of an incompetent; even less can it, of itself, make the decisions which are required to trigger necessary action. On the other hand, disorganization can scarcely fail to result in inefficiency and can easily lead to disaster. Organization makes more efficient the gathering and analysis of facts, and the arranging of the findings of experts in logical fashion. Therefore organization helps the responsible individual make the necessary decision, and helps assure that it is satisfactorily carried out.

Did Eisenhower, as was so commonly alleged, delegate to aides decisions that he should have made? Again, Eisenhower was oblique. He first explained why he neither approved of nor engaged in leaving decision making to his staff, then discussed possible reasons for the existence of a mistaken organizational theory.

> I have read about "staff decisions" but I have never understood exactly what was meant by the expression, unless it is the assumption that decisions are sometimes made by group voting, as in a congressional committee, where a majority of votes controls the action. In my own experience—extending over half a century in various types of group mechanisms, large and small— I have never known any successful executive who has depended upon the taking of a vote in any gathering to make a decision for him.

Quoting the familiar anecdote about Lincoln's overruling a unanimous cabinet, Eisenhower summed up his oblique rejoinder by saying, "The Presidency still works the same way today."

And what of the familiar assertion that formalized organizational procedures generate uncreative policies and delay their execution? Maintaining his pedagogical tone, Eisenhower stated that he had

> been astonished to read some contentions which seem to suggest that a smooth organization guarantees that nothing is happening, whereas ferment and disorder indicate progress . . . I

have often wondered, with occasional amusement, why so many who write on politics and public affairs apparently feel themselves expert on organization. Normally a writer is an individualistic rather than an organizational worker, and rarely has he gone deeply into the problems of organizing people into a great business or a large road gang, a vast military formation or a squad, a university or a governmental agency. Yet there are more than a few who seem to feel a compulsion, at times, to pontificate about organization.[22]

Well before he became president, Eisenhower was familiar with criticisms of overstaffing. A lengthy memorandum he sent to Secretary of Defense James Forrestal on February 8, 1948, the day before he retired as army chief of staff, illuminates Eisenhower's propensity to think abstractly about such matters. Eisenhower warned Forrestal that the new Defense Department and unified military establishment would need a "highly efficient staff" and that the staff itself should have a head.

But for obvious psychological reasons and, indeed, legal prescription, the head of such a staff should not be called a Chief of Staff. My personal choice would be for the title "Administrative Assistant," but he should come from the military services. He must, at all costs, be a useful assistant in accumulating, briefing, and presenting to you the options and recommendations of military professionals. His rank should not be so high as to cause suspicion on the part of the Joint Chiefs of Staff that he might be tempted to intervene between any of these Chiefs of Staff and yourself. On the other hand he should be of such experience and rank as to have the respect of everybody in the military services . . .

Foreshadowing the observation in his presidential memoirs that a leader who engages in effective staff practices will be criticized, Eisenhower warned:

Assistants who are personally close to the Secretary of a governmental department always oppose the formation of an advisory and coordinating staff group under a single head, since this development, they feel, thrusts them one step away from the throne . . . Such words as "over-organization," "red-tape," and "duplication" are used to condemn the ideas of staff organization.

These ideas are not sound. First of all, the top man in any organization—and this applies with particular force to cabinet officers in Washington—has "prescribed" responsibilities with respect to the organization he heads; but he has a tremendous number of duties that force him continually to face outward . . . As a result the details fall into confusion; policy cannot be efficiently applied. Moreover, if there is no integrated staff, all principal *operating* subordinates . . . are compelled to decide which one of the chief's various "assistants" takes cognizance of a particular subject . . . My own experience has been that once these special assistants understand and begin working in an integrated staff, under a staff chief who is a real leader, they adopt the system wholeheartedly and enthusiastically.[23]

Clarity in the formal structure of organizations was important to Eisenhower. But he was not under the illusion that the official skeleton of an organization was in itself an organism in the absence of muscles, nerves, and vital organs. Rather, he thought in terms of the complementarity of formal and informal organization—of the elements of personal and group psychology that infuse an institution with purpose and motivation. These human relations considerations were if anything more prominent in his leadership theory and practice than was his passion for organization.

The Place of Debate and Consensus in "Teams"

The academic analyst of the presidency is likely to find the term *teamwork* vague and platitudinous, with an aura of Boy Scout troops and athletic coaches. Eisenhower (a onetime football coach) used the term to refer to several related practices he considered of crucial importance in both his prepresidential and presidential leadership. In the Eisenhower presidency, the cabinet meeting was a particular locus for fostering "team spirit."[24]

Washington lore has it that the items on Eisenhower's cabinet meeting agendas were trivial, and the cabinet discussions vacuous. Eisenhower himself, his personal secretary once reported, "feels that to fill out an agenda, items are sometimes included that are not necessarily of the caliber that should come before the Cabinet."[25] Yet all the issues that constituted the president's annual program and many others found their way to the cabinet. They were discussed with care and sometimes debated intensely, although Eisenhower made the final decisions and there was no voting. As well as being forums for debate, Eisenhower's cabinet meetings were occasions for bringing the debaters into agreement on the president's policies. And when not in agreement they were expected to close ranks once a decision was made, although slippage inevitably occurred.[26]

Still another team purpose of the cabinet meetings was to develop goodwill among the leading members of the administration. As a necessary (though obviously not sufficient) condition for the president and his associates to work in concert, Eisenhower put a premium on amiable personal relationships among them. This approach was the opposite of Roosevelt's competitive mode of energizing his associates by fostering rivalries among them. The theme of friendship as the lubricant of leadership groups recurs in Eisenhower's observations. In a memorandum to himself, occasioned by his observation that "in two more days I complete my first year as President," Eisenhower wrote that,

> as [the cabinet is] now constituted [the one dissident, Secretary of Labor Martin Durkin, had resigned], I cannot think of a single position that I could strengthen by removal of the present incumbent and appointment of another. I trust this will be so for the next three years, but, of course, in human affairs of this kind one is sometimes compelled to change his mind.
>
> By no means do I mean to imply that any one of my associates is perfect in his job—anymore than I deem myself to be perfectly suited to my own! I mean merely to say that I have had a good many years of experience in selecting people for positions of heavy responsibility, and I think the results so far achieved by this Cabinet and by other close associates, justify my conviction that we have an extraordinarily good combination of personalities . . . I think the individuals in the Cabinet and in other important offices like each other. At least, I can detect no sign of mutual dislike among the group. I know that I like them all; I like to be with them; I like to converse with them; I like their attitude toward their duty and toward governmental service.[27]

Six years earlier, in his memorandum to Forrestal on how to manage the Defense Department, Eisenhower had exhibited his conviction that it is vital to foster amiable relations among the members of groups that, like the cabinet, are vulnerable to disruption from the diverse organizational loyalties of the participants. In advising the defense secretary about how to work with the service chiefs, he foreshadowed how he would comport himself in cabinet meetings. Eisenhower urged Forrestal to meet once a week with the chiefs (provision had not yet been made for a Joint Chiefs of Staff chairman):

> The effort should be to promote the concept that the four individuals present, without regard to their respective responsibilities and specific duties, were meeting as a group to talk over broad security problems in an atmosphere of complete friendliness and objectivity. Whenever at such a meeting any individual showed a tendency to become a special pleader, the subject should be skillfully changed and constant effort made to achieve unanimity of conclusion, first upon broad generalities and then gradually brought closer to concrete application to particular problems . . . The men composing this staff have reached the pinnacle of their respective careers. They should consider every problem from its broad national viewpoint; but habits of years will have to be overcome by some patience and a sense of humor. If the Secretary habitually and casually brings out into the open, at informal meetings, major controversial issues in the attitude of one seeking *general* professional assistance so that he may make decisions on the basis of the national welfare, he will eventually profit immeasurably.[28]

Eisenhower did not like "yes men" in his counsels, but private and public disagreement were different matters. When his brother and informal adviser, Milton, complained that Treasury Secretary Humphrey had privately expressed views that diverged from the president's program, Eisenhower responded that "so long as he is the good soldier that I believe him to be, I must say that I don't see that anything is hurt by the presence in the highest councils of different kinds of thinking. It is in the combination of these various attitudes that we hammer out acceptable policies; enthusiasts for or against anything usually go too far."[29]

Efforts to build solidarity were of course not limited to cabinet (and NSC) meetings. In his weekly meetings with the Republican legislative leaders, individuals who were not and in some cases never would have been chosen by Eisenhower as team members, he advanced his own views with force, but in a spirit of consultation and cooperation, and with considerable success. He viewed failure to consult informally with the legislators and seek to win them over as a serious error, as his remarks to Defense Secretary Charles Wilson on a policy leak illustrate: "I was shocked to find a story in the paper of a project that we have been discussing before the NSC. This shakes me considerably because, as you know, it is my belief that there is no hope of getting a reserve program enacted into law until after we have appropriate confidential consultations with our congressional leaders and other interested groups and individuals. Now, with this sudden release, we are practically sure of antagonisms and resentments which will be difficult to overcome."[30]

The importance of teamwork was relative to circumstances, however. A few days before taking office in 1953, Eisenhower met with Winston Churchill. In his notes on the conversation he remarked that Churchill appeared to be living in the past in terms of his views of the special relationship between Britain and the United States. Churchill wanted to maximize joint decisions and action. Eisenhower held that this would antagonize other countries: "There is great danger in the two most powerful free nations banding together to present their case in a "take-it-or-leave-it" fashion. It will be far better for us to proceed independently toward the solution of knotty problems but to agree on fundamental factors and proposals before we make public our separate suggestions. In this way we will create confidence and even if occasionally there is a lack of uniformity in the detailed methods we suggest, this will be an advantage rather than the contrary."[31]

Delegation

On one occasion Eisenhower expressed a view very much like Truman's assertion that the buck must stop at the Oval Office. His secretary's notes on a meeting with his economic aide, Gabriel Hauge, show him observing that in the army Eisenhower "always had a rule that he would never decide any question upon which he was not fully acquainted; that made his aides make the decision—that is, the person who saw the problem, realized its full implications, was responsible for the decision. Here [in the Presidency] was a different case; he must know, or pretend to know, everything about literally everything."[32] On another occasion, however, he spoke of delegation in far more expansive terms:

The government of the United States has become too big, too complex, and too pervasive in its influence on all our lives for one individual to pretend to direct the details of its important and critical programming. Competent assistants are mandatory; without them the Executive Branch would bog down. To command the loyalties and dedication and best efforts of capable and outstanding individuals requires patience, understanding, a readiness to delegate, and an acceptance of responsibility for any honest errors—real or apparent—those associates and subordinates might make. Such loyalty from such people cannot be won by shifting the responsibility, whining, scolding or demagoguery. Principal subordinates must have confidence that they and their positions are widely respected, and the chief must do his part in assuring that this is so.[33]

The first statement emerged from a discussion in which Eisenhower was carrying out his official responsibility of refereeing a Tariff Commission decision; he was complaining about the inappropriateness of requiring the president to reach final judgment on problems with a highly specialized component. The second observation was contained in Eisenhower's 1960 stock-taking letter to Henry Luce. Here his concern was with overall organizational leadership. It was his policy to delegate to the extent to which the circumstances made this possible. He considered it essential to select line executives with care, give them general direction, and back them up when they made occasional human errors.

Eisenhower's critics took it for granted that his acts of delegation were so "generous" that there remained little for him to do as chief executive. Eisenhower never commented at length about delegation, either in general or in terms of specific matters such as how staff aides could be employed so that they effectively took the burdens of detailed policy execution from their boss without preempting decisions and how line officers should make policy without undermining the program of the president. But both his interstitial comments on his acts of delegation and his actions themselves are instructive.

First, consider Eisenhower's delegation to his high-level staff officers such as Adams, Smith, Gruenther, or the administrative assistant that Eisenhower suggested Forrestal should employ. The case of Sherman Adams is typical. A staff official such as Adams was his chief's deputy, not an independent policymaker. Adams was present at a large proportion of Eisenhower's meetings and received minutes of others. Although his job was never defined in detail by Eisenhower, Adams learned the president's positions on various matters, including those concerning what was or was not to reach the latter's desk. He was often able to proceed by deduction in responding to new situations. The overriding procedural principle was stated in a note from Eisenhower to General Walter Bedell Smith in 1942: "I am particularly anxious that you always understand these things in person, so that you can enlarge and elaborate on them when the occasion demands."[34]

Eisenhower also regularly outlined policy to his deputies and set them to work seeing that it was implemented. He authorized them to emphasize to all concerned that they had the support of their superior. Eisenhower's military correspondence contains countless memoranda to General Smith doing precisely these things.

A teletype from Eisenhower to Adams shows how the latter was instructed to implement a direct command from his chief. Eisenhower first forwarded suggestions from newspaper publisher Roy Roberts about how the administration's controversial farm policy might be more effectively promoted. He then expressed irritation that a suggestion from the labor secretary about Defense Department spending during the preelection half of the fiscal year had not been implemented. Eisenhower instructed Adams to act in both matters. Roberts's letter was to be circulated to a number of administration officials because

> it seems to me there is a tremendous amount of material that will be helpful in selling the farm program properly. I shall speak to Ezra [Taft Benson, secretary of agriculture] on Monday, but I hope that you will see that his Department put the full force of their leadership behind this business. [Shifting to the second topic] This morning you and I talked briefly about the program for stepping up expenditures to stimulate industrial activity. You stated you would soon see Secretary [of Labor James] Mitchell. Please ask him to show you the memorandum he wrote me under the date of September 16, which came to my attention this morning. I should very much like to push in the direction he advocates. For six months I have been urging the Defense Department to do the major portion of its buying now and not wait until the last half of the fiscal year. This does not seem to be happening and I think it is time that it was. Do not hesitate to use any legal authority I have to get this going and be sure to notify everybody of my personal anxiety.[35]

Second, consider delegation to line officials, notably cabinet sec-retaries. The variation in the extent of autonomy he granted cabinet members strikingly illustrates how Eisenhower acted on the premise that the personalities of superior and subordinate should be an in-tegral part of leadership transactions. The memorandum to Adams just quoted refers to a Defense Department matter. Eisenhower pe-riodically expressed impatience at Defense Secretary Charles Wil-son's proclivity to bring problems to the White House that might have been settled by Wilson himself.

But the reverse of the coin was that Eisenhower *wanted* to deal with the military in some detail. He knew precisely what he favored on a wide range of military issues, from details of the internal man-agement of the services to the nation's overall strategic stance. Therefore, he delegated little policy-making power to Wilson. The Eisenhower Library files are replete with presidential directives spec-ifying a particular Defense Department policy or procedure. These directives were not, as was usually the case even when Eisenhower meant to tell a subordinate what to do, worded as suggestions. They were orders.[36]

Attorney General Herbert Brownell was at the other end of the continuum. Eisenhower had great confidence in him and recognized that his special field of knowledge—the rendering of legal judg-ments—was outside his own expertise. Brownell enjoyed much greater leeway in policy-making than he had expected, although in their first conversation about his duties Eisenhower made it clear that Brownell would hear from him if he felt Brownell's actions had been inappropriate. In fact Brownell was rarely corrected. When he was, the correction was likely to be in a broader capacity in which Ei-senhower frequently employed him—that of a wise judge about how to proceed in decisions that involved balancing political consider-ations.

When Brownell was corrected in his capacity as a political oper-ative, the admonition was phrased mildly but unequivocally. Thus, during a period of intense bargaining and legal maneuvering over possible ways to rephrase the Bricker Amendment to make it ac-ceptable to the administration, Eisenhower signed a letter to Senate Minority Leader William Knowland that Brownell had drafted for him. He then discovered that Knowland was at that very moment making the letter public in a press conference. Eisenhower felt that if he had known in advance that the letter was for publication he would have reworded it. In a letter to Brownell he simply asked:

"When you asked me to sign the letter . . . did you know that he intended to publish it this evening? . . . While I have no particular objection to his action, I do think I should have been carefully informed as to the ultimate purpose of the letter when I signed it . . . Please do not do anything about the matter—I was just wondering whether I stupidly missed something this morning that I should have picked up from the conversation."[37]

With an experienced staff associate such as Staff Secretary Paul Carroll, who had served with Eisenhower at the Pentagon and at NATO, a "small" decision could be wholly delegated, since Carroll was fully cognizant of Eisenhower's basic predilections and could be counted on to adhere to the overall administrative line. If, for example, Eisenhower noted that a paragraph of a letter drafted by the Bureau of the Budget seemed to contradict administration policy, he might ask Carroll to draft a substitute paragraph. But Carroll was also to confer with the BOB, since Eisenhower realized that "it is possible there is something in the whole affair that I do not sense." Then Carroll was to use the paragraph he drafted in whatever way was consistent with Eisenhower's policies.[38]

The Hidden Hand

Richard Nixon asserted correctly that Eisenhower "usually preferred the indirect approach where it would serve him better." Eisenhower took many actions of which contemporary observers, both outside and inside his administration, were unaware. One example of his "hidden-hand" mode of leadership is to be found in an exchange of letters and telephone calls with South Carolina Governor James F. Byrnes in the summer and fall of 1953. This exchange concerned the explosive problem of balancing federal desegregation policy with "states' rights," then a southern white code word for resistance to desegregation. Eisenhower had the conflicting aims of gradually remedying discrimination against blacks while seeking to align conservative (hence segregationist) whites with "modern" nonsouthern Republicans.

A key letter to Byrnes on this topic appears in Eisenhower's memoir *Waging Peace*.[39] The classification "personal and confidential," which appears at the head of the letter, is not shown in the portion printed, however. Nor does the memoir allude to Byrnes's strongly argued rejoinder and the numerous telephone conversations between the two. The exchanges in their entirety demonstrate both the continuing elements of the disagreement and the two men's respect for each other. Eisenhower stressed that his obligation as president was to enforce desegregation of federal facilities, regardless of his personal convictions; but he also propitiated Byrnes, voicing his personal opinion that abrupt jolts to regional mores were likely to retard rather than advance interracial amity.

A note from Eisenhower to Maxwell Rabb, whose White House duties involved minority group relations, indicates how the letter came to be officially labeled as off the record.

In view of what you have to say on my proposed letter to Governor Byrnes, I think we had better mark the letter "Personal and Confidential." I return the draft herewith with certain corrections, and assuming that it now meets the approval of interested staff agencies, please have it put in finished form and returned to me . . .

In the event that this letter is not to be a "personal and confidential" one, perhaps I should handle the whole matter by telephone. After all, we are not after publicity for this particular letter; what we want is the Governor to go along with us completely in the enforcement of *federal regulations*. Our job is to convince not to publicize.[40]

Some of the most instructive examples of Eisenhower's hidden-hand leadership occurred during the McCarthy episode. Eisenhower worked through his press secretary, James Hagerty, to help manage the congressional hearings that culminated in McCarthy's censure in December 1954 and otherwise directed the fight against McCarthy.[41] An example of Eisenhower's covert involvement in this issue is his response to a May 6 speech by Adlai Stevenson questioning whether Eisenhower or McCarthy was the true leader of the GOP. Eisenhower's telephone log for Monday, May 8, shows how he quietly intervened. Early that morning Eisenhower called Republican National Chairman Leonard Hall and asked him to see if the networks were granting equal time for a reply. In the past, free network time had been granted to McCarthy to respond to such Democratic claims. The president told Hall to establish that the National Committee, and *not* McCarthy, was to be given the time. Hall was to get back to Eisenhower, who would contact the network heads, NBC's David Sarnoff and CBS's William Paley, if Hall himself could not obtain a grant of equal time for the National Committee. Hall was successful.

After conferring with Adams, Eisenhower called the vice-president to his office. Nixon had been assiduously seeking to maintain his ties with both the pro-McCarthy and anti-McCarthy forces in the party. Eisenhower said that he realized Nixon did not want to become involved in public exchanges. Nevertheless, Eisenhower continued, he felt that Nixon was the proper party representative. He advised Nixon to follow the general approach that Eisenhower himself sought to follow, ignoring McCarthy as an individual and "speaking positively" about the party's program and its position and performance on the issues of internal subversion, preserving the rights of civil servants, and other matters bearing on the Stevenson speech and McCarthy's continued claims and charges.[42]

In addition to working behind the scenes to see that McCarthy did not get the attention that would accrue to the Republican who replied to Stevenson, Eisenhower also appears to have been responsible for the content of Nixon's remarks. Although these made no explicit reference to McCarthy, they castigated reckless anti-Communists in an indirect criticism that added to the mounting attacks on the Wisconsin senator during his ill-fated 1954 confrontation with the army.

In peace as in war, Eisenhower was consistently at pains to analyze not only what policies and actions were needed, but also whether actions should be publicized at all. He was acutely attentive to the need for confidentiality in both covert operations and activities in which tact was required. In 1953, for example, he suggested to General Gruenther at NATO headquarters that when newly appointed Ambassador Douglas Dillon arrived in France he be included in a series of off-the-record meetings of American ambassadors to neighboring nations:

> I have suggested to him the institution of a "get together" plan for the American representatives in Britain, France, West Germany, and sometimes including those of Italy and Belgium. Of course on special occasions the list could be made even more extensive.
>
> My idea is that about once every two months he could, on a fairly confidential basis, invite both Mr. Aldrich and Dr. Conant to come in for a weekend, thus giving them a chance to discuss various problems from the viewpoints of the different

areas. The reason I am writing to you about this idea is that occasionally you might want to take advantage of such a meeting to get a little help in some of your own military projects . . .

Of course the meetings would lose all value and would, indeed, become almost impossible if they should become publicized. Other Ambassadors would feel neglected and other countries would feel that there was some nefarious plot afoot.[43]

The Caressing (and Cuffing) Hand

Shortly after becoming army chief of staff in 1945, Eisenhower suggested to General Maxwell Taylor, the new superintendent of the U.S. Military Academy, that a course in "tactical or applied psychology" be introduced there. The first step would be to bring in as consultants "experts both from other schools and . . . persons who have made an outstanding success in industrial and economic life. Too frequently we find young officers trying to use empirical and ritualistic methods in the handling of individuals—I think that both theoretical and practical instruction along this line could, at the very least, awaken the majority of Cadets to the necessity of handling human problems on a human basis and do much to improve leadership and personnel handling in the army at large."[44]

He made a similar point in his long 1948 memorandum to Forrestal, extending it to leadership in general: "In organizing teams, personality is equally important with ability. Too many people believe that strength of character is synonymous with arrogance and insufferable deportment. Leadership is as vital in conference as it is in battle . . . I simply cannot over-stress the importance of this point; I have had personally to relieve officers of ability from high staff positions because of the dislike for themselves they generated among their associates."[45]

During Eisenhower's short collaboration with Senate Majority Leader Robert Taft in early 1953, before the latter suddenly succumbed to cancer, Eisenhower came increasingly to respect Taft. But he felt that Taft's inability to discipline his anger was a major shortcoming, as was his impulse to speak in public about disagreements that should be reconciled without publicity.

Senator Taft never disagrees with me when we discuss such affairs academically or theoretically. He believes in the theory of cooperative security and mutual aid. However, when we take up each individual problem or case, he easily loses his temper and makes extravagant statements. He always does this when he starts making a public speech—he seems to work himself into a storm of resentment and irritation . . . The result of this is that all our allies fear him . . . They think he gives McCarthy ideas, and McCarthy, with his readiness to goad to the extreme of calling names and making false accusations, simply terrifies the ordinary European statesman.[46]

Even when provoked to the point of barely being able to restrain his temper, Eisenhower continued to reach out to be amiable to Taft and achieved something of a friendship with him by the time illness unexpectedly felled the senator.

Eisenhower's own preeminent principle of "tactical or applied psychology" was (in the language of behavioral psychology) to use positive rather than negative reinforcement. The first half of the motto on a plaque on Eisenhower's desk—"Gently in Manner, Strong in Deed"—effectively summarizes the expressions of affection and warm feeling that pervaded his discourse and his constant demonstrations of appreciation and respect for aides and other associates. His long-term friend, supporter, and confidant, *New York Herald Tribune* publisher William E. Robinson, was the recipient of this missive:

Dear Bill:

You are the one individual whom I am inviting for a second time to one of my stag dinners—in fact, I am contemplating a later dinner where I may again ask for your presence. For this there are a number of reasons. The principal one is that your impressions and options on matters of general interest are always of such value to me that I feel a distinct confidence when you are present on such occasions in order to analyze what might be called the group thinking.[47]

To the often beleaguered secretary of health, education and welfare, Mrs. Oveta Culp Hobby, he wrote:

Dear Oveta:

When I spoke to you the other day about taking a short breather, you said you would take Thursday off—meaning Thanksgiving Day. Now I admit that when anyone gets as high ranking as you are, such a person has gotten beyond the place where he or she can be "ordered about." But I would deem it a very great personal favor if you would get out of this place no later than tomorrow morning (Wednesday) and not be back before Monday. My whole purpose in making this request would be defeated if you would lug off with your briefcase full of papers (anyway briefcases belong only to diplomatic service) or if you continue to contact with your office by telephone. This request is based on truly selfish reasons—on reasons that are shared by the entire Cabinet and your other associates. Briefly stated, they are nothing more than our conviction that you are absolutely necessary to this administration and we want you to get enough variation, recreation and rest in your life that you don't become bored, sick or just plain tired of your job.[48]

When his special assistant for national security affairs, Robert Cutler, wrote saying he was considering resigning but would stay on if needed until the end of the administration, Eisenhower replied:

Dear Bobby:

I think my blood pressure would have showed less violent variation had you reversed the order in which you expressed the thoughts containing your March 20th letter. Throughout the first part, I had the sinking feeling of "Et tu, Brute!"

But Eisenhower was reassured by the conclusion of the letter that Cutler would continue "working my head off" if need be. This, he continued,

restored me to something like normal. By which I mean I am selfish enough to want to keep you doing just that, even though I do most seriously urge that you, for one, practice a modicum of malingering.

When I try to deal with the sentiments of personal appreciation you express toward me I am completely helpless. Perhaps I should just say that I lean on you far more than you could possibly know and with far greater reason.[49]

But Eisenhower's hand could also cuff instead of caress. During his civilian leadership, Eisenhower's reprimands rarely went beyond a stern word or a barbed phrase. His private expressions of temper were legendary, but his control over his temper was powerful. That Eisenhower could—deliberately more than intemperately—administer a harsh reprimand is clear from his famous dressing down of Patton in World War II:

Dear General Patton:

You first came into my command at my own insistence because I believed in your fighting qualities and your ability to lead troops in battle. At the same time I have always been fully aware of your habit of dramatizing yourself and of committing indiscretions for no other apparent purpose than that of calling attention to yourself. I am thoroughly weary of your failure to control your tongue and I have begun to doubt your all-round judgment, so essential in high military position.[50]

"No Personalities"

Eisenhower used this phrase to summarize his practice of refusing to criticize people in public, even if they had criticized him or had behaved in ways that he considered reprehensible. Instead, he would criticize the kinds of acts they had committed. He might be scathing in his private comments about them, but he would not publicly "engage in personalities."[51]

This precept was most taxed during the McCarthy episode. Because many of Eisenhower's closest supporters urged him to strike back, especially before McCarthy was put on the defensive early in 1954, his private correspondence from this period contains a well-elaborated set of general statements explaining why he never mentioned McCarthy by name but did openly attack "book burners" and publicly castigate people who urged that public servants divulge confidential information to congressional committees.

Eisenhower presented a variety of reasons that were specific to the McCarthy case: McCarthy had flourished on publicity; more publicity would give him the underdog sympathy that is accorded to Davids who are set upon by Goliaths; and personal attacks on politicians would weaken the dignity of the presidency. He stated his general reasoning in a letter to Governor George Craig of Indiana, commenting that attacking McCarthy would violate "a principle to which I have adhered all my adult life":

To explain the development of this, to me fundamental rule, I have to go back to war experiences and certain lessons I learned throughout those years. Of these, the first and foremost is that the support and teaching of a constructive program is a *long-term* thing. Moreover, it is seldom, if ever that a worthwhile conception can be advanced by indulging in hateful or hyper-critical remarks concerning some other *individual*. Out of these experiences, I developed a practice which, so far as I know, I have never varied. This practice is to avoid public mention of any name *unless it can be done with favorable intent and connotation*. This, of course, means that whatever criticism is necessary must be done in the private conference.[52]

Eisenhower's reluctance to criticize adversaries by name was linked to his profoundly issue-oriented concern with seeking what he considered to be rational solutions to the complex problems of advancing needed public policies. He was therefore wary of being enmeshed in the irrational facets of individual and group political psychology. From his standpoint, the ends of politics were too important to be compromised by emotional indulgence. Given the intensity of his preoccupation with seeking solutions to—or at least buying time against—threats to the forms of governments and societies with which he was identified, he simply could not afford to indulge animus. The individual whose motives were attacked in a political conflict, Eisenhower held, would inevitably nurse a grudge and seek revenge, or at a minimum refuse to join in future collective endeavors.

Eisenhower sought personally to transcend "personality" conflict and recommended to others that they avoid stirring emotionally-based political contention. The best ways to deal with attacks on one's person were, if possible, to ignore them or to accentuate the positive by favorably presenting one's policies.

In World War II, when the calculus of effective leadership was the actual or potential loss or saving of lives, Eisenhower had experienced with special intensity the tension between cool calculation of how best to attain a long-run effect and the impulse toward heated response to the other people's errors, slights, and antagonisms. He concluded that when he was under public fire his best bet was not to reply, but rather to use informal means of winning support, letting his adversaries exhaust their ammunition. Meanwhile, he employed his extraordinary capacity to convey to his own forces and to the larger public a sense of his sincerity, warmth, and integrity.

Shortly after the war as army chief of staff, Eisenhower had occasion to commend his experience to General Mark Clark, whose troops, particularly Texas national guard divisions, had suffered severe losses in the Italian campaign. When Clark's strategy in the Rapido River crossing was condemned by a Texas veterans' group and became the subject of congressional hearings, Eisenhower urged Clark to make no comment: "To initiate unnecessarily a public quarrel will have many unfortunate effects, among these being a tendency to drag forward as a volunteer witness every single individual who may through venom, spite, or mere love of personal publicity, see a chance of doing a bit of damage . . . You must remember that on our side we have only facts and honest conclusion with which to combat argument based largely on sentiment and emotional appeal."[53]

Later in the year, when Clark's promotion to permanent major general was confirmed by the Senate, Eisenhower, in replying to a note of thanks from Clark, said that (as was later to be the case in the McCarthy episode) he had deliberately held his fire while also engaging in behind-the-scenes work:

> I always knew we would get [the promotion] over, and I wanted very much to avoid a name calling campaign. However, I did talk personally to several members of the committee, and they knew I was prepared to go down to do my stuff if it became necessary. What I was going to do was dwell upon Grant's second charge at Cold Harbor and Pickett's Charge at Gettysburg, directed by Lee. I figure that the proper treatment of these two incidents would do more than to argue about the specific tactical situation existing in the Rapido.[54]

In short, Chief of Staff Eisenhower let the attacks on General Clark subside without public appeal and developed congressional allies privately. If necessary he would have testified on the Hill but even then his plan was to "stonewall," speaking authoritatively, but of Civil War events and not of the Rapido incident or Clark's accusers.

The High Ground and the Middle Way

The second half of Eisenhower's motto—"Strength in Deed"—may seem to be contradicted by his reputation as a seeker of consensus policies. Eisenhower did not view his policies as wishy-washy. His political beliefs were strong, but so was his procedural commitment to a pragmatic political truism: unless one can win support for a policy, the strength to carry it through will not be forthcoming.

His highest achievement had been that of commanding the forces that liberated Europe in World War II. This effort called for complex, careful overall planning, but flexibility in operation. At various stages he was subjected to intense pressure by fractious subordinates and demanding superiors to alter his basic strategy, but he won out over those who opposed his broad-front advance through Western Europe, which aimed at demolishing the bulk of German forces west of the Rhine. On the one hand, he resisted Churchill's efforts to ward off a cross-Channel landing and follow a strategy of attack from the "underbelly" of Europe. On the other, he refused to gamble on the lightning thrust across the Rhine to Berlin that Field Marshal Bernard Montgomery confidently predicted would end the war.

During his brief stint as president of Columbia University, a position constantly interrupted by travel to Washington on special Defense Department assignments, Eisenhower was especially proud of establishing the American Assembly, a forum at which leaders from diverse fields gather in seclusion and work out policy recommendations on major contemporary issues. His aim in forming this body was not only to encourage thought about policy, but also to build consensus by fostering discourse among leaders from many segments of society who, meeting "free of telephone calls and urgent summons to make instant decisions . . . might examine the larger problems, find a common agreement about answers, and arrive at working conclusions."[55]

The overriding "larger problem" Eisenhower perceived during his years at Columbia was the development and maintenance of the Western alliance. He viewed this aspect of the Cold War as a continuation and extension of the fight he led in World War II against statist authoritarianism. The summons to leave Columbia and head NATO meant a return to alliance management, but his military role now had a far more manifestly political component than it had in his wartime dealings with Churchill, Roosevelt, and De Gaulle. The goal of his newest crusade was a united Europe, allied with the United States.

His conservative predilections, revealed mainly in speeches while he was at Columbia, made him the target of Republican (rather than, as in 1948, Democratic) appeals that he seek nomination for the presidency. He agreed to do so after concluding that a continuation of Democratic party rule would be inconsistent with his view of the national interest and that the otherwise certain Republican nominee, Senator Taft, even if electable, might destroy the nascent Western alliance. Further, he persuaded himself (or allowed his political and business supporters to persuade him) that only he could assemble a new centrist coalition capable of winning widespread support and providing a balance between sound domestic policy and firm support for the nation's international commitments. Domestically, Eisenhower's commitment to building a majority party led him to support public policies that were more liberal than his private convictions. Internationally, his public policies and commitments usually coincided. Overall, his nonconflictual leadership and his centrist policies were congruent.[56] As he once put it: "Clearly there are different ways to try to be a leader. In my view, a fair, decent, and reasonable dealing with men, reasonable recognition that views may diverge, a constant seeking for a high ground on which to work together, is the best way to lead our country in the difficult times ahead of us. A living democracy needs diversity to keep it strong. For survival, it also needs to have the diversities brought together for a common purpose, so fair, so reasonable, and so appealing that all can rally to it."[57]

At one point, commenting on public statements by Nelson Rockefeller that were too liberal for his taste, Eisenhower expatiated on his centrist view of the relationship between what is ideal and what is practical. Exhibiting his analytic bent, he compared pragmatism in policy-making to the statistical properties of the normal distribution curve, in which the bulk of phenomena (such as the height and weight of individuals in a population) are at the center, not the high or low end, of a continuum. Describing Rockefeller's aims as "admirable" when viewed "as generalizations defining great objectives," Eisenhower observed:

Difficulties arise, of course, when we begin to apply basic truths to human problems. This is natural because in almost every field of thought and actions humans seem to distribute themselves almost according to a natural law, from one extreme to another. The noticeable fact is that under what has been called "nature's curve," the extremes comprise small percentages of the whole; what might be called compatible groups is about two-thirds of the aggregate. Most people believe that in a general way they belong to the "middle-of-the-road" group.

While in the field of moral truth of basic principle the statement tends to be black or white, the task of the political leader is to devise plans among which humans can make constructive progress. This means that the plan or program itself tends to fall in the "gray" category, even though an earnest attempt is made to apply the black and white values of moral truths. This is not because there is any challenge to the principle or the moral truth, but because human nature itself is far from perfect.

The principal objective is to make progress along the lines that principle and truth point out. Perfection is not quickly reached; the plan is therefore "gray" or "middle-of-the-road." But it is *progressive!* Just as a tree does not instantly reach full stature when it is planted as a seedling, progress must be attained by small steps, some of the times discouragingly small. But as long as we do attain discernible progress and fight stagnation and recession with all our strength, I believe that we are on the right road—and people who seek to live by this doctrine should claim and deserve the name of progressives.[58]

The Public Role of the Leader, the Dignity of the Presidency

The foundation on which Eisenhower's governance rested was his own extraordinary appeal both to the larger public and to those with whom he met face-to-face. Modesty or the lack of need to reflect extensively about the uniquely personal sources of his popularity may have kept him from making many general pronouncements about how he won over both small groups and large populations.[59] The pattern was set in the war. Of face-to-face leadership, he dictated the following notes for his wartime diary:

Rich organizational experience and an orderly, logical mind are absolutely essential to success. The flashy, publicity-seeking adventurer can grab the headlines and be a hero in the eyes of the public, but he simply can't deliver the goods in high command. On the other hand the slow, methodical, ritualistic person is absolutely valueless in a key position. There must be a fine balance . . . In addition . . . a person in such [high] position must have an inexhaustible fund of nervous energy. He is called upon day and night to absorb the disappointments, the discouragements and the doubts of his subordinates and to force them on to accomplishments, which they regard as impossible.[60]

On leadership of people en masse, Eisenhower made it known that he deplored flashy press relations, but also that he allowed himself to be personally publicized when he thought it desirable to advance national concerns. For example, he granted a request by newsman John Gunther that he personally land and make contact with troops shortly after an area in Sicily had been secured, because he agreed with Gunther that the ensuing press coverage would serve the interests of "psychological warfare."[61] In other words, he depreciated getting headlines for their own sake but recognized that he was becoming a celebrity and that his personal prestige had instrumental value. He explained to his brother Edgar (perhaps disingenuously) that modesty and getting media attention were not necessarily in conflict with each other:

> To the extent possible in a position such as mine, I have constantly shunned the headlines. This has not been entirely due to a sense of modesty, but because of the nature of an Allied Command. Any "glory grabbing" on the part of the top man would quickly wreck an institution such as this. Happily, the official requirement has coincided exactly with my personal desire. One result is that, almost without exception, the five hundred newspaper and radio men accredited to this organization are my friends. Quite frequently they seem to be moved by a desire to see that I get "full credit" so they write special articles and even books. Strangely enough, the vast majority of them will eventually turn upon a man who shows any indication of courting them in his own self-interest, no matter how "colorful" they may deem him at first. What I am trying to say is that some publicity is mandatory—otherwise, American soldiers would not know they had an American commander, interested in their welfare. The problem is to take it and use it in the amount required by the job; but to avoid distortion and self-glorification.[62]

During his presidency Eisenhower was acutely attentive to winning and maintaining public support. As during the war, he avoided actions that might be easily interpreted as gimmicks. He sought to act as a symbol of the nation *qua* nation and to play down the controversial (and hence divisive) aspects of presidential leadership. One aspect of his comportment is captured in his 1960 letter to Henry Luce: "Among the qualities that the American government must exhibit is dignity. In turn the principal governmental spokesmen must strive to display it."[63] Another (acknowledged as effective even by contemporaries who depreciated his leadership) was making regular use of his visual trademarks, the beaming smile and the other body language that enabled him to instill happy enthusiasm into crowds. The Eisenhower grin was not wholly a spontaneous emanation. In an instructive passage in one of his memoirs, Eisenhower referred to the "ache in his bones" that the campaigner's grin conceals,[64] and his campaign aide Bryce Harlow remembers that Eisenhower, the ostensible amateur, gave advice to political professionals on the importance of giving an animated impression to campaign audiences.[65]

Eisenhower's leadership style was evident to varying degrees to his closest associates, but not to the wider public. As president he drew extensively on an explicit conception of the means and ends of leadership that he had developed before assuming office. The record supports his assertion in his 1960 letter to Henry Luce that his "practices . . . were or are deliberate, or, rather, natural to me. They are not accidental."[66]

The amount and quality of his own writings, both private and public, demonstrate beyond question that Eisenhower was fully capable of explaining his political performance clearly and with analytic detachment. Why would such an individual not advertise these enviable personal qualities? Why did he not anticipate Kennedy, who consciously displayed his abilities, for example, by using his press conferences to exhibit both his grasp of policy specifics and an engaging wit that bespoke a first-rate mind? Why did Eisenhower not seek to refute public depictions of him as the bewildered, disoriented, if amiable bumbler of (for example) the Herblock cartoons that greeted him in each morning's *Washington Post?*

There appear to be three answers. First, he was seeking to please the general public, an audience that did not consume what today is called within-the-Beltway political folklore, and did admire unpretentious folksiness. Second, Eisenhower's operating code required that its practitioners subordinate displays of public skill to whatever method produced the desired outcome. As Eisenhower wrote to his aide, Maxwell Rabb, the "job is to convince, not to publicize." Finally, Eisenhower cared greatly about his policy aims, but he seemed singularly unmoved by the need to use his presidency to establish a place in history. In his opinion, he had achieved that place by 1945.

I have argued in *The Hidden-Hand Presidency* that by obscuring his steady involvement in political machinations while publicizing his ecumenical appeal to all Americans and his congenial outward manner, Eisenhower escaped a catch-22 built into the presidency. Rather than allowing the presidential roles as nonpolitical chief of state and political leader to undermine each other, he enabled them to coincide. (I do *not* claim that Eisenhower himself conceived of his practices in these terms.) Surely his capacity to maintain an impression of distance from the contentiousness of politics helps explain why he garnered more continuingly positive public approval ratings than has any other president during the years (from Truman to Reagan) for which the Gallup Poll has assessed presidential support.

The embattled final period of Johnson's presidency, Watergate, and more recent controversy over what President Reagan may have known, and when, provide after-the-fact reminders that there are gains for the polity simply in having a chief executive who enjoys public confidence and therefore is taken seriously by leaders in his own and other nations. But a policy of "hoarding" popularity and not seeking to respond intelligently to challenges that face the nation scarcely commends itself as a model for effective presidential leadership. It is one thing to show that Eisenhower engaged in team building and sought to influence events while hiding these efforts; it is quite another to show that the procedures produced the desired results and did not produce unhappy outcomes.

Often questions about presidential "success" are answered with sweeping pronouncements on an administration's policies judged in terms of the evaluator's own policy preferences. Such assessments also often make easy use of hindsight rather than relying on realistic reconstructions of what might or might not have been possible, given the president's historical context. It is possible to do better, but only by closely examining specific cases and events. I undertake this in *The Hidden-Hand Presidency* for a single case in which most commentators have found Eisenhower's performance deficient—his response to Wisconsin Senator Joseph McCarthy's assaults on the executive branch.[67] What emerges is a balance sheet, not a unitary judgment. There is much to be said for the argument that, by refusing to fight publicly with McCarthy but engaging in covert wire-pulling, Eisenhower hastened the senator's political demise. But more was at stake in the issue of McCarthyism than the senator. Surely Eisenhower's comportment during his first year of office, when he was not even attacking McCarthy obliquely, permitted grave damage to the morale of civil servants, especially of those in the foreign service.

But another sequence of events occurring at the same time that McCarthy's support was unraveling, in Eisenhower's second year in office, complicates an assessment of his performance in the Mc-Carthy case. At the time of the Army-McCarthy hearings, and out of the public eye, Eisenhower was also addressing the question of how the nation should respond to the incipient collapse of the American-supported, anti-Communist French forces and their indigenous allies in Indochina.

If Eisenhower had chosen to respond positively to those in his administration who favored American military intervention (including Joint Chief of Staff Chairman Admiral Arthur Radford and Vice-President Richard Nixon), he would have needed the consolidated support of Senate Republicans, who were sharply divided on how to respond to McCarthy. His actual course of action—that of rejecting military intervention—made it equally urgent that he hold his party together and not be the object of criticism of an anti-Communist demagogue.

Eisenhower emerged from the sequence of events that led to a communist government in North Vietnam without being successfully attacked with "Who lost Indochina?" charges. Rather, two streams of political activity with an explosive potential for convergence—the fall of Dien Bien Phu and the Army-McCarthy hearings—remained separate. And the political backfire over the Geneva settlement dissipated within days.

This survey of Eisenhower's leadership style is necessarily inconclusive. The next major step in the study of Eisenhower's leadership is to examine his practices and policies in depth, with close attention to simultaneous events and actions. Such study can illuminate the capacity of presidents to maintain support in the face of potentially damaging conflict—no small feat in the second half of the twentieth century.

4

JOHN F. KENNEDY

The Endurance of Inspirational Leadership

Carl M. Brauer

Both during his presidency and since, John F. Kennedy has attracted more attention than most of his counterparts, and certainly far more than his truncated term of less than three years would appear to justify. To some extent, the Kennedy phenomenon stems from the tragic manner of his death. Yet William McKinley and James Garfield died similarly without evoking anything like the public reaction that succeeded Kennedy's death. Of the presidents who have died in office, only Abraham Lincoln and Franklin D. Roosevelt aroused comparable grief or comparable speculation about what they might have done had they completed their terms. Of the presidential assassinations, only Lincoln's inspired such constant public fascination with surrounding circumstances and with weaknesses in the subsequent official inquiries.[1]

Typically, presidents have been treated rather unkindly by scholars and commentators immediately after leaving office and have then been partly or wholly rehabilitated over time. In Kennedy's case, however, this pattern was reversed—his reputation skyrocketed, then plummeted. This reversal had much to do with the circumstances of his death and the grief it inspired, and to some extent with the considerable literary skill of his early chroniclers, especially his aides, Arthur Schlesinger, Jr., and Theodore Sorensen, who established a powerful pro-Kennedy orthodoxy. The repudiation of that orthodoxy accompanied developments occurring a few years after Kennedy's death, especially the expansion of the Vietnam war and the divisions it opened in American society, a discrediting of government from both ends of the political spectrum, and a growing popular fascination with the personal shortcomings of the powerful and famous. Having been mythologized, Kennedy became a sitting duck for demythologizing.[2]

The many revisionist assessments and the shortness of his tenure have had a strong effect on Kennedy's rating among historians. In 1982 a nationwide survey of American historians found that Kennedy ranked only thirteenth in presidential performance, in the lusterless "above average" category. (Among presidents of the last fifty years, he was behind Roosevelt, Truman, Johnson, and Eisenhower but ahead of Ford, Carter, and Nixon.)[3]

Kennedy revisionism, however, has had no discernible effect on public opinion. Since 1972 the pollster Louis Harris has periodically asked the public to rate the presidents since Franklin D. Roosevelt, and Kennedy has consistently led the field. In the 1985 survey, for example, Kennedy came in first on most of Harris's criteria: inspiring confidence in the White House, personality, trustworthiness in a crisis, ability to get things done, handling of domestic affairs, setting high moral standards. Even Americans under age thirty, who were at most eight when he died, remembered Kennedy very favorably. It is little wonder, then, that so many presidential candidates continue to evoke his memory. In addition to trying to create an association with Kennedy in the minds of the voting public, many were themselves inspired and influenced by him in their youth.[4]

The enormous grief over Kennedy's death and the persistence of his popularity despite his demythologizing suggest that he succeeded in profoundly affecting people during his lifetime. Beyond question, Kennedy was inspirational in a way that few presidents have been. He raised people's hopes, not just in America but in many countries, about peace, the promise of democratic government, social justice, economic progress, and the exploration of "New Frontiers" on earth and in space. Especially among the large postwar generation, which was coming of age when he became president, he inspired idealism about the importance of trying to achieve great things for society as a whole. For this generation, he ennobled politics and public service.

The ability to inspire masses of people and to endure in their memories as inspiring constitute the very essence of leadership. Presidents who lack those attributes can certainly be good presidents. They may possess courage and wisdom, demonstrate statesmanship and decisiveness, get programs enacted and conduct the operations of government effectively. But they are not leaders in the sense that Lincoln, the two Roosevelts, Wilson, and Kennedy were. (Since Kennedy, Reagan clearly has been the most inspirational of our presidents, the most interested in using the bully pulpit, and the most talented at it. But only time will tell whether he will be remembered as inspirational by large numbers of people.)

Kennedy's inspirational capability seems paradoxical, for he favored rational arguments and affected a cool style. He had an ironic and fatalistic view of life, an irreverent wit, and a wry sense of humor. Summed up by his wife best as "an idealist without illusions," he disliked cant, was uncomfortable with ideology, and sought practical, realistic, and often technical solutions to national and international problems.[5] Yet he also invoked moral arguments, appealed to people's idealism about serving big causes, and set exciting, ambitious goals for the nation and the world. He was leery of using the bully pulpit to excess, but when he chose to use it, he used it dramatically and well. His rationalism and wit mitigated any implied grandiosity in his high oratory. He softened certitude and passion with skepticism, ambiguity, and humor.

Kennedy appreciated and exploited the symbolic aspects of his office to set the nation's tone—by promoting "vigor," by honoring its best minds and creative talents, and by respecting and preserving its cultural and political heritage. Although his personal tastes were middlebrow, he associated himself with the highbrow. Being cosmopolitan, urbane, intellectual, and tolerant himself, he advanced those qualities in a country where provincialism, ill manners, anti-intellectualism, and intolerance are traditionally abundant.

Many of Kennedy's critics regard such activities as empty public relations serving only to cover up substantive deficiencies. Those who view Kennedy favorably they dismiss as court historians for Camelot (a metaphor that Arthur Schlesinger reminds us first came into use after Kennedy's death and that Kennedy himself would probably have derided).[6] Kennedy's critics have succeeded to the point of placing his supporters on the defensive. Yet without its rhetorical and symbolic aspects, the presidency is just another political office. And symbols, style, and rhetoric are nothing without purposeful political leadership that gets results. This chapter examines selective aspects of Kennedy's performance as president— how he created a mandate and conducted himself in office, his domestic policy and relations with Congress, and his record and approach to and achievements in foreign policy.

Creating a Mandate

Kennedy rode to the presidency on the crest of a wave of popular doubts about America's goals and performance. A sluggish economy; a perception that important public needs in areas such as education, medical care, and civil rights were not being met; and concern about excessive devotion to consumer goods all contributed to a fairly wide perception in the late 1950s that America had grown complacent and that it was time for a change. What is more, America seemed to face a greater challenge from abroad. Many Americans wondered whether the United States could meet the Soviet Union's technical, educational, and military challenge, vividly symbolized by the launching of Sputnik in 1957. Congressional hearings popularized the notion of a missile gap, and Democratic campaign ads in 1960 highlighted the failures of the American space program. Kennedy capitalized on these fears by building his campaign around the idea that it was time "to get America moving again."

The wave that Kennedy rode to the presidency, however, barely carried him ashore. He won by fewer than 120,000 votes out of nearly 69 million cast. Although he led more comfortably in the electoral college, 303–219, his victory there rested on very thin popular margins in several larger states, which his opponent, Vice-President Richard M. Nixon, briefly considered challenging in court. Moreover, for the first time in this century the president's party failed to gain seats in Congress. Kennedy's coattails were more of a liability than an asset for his party. Although Democrats maintained large paper majorities in both houses—65–35 in the Senate and 262–174 in the House—their majorities were smaller (by one in the Senate and by twenty-two in the House) than in the previous Congress. In addition, even in 1959 and 1960 a conservative coalition of Republicans and Southern Democrats had been able to thwart the sort of domestic initiatives on which Kennedy campaigned in 1960; so the outlook for his being able to enact a significant program was not bright on the day after the election.

Kennedy publicly rejected the notion that he had failed to obtain a mandate. "The margin is narrow, but the responsibility is clear," he said. "There may be difficulties with the Congress, but a margin of only one vote would still be a mandate."[7] Nevertheless, the narrowness of his victory and the bleakness of his legislative prospects shaped how he went about assuming power: he had to build much broader popular support than he had received at the polls; he had to avoid partisanship and reach out to Republicans and conservative Democrats; and he had to demonstrate, through force of personality, that he was in command.

Characteristically, Kennedy dealt with the mandate problem intuitively rather than in a highly rational or methodical way. In the days after the election he did not sit down with his aides to develop a strategy to deal with the lack of a robust mandate; he was more of an improviser than a systematic calculator. (Nor was he apt to devise elaborate rationalizations after the fact.) But despite the absence of a coherent plan—indeed of any plan as such—he fashioned an intelligent and effective response to the mandate problem, a response in which actions and words complemented each other.

First, there was the matter of appointments. Kennedy sought to reassure the country of his nonpartisanship and moderation by reappointing certain incumbents and by naming some Republicans. Thus, two days after the election he announced that he was retaining Allen Dulles as CIA director and J. Edgar Hoover as FBI director. Similarly, he sought out leading financiers and lawyers who had served presidents of both parties in the past, such as John McCloy and Robert Lovett. He gave Lovett his choice of the most senior departments; Lovett declined to serve on grounds of health, but became an influential adviser to Kennedy on who should fill these posts. He was a strong proponent of Robert McNamara, who had recently become president of Ford Motor Company and who was nominally a Democrat. McNamara, of course, became secretary of defense. Perhaps most remarkably, Kennedy chose C. Douglas Dillon as his treasury secretary. A Republican and a Wall Street investment banker, Dillon had made financial contributions to Nixon's campaign and at the time of his appointment by Kennedy was Eisenhower's under secretary of State.

Not all of these appointments were made solely to reassure the country. Hoover may have retained his position partly because he had made himself into such an untouchable institution and partly because he had embarrassing information about Kennedy in his files. Dulles, too, was a legendary figure, though one Kennedy liked. Dillon's candidacy was championed by Joseph Alsop, the influential columnist who had done much for Kennedy, but Dillon would not have been appointed had Kennedy not hit it off with him and had he not assured Kennedy that he would leave quietly if he found himself disagreeing with administration policy. McNamara's appointment would not have been made at all had he been a Catholic, for Kennedy, as the first Catholic president, was wary of the country's religious sensitivities. Kennedy would have won very comfortably had he not lost millions of Protestant votes on account of religious prejudice. (In office, Kennedy sometimes bent over backward to prove that he was not pro-Catholic, as in the stand he took against federal aid to parochial schools, which helped kill federal aid to education during his presidency.)

From Kennedy's perspective, only two of these personnel decisions turned out satisfactorily. Kennedy came to have the highest regard for Dillon and McNamara. Hoover, on the other hand, became a problem to be managed and endured. Dulles proved to be a mistake not only because he advocated the disastrous Bay of Pigs invasion, but because Kennedy felt he could not have been sure of Dulles's personal loyalty had he vetoed the invasion. Kennedy feared that Dulles would tell his Republican allies that Kennedy lacked Eisenhower's courage, for Eisenhower had approved a CIA overthrow in Guatemala that Dulles had given less chance of success.[8]

Overall, Kennedy's appointees were substantially less likely to have been Democrats than Eisenhower's were to have been Republican. Their median age was four years lower than that of Eisenhower's appointees at the start of his administration. On the other hand, they typically had more government experience than Eisenhower's, a reflection both of the Democrats' shorter absence from power in the executive branch and of Kennedy's greater belief in the intrinsic value of previous government experience.[9]

Kennedy did follow the normal practice of using political appointments to repay political debts, both to individuals and to various parts of his constituency. He sometimes yielded to political pressures from Capitol Hill and from party leaders. But overall his appointments indicated a commitment to competence, experience, nonpartisanship, and youth. Rhodes scholars and professors from prestigious universities abounded; they were the "action intellectuals," men of ideas—there were very few women—who could get things done. While the appointment or reappointment of familiar figures was reassuring to the country and to Congress and the press, it was not long before the brilliant new men, particularly around the White House, in the defense and justice departments, and even in certain regulatory agencies, captured public attention and the popular imagination. In a way, then, by reassuring the country with appointees such as Dillon, Dulles, and Hoover, Kennedy made it easier for an energetic new generation to make its mark in government.

Kennedy's approach to appointments is worth noting because it resembled his operating style in the White House. He had little respect for or patience with bureaucracy, hierarchy, or formal organizational structure. In contrast to Eisenhower, who had been a student and master of one of the most structured of organizations, the military, Kennedy came away from his wartime experience thoroughly unimpressed with and even contemptuous of military bureaucracy and inefficiency. When he and Lovett got to know each other after the election, they laughed together at the old wartime crack about "a committee being a group of men who, as individuals, can do nothing but who, as a committee, can meet formally and decide that nothing can be done."[10]

Kennedy's disdain for formal organization was unshaped by experience in the executive branch of government. Aside from certain urban machines, participation in Democratic party politics had never offered much schooling in the organizational arena. All of Kennedy's campaigns for office, including the presidency, were highly personal undertakings and were run by members of his family, especially his brother Robert. As campaigns go, they were well run, even producing talk of a "Kennedy machine," but their organizational efficiency always seemed more impressive to observers than to insiders. In the House and Senate, Kennedy often demonstrated wit; he occasionally showed mastery of legislative detail. But he evidenced little organizational skill or interest.[11]

In selecting people to serve under him, Kennedy thought in terms of people, not in terms of organization. His approach was to find interesting people and then see where they could be plugged into an organization, rather than to determine what the needs of an organization were and then find the right people to meet those needs. Sargent Shriver launched a talent hunt on behalf of his brother-in-law; "Shriver knew the kind of man Kennedy wanted," Harris Wofford, who assisted him, later wrote. "More accurately, since Kennedy worked well with and respected a wide range of types, Shriver knew the kind *not* wanted: the too ideological, too earnest, too emotional, and too talkative—and the dull."[12]

For his own White House staff, Kennedy followed the usual practice of turning to his campaign staff, including Kenneth O'Donnell, Theodore Sorensen, Pierre Salinger, Lawrence O'Brien, Myer Feldman, and Ralph Dungan. Though young, many of them had had Washington experience, often as congressional aides. The one important newcomer was his national security adviser, McGeorge Bundy, the young dean of faculty at Harvard; but Bundy had served in Washington during World War II, had coauthored Henry Stimson's memoirs, and was very much a part of the elite group that had long dominated American foreign policy. An indication of Kennedy's administrative ignorance and indifference was that before he made Bundy his national security adviser he first asked him to take a nonexistent undersecretaryship in the State Department.[13]

Kennedy, of course, became known for his loose organizational style. Eschewing a hierarchical staff system, Kennedy described himself as the hub of a wheel with a series of spokes, his assistants. In fact not all had equal access or equal influence. Kennedy welcomed disagreements among his staff and liked to hear issues rigorously debated by them. "When you people stop arguing, I'll start worrying," he once commented to Pierre Salinger, his press secretary. He never had a staff meeting and "held to the belief," as Salinger put it, "that the productivity of all meetings is in direct inverse ratio to the number of participants." Veterans of more structured administrations, such as Dean Acheson, regarded Kennedy's as a cacophonous *ad hocracy*.[14]

The lack of structure sometimes caused difficulties, but Kennedy could get away with his loose system because he kept the White House staff coherent and small—about the same size as Eisenhower's and much smaller than it would become under Nixon and subsequent presidents. Kennedy himself had a voracious appetite for information and commonly reached well down into government organizations to get the information he wanted directly from the most knowledgeable source. Unusually inquisitive, he was once described by George Kennan as "the best listener I've ever seen in a high position anywhere." He was straightforward in his dealings with subordinates, who knew where they stood with him. He was decent and loyal though not effusive to his staff, who became extremely devoted and loyal to him.[15]

In making appointments at the start of his administration, Kennedy cast his net widely, consulted a broad range of sources, and created competing search and placement operations. He gave some secretaries-designate, such as McNamara, wide discretion in naming subordinates; for others, such as Dean Rusk at State, Kennedy and his staff chose most of their subordinates. Kennedy was personally

involved in choosing his cabinet and perhaps several dozen subcabinet, agency, and executive branch officers. In filling these jobs, his
most influential advisers were his brother Robert, his father, his
brother-in-law Sargent Shriver, his personal staff, and certain older
former high officials who were not interested in positions for themselves, especially Lovett, but also Clark Clifford, Dean Acheson, and
John McCloy. Finally, he was influenced by members of the press,
including Joseph Alsop, Philip Graham, and Walter Lippmann, and
by certain politicians. What set Kennedy apart from most presidents-
elect was the degree to which he relied on family members and
journalists.

Kennedy did not just rely on family members for advice about
prospective appointees; he also appointed them to office themselves.
His most controversial cabinet nomination was that of his brother
Robert for attorney general. At thirty-five, Robert Kennedy was the
youngest attorney general since the early nineteenth century, when
the office had been held by private lawyers on presidential retainer.
Having his own brother enforce civil rights laws in the South eventually added to the president's political difficulties, but Robert Kennedy became such an important member of the administration that
it seemed a small price to pay. He invigorated the Justice Department
and served the president as troubleshooter, confidant, and bureaucratic prodder in a variety of areas. Although his brashness made
him some enemies, his youthful idealism, boldness, and vigor epitomized the spirit of what John Kennedy called the New Frontier.[16]

The association of the Kennedy name with bold new idealistic
ventures also came through the appointment of Sargent Shriver as
director of the Peace Corps, which Kennedy created by executive
order in March 1961. Thousands of Americans, most of them young,
went to Third World countries as Peace Corps volunteers and worked
as teachers, engineers, and technicians, and in health care and other
areas of critical need. The Peace Corps was brash, adventurous, idealistic, and highly publicized; it has also endured. As a historian of
the Peace Corps recently concluded, "such was the force of the idea,
that decades after Kennedy's death, his name continues to be the
one most commonly associated with the agency. As the people of
the Dominican Republic . . . said, the Volunteers were 'hijos de Kennedy'—Kennedy's children.'"[17]

Kennedy's youthfulness itself conveyed a positive impression. Forty-
three years old when he took the oath of office, he was the youngest

president since Theodore Roosevelt, and he succeeded the oldest up to that time. Whereas Eisenhower had been one of the great generals of World War II, Kennedy was a member of the much larger group of men who had been in battle. Kennedy's own wartime heroism, though somewhat exaggerated, remained a useful political asset. His attractive young family captivated the public. It was a constant challenge for the family to preserve some privacy, although in that era the press did not try to "tell all" about either Kennedy's private life or his health.[18]

Kennedy's press relations and his direct communications with the public helped him augment his mandate and played central roles in his assertion of leadership. Two of Kennedy's successors, Johnson and Nixon, believed that the press was infatuated with Kennedy and had treated him with kid gloves (in contrast to their own experience). In fact Kennedy received a normal amount of criticism in print and collided with the press on news management (which he practiced), press self-censorship (which he advocated), and other matters. At one point, the *New York Herald Tribune* so angered and frustrated him that he canceled the White House subscription to it.[19]

Yet it is also true that Kennedy had an unusual affinity for the press. He had briefly been a reporter himself and retained the ability to think like one. He followed the press closely, made friends among journalists, and turned to them for advice. He relied upon newspapers and magazines both as a source of information and as a kind of report card on his performance. Benjamin Bradlee, the journalist and Kennedy friend, has astutely contrasted Kennedy's press relations with Nixon's in 1960:

Kennedy loved to shoot the breeze with reporters. He knew about the politics of each newspaper and magazine, the political politics and the office politics. And he knew this instinctively, without briefings. Nixon, on the other hand, then as later, was plagued by his discomfort with the press. On the rare occasions when he tried to be "one of the boys," the boys and girls of the press felt he was putting on an act, as he was. And all of this, despite the fact that the Nixon press operation was far smoother than the Kennedy operation. On the Nixon press plane, there was order; press releases were issued in good time; schedules were issued well in advance, and adhered to rigidly. And the press grumbled, openly hoping for assignment to the JFK camp.

On the Kennedy press plane there was informal, friendly chaos, and the press loved it. In short, Kennedy was stimulated by reporters; Nixon was annoyed by them.[20]

Given his interest in and enjoyment of the press, it is not surprising that Kennedy had good press relations. Although he had his critics and was sometimes pained by the press like any other president, he probably did have an unusually large number of friends and allies within the working press. Had he lacked them, he would have suffered much greater damage than he did when he erred, as in the Bay of Pigs debacle early in his administration.

After the election Kennedy made a decision that thoroughly displeased many print journalists but paid him handsome rewards: he allowed presidential press conferences to be televised live. Eisenhower's press conferences had been filmed, and the White House had retained the power to edit them and revise the transcript. Relatively little of his press conferences appeared on the national fifteen-minute news shows of the day. In making his decision, Kennedy disregarded the objections of journalists such as James Reston of the *New York Times*, who called it "the goofiest idea since the hula hoop."[21] He dismissed as well the worries of national security advisers, including Bundy, who feared that he might commit an egregious slip of the tongue in the foreign policy area. As a result of his successful performances in the televised campaign debates with Nixon, he had great self-confidence and had come to see the television medium itself as an ally. He hoped to use the live press conference as a way of communicating directly with the public.[22]

His hopes for the televised press conference were fully realized. "We became spearcarriers in a great televised opera," Peter Lisagor, the veteran newspaper reporter, later observed. "We were props in a show, in a performance. Kennedy mastered the art of this performance early, and he used it with great effectiveness." The public heard and saw more of Kennedy through these press conferences than in any other way, and his pleasing personality, quick-wittedness, and impressive knowledge of government set a standard that his successors have struggled to meet. By May 1961 three out of four adults had seen at least one of his press conferences, with 91 percent forming a favorable impression and only 4 percent an unfavorable one.[23]

Televised press conferences served as a way for Kennedy to communicate with his own administration, with Congress, and with foreign governments. They even allowed him to dominate the front pages of newspapers, generating much more newspaper coverage than the more private sessions of his predecessors, including that great master of the form, Franklin D. Roosevelt. Eisenhower had been the first president to appear with some regularity on television, but under Kennedy, television exposure of presidents greatly increased. (Partly because of him, television coverage of public affairs also expanded dramatically.) Indeed, it was under and because of Kennedy that television became an essential determinant—probably *the* essential determinant—of a president's ability to lead the nation.

Kennedy also communicated with the public through prepared speeches, the most important of which was his Inaugural Address, which was broadcast on television and set the tone for his administration. He decided against outlining domestic goals in the Inaugural Address because they made it seem too divisive and partisan, too much like the campaign. It was a remarkable speech, and many of Kennedy's phrases immediately entered the political lexicon. His concise eloquence and stirring delivery inspired many people, both in the United States and abroad. In later years, when America became heavily involved in the war in Vietnam, Kennedy's unqualifiedly universalistic rhetoric came back to haunt his reputation. Although the speech was a strong blast of Cold War rhetoric, it also held out an olive branch to the Soviet Union. Among its most memorable passages are these:

Let the word go forth from this time and place, to friend and foe alike, that the torch has been passed to a new generation of Americans, born in this century, tempered by war, disciplined by a hard and bitter peace, proud of our ancient heritage, and unwilling to witness or permit the slow undoing of those human rights to which this nation has always been committed, and to which we are committed today at home and around the world . . .

Let every nation know, whether it wishes us well or ill, that we shall pay any price, bear any burden, meet any hardship, support any friend, oppose any foe to assure the survival and success of liberty . . .

If a free society cannot help the many who are poor, it cannot save the few who are rich . . .

Let us never negotiate out of fear, but let us never fear to negotiate . . .

In the long history of the world, only a few generations have

been granted the role of defending freedom in its hour of maximum danger. I do not shrink from this responsibility; I welcome it. I do not believe that any of us would exchange places
with any other people or any other generation . . .

And so, my fellow Americans, ask not what your country
can do for you; ask what you can do for your country.

My fellow citizens of the world, ask not what America will
do for you, but what together we can do for the freedom of
man.[24]

Kennedy's speech moved a generation. Years later it was still being
cited, by many who were young when they heard it, as a turning
point in their lives. For some, its immediate impact was very tan-
gible. The day after Kennedy gave it, James H. Meredith, a black
twenty-eight-year-old air force veteran, decided to seek admission
to the all-white University of Mississippi. His matriculation the next
year caused rioting by whites, compelling Kennedy to dispatch federal troops. A month after the Inaugural Address, a Gallup poll asked
Americans if they could think of anything they could do for the
country, and 63 percent said they could, offering a variety of suggestions.[25] The 1960s were characterized by an unusual amount of
social and political activism, which might have occurred under any
president. But by kindling the nation's idealism and challenging the
status quo, Kennedy clearly encouraged such activism.

With respect to the more immediate problem of augmenting—or
creating—the mandate that had eluded him in November, the Inaugural Address undoubtedly benefited Kennedy, as did the other
first impressions he made on the public. In mid-February he received
a higher approval rating from the public (72 percent favorable, 6
percent negative) than did Eisenhower in mid-January (50 percent
approval, 27 percent disapproval). And although all newly inaugurated presidents tend to have high approval ratings, Kennedy managed to preserve his quite well.[26]

Congress and Domestic Policy

One of the most frequent criticisms of Kennedy, both when he was
president and since, has been that he failed as a legislative leader.
This criticism was largely based on the fact that several controversial
measures he sought, particularly Medicare and federal aid to edu-

cation, were stalled during his administration, and that two others, civil rights and tax reduction, had not been passed at the time of his death. Moreover, all of these controversial measures *were* enacted under Lyndon B. Johnson.[27]

In retrospect, Kennedy's legislative record and performance look reasonably good given the conservative Congresses with which he had to deal. As James Sundquist has shown, Johnson's enormous successes with Congress were attributable not simply to Johnson's great skill as a legislative leader, but also to the Democrats' huge gains in the House and Senate in the 1964 election, which opened the floodgates for liberal legislation. "I would take nothing from Lyndon Johnson's brilliant and tireless performance with Congress," wrote Lawrence O'Brien, who served both Kennedy and Johnson as chief legislative aide, "but I believe that, had Kennedy lived, his record in his second term would have been comparable to the record Johnson established."[28]

Kennedy did not have Johnson's legislative expertise or interest—few, if any, other presidents have—but he was certainly not indifferent to Congress or maladroit in his dealings with it. He knew, however, from the opening battle over expanding the House Rules Committee, in which he played a behind-the-scenes role, that it would not be an easy Congress in which to pass liberal legislation. Kennedy was therefore cautious in what he asked of it. For example, he did not request civil rights legislation when he first took office, because he believed, reasonably enough, that it could not be passed and would only jeopardize other parts of his program that did have a chance to pass. Indeed, he did score some early successes with Congress, but in areas in which he commanded large Democratic majorities, namely antirecessionary measures, defense, and space. In 1962 he got Congress to give the president greater authority to negotiate tariff reductions with foreign countries.

Several presidents since Kennedy have set dramatic goals for the country—ending poverty, curing cancer, or making the country energy self-sufficient—but Kennedy alone set one that was actually met, and met on time: landing a man on the moon before the decade ended. When he entered the White House, Kennedy knew relatively little about the space program other than that it lagged behind the Soviet Union's, that Eisenhower had treated it parsimoniously, and that American prestige had suffered. The most important job he gave Lyndon Johnson, who had become very knowledgeable about the issue while he was in the Senate, was to review the space program and look for some spectacular goal at which the United States might be able to best the Soviet Union. Two prestige-jarring events hastened Kennedy's adoption of Johnson's recommendation of a lunar landing: the first successful manned orbital flight by Soviet Cosmonaut Yuri Gagarin and the shattering defeat at the Bay of Pigs of an anti-Castro force of Cubans trained, armed, and transported by the United States.

When Kennedy announced the lunar goal in person before Congress in May, he stressed national prestige more than the intrinsic value of space exploration. Congress and the public proved very receptive. Although the lunar program had its critics—and still has—there is no doubt that a popular majority of Americans favored it, thanks in considerable part to television, which dramatically brought the developing story into the nation's homes. It certainly also met its original purpose of enhancing American prestige internationally. It harnessed American technological and organizational skill, showed how effective government could be, and harmed nothing. Some people argued that it drained funds from more pressing objectives, but Kennedy was almost certainly right that Congress would not have appropriated funds for those objectives in any case. Indeed, he grew to like the lunar program in part because it pumped into the economy dollars that would not have been available otherwise.[29]

The initial antirecession measures Kennedy proposed and won—on minimum wages, Social Security, and area redevelopment—did not satisfy the Keynesian economists on Kennedy's Council of Economic Advisers. They had urged a tax cut, but Kennedy did not see how he could reconcile such a measure with his sacrifice theme. Nor did he originally comprehend his experts' arguments. Finally, he believed a tax cut would be attacked as fiscally irresponsible. "Tell them to count the votes on the Hill," Kennedy told Walter Heller, chairman of the council, "and see how far we would get with a tax cut program."[30]

By the summer of 1962, however, Kennedy's economists had persuaded him of the merits of a tax cut, and in fact the economy, though not bad, was not performing as well as he had expected or as well as he had promised during his campaign. He therefore reversed his initial stand and proposed the largest tax cut in history, announcing his intentions to a New York business audience after the fall elections. John Kenneth Galbraith, who did not see eye to eye with his fellow economists in the administration, called it "the most Republican speech since McKinley."[31] Kennedy originally coupled tax cuts with progressive tax reforms, which were favored by his Republican treasury secretary. In the face of congressional opposition, however, Kennedy again demonstrated his realism by yielding on reform in order to salvage cuts, which garnered more political and business backing.

Enacted soon after his death, Kennedy's tax cuts proved highly successful in enhancing economic growth. Though not an expression of moral courage, these cuts required a certain boldness, a willingness to lead public and congressional opinion. They also manifested Kennedy's openness and rationality. Determined to achieve a higher growth rate in the economy, Kennedy allowed himself to be educated by his economists, and then he educated the country. Breaking with old shibboleths and ideological verities, he raised the level of sophistication in managing the modern economy.

While professional economists taught Kennedy how to use fiscal policy to boost economic growth, the civil rights movement and the recalcitrance of southern whites taught him to expand the role of the federal government to assure the civil rights of its citizens, irrespective of race. Although he had promised executive, moral, and legislative leadership to combat racial discrimination during his campaign for president, congressional realities initially persuaded him to forgo attempts at legislation. He did, however, provide executive and moral leadership. He appointed an unprecedented number of blacks, including Thurgood Marshall, whom he made a federal judge. This was important symbolically because Marshall had directed the Legal Defense Fund of the National Association for the Advancement of Colored People and was the preeminent civil rights lawyer of his time. Kennedy also took significant steps against racial discrimination in federal employment and among federal contractors. He welcomed blacks to the White House and, in contrast to Eisenhower, endorsed the Supreme Court's *Brown* decision.

Meanwhile, Robert Kennedy dramatically stepped up Justice Department enforcement of existing voting rights laws and helped create the Voter Education Project, which eventually registered hundreds of thousands of blacks to vote in the South. In a speech at the University of Georgia the attorney general endorsed school desegregation. His department did hard, behind-the-scenes work to bring about voluntary compliance with court-ordered desegregation in schools and public transportation facilities.[32]

The Kennedy administration's support and involvement persuaded civil rights leaders that they had an ally in Washington, although this alliance also underwent strain. Some activists in the South were bitterly disappointed that the federal government did not protect them from violence at the hands of local officials and vigilantes. Explanations from administration spokesmen about the federal government's limited legal authority failed to assuage them.[33]

State and local officials sometimes not only failed to prevent mob violence against peaceful black citizens and civil rights demonstrators but also actually encouraged such violence. Several times, President Kennedy found he had no choice but to use large forces of federal marshals or military troops—during the Freedom Rides in 1961, the desegregation of the University of Mississippi in 1962, and the desegregation of the University of Alabama in 1963. Frustrated by southern whites' resistance to federal law and simple justice, President Kennedy privately began to wonder "whether all that he had been taught and all that he had believed about the evils of reconstruction were really true."[34]

In Albany, Georgia, in 1962, the civil rights movement adopted new tactics in its efforts to end racially discriminatory practices by local governments and businesses—repeated public demonstrations and civil disobedience. These tactics did not succeed there because the police, without engaging in public violence, simply arrested all the demonstrators and even, in a shrewd ploy, arranged for the release from jail of the demonstrators' most important leader, Martin Luther King, Jr. In Birmingham, Alabama, the following spring, however, the same tactics led to a very different result. At first, police commissioner T. Eugene ("Bull") Connor decorously arrested the demonstrators. But when King decided to include schoolchildren in the protests, Connor became enraged and began to have protestors repulsed rather than arrested, using high-pressure fire hoses and police dogs. The violent actions by the police were graphically documented on television and by news photographs that appeared around the world.[35]

President Kennedy sent representatives to the city to mediate the dispute and also initiated an effort to persuade business executives with Birmingham subsidiaries to bring pressure on their local subordinates to make a settlement. These efforts helped produce some results, but they were quickly endangered by white terrorist bombings directed at blacks, some of whom responded by rioting.

Kennedy's confrontations with southern white resistance and the growing pace and intensity of the civil rights movement itself convinced him that the time had come to place the full moral authority of the presidency behind the cause of racial justice. On the night that the University of Alabama was peacefully desegregated, Kennedy went on television to preach more boldly on civil rights than any president before him:

> The heart of the question is whether all Americans are to be afforded equal rights and equal opportunities, whether we are going to treat our fellow Americans as we want to be treated. If an American, because his skin is dark, cannot eat lunch in a restaurant open to the public, if he cannot send his children to the best public school available, if he cannot vote for the public officials who represent him, if, in short, he cannot enjoy the full and free life which all of us want, then who among us would be content to have the color of his skin changed and stand in his place? Who among us would then be content with the counsels of patience and delay?[36]

This speech marked a turning point for Kennedy and the country, for it began the drive for the most comprehensive civil rights legislation since Reconstruction, the 1964 Civil Rights Act, which became the legislative cornerstone of the Second Reconstruction. Many of Kennedy's aides and advisers warned him that civil rights legislation would tie up the rest of his program, that it was ill timed or ill fated. Some cautioned him that it would cost him the 1964 election. But Kennedy disregarded these warnings; he agreed with his brother Robert that he simply had to go ahead with it.

Until Birmingham, the administration had managed to stay abreast or slightly ahead of the evolving pressures for civil rights. But with Birmingham, massive street demonstrations became a popular, dramatic, and successful tactic, and there were bound to be more of them (as indeed there were). Kennedy perceived an atmosphere developing in which he could only respond to events rather than shape and direct them. He did not want to find himself in a weak and defensive position given that his personality and his view of the presidency called for decisive leadership and a measure of control over events. "The situation was rapidly reaching a boil," recalled Theodore Sorensen, "which the President felt the federal government should not permit if it was to lead and not be swamped."[37] And, of course, Kennedy fully believed in the moral arguments he was making to the nation: "We preach freedom around the world, and we mean it, and we cherish our freedom here at home, but are we to say to the world, and much more importantly, to each other

that this is a land of the free except for the Negroes; that we have
no second-class citizens except Negroes; that we have no class or
caste system, no ghettoes, no master race except with respect to
Negroes?"[38]

In the ensuing months the White House spearheaded a major effort
to pass its broad civil rights bill, so Kennedy was in effect at the
center of the action, where he wanted to be, not at its periphery. He
arranged for and participated in an unprecedented series of meetings
at the White House with groups of lawyers, clergymen, women,
educators, businessmen, and labor leaders to enlist their support for
the legislation and for voluntary action against racial discrimination.

Kennedy never expected Congress to fall in line immediately. A
vital part of his legislative strategy was to incorporate suggestions
from Republicans so as to win their support for the legislation as a
whole, for without such support the legislation was doomed. By the
time of his death in November, this strategy had paid off in the
House, resulting in a stronger bill than Kennedy originally submitted, with excellent chances for passage. In the Senate, where a filibuster loomed, final passage was more remote. But Everett Dirksen,
the Senate Republican leader, had privately given his word that the
legislation would be brought to a vote. In other words, a filibuster
would not be allowed to kill the legislation.

What might have happened to the bill had Kennedy not been
assassinated must remain a matter for speculation. It is possible that
Kennedy's death both strengthened the legislation and improved its
chances for passage. President Johnson wisely made the bill's enactment a memorial to Kennedy. His commitment to the legislation
showed that Johnson, a Texan, had a national, not a southern, perspective. But civil rights and the Second Reconstruction had come
so far under Kennedy that it would have been politically dangerous
for Johnson to turn back even had he wanted to, which he did not.

There was a kind of symbiotic relationship between Kennedy and
the civil rights movement. Kennedy encouraged and emboldened
the movement and in turn responded to its heightened expectations,
hopes, and demands. Conservative critics in 1963 who charged Kennedy with encouraging massive lawbreaking were in a sense not so
wide of the mark. Kennedy never urged blacks to march in the
streets, but he fostered an atmosphere in which protests against the
status quo could occur. He created that atmosphere through symbolic acts such as appointing Thurgood Marshall to the federal bench
and opening the White House to blacks, and through substantive

deeds such as establishing a close working relationship between the Justice Department and civil rights activists, sending federal marshals and troops into the South, and using the executive powers of his office to combat discrimination. Operating within the bounds of a democratic political system, Kennedy both encouraged and responded to black aspirations and led the nation into its Second Reconstruction. It was one of his most important achievements.[39]

Foreign Policy

Kennedy's record in foreign policy has probably been the most debated aspect of his presidency. His defenders have credited him with piloting the United States safely through international crises not of his own making, for beginning the process of detente with the Soviet Union and negotiating the first arms control agreement, and for recognizing the importance of nationalism and thereby improving America's standing in the Third World. His critics, on the other hand, have charged him with being as much of a Cold Warrior as Eisenhower, though far less prudent than his predecessor in applying American power. The universalistic language of his Inaugural Address was applied, they assert, and the world was a more dangerous place as a result. Kennedy has been charged with crisis mongering, with escalating the arms race, and with increasing U.S. involvement in the Vietnam war.

The literature on Kennedy's foreign policy is vast, with many volumes devoted to single episodes or aspects such as the Cuban missile crisis or Third World policy. The sheer amount of writing on Kennedy's foreign policy may reflect both on Kennedy's ability to stir things up and on the ambiguity of his record. Because many diplomatic records in this country and abroad remain classified or, as in the Soviet Union, closed to independent scholars, the debates about Kennedy's foreign policy are not apt to be settled soon. Changing values and ideology, and the impact of intervening events also affect sholarly interpretations. In a recent article, David Horowitz and Peter Collier, who were prominent members of the New Left and later wrote a highly popular and critical history of the Kennedy family, offer a striking example of the way events can change perceptions:

New Left orthodoxy had scorned the idea that the [Vietnam] war was at least partly about Soviet expansion, but soon after the American pullout, the Soviets were in Da Nang and Cam Ranh Bay and had secured the rights to exploit the resources of Indochina in unmistakably imperial style. Other things we had claimed were impossible were also now happening with dizzying velocity. Far from being liberated, South Vietnam was occupied by its former "ally" in the North. Large numbers of "indigenous" revolutionaries of the NLF whom we had supported were in "political reeducation" camps set up by Hanoi or taking their chances on the open seas with hundreds of thousands of other Vietnamese refugees fleeing the revolution in flimsy boats. In Cambodia two million peasants were dead, slaughtered by the Communist Khmer Rouge, protégés of Hanoi and beneficiaries of the New Left's "solidarity." It was a daunting lesson: more people had been killed in three years of a Communist peace than in thirteen years of American war.[40]

Collier and Horowitz do not go so far as to say that American intervention was morally justified, but their acknowledgment of Communist imperialism and atrocities gives American intervention a plausibility that few of its numerous and vociferous critics in the 1960s and 1970s, including the authors themselves, would have allowed then. Events in Vietnam and Southeast Asia since 1975 have certainly dispelled the once popular notion among war critics that the United States was fighting on the wrong side morally. Retrospectively, American intervention looks bad today, not on moral grounds, but on realistic ones such as these: Vietnam did not involve critical American interests; the war was unwinnable; direct and indirect costs to the United States far exceeded benefits.

Kennedy, of course, was not solely or even primarily responsible for American involvement in Vietnam. That involvement can be traced back to the end of World War II and the Roosevelt administration. Originally it had much to do with Franco-American relations; then it became a function of the Cold War. After the French withdrew following their defeat at Dien Bien Phu in 1954, the United States moved in, repudiated key political agreements reached at Geneva, and helped create and then support an anticommunist regime in South Vietnam. A Communist-backed war against that regime was under way when Kennedy became president.

Although Kennedy from time to time privately expressed skepticism about direct involvement in Vietnam and talked about a complete American withdrawal after the 1964 elections, he publicly endorsed the "domino theory" propounded by Eisenhower, sent over 16,000 American military "advisers" there to assist the South Vietnamese army in counterinsurgency warfare, and encouraged a military coup against the Diem government in Saigon after that government engaged in its highly publicized repression of Buddhists. "Though he privately thought the United States 'overcommitted' in Southeast Asia," Arthur Schlesinger, a dovish Kennedy defender, recently wrote, "he permitted the commitment to grow. It was the fatal error of his Presidency."[41]

In Vietnam, as elsewhere, one of the most striking things about Kennedy's conduct of foreign affairs was his cautiousness in challenging and overturning inherited policies or doctrines. This cautiousness derived in part from his fears of a right-wing political backlash. The backlash over the "loss of China" was a fresh memory, as were the 1960 election returns. Moreover, the right wing had considerable power in Congress, and a right-wing movement was developing grass-roots appeal around the country. But Kennedy's cautiousness was also personal; his style, as James Reston once wrote, was "to make decisions at the margin, committing himself to little and leaving room for escape."[42]

But Kennedy also firmly believed that nationalism was the major force of the twentieth century. In his view it was therefore not enough to oppose communism in the Third World; rather, the United States had to ally itself with the nationalist aspirations of countries emerging from colonialism. Kennedy's articulation of this position, his idealism, and his personal interest and involvement in Third World countries won him and the United States new friends among them, although his policies themselves were often shaped more by Cold War imperatives and by bureaucratic and political considerations than by his belief in the importance of nationalism. "In the end, the expectations proved far greater than the achievements," Richard Mahoney concludes in a recent monograph on Kennedy's African policy. "But Kennedy did succeed in identifying nationalism as the central reality of his age and in doing what no other American president before or after him has done—establishing a common ground between African ideals and American self-interest in the midst of the Cold War."[43]

In Latin America, where Kennedy created the Alliance for Progress as a new vehicle for American aid, expectations again exceeded achievements. The ideals were not faulty, but the problems were so vast. Dominated by elites, many Latin American governments were naturally reluctant to institute democratic reforms because they might undermine their own authority and power. Knowing that anticommunism was a higher American priority than reform, they simply accepted U.S. economic and technical assistance while safely ignoring its reformist suggestions. Kennedy became a much more popular figure in Latin America than Eisenhower ever was, in part because of the ideals publicly expressed in the Alliance for Progress, but his policies there did not deviate significantly from Eisenhower's in the late 1950s.[44]

Kennedy's adherence to inherited policy landed him in serious trouble early in his administration when he allowed the CIA-sponsored invasion of Cuba to proceed. The story of the "perfect failure" at the Bay of Pigs has been told so many times that it requires no retelling here. But it is worth noting the lessons Kennedy learned from this debacle. One was the importance of having his own people at the head of intelligence and the military. After a decent interval he replaced Dulles and Bissell at the CIA and made General Maxwell Taylor his military adviser and then chairman of the Joint Chiefs of Staff. He also began to bring Robert Kennedy and Theodore Sorensen into critical foreign policy deliberations. In response to the disorganization of the decision-making process leading up to the Bay of Pigs, Kennedy reestablished preexisting oversight and coordinating committees. He strengthened Bundy's roles as a watchdog and channel and created an analogous role for Taylor.[45]

The Bay of Pigs debacle appears, however, only to have strengthened Kennedy's predisposition toward a personal involvement in the details of foreign policy. Kennedy was his own secretary of state. Dean Rusk, who held the title, was intelligent, loyal, and diffident and an articulate spokesman for the administration. He saw himself as Kennedy's principal foreign policy adviser but never established the kind of personal relationship with Kennedy that might have won him the hearing he wanted. He was the only member of the cabinet whom Kennedy did not call by his first name, and Rusk preferred it that way. He refused to be drawn into policy debates within the administration lest it appear that he had lost a debate on the occasions when Kennedy followed someone else's advice. Kennedy sarcastically observed of Rusk's reticence that when they were alone Rusk would whisper that there were still too many persons present.

Kennedy came to office with a decided preference for foreign policy. Issues of war and peace, not domestic policy, had interested him since his youth, and the responsibility of being president in the nuclear age only reinforced that interest. "Domestic policy," Kennedy liked to say, "can only defeat us; foreign policy can kill us."[46] He therefore fully involved himself in the details of foreign policy; he created special task forces reporting directly to him, used Bundy and his staff to monitor the State Department and see that his wishes were carried out, and closely watched and personally directed sensitive diplomatic situations. In Laos, for example, where Kennedy sought and achieved neutralization and a ceasefire in that country's civil war, Winthrop Brown, the American ambassador, later explained how much help it was "when the President is your desk officer."[47] According to Robert Kennedy, in a 1964 oral history interview, the President "really felt at the end that the ten or twelve people in the White House who worked under his direction with Mac Bundy . . . really performed all the functions of the State Department." (It is worth noting that Bundy largely drew his staff from the ranks of career officials throughout the government.)[48]

Regarding the most important foreign relationship of the early 1960s, the one between the United States and the Soviet Union, Kennedy adhered to the set of beliefs that had prevailed since the dawn of the nuclear age in the late 1940s—that the Soviet Union represented a threat to the United States and its allies, was expansionist, and must therefore be contained. Like many Democrats and some Republicans in the late 1950s he subscribed to the military doctrine of "flexible response," that is, that the United States needed a buildup of conventional forces in order to reduce the risk of nuclear confrontation and exchange. Kennedy also believed in the utility of counterinsurgency warfare in resisting communist expansion via wars of national liberation, such as was being waged in Vietnam.

Although Kennedy was generally skeptical of theory and insistent upon facts, political expediency sometimes outweighed facts, most notably in the case of the missile gap issue, which had been an important part of the 1960 campaign. Soon after taking office Kennedy accelerated missile deployments more on the strength of campaign momentum than on the basis of hard intelligence. Indeed, intelligence analysis quickly revealed the missile gap to be a myth. But by then the American buildup was under way and may have stimulated a countervailing Soviet one. Moreover, Kennedy failed to educate the public on the nonexistence of the gap.[49]

Although his handling of the missile gap issue did not constitute statesmanship, Kennedy did demonstrate prudent but effective leadership when the Soviet Union threatened Berlin in 1961 and when it provocatively began to install missiles in Cuba in 1962. In handling these Soviet-created crises effectively, Kennedy was aided by his insistence upon facts, by his natural cautiousness, and by his desire to control foreign policy directly. He was aided as well by his knowledge of history, which taught him that wars could come about as a result of miscalculation. Finally, he was well served by his cool, dispassionate style and by his ability to see things from his adversary's perspective.[50]

In the Cuban missile crisis, in particular, Kennedy did demonstrate genuine statesmanship. He looked at things from the Soviet side, compromised on secondary issues, did not play politics, and, when he succeeded in getting the missiles removed, did not gloat or boast. The missile crisis had numerous consequences, but one of the most important was to impel Kennedy to take new initiatives in seeking a reduction in Soviet-American tensions. At American University in June 1963, Kennedy declared that "we must deal with the world as it is, and not as it might have been had the history of the last eighteen years been different."[51]

Kennedy proposed complete disarmament, to be achieved through stages, the first of which would be a ban on atmospheric nuclear tests. He demonstrated America's good faith by suspending U.S. atmospheric tests. Very soon thereafter, the United States and the Soviet Union agreed to their first arms control agreement—on atmospheric nuclear tests. Retrospectively, it is easy to fault this agreement for not also banning underground tests, but it was as far as Kennedy could get his own military establishment and the Senate to go. Like many of his foreign policy accomplishments, the test ban treaty was only a small step forward, but it raised hopes for much greater progress in the future.[53]

The criteria by which scholars evaluate presidents are many and subjective. Among them are: conduct of office and faithfulness to law and the Constitution; vision and ability to communicate that vision and to lead public opinion; relations with Congress and ability to get a program enacted; conduct of foreign policy and diplomacy; performance as commander in chief and defender of national security, as party leader, as economic manager, and as defender of the weakest and most vulnerable members of society; personality and character; leadership of the executive branch of government; institutional, political, and cultural legacy; popularity and endurance; crisis management.

For all that has been written about Kennedy, there is still much to be known. The passage of time and further research will no doubt provide a richer and clearer picture of his presidency. We shall never know what he would have done had he lived and served out two full terms. But it should become clearer just how and why he was able to inspire the popular imagination and be so well remembered today, twenty-five years after his assassination, even though (and perhaps to some extent because) he served a mere two years and ten months in office. His enduring popularity, despite best-selling exposés, critical biographies, unflattering docudramas, and defamatory publicity, suggests that there was more to Kennedy's presidency than either orthodox or revisionist historians currently perceive.

Kennedy had faults, made mistakes, and did not always live up to his flattering and carefully nurtured public image. His cautiousness and his tendency to work at the margins (which in particular has been too little understood by revisionist critics) at times kept him from exercising the bold leadership he was capable of, especially in foreign and defense matters, where he accepted too many of the "givens." His administrative indifference incurred costs that have not been fully calculated. He did not, for example, exercise due diligence over the nation's domestic and foreign intelligence services, and he tolerated, if he did not condone, certain innappropriate and unwise actions by them.

On the other hand, many aspects of Kennedy's presidency stand up well, including personal qualities of graciousness and humor, tolerance and decency, openness, intellectual growth, and flexibility. He set idealistic but attainable goals for the nation, improved America's image in the developing world, and inspired young people here and abroad to do public service. He led the nation into its Second Reconstruction to assure black citizens their full rights and opportunities, and he introduced important new tools for achieving sustained economic growth. In international affairs, he was a sophisticated diplomat and a careful crisis manager who at least raised, if he did not fulfill, widespread hopes for peace, justice, reform, and human progress. In a variety of ways, both deliberate and unconscious, he raised public expectations of presidential performance and leadership.

5

LYNDON B. JOHNSON

Paths Chosen and Opportunities Lost

Larry Berman

The tragedy in Dallas on November 22, 1963, martyred John Kennedy and left the nation in the hands of Lyndon Baines Johnson. Although Johnson had actively sought the Democratic presidential nomination in 1960, by 1963 he had given up his aspirations for the nation's highest office. After the anticipated completion of Kennedy's two terms, he looked forward to retirement at the LBJ ranch.

Now Johnson needed to establish his right to govern as president, and he acknowledged that doing so "presented special problems. In spite of more than three decades of public service, I knew I was an unknown quantity to many of my countrymen and to much of the world when I assumed office. I suffered another handicap, since I had come to the Presidency not through the collective will of the people but in the wake of tragedy. I had no mandate from the voters."[1] In the months after the assassination he set about establishing his political legitimacy and forging a national political consensus. His first task was the completion of key elements in Kennedy's New Frontier—civil rights, the 1964 tax cut, Medicare, and voting rights. "No memorial oration or eulogy," LBJ told the nation, "could more eloquently honor President Kennedy's memory than the earliest possible passage of the civil rights bill."[2]

When Kennedy died, the civil rights bill was bogged down in Senate parochialism and procedures. In the spring of 1964 Johnson worked with members of Congress who did not share his commitment but were willing to strike a deal. He wooed Senators Richard Russell and Everett Dirksen in order to enlist moderate Republicans in the civil rights cause. The president eventually convinced minority leader Dirksen to call for cloture (the first time the Senate had ever voted to limit debate on a civil rights bill). On July 2, 1964, Congress passed and Johnson soon signed the Civil Rights Act of 1964. The achievement endeared the new president to liberals and earned him the respect of the Washington community.

In the 1964 presidential campaign Johnson's Republican opponent, Barry Goldwater, moved further and further to the right. Remarks such as "I want to lob one into the men's room of the Kremlin and make sure I hit it" persuaded voters that he would start a nuclear war.[3] Johnson, on the other hand, took care to present himself as the leader of a national consensus. He promised that American boys would not be sent overseas to fight a ground war in Vietnam. Johnson left the rhetoric of escalation to Goldwater.

In 1964 Johnson received 7 million more votes than Kennedy had in 1960. He later wrote: Our victory was . . . a mandate for action, and I meant to use it that way."[4] In fact he was determined to transform American society. But Johnson believed it would be impossible to pass a liberal domestic legislative program if South Vietnam was lost. He told Special Assistant Harry McPherson, "I'm not going to be the Democratic President pushing liberal social legislation who's letting go of a part of Southeast Asia that my predecessor John Kennedy and his predecessor Dwight Eisenhower said was critical to the free world."[5] Thus on July 28, 1965, when he decided to commit American ground forces to the war in South Vietnam, he launched a process of slow political suicide.

The unparalleled legislative record of the Eighty-ninth Congress was in part a tribute to the president's skill at minimizing the anticipated military buildup in Vietnam. In 1965 Congress approved eighty of the administration's eighty-three major proposals, including Medicare, Medicaid, the Civil Rights Act of 1965, The Elementary and Secondary Education Act, the Higher Education Act, the War on Poverty, Head Start, the Neighborhood Youth Corps, the Air Pollution and Control Act, the Educational Opportunity Act, the Jobs Program, the Safe Street Act, Model Cities, Aid to Appalachia, the Economic Development Act, the Department of Housing and Urban Development, the Department of Transportation, aid to urban mass transit, the National Endowment for the Arts, the National Endowment for the Humanities, the Federal Water Pollution Control Act, and the High Speed Ground Transportation Act. There was something for everybody until Johnson lost control of events in Vietnam.

In 1965 Lyndon Johnson embodied creative leadership in the modern presidency, combining formidable personal political skills with the extraordinay powers of his office. He had become the consensus leader of America; he stood atop the political process. Johnson yearned to be remembered as the president who used the power of the chief executive to remove barriers to racial injustice in voting, education, and vocation. He wanted to be the leader of national reconciliation in America, the greatest reforming president in history, exceeding even the accomplishments of his mentor, Franklin D. Roosevelt. In return he sought confirmation that in a world of doers and thinkers, the latter owed a large debt to the former. Johnson's Great Society was a historic legislatve success, but Vietnam largely obscured it. Johnson was unable to wage both a war against aggression abroad and a war against poverty at home. The magnitude of his failure reflects his shortcomings in the requisites of presidential leadership. The puzzle remains why he failed to see beyond the technical application of his skills. "How and why," recently asked former presidential assistant John Roche, "would a man as shrewd and intelligent as Lyndon Johnson persist for three years in the military equivalent of playing middle hand in high-low poker?"[6]

As a war leader Johnson abandoned the approach that had earned him respect as Senate leader. "Johnson was a legislative pragmatist," wrote Ralph Huitt. "He believed it possible to do anything that was worth the effort and the price, and so considered every problem from the standpoint of what was necessary to achieve the desired objective, and whether the objective was worth the cost. He learned early and never forgot the basic skill of the politician, the ability to divide any number by two and add one."[7] The equation did not work in Vietnam, primarily because Ho Chi Minh was, by Johnson's standards, essentially nonpragmatic. Ho lacked any incentive to bargain; he wanted only to win, whereas Johnson sought only not to lose. Johnson, recalled Abe Fortas, "was an operator president. And . . . I think perhaps he overestimated that possibility in some areas; perhaps the presidency also requires a type of conceptual deployment which is not needed in the role of majority leader . . . Vietnam may be an instance in which Johnson's concept of power and of the power of power misled him. That is to say, it is not true, I am afraid, that the application of irresistible power is always irresistible."[8]

Johnson, though unsurpassed in his ability to persuade individuals in the corridors of the Senate and behind the closed doors of the White House, was unable to present himself effectively to large public audiences. This inability to project his leadership, particularly through television, helped undermine whatever credibility existed in his policy. Leading a nation of 200 million required skills different from those needed to convince 100 senators to coalesce around civil rights legislation. According to John Roche, Johnson

> never understood the difference between the Hill and the White House . . . the tactics of a Senate majority leader automatically created a credibility gap as President. If something like a Social Security Bill came up in the Senate, he used to be able to say to [Senator] Harry Byrd, "I'll tell you what, you make your speech, and you can make a motion to recommit, but then when the final vote comes up, you go with it, huh?" and simultaneously he could say to Paul Douglas, "You make your motion, and you make your speech, but when the time comes, this is the way it's got to be, and you go with it, huh?" and both of them thought Lyndon was with them, and he got his bill through. That's the way you do business in the Senate; but when you're President, newspapermen start comparing different versions of what you say, and they check Source A against Source B against Source C. Lyndon has no sense of historic inevitability as a President should.[9]

Smart policies have a way of making presidents look like effective leaders; Vietnam was not such a case. LBJ's problem in communicating must be viewed as a component of leadership style as well as of the policy itself. Johnson later acknowledged that he had "a general inability to stimulate, inspire and unite all the people of the country, which I think is an essential function of the presidency."[10] Unlike Roosevelt, he never learned that presidential leadership is, to a crucial degree, a matter of educating the public; that the legitimacy of leadership is frequently based on not getting too far ahead of followers. Notwithstanding all Johnson's domestic legislative skills and successes, the Vietnam war exposed his weakness as a leader; by 1967 it had eroded most of his political credibility. Inevitably that conflict must be the ultimate standard by which LBJ's presidency is measured.

Personality and Operating Style

Johnson's style of presidential leadership—an emphasis on consensus, a tight rein on the White House staff, an extreme sensitivity to criticism, a need for controlling information to and from the White House, and a preoccupation with secrecy—was of course dictated by his personality. Johnson, the man, defies tidy descriptions. David Halberstam characterizes him as "the elemental man, a man of endless, restless ambition . . . a politician the like of which we shall not see again in this century . . . a man of stunning force, drive and intelligence, and of equally stunning insecurity . . . he was, in that sense, the most human of politicians."[11] But the "megatonnage" of his personality has posed a constant challenge to his biographers. According to Robert Donovan, "Johnson was a tragic political genius of bottomless pettiness, volcanic energy, brilliant intellect, disgusting manners, wild emotions, voracious appetites, habitual mendacity, restless cunning, nagging insecurity, great achievements, and sometimes near lunacy."[12] Another Johnson biographer, Robert Caro, has discerned "a hunger of power in its naked form, for power not to improve the lives of others, but to manipulate and dominate them, to bend them to his will."[13]

Johnson's extraordinary complexity, talent, and energy inspired extreme and contradictory responses. Doris Kearns explains:

> there was a strange texture to the mere act of standing next to him; it seemed as if he were violating the physical space of those around him by closing in—clasping and even hugging tightly. People felt they had no private space left in Johnson's presence. The other side of that fascination was fright. For the very compulsion involved in the large power, the bending of other people's wills to his, was a frightening thing to observe. His associates often worried themselves sick about entering his office, worried that he would deride their work. I heard real fear in their voices and saw it in their faces. Lyndon Johnson made you feel larger at first, because he paid so much attention to you, almost as though he were courting. And he did that with everybody, man or woman alike, until he had won them. And then, almost as if these were all passing high school romances, people's feelings suddenly became of little interest to him. You felt diminished rather than enlarged as a result of being with him.[14]

Johnson used his overpowering personality to dominate those around him. He once remarked to Bill Gulley, then director of the White House Military Office, "just you remember this: There's only two kinds at the White House. There's elephants and there's piss-

ants. And I'm the only elephant."[15] It is difficult to know which
Johnson enjoyed more—acting the elephant or treating others as
"pissants." Clearly he relished the act of dominance, seemingly gain-
ing from others' indignities a sense of his own self-esteem. A great
deal of his behavior was calculated rather than spontaneous. "As a
human being," writes George Reedy, "he was a miserable person—
a bully, sadist, lout and egoist . . . His lapses from civilized conduct
were deliberate and usually intended to subordinate someone else
to do his will. He did disgusting things because he realized that other
people had to pretend that they did not mind. It was his method of
bending them to his designs."[16]

In the cloakroom of the Senate chamber or face to face with a
political adversary, Johnson was an overpowering force. He possessed an uncanny ability to size up his adversary and, through a
variety of techniques that ranged from squeezing the thigh, reasoning nose to nose, horse-trading, or—when all civilized forms of negotiation failed—humiliation, usually got what he wanted; and the
individual giving it never forgot how LBJ exacted his price.

Johnson could be relentless. President Eisenhower once ordered
his attorney general, William Rogers, to stand between himself and
Senator Johnson so that LBJ would not tug at Eisenhower's lapels.[17]
Johnson was also noted for "the treatment," "an almost hypnotic
experience [that] rendered the target stunned and helpless."[18] Special
Assistant John Roche once wote a memorandum to the president
trying to explain the impact of Johnson's persona.

> The press wants proof that you are not (1) a yahoo; (2) a Simon
> Legree vis-à-vis your staff; (3) a supine leader who follows the
> polls; (4) an egomaniac who disregards public opinion en-
> tirely . . . let them lead, and don't get carried away and hyp-
> notize them with your unique magic. You can completely
> persuade them, but then—the morning after—they come to
> and resent bitterly the fact that anybody can get to them the
> way you can. This, by the way, is in my judgment the basis of
> most of your problems with the press—no "hard-boiled, real-
> istic" reporter who had ever succumbed to your magic (and I
> use this word admiringly not critically . . . it is the quality of
> *politikos*, the Greek ideal of a statesman) can forgive you for
> it: You have left too deep a scar on his ego.[19]

By every account, Johnson was a workaholic. After his major heart
attack in 1955, he had given up his favorite hot chili, stopped a

three-pack-a-day smoking habit, lost forty pounds, and reduced his working hours from eighteen to "only" fourteen a day. But as president he again compressed two days into one. In an interview with *Washington Star* reporters on November 15, 1967, Johnson described a typical day:

> My day begins at 6:30, when I arise to read the morning intelligence reports and the newspapers. In addition, I finish up night reading, read special North Vietnam reports, a special Defense report, the Congressional Record, and a State Department report. Marvin Watson and his press secretaries come over to go over work. I work from 6:30 until 3:30 P.M. going to the office around 10:30 or 11 A.M. I have lunch, go to bed after reading the *Washington Star* and listening to news on radio. Then after the nap I return to the office, often working until around 11 P.M. when I return to the mansion to watch the network newscasts. I get a massage every night, working on night reading while getting the rub-down. Last night I worked until 3 A.M.[20]

Reprinted below is a typical schedule, for June 1, 1967.[21]

7:28 A.M.   Called Leonard Marks, Director of the U.S.I.A. [U.S. Information Agency]

8:00 A.M.   Marvin Watson to the President's bedroom.

8:57 A.M.   Called Farris Bryant, Director of Office of Emergency Planning.

9:40 A.M.   Was called by Walt Rostow.

9:55 A.M.   Was called by Joe Califano (re District reorganization).

10:00 A.M.   George Christian and Tom Johnson to the President's bedroom. Marvin Watson departed.

10:18 A.M.   Called by Walt Rostow.

10:27 A.M.   Called by Richard Helms, Director of C.I.A.

11:00 A.M.   Christian and Tom Johnson out.

11:17 A.M.   Called Marvin Watson (re appointments).

11:18 A.M.   Called by Marvin Watson.

11:20 A.M.   Called Marvin Watson.

11:25 A.M.   President and Mrs. Johnson went to the Diplomatic entrance on the South Grounds to greet Prime Minister and Mrs. Harold Holt of Australia, and they exchanged pleasantries. After the anthems, the review of the honor guard, and the remarks by the two leaders, the President escorted the Prime Minister from the platform at 11:50 A.M.

12:00 noon	President and Prime Minister met privately in the Oval Office. Simultaneously, the following were meeting in the Cabinet room:

Under Secretary of State Nicholas deB. Katzenbach
Ambassador Keith Waller, Ambassador to the U.S.
Sir Laurence McIntyre, Deputy Secretary, Department of External Affairs, Australia
Ambassador Edward Clark, Ambassador of U.S.
Honorable William Bundy, Assistant Secretary of State for Far Eastern and Pacific Affairs
Honorable James Symington, Chief of Protocol
William Jorden, N.S.C.

12:43 P.M.   The President called Henry Wilson.

12:44 P.M.   The President called Barefoot Sanders.

12:45 P.M.   President called Joe Califano.

12:50 P.M.   President called Mike Manatos.

12:55 P.M.   President called Joe Califano. (These calls related to pending legislation.)

1:20 P.M.   Called George Christian.

1:21 P.M.   The President went to Marvin Watson's office and talked to George Christian and Lincoln Gordon. He then took Secretary Gordon into his private office to tell him goodbye. The President autographed a copy of the Punta del Este Summit pamphlet: "To Lincoln Gordon with deep appreciation for your help in making the Summit a success, Lyndon B. Johnson." During this time Prime Minister Holt was in Marvin Watson's office talking with George Christian and Tony Eggleton, Holt's press man.

1:35 P.M.   The President and the Prime Minister returned to the President's office, then went to the Flower Garden for pictures by the press photographers.

1:43 P.M.   The President and the Prime Minister went to the second floor of the Mansion with George Christian and Tony Eggleton.

1:55 P.M.	They were joined by Edward Clark, Ambassador to Australia; and John Keith Waller, Ambassador to Australia.
2:00 to 3:30 P.M.	The President had lunch with Holt, Clark, Waller, Christian, and Eggleton. During the luncheon, he talked to Francis Bator twice by telephone to get information on trade questions he was discussing with the Prime Minister.
4:10 to 5:18 P.M.	The President napped
5:18 P.M.	Called George Christian.
5:27 P.M.	Called Joe Califano.
5:40 P.M.	Called George Christian.
5:50 P.M.	Called Bess Abell.
5:51 P.M.	Called by Secretary McNamara.
6:00 P.M.	Returned to his office.
6:05 P.M.	Called Secretary McNamara.
6:10 P.M.	Met with Admiral Thomas H. Moorer.
6:37 P.M.	Met with a *Life Magazine* writer, Thomas Morgan, who was doing a story on Walt Rostow. The President discussed generally with him the functions of the National Security Council staff and his high opinion of Rostow.
7:02 to 7:25 P.M.	Met with Secretary Rusk, Eugene Rostow and Walt Rostow. This was on the subject of Foreign Minister Adam Pachachi, Foreign Minister of Iraq, who had come to Washington.
7:26 to 8:00 P.M.	The President met with the Foreign Minister and Ambassador Nasir Hani of Iraq, Walt Rostow and Robert Houghton, State Department Country Director of Iraq. This, obviously, was on the mounting tensions in the Middle East.
8:02 P.M.	The President went to the mansion to change clothes for the State Dinner for Prime Minister Holt.

8:15 P.M.   The President and Mrs. Johnson went to the North
Portico to greet the Prime Minister and his wife, then
returned to the second floor with the Holts and the
official party. For about 20 minutes he talked with the
party, which included Ambassador Waller, Sir John
Bunting, Vice President Hubert Humphrey, Ambassador Clark and Secretary Rusk. The President and
the Prime Minister exchanged gifts. The President's
gift to Holt included an oil painting, a coffee set,
and some skin-diving equipment. The Holts gave
the President and Mrs. Johnson a pair of gold candle-
sticks.

8:41 P.M.   To The East Room to receive guests for the State Dinner.

10:20 P.M.   Toasts.

10:45 P.M.   Coffee in the parlor.

11:05 to   Entertainment in the East Room ("Salute to American
midnight   Musical Theatre," a review composed of highlights from
American musical comedies).

About 1 A.M. the President returned to the second floor,
went over his night reading, and retired at 2:05 A.M.

During this day, two submissions to the Congress were
made: a reorganization plan for the government of the
District of Columbia, and a budget amendment calling
for a decrease of $5.7 million in the 1968 appropriation
request for the Peace Corps.

Johnson acknowledged that his most loyal aides also worked "like
dogs," often remaining at the White House until midnight.[22] For
most of them, there was no middle ground; once in Johnson's world,
you were in for the duration. Harry McPherson recalled that Johnson
was "an overpowering influence in my life, one whom I had to fight
to keep from utterly dominating me. He is consuming to be with.
His preoccupations become yours. Whatever he happens to be working on becomes the only thing that anybody works on around him,
or thinks about."[23] According to Leonard Marks, former director of
USIA, "Lyndon Johnson surrounded you. You became part of his
family. He would possess you. Your time was no longer your
own . . . He didn't understand why people had to go home at 6:00.
He would be there until midnight; why shouldn't they?"[24]

The source of Johnson's drive, which is not necessarily a negative attribute in presidential leadership, remains unclear despite much scholarly attention.[25] Whatever his underlying motivations, Lyndon Johnson never satisfactorily completed the transition from legislative tactician to presidential leader. His character, political style, and personal makeup were ill suited to the presidential environment.

One can argue that any number of men with Lyndon Johnson's world view would have stayed the course in Vietnam; but few would have persisted with such private misgivings. Sleepless nights found Johnson walking the halls of the White House or calling down to the situation room. Horace Busby recalled that "one of the things that drove me up the wall after the bombing began was that he was waking up at 3:00 in the morning and calling the situation room. 'Did the boys get back?' There was too much concern."[26] George Reedy recalled that every casualty was like a stab to Johnson's heart. "When they were bad, he would come to work the next morning, with the features of a haunted man. Sometimes he would pass old friends without even an eyeball of recognition."[27] According to Secretary of State Dean Rusk, "Beyond the men and women and their families who carried the battle for us, I don't know anyone who agonized over Vietnam more than Lyndon Johnson. We couldn't break him of the habit, even for health reasons, of getting up at 4:30 or 5:00 every morning to go down to the operations room and check on the casualties from Vietnam, each one of which took a little piece out of him."[28] As the personal pressures grew, LBJ sought private solace in late-night prayer at St. Dominic's Church, in southwest Washington. Accompanied only by the secret service, the president and his "little monks" would read scriptures, psalms, and hymns.[29]

Notwithstanding his massive legislative achievements, Johnson remained basically insecure. He tended to view himself as the victim of circumstances—of his background, of Vietnam, and of the credibility gap. This insecurity became especially apparent in his excessive sensitivity to criticism by the press. Thus, in a private interview with Max Frankel of the *New York Times* on September 15, 1967, when Frankel asked why there was so much "hate talk" about the president, Johnson replied, "I think it is because of Texas, because of the label of professional politician and a good deal of my impatience." He went on to assert that the *Times* "plays a leading part in prejudicing people against [me]. Editors won't use the words 'President Johnson' in anything that is good. Bigotry is born in some of *The New York Times* people. I told Scotty Reston at a meeting two months after my election that it wouldn't be long before my geography and parentage catches up with me in the minds of these people." Johnson fretted that "newspapermen are the only group in the country who operate without license. Reporters can show complete irresponsibility and lie and mis-state facts and have no one to be answerable to. The same groups continue to call [me] 'that lying SOB.' These are the preachers, liberals and professors who are the first to cry discrimination if anybody says anything about them."[30]

Johnson's insecurity also manifested itself in distrust of intellectuals. The graduate of San Marcos State Teachers College needed to show the eastern intellectual liberal establishment, centered in Harvard, that he could do more for social justice than their hero, John F. Kennedy. In return, he expected, even demanded, from them the affection and loyalty accorded Franklin D. Roosevelt, who, upon meeting the young, energetic, and ambitious Johnson, told his aide, "I might have been like him if I hadn't gone to Harvard."[31] Johnson once told Hugh Sidey of *Life*, "I don't believe that I'll ever get credit for anything in foreign affairs, no matter how successful it is, because I didn't go to Harvard."[32] Yet Johnson relied on a range of independent thinkers, many of them graduates of Harvard, including Robert McNamara and McGeorge Bundy. He accorded these men respect and valued their counsel. Moreover, Johnson created task forces that tapped new sources of talent and ideas in universities across the country.

Johnson once used his skills in persuasion to try to win the hearts and minds of Harvard faculty. On September 5, 1967, John Roche convinced him to see "as fine and distinguished a group of academicians as the United States could produce (not a Kennedy flunky in the crowd) . . . I am certain that an hour with you would bring most of them into camp—they live outside the snare drum in Cambridge and need reassurance of the sort that only contact with you can provide." Johnson soon met with the Harvard contingent; afterward Roche wrote: "you did an extraordinary job . . . I practically had to carry them out—Talcott Parsons, the distinguished sociologist, grabbed me by the shoulder and said, 'this has been the greatest experience of my life.' "[33]

Johnson lashed out at some real, but mostly anonymous "intellectuals" for what they symbolized—the freedom to dissent without fear of reprisal. It pained him that those he believed had been helped the most by his presidency were leading opposition to the war. College students had received loans and scholarships; now they chanted

slogans for Ho Chi Minh. No president had done more for civil rights;
now Martin Luther King, Jr., urged blacks to oppose the war. Johnson
typically blamed the Ivy League for his troubles. On February 13,
1968, he told Charles Bartlett: "Gale McGee told me he had been
on 169 college campuses. And outside [the] Ivy League, students
stand two to one and three to one in favor of our Vietnam policies.
In the Ivy League it was maybe 50–50."[34] Some advisers played to
these prejudices. On September 22, 1966, Walt Rostow declined
Johnson's offer of an administrative position in the planned LBJ
School of Administration. Rostow explained that he intended to use
the time after his White House service for writing and teaching, but
"above all, we would want you to know that our reservation about
considering this project in no way stems from our being, simply,
'children of the East.' "[35]

Johnson labeled those who dissented "nervous nellies," "half-
brights," and "knee-jerk liberals." In an August 19, 1967, meeting
with Rusk, McNamara, Wheeler, and Rostow, he bemoaned the lack
of congressional support for administration policy. "In war, politics
stops at the water's edge," he asserted, noting that as Senate minority
and majority leader he had supported President Eisenhower 79 percent of the time on foreign policy. When Secretary McNamara was
called to testify on the Hill Johnson told his staff, "there is something
wrong with our system when our leaders are testifying instead of
thinking about the war."[36]

Having succeeded such a popular president, Johnson often felt
that his style and his policy were always compared unfavorably with
Kennedy's and he was under an unremitting compulsion to justify
himself. He often told journalist Chalmers Roberts that he wanted
to prove to JFK, "looking down on us from up there in heaven," that
Kennedy had made the correct choice in his vice-president. At other
times he was much more caustic. "They say Kennedy knew about
foreign policy and I don't. I was up there participating in all the
Eisenhower decisions—Lebanon, Korea . . . I appointed Kennedy to
the Foreign Relations Committee and he only attended a few meetings. They say he called the fifth desk officer [in the State Depart-
ment] about things. I call Rusk."[37] As Vietnam evolved into Lyndon
Johnson's war, the president lashed out at those who sought to revise
history by invoking "had Kennedy lived" scenarios. Johnson believed that Kennedy had soft-pedaled Vietnam with rhetoric about
"getting out" while quietly and decisively increasing our commitment in numbers and money and, most important, by the assassi-

nation of South Vietnam's President Nguyen Van Diem. American complicity in the coup seemed to tie the United States to each succeeding regime. Kennedy was murdered in Dallas just three weeks after Diem's death.

Johnson became obsessed with proving that Kennedy could not and never planned to abandon Vietnam. On February 7, 1967, John Roche wrote to him that "there is now a major industry devoted to inventing quotes—mostly on Vietnam—by John Kennedy, Adlai Stevenson and others who are in no position to object. Schlesinger and Goodwin are expanding Kennedy's views full time while Clayton Fritchey has the Stevenson franchise. I think it is time some good columnist (Alsop, Howard Smith, Drummond) took off after this outrageous manipulation of the distinguished dead."[38] The president instructed Walt Rostow to compile all statements made by President Kennedy regarding Vietnam and U.S. interests there. On September 15, 1967, Rostow wrote to the president:

> herewith a rather full compilation of statements by President Kennedy regarding Viet Nam and U.S. interests and commitments in Southeast Asia . . . What emerged for me more sharply even than what I would have predicted are these basic elements in President Kennedy's position: his explicit linkage of the commitment in Viet Nam to the SEATO treaty; his flat acceptance of the domino theory in Southeast Asia; his recurrent linkage of Viet Nam to Berlin, and the general theme that the fate of our own liberty was involved in Viet Nam. I don't believe any objective person can read this record without knowing that President Kennedy would have seen this through whatever the cost.[39]

Johnson never adopted a mode for deflecting criticism; he sought instead to discredit each messenger, particularly when the messenger was the press. Thus his legendary statements "Cast your bread on the water and the sharks will get it" and his parting words "Don't let the newspapermen divide us" to Generals Thieu, Ky, and Westmoreland during a meeting in Honolulu on October 23, 1966. On August 21, 1967, he complained to Bob Thompson of Hearst Publications: "Eighy-five percent of the papers are Republican . . . have explained Vietnam fifty times. It is hell when a President has to spend all of his time keeping his own people juiced up. But it doesn't matter whether the poll is 10 or 40, I am going to try to do the right thing."[40]

During a November 4, 1967, luncheon meeting with Rusk, McNamara, Rostow, and Helms, LBJ bemoaned his political fortunes: "Gallup and Harris say anyone could beat us. Gallup takes these polls a month old, juggles them a little, and makes it look that way and the public believes them." He urged his advisers to answer Senators Hartke, Fulbright, and McCarthy, who "are going to all the colleges and stirring up problems and we are not answering them." Then he turned to the troubles at home: "I'm not going to let the Communists take this government and they're doing it right now." The president pointed out that he had been protecting civil liberties since he was nine years old, but "I told the Attorney General that I am not going to let 200,000 of these people ruin everything for the 200 million Americans. I've got my belly full of seeing these people put on a Communist plane and shipped all over this country. I want someone to carefully look at who leaves this country, where they go, why they are going, and, if they're going to Hanoi, how are we going to keep them from getting back into this country." Johnson then revealed why he had not yet picked a new Marine commandant: "I'm going to take that man's blood pressure and make sure he's loyal. It doesn't do any good to win the fighting over there and lose it over here." On February 9, 1968, LBJ told his principal advisers, "Well, it looks as if all of you have counseled, advised, consulted and then—as usual—placed the monkey on my back."[41]

All presidents feel ill treated by the press, but with Johnson it was an obsession. In March 1965 Johnson met privately with Chalmers Roberts of the *Washington Post* and read him letters of support from soldiers in Vietnam. "In each case," Roberts later wrote, "the soldier had written home that things were going better than the stories said, that the United States should stick it out and could win, that the United States had better draw the line where it was or it wouldn't hold anywhere. LBJ read one soldier's letter together with the mother's words on how she had been for negotiation and getting out but now had changed her mind. Then LBJ thrust his head at me and said, 'now doesn't that make you [critics] feel like a shit-ass?' "[42]

In an interview with the Australian Broadcast Group on September 20, 1967, Johnson claimed that "NBC and the *New York Times* are committed to an editorial policy of making us surrender." He argued that Ho Chi Minh received fairer treatment in the U.S. media than did the president of the United States: "But the television doesn't want that story. I can prove that Ho is a son-of-a-bitch if you let me put it on the screen—but they want me to be the son-of-a-bitch. Press coverage of Vietnam is a reflection of broader and deeper public attitudes, a refusal by many Americans 'to see the enemy as the enemy.' " Johnson analyzed this public mood as being rooted in "a maternalistic attitude toward the enemy unlike anything we have had in other wars. You can blame it on liberal [permissiveness]. But the best way to turn a peacenik into a realist is to tell him the truth about the chances of his wife being ravaged by V.C. if she were over there."[43]

Johnson tried to control the flow of information both to and from the White House—an operating principle that affected most functional staff responsibilities.[44] His insistence that important announcements originate from the White House, not from the departments, was often counterproductive. Johnson's refusal to use cabinet officers as lightning rods meant that the president, not his staff, caught flack on many issues. White House staff member Bob Hardesty wrote to Special Assistant Robert Kintner that although "the President is fond of saying that you never hear of a Harold Ickes and Harry Hopkins fist-fighting in the Rose Garden in this Administration . . . you never hear of an Ickes or Hopkins taking the heat off the President, either." Presidential Special Assistant Tom Johnson informed the president, "it is my view that you have become so closely associated with all the major issues which face this country that you are suffering from it . . . I believe a better course would be to have your decisions and feeling on a particular matter voiced through the Cabinet and through the agency heads who are most directly concerned with the issue. Let them shoulder more of the burden for the faults of their programs. Rather than the President losing popularity for weaknesses, it seems more appropriate for the department head to receive the criticism."[45]

Johnson's tendency to discredit the messenger imbued his operating style. The record shows that he scattered blame for his faltering popularity among his press secretaries, journalists, and members of Congress. In a December 1968 interview with Helen Thomas, Johnson implied that "some of his early press secretaries were responsible for the credibility gap." Following Walter Lippmann's credibility gap series in March 1967, that journalist became a personal target of the administration.[46] And J. William Fulbright, chairman of the Senate Foreign Relations Committee, increased his vocal opposition to the war, Johnson and his staff sought to discredit him also. When Fulbright later demanded televised hearings on the capture of the *Pueblo* (and the conduct of American foreign policy in general), Johnson had his staff dig up a 1961 article in which the senator had argued that presidential power in foreign affairs was too constricted by congressional power. Johnson thought the effort so good that he instructed McPherson to "make copies for Rusk, Clifford, McNamara, McGeorge [Bundy], et al." On August 21, 1967, Johnson told Bob Thompson of Hearst Publications that "Fulbright has never found any President who didn't appoint him Secretary of State to be satisfactory. I recommended him to Kennedy to be Secretary of State, but Kennedy told me he had a good view of Europe but nothing else, and that he was parochial in his views."[47]

Johnson's preoccupation with gathering information is legend. According to Doris Kearns, "Television and radio were his constant companions. Hugging a transistor radio to his ears as he walked through the fields of his ranch or around the grounds of the White House, Johnson was a presidential teenager, listening not for music but for news."[48] His White House office resembled an information command center—three television sets running simultaneously, their channels changed by the click of a presidential remote control, the only competing sound the tickers spewing forth information from Vietnam—all while Johnson carried on other presidential business. The result of Johnson's preoccupation was that the more he heard, the less he was bound to like. Television news is not the best refuge for the overly sensitive. By increasing the number of inputs, LBJ increased the probability of sensory overload. General William Westmoreland recalled that Johnson "had three TV sets, one turned to NBC, one to CBS, and one to ABC. He even had a television set in his bathroom. So the sensational reporting had a greater impact on Mr. Johnson than any official reports, because he was pounded, pounded, pounded with the sensational, the overstatement, the negative."[49] Obsessed with the media's perception of him, Johnson never received from the media confirmation of his self-image. Johnson saw himself as deserving much greater respect than he received from television.

Johnson subscribed to the dictum that a man's judgment is no better than his information. But no one could ever supply him with enough information. According to Special Assistant for National Security Walt Rostow, the president fought for "every piece of information he could, from me and others." Whenever Secretary of State Rusk or CIA Director Richard Helms told him, "There is a new piece of intelligence," the president "would lean across and look very earnestly and listened very carefully and thanked them. He would wink at me at the end of the table because he had it beforehand and God help me if he didn't. It was pretty brisk in the intelligence agency but it wasn't as fast as Art McAfferty to Rostow to the President."[50] But Johnson did not entirely trust the overly optimistic and panglossian Rostow. He would call Rostow's subordinate, NSC staffer Robert Ginsburgh, at home for the latest updates about Vietnam. Of course Ginsburgh had no additional information: he would have given it to the president or Rostow. Ginsburgh recalled that during the twenty-four-hour watch during the battle for Khe Sanh, "I had the night-time watch. And so, every two hours I was either in touch with the President on the phone, that is, he would call me or I would have sent him a message, a little memo to try and preclude his calling. He wanted to know, 'how is it going, what is happening?' "[51]

The telephone also served Johnson's insatiable need for information. "Cutting off his telephone communications," according to Bill Gulley, "would have been like cutting off his supply of oxygen." Johnson secretly recorded telephone conversations and cabinet meeting conversations (six boxes of dictabelt recordings and one box of 1968 cabinet meeting conversations on Vietnam are locked in the LBJ Library vault). Gulley recalls that "Johnson had an extensive, really extensive system, one that made the Nixon system look like the shabby job it was." Installed by the White House Communications Agency, the system was referred to as "Big and Little"; the latter covered the Cabinet Room, the former his private office. Johnson also recorded his telephone conversations at the ranch, in the Oval Office, in the family quarters, at Camp David, even on the road.[52]

By 1967, coverage of Vietnam had evolved into a public relations war, and the administration was bound to lose with Johnson as its spokesman on national television. Jack Valenti later reflected on Johnson's shortcomings on television:

I always felt that the President ought to do more live press conferences, I thought he was excellent in them. He recoiled from that. I really don't know why. Maybe he felt that Kennedy phantom which ran down every corridor in that White House all the years we were there would come alive like Banquo's ghost at every one of these press conferences and they would compare him unfavorably with Kennedy. The whole business of his communication with the people I think affected him . . . in a small room with a hundred people or ten people Johnson was magnificent—the most persuasive man I have ever met. But when he went before television, something happened. He took on a presidential air, he fused a kind of a new Johnson which wasn't the real Johnson. He became kind of stiff and foreboding.[53]

Writing to Johnson on May 11, 1967, Bill Moyers, then publisher of *Newsday*, suggested that he talk to the nation about Vietnam,

not from behind a podium with a teleprompter and not during a press conference which always has to seem artificial, but in a more direct and informal setting which gives them the feeling that you are talking things over with them. I have in mind, of course, the format you used in the spring of 1964 during the "Conversation with the President." You have never done as well since as you did then on television, not in making headlines but in providing the people with a sense of relief . . . It has been some time since the people have authentically heard from you; let them see you again "safe and sound" as only an informal report can do. The dissenters will not retreat, but the great majority of the middle will be reassured that the dark road ahead can be safely traversed. It is a question of purpose not popularity, of strength not safety, and only the President can reaffirm purposes and provide strength.

I believe that such a conversation would help not only the country but you as well.[54]

Johnson's associates frequently exhorted him to wear eyeglasses, address reporters by name, and move around with a lavaliere microphone during televised conferences. On November 17, 1967, during one of his rare ad lib press conferences on Vietnam, he seems to have taken their advice. The next day the *Philadelphia Inquirer* noted Johnson's dramatic style of "removing his glasses, stepping away from the podium which held his notes, clapping his hands for emphasis and speaking with great earnestness." Johnson never repeated this format because he believed it made the president look like an actor. And he took offense when the next day's *New York Times* likened his style to Kennedy's. Watching the same press conference was NSC staffer Bob Ginsburgh, who wrote to Rostow:

if the President would conduct a press conference each month like his last one, I believe the "credibility gap" would disappear very shortly. From a professional newsman: "I can think of only two times when I was more impressed by a Presidential performance—and both were in times of crisis—Roosevelt after Pearl Harbor, and Kennedy during the Cuban missile crisis." From an Air Force officer: "We were all cheering the President on like it was an Air Force football game." From my wife's brokerage firm: "I've voted Republican all my life, but this time I'm going to vote for LBJ." From a lawyer: "The President handled beautifully the question of dissent."[55]

When newsman Howard K. Smith complimented LBJ on the effectiveness of his lavaliere mike, the president retorted, "There was no magic . . . It was fair to say that we never had plain speaking on television before."[56]

Lyndon Johnson's War

Johnson's extraordinary skill at building political consensus in 1965 helped legitimize the Americanization of the war in Vietnam. By 1967 the president was trapped politically at home, strategically in Vietnam. On November 2 he told his advisers, "I am like the steering wheel of a car without any control."[57] Johnson's loss of control over events in Vietnam dramatically affected his style of leadership. George Herring observes: "Johnson's decisions of 1967, even more than those of 1965, were improvisations that defied military logic and did not face, much less resolve, the contradictions in American strategy. The bombing was sustained not because anyone thought it would work but because Johnson deemed it necessary to pacify certain domestic factions and because it might be regarded as a sign of weakness. The President refused to give his field commander the troops he considered necessary to make his strategy work, but he did not confront the inconsistencies in the strategy itself."[58]

In 1967 Johnson's political consensus crumbled under the strain of the credibility gap. Private White House councils among the principals ranged widely and wildly over the issues of media bias, the enemy's resolve and what would stop it, the attitude of American troops in Vietnam and of the Senate Foreign Relations Committee. At the meeting of November 2, 1967, McGeorge Bundy acknowledged that negotiations were no longer a serious short-term objective: "I suppose we can't say that publicly because the judges of public opinion in the nation won't believe it." He urged Johnson:

"Don't let communications people in New York set the tone of the debate. Emphasize the 'light at the end of the tunnel' instead of the battles, deaths and danger." Douglas Dillon agreed that "the feeling [among] both the doves and hawks [is] that the situation over there is hopeless. We must show some progress. To talk of 15 years seems like forever." Walt Rostow also discussed the necessity, as a matter of administration strategy, of showing progress: "There are ways of guiding the press to show light at the end of the tunnel." As the meeting ended, George Ball, who had been unusually quiet during the dialogue, confronted his colleagues: "I've been watching you across the table. You're like a flock of buzzards sitting on a fence, sending the young men off to be killed. You ought to be ashamed of yourselves."[59]

The war in Southeast Asia had become Lyndon Johnson's war; the president found himself trapped between the same policy alternatives he had avoided in July 1965—withdrawal and major military escalation—but the ante had been raised from 125,000 to 575,000 troops. During a meeting with labor leaders in the State Department dining room on August 9, 1967, LBJ reflected on the dilemmas of political leadership. In doing so he revealed the personal reservations of a man who had misplayed the hand:

Some people say that we should turn the bombers loose. But I can't do that. Some people say to pull out. But I can't do that either. And some people say stop the bombing but I can't tie General Westmoreland's right arm behind his back right now. I wish somebody would stop saying what President Johnson should do and spend a little of their time trying to get Ho to do something. Don't put all the heat on me. I'm doing eveything I can. And I know that everything we are using is not enough. We have tried five bombing pauses. We have sent Goldberg to 37 countries and Ambassador Harriman to 50 countries. The Communists are determined to take Southeast Asia. I don't want to invade North Vietnam. I don't want to bomb population centers. I don't want to get China into a war. All I want to do is to show them they can't take Vietnam by force. If they would stop coming across into South Vietnam, there would be no war. But Ho is not interested in anything. Don't sympathize with those people. We have got 500,000 of our boys out there. Stop and think a little bit. There is no man in this White House who wouldn't want to stop the shooting tomorrow if we could. Ho won't talk to anybody. He wouldn't even listen to Kosygin. I'm the guy who's got to ride with this thing. The first thing that comes to me each morning is the list of how many of our men died out there the day before. Remember that every time you criticize me it is just another sack of cement that I carry.[60]

In a war with no clear fixed front, the president could not show territorial advances; therefore, statistical indicators were needed to demonstrate progress. The promised light at the end of the tunnel was based on several factors, but primarily on winning a war of attrition in which U.S. forces would eventually kill more enemy forces than could be replaced. When that crossover point was reached, the enemy would negotiate. By mid-1967 Lyndon Johnson's worst fears were realized when the press raised for public debate the possibility of stalemate in Vietnam.

Johnson brought General Westmoreland back to Washington in April 1967 for a face-to-face discussion of the situation in Vietnam. The transcripts of their conversation reveal a remarkably barren political base for the president.[61] American troop strength already stood at approximately 470,000; Westmoreland requested a minimum force of 565,000; another 100,000 would probably be needed in fiscal year 1969. LBJ asked Westmoreland, "How much will be enough?" Westmoreland explained, "With the troops now in the country, we are not going to lose, but progress will be slowed down. This is not an encouraging outlook, but it is a realistic one." Westmoreland also told LBJ that "last month we reached the crossover point. In areas excluding the two northern provinces, attrition will be greater than additions to the force."

The president ws not buoyed. Instead he asked, "Where does it all end? When we add divisions, can't the enemy add divisions? If so, where does it all end?" Westmoreland answered, "if we add 2⅓ divisions, it is likely the enemy will react by adding troops." Johnson shot back, "At what point does the enemy ask for volunteers?" "That is a good question," noted Westmoreland. "With the present program of 470,000 men, we would be setting up a meat grinder. We would do a little better than hold our own. We would make progress, but we would have to use a fire brigade technique. Unless the will of the enemy was broken or unless there was an unraveling of the VC [Viet Cong] structure, the war could go on for five years. If our forces were increased, that period could be reduced, although not necessarily in proportion to increases in strength. With a force level of 565,000 men, the war could well go on for three years. With the second increment of 2⅓ divisions, leading to a total of 665,000 men, it could go on for two years."

Seemingly stunned by the pessimistic scenarios, LBJ asked, "What if we do not add the 2⅓ divisions?" General Wheeler provided a disheartening answer: "The momentum will die; in some areas the enemy will recapture the initiative. We won't lose the war, but it will be a longer one."

President Johnson now recognized that his decision of July 1965 had, in the proverbial sense, come home to roost. The credibility of U.S. policy as well as that of its principal architects stood at a crucial juncture. As Johnson lost control of his ability to demonstrate progress in Vietnam, his advisers addressed the problem of presidential leadership. On November 16, 1967, Under Secretary of State Nicholas Katzenbach wrote to Johnson concerning the need to restore the political center in the United States. Dissipating levels of popular and congressional support played directly into Hanoi's strategy of winning in the United States, not in Vietnam. "Hanoi uses time the way the Russians used terrain before Napoleon's advance on Moscow, always retreating, losing every battle, but eventually creating conditions in which the enemy can no longer function. For Napoleon it was his long supply lines and the cold Russian winter; Hanoi hopes that for us it will be the mounting dissension, impatience, and frustration caused by a protracted war without fronts or other visible signs of success; a growing need to choose between guns and butter; and an increasing American repugnance of finding, for the first time, their own country cast as 'the heavy' with massive fire power brought to bear against a 'small Asian nation.' " In Katzenbach's view, "time is the crucial element at this stage of our involvement in Vietnam. Can the tortoise of progress in Vietnam stay ahead of the hare of dissent at home?"[62]

In mid-June 1967 a draft of Special National Intelligence Estimate (SNIE) 14.3-67 had been prepared by the CIA. This study of enemy capabilities in South Vietnam estimated enemy strength at between 460,000 and 570,000. These CIA figures stood in stark contrast to General Westmoreland's official MACV (Military Assistance Command, Vietnam) order of battle of 298,000. Three days later Secretary of Defense Robert McNamara authorized the formation of a task force to study U.S. involvement in Vietnam, later published as *The Pentagon Papers*.

On August 29, 1967, Ambassador Bunker cabled Walt Rostow

regarding the "potentially serious problem created by the new NIE on verge of completion." The CIA was insisting on bringing out estimates of enemy strength that were much higher than MACV's estimates. "I need hardly mention the devastating impact if it should leak out (as these things so often do) that despite all our success in grinding down VC/NVA [North Vienamese Army] here, CIA figures are used to show that they are really much stronger than ever. Despite all caveats, this is an inevitable conclusion to which most press would react." Bunker then said, "I intend to mention it to the President in my coming weekly. The credibility gap would be enormous, and is quite inconsistent with all the hard evidence we have about growing enemy losses, declining VC recruitments and the like."[63]

The 1984 libel trial involving CBS and General Westmoreland brought virtually all the principal architects of policy into a court of law to decide whether General Westmoreland conspired to deceive President Johnson and the public on enemy troop strength. By accepting General Westmoreland's reduced order of battle, the unsuspecting president was led to believe that the crossover point had been reached—enemy losses could not be replaced at their rate of attrition. Having been lulled into this false sense of security, LBJ and the nation were unprepared for the size of the enemy onslaught during the Tet offensive of January 31, 1968. Two months later Johnson announced that he would not seek another term.

There are crucial distinctions between an intelligence conspiracy, the misreading of intelligence, and poor intelligence. Had the war been so rotten that intelligence estimates and analyses were compromised? Had MACV intelligence officers, because of political pressure, fudged their estimates in order to show progress? And had they succeeded in keeping from their commander in chief data that might have offset the shock of the massive Tet offensive in January 1968? Had General Westmoreland and other members of the military command engaged in treasonable offenses? Could MACV intelligence officers have deliberately downgraded and then successfully hidden from the president the strength of enemy forces? Would the CIA actually "cave in" to MACV's official estimates? And could this conspiracy have been kept from "big ears" Johnson?

Westmoreland was under extraordinary pressure to show progress in the war; the president was demanding evidence that a troop strength of 525,000 was making a difference in the war's outcome. CBS maintained that when Westmoreland learned from MACV intelligence

officers that enemy troop strength was actually much greater than
previously believed, he could hardly have gone to LBJ with the news.
The press would crucify the administration once it learned that
525,000 U.S. troops were not nearly enough to force the enemy to
the conference table. CBS charged that when confronted with a disintegrating military strategy and sensitive to its domestic underbelly, Westmoreland was forced to cook the order of battle books.

CBS extrapolated from a well-worn political debate initiated during the Pike Committee hearings in 1975. It is absurd to believe that
LBJ was deceived by Westmoreland or that the latter even tried to
deceive his commander in chief. Even if the National Intelligence
Estimate had been dishonest, it was one small input into LBJ's daily
intelligence menu. The order of battle was well known and well
worn among decision makers. Moreover, Westmoreland could not
possibly have suppressed reports of North Vietnamese regular army
infiltration of 25,000 a month between August and January 1968.
Instead, the intelligence-gathering process in a guerrilla war was the
major problem. To Westmoreland it was tantamount to "trying to
estimate roaches in your kitchen." The CIA believed that a Vietnamese civilian who struck a *panji* stick (a boobytrap) in the ground
belonged in the order of battle; Westmoreland did not.[64] The problem of defining who was and was not a soldier constituted a mi-
crocosm of the war itself. Counting the size of the enemy forces and
the rate of infiltration was an inexact process.

The failure of *method* particularly troubled Secretary of Defense
Robert McNamara because this meant there could be no military
solution to the problem. "I had been very skeptical for a long, long
time about the data relating to operations in South Vietnam. And
when one took the reported figures of infiltration, the reported figures of enemy losses, the reported enemy strength—they didn't add
up. And it simply caused me to question these as measures of progress, and some people not questioning them as I did came to one set
of conclusions—that is to say, progress was being made in the war
at a satisfactory rate and was pointing to ultimate victory; others,
particularly myself, concluded the opposite. Progress was not being
made at a satisfactory rate; we were not progressing toward a probable military victory."[65]

The available documents show that LBJ was receiving a voluminous amount of statistical material on Vietnam. It is inconceivable that MACV could have hidden something of this magnitude
from the president. Moreover, both sides of the debate had bureau-

cratic advocates who were in the business of slanting data toward their perspective. McNamara later recalled that "I didn't believe we had reached a cross over point, I didn't believe the strength would decline, I didn't believe that the bombing would prevent North Vietnam from supplying the forces in South Vietnam with whatever strength North Vietnam wished to have there . . . the cross over point implies where there is light at the end of the tunnel, we are moving toward victory and things are great. As far as I know, nobody asked me whether I thought that there was light at the end of the tunnel."[66]

In retrospect, it seems clear that the intelligence-gathering process was corrupted from above by an excessively paranoid president and from within by the choice of attrition as the means of measuring progress.[67] The available documents show that LBJ was briefed on the bureaucratic dispute between the CIA and MACV concerning the size of enemy forces. Not only did NSC Adviser Walt Rostow provide night reading, but almost every scrap of meeting notes shows that LBJ placed extraordinary pressure on MACV for demonstrations of military progress in order to buttress his political fortunes at home. That pressure might have made Westmoreland feel uncomfortable, even pressured, but he could hardly have led a bureaucratic conspiracy. All participants recognized that they could not lose American public opinion. Everyone was under pressure to demonstrate progress, and by the summer of 1967 virtually every unit of the U.S. government was involved in doing so.

Between August and December 1967 the administration embarked on a massive public relations effort to discredit the stalemate thesis. Meeting with the principals in the White House on August 26, Johnson insisted on developing optimistic scenarios: "We have reports that the guerrilla infra-structure is on the verge of collapse. All I can say to that is that if there is a stalemate, as the press reports, then every single one of our men we have out there is wrong. Bunker and Westmoreland do not agree, nor does anybody else who works for us out there—and they have no other purpose than to report the facts."[68]

The very nature of the war served Hanoi's long-term interest of creating dissension within the United States. Johnson's obsession with demonstrating progress in the war of attrition meant, by definition, rebutting the stalemate thesis. With the 1968 presidential election less than a year away, Johnson believed that the war would be won or lost in the United States, where the average citizen needed to see a light at the end of the tunnel. Statistical demonstration of progress was seen as a requisite for successful presidential leadership. Fighting a guerrilla war meant that few crucial victories could be identified; instead, such statistical indicators as kill ratios, order-of-battle infiltration rates, and weapons losses were intended to move the United States toward the elusive crossover point.

Lyndon Johnson orchestrated the demands for demonstrations of progress. On September 27, 1967, for example, a confidential cable to Ambassador Bunker arrived from Walt Rostow with explicit instructions: "The President requests you, Westy, Bob Komer to search urgently for occasions to present sound evidence of progress in Vietnam . . . President's judgment is that this is at present stage a critically important decision of fighting the war."[69] On October 12 Rostow wrote McNamara, Rusk, Helms, and Ambassador Leonhart: "The President has an urgent need for reliable, usable data on Vietnam and ways of measuring the evolution of the Vietnam conflict . . . We must proceed as rapidly as possible to purify existing data so that our present displays can be refined and new, more valid statistical displays can be developed. Individual new statistical series should be added to those currently in use as they become ready."[70]

During lunch on October 31, 1967, Robert McNamara told Johnson "that continuation of our present course of action in Southeast Asia would be dangerous, costly in lives, and unsatisfactory to the American people."[71] McNamara's position constituted a major break within the ranks of the best and brightest. Johnson already believed that what Haoi could not win on the battlefield it could win by outlasting American resolve. It had been one thing for college professors, "nervous nellies" and hippy demonstrators to challenge the war's progress, but now one of the chief architects of that policy faced its inevitable contradictions. The resolve of Secretary McNamara had broken; the credibility of U.S. foreign policy stood in the balance.

McNamara's November 1, 1967, memo to the president raised "fundamental questions of policy with reference to the conduct of the war in Vietnam."[72] The secretary began from the premise "that continuing our present course of action will not bring us by the end of 1968 enough closer to success, in the eyes of the American public, to prevent the continued erosion of popular support for our involvement in Vietnam." Endorsing a policy of *stabilization* in military effort, McNamara recommended a halt to increases in force levels and no further expansion of air operations against North Vietnam.

McNamara's memorandum showed sensitivity to the public relations war. The secretary was not arguing that U.S. policy had failed; instead, progress would be so slow that it "will not be readily visible to the general public either in the United States or abroad." After 525,000 troops and three years of bombing, how could the American public *not* see progress? Bombing had not sufficiently interrupted the flow of supplies and men to the degree that it hindered enemy military action in the South. Moreover, infliction of additional casualties and increasing air bombardment would not break the will of the North Vietnamese and the Viet Cong:

> Nothing can be expected to break this will other than the conviction that they cannot succeed. This conviction will not be created unless and until they come to the conclusion that the U.S. is prepared to remain in Vietnam for whatever period of time is necessary to assure the independent choice of the South Vietnamese people. The enemy cannot be expected to arrive at that conclusion in advance of the American public. And the American public, frustrated by the slow rate of progress, fearing continued escalation, and doubting that all approaches to peace have been sincerely probed, does not give the appearance of having the will to persist. As the months go by, there will be both increasing pressure for widening the war and continued loss of support for American participation in the struggle. There will be increasing calls for American withdrawal.

Johnson was determined to give McNamara's memorandum a complete airing. He instructed Rostow to circulate the memo amongst the principal foreign policy advisors. One of the most forceful responses came from Johnson's longtime friend, Supreme Court Justice Abe Fortas. Writing to the president on November 5, 1967, Fortas derided McNamara's proposal as "an invitation to slaughter."[73] The secretary's analysis and recommendations were based "almost entirely, upon an assessment of U.S. public opinion and an *unspoken assumption* as to the effect that should be given to it." Fortas rejected the premise that the American people were "unwilling to sustain an indefinitely prolonged war." Moreover, "*our duty is to do what we consider right . . . not what we consider (on a highly dubious basis with which I do not agree) the 'American people' want.*" Military decisions could not be made on the basis of a perceived public opinion. A program of stabilization would, according to Fortas, "*produce demands in this country to withdraw—*

and, in fact, *it must be appraised for what it is: a step in the process of withdrawal."*

Fortas suggested that the time had come to clean house. "I must frankly state again that I am not convinced that our military program in South Vietnam is as flexible or ingenious as it could be. I know that new proposals have been sought from our military. But perhaps a new and fresh look, including new people—civilian as well as military—might be warranted." When Fortas talked, LBJ listened. McNamara and Westmoreland would soon be gone, but the war remained indelibly linked with Lyndon Johnson.

The president decided to orchestrate dramatic attempts to sell the war's progress to the American people. In doing so, Johnson committed a tactical error in leadership: the Tet offensive of January 1968 contradicted the president's public pronouncements. "I am convinced I made a mistake," Johnson later wrote, "by not saying more about Vietnam in my State of the Union report on January 17, 1968. Cable traffic and intelligence reports all confirmed a buildup of enemy forces, but Johnson relied on background press briefings instead of public announcements. After selling optimistic scenarios in November, he could hardly have done otherwise. "This was one of those delicate situations" Johnson wrote, "in which we had to try to inform our own people without alerting the enemy to our knowledge of its plans. In retrospect, I think I was too cautious. If I had forecast the possibilities, the American people would have been better prepared for what was soon to come."[74] Tet revealed that despite over 500,000 men, billions of dollars, and extensive bombing, the United States had not stopped the enemy from replacing its forces. The rate of the war and the capacity to sustain it were controlled not by our superior technology, but by the enemy.

President Johnson failed to control public perceptions of the war's progress. He appears to have believed that he could use the prestige of the presidency to legitimize statistics—as though they could stand alone as proof that there was no policy stalemate. Faith in numbers replaced a visible demonstration of presidential leadership. As early as May 4, 1967, McGeorge Bundy tried to warn Johnson:

The Commander-in-Chief should visibly take command of a contest that is more political in its character than any in our history except the Civil War (where Lincoln interfered *much* more than you have). I think the visible exercise of his authority is not only best for the war but also best for public opinion—

and also best for the internal confidence of the Government. Briefings which cite the latest statistics have lost their power to persuade. So have spectacular summits. These things are not worth one-quarter of what could be gained by the gradual emergence of the fact that the President himself—in his capacity as political leader and Commander-in-Chief—is shaping a campaign which is gradually increasing in its success and gradually decreasing in its cost in American lives and money.[76]

Bundy warned Johnson, "I think we have tried too hard to convert public opinion by statistics and by spectacular visits of all sorts. I do have to say also that I think public discontent with the war is now wide and deep."

On March 31, 1968, Johnson announced that he would not seek reelection. His dream of the Great Society had been shattered by the war. He had been unable to use his extraordinary political ingenuity to anticipate his future costs. Leonard Marks, Johnson's director of the USIA, relates a story that shows how Johnson himself came to be aware of his lost opportunities. Senator George Aiken of Vermont had just made his historic statement, "Let's declare that we have achieved our objectives in Vietnam and go home." Marks liked the idea and at the first opportunity raised it with the president. "He looked at me—he had a way of staring at you—and finally I blinked. I said, 'What do you think?' He said, 'Get out of here.' I picked up my papers and left. That's the first and only time he'd ever been harsh with me . . . Several years after he left the White House I was invited to spend a weekend at the ranch. We were by ourselves. It was on my conscience and I said, 'Mr. President, I have to ask you something. In all the years we've been together, only once did you act in a way that I could really complain,' and I recalled this experience. 'Why did you do it?' He looked at me and he said, 'Because you and George Aiken were right.' "[77] Therein rested the tragic legacy of Lyndon Johnson's presidential leadership.

6

RICHARD M. NIXON

The Corporate Presidency

Joan Hoff-Wilson

Richard Milhous Nixon became president of the United States at a critical juncture in American history. Following World War II there was a general agreement between popular and elite opinion on two things: the effectiveness of most New Deal domestic policies and the necessity of most Cold War foreign policies. During the 1960s, however, these two crucial postwar consensual constructs began to break down; and the war in Indochina, with its disruptive impact on the nation's political economy, hastened their disintegration. By 1968 the traditional bipartisan, Cold War approach to the conduct of foreign affairs had been seriously undermined. Similarly, the "bigger and better" New Deal approach to the modern welfare state had reached a point of diminishing returns, even among liberals.[1]

In 1968, when Richard Nixon finally captured the highest office in the land, he inherited not only Lyndon Johnson's Vietnam war but also LBJ's Great Society. This transfer of power occurred at the very moment when both endeavors had lost substantial support among the public at large and, most important, among a significant number of the elite group of decision makers and leaders of opinion across the country. On previous occasions when such a breakdown had occurred within policy- and opinion-making circles—before the Civil and Spanish American Wars and in the early years of the Great Depression—domestic or foreign upheavals had followed.[2] Beginning in the 1960s the country experienced a similar series of failed presidents reminiscent of those in the unstable 1840s and 1850s, 1890s, and 1920s.

In various ways all the presidents in these transitional periods failed as crisis managers, often because they refused to take risks. Nixon, in contrast, "[couldn't] understand people who won't take risks."[3] His proclivity for risk taking was not emphasized by scholars, journalists, and psychologists until after he was forced to resign as president. "I am not necessarily a respecter of the status quo," Nixon told Stuart Alsop in 1958; "I am a chance taker." Although this statement was made primarily in reference to foreign affairs, Nixon's entire political career has been characterized by a series of personal and professional crises and risky political policies.[4] It is therefore not surprising that as president he rationalized many of his major foreign and domestic initiatives as crises (or at least as intolerable impasses) that could be resolved only by dramatic and sometimes drastic measures.

A breakdown in either the foreign or domestic policy consensus offers both opportunity and danger to any incumbent president. Nixon had more opportunity for risk-taking changes at home and abroad during his first administration than he would have had if elected in 1960 because of the disruptive impact of war and domestic reforms during the intervening eight years. Also, he inherited a wartime presidency, with all its temporarily enhanced extralegal powers. Although the Cold War in general has permanently increased the potential for constitutional violations by presidents, only those in the midst of a full-scale war (whether declared or undeclared) have exercised with impunity what Garry Wills has called "semi-constitutional" actions.[5] Although Nixon was a wartime president for all but twenty months of his five and one-half years in office, he found that impunity for constitutional violations was not automatically accorded a president engaged in an undeclared, unsatisfying, and seemingly endless war.[6] In fact, he is not usually even thought of, or referred to, as a wartime president.[7]

Periods of war and reform have usually alternated in the United States,[8] but in the 1960s they burgeoned simultaneously, hastening the breakdown of consensus that was so evident by the time of the 1968 election. This unusual situation transformed Nixon's largely unexamined and rather commonplace management views into more rigid and controversial ones. It also reinforced his natural predilection to bring about change through executive fiat. Thus a historical accident accounts in part for many of Nixon's unilateral administrative actions during his first term and for the events leading to his disgrace and resignation during his second.

The first few months in the Oval Office are often intoxicating, and a new president can use them in a variety of ways. But during the socioeconomic confusion and conflict of the late 1960s and early 1970s, some of the newly appointed Republican policy managers (generalists) and the frustrated holdover Democratic policy specialists (experts) in the bureaucracy unexpectedly came together and began to consider dramatic policy changes at home and abroad.[9] Complex interactions between these very different groups produced several significant shifts in domestic and foreign affairs during the spring and summer of 1969. A radical welfare plan and dramatic foreign policy initiatives took shape.

The country had elected only one other Republican president since the onset of FDR's reform administrations thirty-six years earlier. Consequently, Nixon faced not only unprecedented opportunities for changing domestic policy as a result of the breakdown in the New Deal consensus, but also the traditional problems of presidential governance, exacerbated in this instance by bureaucratic pockets of resistance from an unusual number of holdover Democrats. Such resistance was not new, but its magnitude was particularly threatening to a distrusted (and distrustful) Republican president who did not control either house of Congress. Nixon's organizational recommendations for containing the bureaucracy disturbed his political opponents and the liberal press as much as, if not more than, their doubts about the motivation behind many of his substantive and innovative suggestions on other domestic issues such as welfare and the environment.

Because much of the press and both houses of Congress were suspicious of him, Nixon naturally viewed administrative action as one way of obtaining significant domestic reform. Moreover, some of his initial accomplishments in administratively redirecting U.S. foreign policy ultimately led him to rely more on administrative actions at home than he might have otherwise. In any case, this approach drew criticism from those who already distrusted his policies and priorities. Nixon's covert and overt expansion and prolongation of the war during this period reinforced existing suspicions about his personality and political ethics. In this sense, liberal paranoia about his domestic programs fueled Nixon's paranoia about liberal opposition to the war, and vice versa. By 1972, Nixon's success in effecting structural and substantive change in foreign policy through the exercise of unilateral executive power increasingly led him to think that he could use the same preemptive administrative approach to resolve remaining domestic problems, especially following his landslide electoral victory.

A Manager of Crises

A man less in tune with both popular and elite attitudes might have responded more cautiously than Nixon did to the various manifestations of domestic discontent with the war and welfare. Nixon's sense of timing was all the more acute in the election years of 1968 and 1972 as a result of his close loss to Kennedy in 1960 and his overwhelming defeat in the California gubernatorial race in 1962. By 1968 he realized that old Republican campaign slogans and traditional anti-Communist shibboleths would not suffice. During the presidential campaign he deliberately kept his domestic policy statements palatable to the general public by talking in vague terms about dispersing power.[10]

With respect to foreign policy, however, Nixon had already given notice to elite policy formulators in a widely circulated 1967 article that it was time to question such sacrosanct Cold War assumptions as nonrecognition of mainland China.[11] During the 1968 campaign his more liberal opponent, Hubert Humphrey, appeared to be defending past American efforts to win the war in Vietnam more than was Nixon, whom many considered to be an original Cold Warrior. By implying that he had a "secret plan" for ending the war, a plan based on more diplomacy and less military escalation, Nixon seemed to be stressing victory in Vietnam less than Humphrey was. This left Humphrey wearing the very tattered military mantle of LBJ. All in all, however, during the 1968 campaign Nixon gave few concrete clues to establishment decision makers or to the American public about how he would initiate new policies at home or abroad if elected, let alone what those policies might be.[12]

Sensing the transitional mood of the country and convinced that presidents can accomplish significant deeds only in their first administration, Nixon moved quickly on several fronts even before his inauguration.[13] Later, as president, he and his staff often justified their actions by pointing to existing foreign or domestic crises. "Richard Nixon [was] at his best when things [weren't] going well," H. R. Haldeman reflected in 1975, "and at his worst when they [were]."[14] Hence Nixon's management style as president arose in reaction to an assortment of crises—some actual; others invented by him or his staff. This real and pseudo-crisis atmosphere was the natural by-product of consensual breakdown, but it was reinforced by the fact that Nixon operated most effectively in it.

In addition to the inherited crisis of the war in Vietnam, Nixon or his aides faced several domestic issues they also deemed crises: welfare, the environment, antiwar activities, the economy, population increase, and drug and crime control. In retrospect it appears that a crisis mentality prevailed more on domestic matters than on foreign ones. With the exception of school desegregation and antiwar unrest—areas in which Nixon needed no convincing about the existence of an emergency—high-ranking members of the executive branch actively cultivated a crisis mentality in the White House over other issues on the assumption that Nixon would otherwise not pay sufficient attention to take action.[15]

Consequently, a distinguishing feature of the Nixon presidency became its frequent use of crisis *modus operandi* to justify policy. Although he demonstrated the essential awareness that any successful modern president must have about the importance of managing and controlling bureaucratic processes, too often he exaggerated or rationalized his substantive foreign and domestic policies, as well as his recommendations for structural reform, from an embattled mentality. In a word, Nixon too often cried "wolf" in the name of domestic or national security. In one notable instance, namely Watergate, he finally fooled himself and turned a second-rate, second-story job into a first-rate constitutional crisis of his own making.

With Watergate, years of intermingling meaningful and fabricated crises—first to enhance his political career and then to resolve major foreign and domestic problems—finally placed Nixon on a collision course with history. The result was personal disgrace and public discredit for his significant public policy achievements and his formalistic, corporate management style, both of which had been declared successes in 1972 by such diverse political analysts as Theodore White and I. M. Destler.[16] Indeed, had it not been for Watergate, Nixon would automatically have gone down in history as a successful manager of real and not-so-real crises. He still may, especially if we concede that he was both a transitional and a wartime president.

Richard Nixon has been appropriately called "a management conscious president." Some even maintain that "Watergate . . . was predetermined [by] his managerial system."[17] Ironically, before becoming president he had had little previous management experience. Although his 1962 book, *Six Crises*, has been described as a "study in management crisis,"[18] it is not very informative about what later became his presidential approach to decision making. Rather, like his 1982 book, *Leaders*, it suggests personal characteristics necessary for leadership. In this sense *Six Crises* has been described as a "lesson of personal behavior" and a "saga of moral education."[19] The episodes it documents show how Nixon handled what amounted to personal, short-term, politically difficult situations (not national crises), and that he appears to have thought and fought best when he could convince himself that a crisis existed and that his back was against the wall.

Six Crises tells us more about how Nixon would have *managed himself* had he been elected in 1960 and become president in a traditional, nontransitional period, than about how he would *manage others* as president a decade later in a transitional period plagued by lack of national consensus on major issues. Except for the slush-fund accusations leading to his famous 1952 "Checkers" speech, Nixon manufactured the political traumas he reflected upon in his first best-seller. Thus, long before becoming president Nixon had characteristically exhibited risk-taking, street-fighting, attack-and-overkill tactics in personal situations that he correctly or incorrectly perceived to be political crises.[20] Consequently, substantive administrative ideas are distinguished by their absence in *Six Crises*.

Even though he did not address administrative matters in this book, Nixon had been critical of government red tape and bureaucratic lethargy as a result of his civilian and military experiences during World War II.[21] Nixon's views on governance and on domestic and foreign affairs, like those of most U.S. politicians, appear to have been influenced more by his adult experiences beginning with World War II than by any unresolved childhood psychological crises or ideological influences that he may have experienced as a young man while attending school or establishing himself as a lawyer. As Nixon himself later said:

> I came out of college more liberal than I am today, more liberal in the sense that I thought it was possible for government to do more than I later found it was practical to do. I became more conservative first, after my experience with OPA [Office of Price Administration] . . . I also became greatly disillusioned about

bureaucracy and about what the government could do because I saw the terrible paper work that people had to go through. I also saw the mediocrity of so many civil servants.[22]

According to William Safire, Nixon's disillusionment with the bureaucratic maze he faced as president was reflected in the fact that he used *government* and *bureaucracy* as "half-words," which were complete only when preceded by the expletive *damn*, as in *damngovernment* and *damnbureaucrats.*[23]

Likewise, his years as vice-president under Eisenhower account more negatively than positively for his later management style. Under Ike's demeaning tutelege in the 1950s, Nixon believed that he learned how *not* to operate in the Oval Office in the 1970s. This was particularly true of Eisenhower's National Security Council (NSC) system, which officially included him but privately excluded him from the decision-making process.[24] Acknowledging his exclusion from Ike's inner circle of advisers, Nixon told me that his administrative style was "in reaction to, not an emulation of," Eisenhower's cabinet government. "Cabinet government is a myth and won't work," he said. A president should "never rely on his cabinet . . . no [president] in his right mind submits anything to his cabinet . . . it is ridiculous . . . boring . . . [even] Eisenhower was bored with cabinet meetings and so was I."[25]

Although Nixon's apprenticeship under Eisenhower left him with strong impressions about how the cabinet in general, and the NSC in particular, should function, his vice-presidential years and his political eclipse in the 1960s did not prepare him for systematically managing large numbers of people or agencies. Fortuitously, however, from the time he first entered the political arena with his controversial campaign against Jerry Voorhis in 1946, he had psychologically prepared himself to assume the presidency in a transitional period of war and domestic unrest. By distilling his own personal political experiences over the years, Nixon had developed "a few general principles" for a management style based on a "crisis syndrome." With embarrassing candidness Nixon detailed in *Six Crises* how he politicized certain personal events in his career. By 1968 there was little distinction in his own mind between the two. Having literally transformed the personal into the political, Nixon came to the White House prepared to manage best when managing perceived crises. This mind-set served him unusually well until he faced the most serious crisis of his political career. "History will justifiably record," he wrote in the 1979 preface to *Six Crises*, "that my handling of the Watergate crisis was an unmitigated disaster."[26]

Prior to Watergate, few works on Nixon paid much attention to his administrative style because before 1968 he had exhibited little interest in what was to become almost a private obsession of the president and his closest aides, namely, "to get working control of the Executive Branch of the Federal Government."[27] Since Watergate, most assessments have been negative despite Nixon's many constructive attempts to manage the office of the president better than anyone else before or after. These assessments have also been based on very complicated psychological or structural-functional theories when probably there is a much less convoluted explanation. Nixon simply had a "fascination with How Things Work," or, as John Osborne has noted, he waged a "continuing struggle for neatness" and for "disciplined order and precision."[28] In this search for orderly governing procedures, his experiences under Eisenhower and the political support he had always received from large and small business concerns naturally led him away from cabinet government theories toward corporate ones.

From Cabinet to Corporate Government

Nixon demonstrated a general interest in structural change immediately after his election, when he created the Lindsay Task Force on Organization of the Executive Branch. In April 1969, on the basis of it recommendations, he appointed the President's Advisory Council on Executive Organization (PACEO), also known as the Ash Council. Its members—four top corporate executives and former Democratic governor of Texas John Connally—were to brainstorm about the specifics of executive reorganization.[29] Connally, the only one on the council with political experience, succeeded in convincing a less-than-enthusiastic cabinet to pursue extensive restructuring of the executive branch of government. Although the president supported reorganization, he was pessimistic about its chances for success because the issue had no "sex appeal" and would "upset too many apple carts" if submitted to Congress in any comprehensive form.[30]

In three months the Ash Council targeted six major areas for reorganization. The administration made successful structural changes in four of these: foreign economic policy, environmental protection, social programs, and the executive branch. In August and October

1969, when the Ash Council presented its first suggestions for creating an Office of Executive Management as well as a Domestic Policy Council, the president was most willing to listen.[31] By that time Nixon had concluded that the confusion displayed and the time consumed during the formulation of welfare legislation were direct results of the strongly opposing views of his first executive appointees. They had quickly assumed the unproductive adversarial roles so characteristic of cabinet government in recent years—something Nixon had hoped to avoid. Although he initially claimed that he did not want " 'Yes' men" in his cabinet, he later insisted that he "was willing to trade flamboyance for competence" and did not want "people who were too strong-willed to act as part of the team."[32]

Even if his first cabinet had not confirmed all the doubts he had harbored about cabinets since serving as vice-president, Nixon would have engaged in some kind of government reorganization. He had inherited unwieldily large White House and Executive Office staffs, with major departments resembling badly managed diversified holding companies rather than functionally efficient entities. That he should turn to centralized corporate management techniques is not surprising given the composition of the Ash Council, the need to reassess departmental diversity, and the superfluity of presidential assistants, their staffs, regular employees in the Executive Office, and those "borrowed" from other agencies.[33] From his experience with welfare reform Nixon began to grope his way toward a governing structure based on vertical rather than horizontal functional lines. Each of his subsequent reorganizational attempts from 1970 to 1973 brought him close to this particular corporate ideal, but he never did achieve it fully.

Nixon did not consider reorganization of the executive branch a crisis issue until the beginning of his second term. By following the Ash Council's recommendations, through a combination of legislative and administrative actions during his first four years in office, he had made unprecedented progress, including reorganization of executive agencies by function; creation of the Urban Affairs Council, which was subsumed in the Domestic Council; transformation of the Bureau of the Budget into the Office of Management and Budget (OMB); establishment of the Council on International Economic Policy (CIEP) and the Office of Energy Policy; restructuring of the National Security Council; and subtle but limited manipulations of the civil service personnel system.[34]

There is every indication that most of Nixon's recommendations for government reorganization encouraged a blurring or merging of functions between cabinet officers and members of his White House staff. Although both sets of officials were appointed, not elected, only the former required congressional approval. Therefore, because Congress had delayed or turned down several of his major proposals for reorganizing the executive branch during his first term, after his landslide reelection in 1972 Nixon decided to call for the summary resignation of his entire cabinet and to create a set of four special counselors to the president, or "supersecretaries," to take charge of certain domestic bureaucracies. In addition, he wanted to create a second line of subcabinet officials, consisting mainly of former or current White House aides, to act as presidential assistants responsible for such broad functional areas as domestic affairs, economic affairs, foreign affairs, executive management, and White House coordination. This last plan also called for the supersecretaries or counselors and presidential assistants to operate as a "supercabinet" in order to increase White House control over the bureaucracy.[35]

By the end of his first term Nixon had also decided that he needed loyal "politician managers" in these key supersecretariat positions, as well as in many of the more than two thousand appointive "plum" managerial jobs in the executive branch. Through his appointment powers he hoped to place loyalists thoughout the top levels of government to ensure implementation of his foreign, but particularly, his domestic policies. Nixon had endorsed the idea of using appointed generalists to oversee the work of civil servant specialists from the very beginning of his presidency. The value of this approach had subsequently been impressed upon him by the Ash Council. Initially, however, Nixon thought that he could appoint *both* strong agency and department heads and strong White House staff people to monitor them. After the two inevitably clashed during his first administration, he decided to move members of his White House staff (and other proven loyalists on policy) out into key positions within the executive branch.[36]

This notion of appointing Republican generalists to restrain or replace holdover Democratic specialists did not originate with Watergate. It failed, however, largely because the unfolding of Watergate events generated excessive criticism and suspicion about its intent. "Nixon's attempt to control the bureaucracy by placing loyalists in key position was more than an ideological effort to change government policies and programs," journalist Haynes Johnson insisted as late as 1980. "It was a blueprint for political subversion and executive tyranny."[37] Ironically, such criticism has not prevented Nixon's successors from quietly utilizing most aspects of his corporate reorganization of the executive branch. Indeed, his successors in the Oval Office have discovered that Nixon made "life . . . much more comfortable for them." According to I. M. Destler:

> It is far easier for a chief executive to deal through a few "loyal" aides almost totally dependent on himself, than to conduct extensive personal efforts at bargaining and persuasion which will frequently prove frustrating and occasionally be directly rebuffed. It is easier to work with his White House "court" than with those whose interests diverge from his and must be brought to see the gains for *them* in acting as he wants. And the closed Presidency is likely to give the President a *feeling* of great flexibility and room for maneuver. Those who have not been consulted need not be informed, much less heeded. The political limits on his power do not confront the President directly and daily in his personal relationships. He is encouraged to act as if he has not a Neustadtian license to persuade, but a "mandate" to decide things and have his decisions obeyed. He leads less than he orders. Those who obey are "loyal"; those who do not are enemies.[38]

No president since Nixon has undone the legitimate structural changes he made for conducting both domestic and foreign policy, because they have proved too useful. For example, under the guise of "cabinet" government, the Reagan administration has quietly institutionalized many aspects of Nixon's corporate government. Since 1981, Reagan and his advisers have effectively used the civil service reform initiated by President Carter to reach down beyond the "plum" appointments Nixon originally targeted, appointing GOP loyalists to upward of eight thousand career and noncareer Senior Executive Service positions. Nixon's influence can also be seen in Reagan's designation of some cabinet members as more equal than others and in his appointment of former aides as heads or deputy heads of major agencies and departments (such as Treasury Secretary James A. Baker, Attorney General Edwin Meese III, and William P. Clark—all of whom have occupied several high-level positions for which their primary qualification was that they were close friends or loyal aides of President Reagan).

Because of Watergate, many of Nixon's theories about corporate reorganization were discredited before they had been thoroughly analyzed or tested. The recommendations Nixon received from the Ash Council did not differ significantly in content from those his predecessors had received from similar advisory bodies. However, through a combination of legislative and administrative actions, Nixon's reorganizational plans were more extensive than any president's before or since. It was their quantity more than their quality that frightened and angered a significant number of Washington bureaucrats and politicians. Even without Watergate, therefore, Nixon's experiment with corporate government would have continued to face Democratic Congresses, which had turned down his domestic legislation in his first term and which "caustically regarded" his successive reorganizational plans "because of [their] corporate character, sweeping scope, and ambiguity of basic goals for combined but disparate programs."[39] Much of this ambiguity stemmed from shifts in federal and state functions as the Nixon administration tried to establish new priorities at home and abroad under the rubric of the New Federalism.

Nixon's New Federalism

Nixon's New Federalism was an attempt to resolve a paradox as old as the Constitution itself. Too often, as Senator William Fulbright noted in his famous March 27, 1964, speech, "we are inclined to confuse freedom and democracy, which we regard as moral principles, with the way in which these are practiced in America—with capitalism, federalism and the two-party system, which are not moral principles, but simply the preferred and accepted practices of the American people."[40] Nixon did not. His brand of federalism (like his brand of détente) was a pragmatic, not a moral, concept. He considered pragmatism to be a necessary *modus operandi* for any president dealing with contemporary American problems. Nixon's New Federalism, as Richard Nathan has noted, was "a political program . . . [not] an academic treatise."[41]

In contrast to the founding fathers' federalism, Nixon's did not represent a static approach to the powers of the state versus those of the federal government.[42] Nor did it make the role of military power primary in international affairs, as had traditional cold warriorism. Instead, Nixon's New Federalism, both at home and abroad, was based on ascertaining where the predominant responsibilities logically lay and then determining the appropriate level of domestic or international power at which to handle a specific function or activity. Welfare, for example, was brought under the jurisdiction of the federal government, whereas manpower training devolved to the states. Likewise, some international problems such as the Middle East required decentralized and multilateral negotiations, whereas opening up relations with China did not.

To implement the New Federalism, Nixon and his advisers distinguished between federal functions and state or local ones—between activities requiring large cash transactions and those primarily involving services. Nixon attempted to return to the states some power over service issues (what social scientists call "distributive" issues), such as education, manpower training, and public health, while retaining control at the national level over cash transfers or "nondistributive" issues, such as welfare, energy, and the environment. Above all, unlike Reagan's, Nixon's New Federalism was not intended to cut federal spending programs. Instead, he addressed national problems by spending more and by redistributing power away from Congress and the federal bureaucracy toward local, state, and presidential centers of control.[43] As a result, Nixon is currently credited with or criticized for taking significant steps toward centralized planning and structural decentralization in domestic affairs. According to Otis L. Graham, Nixon personally began to "preside over a more rapid evolution toward planning than [had] any other President since FDR."[44]

The final essential element of Nixon's New Federalism was the desire to preserve natural community structures. As James Reichley has pointed out, the Nixon administration recognized "that contemporary American society required satisfaction of paradoxical sets of needs: a need for both national unity and local diversity; a need to protect both individual equality at the national level and individual uniqueness at the local level; and a need *both* to establish national goals and to decentralize government services."[45] Nixon believed that this type of increased centralization would help him implement many of the decentralized features of his New Federalism, such as special and general revenue sharing with states and local communities instead of categorical grants, income strategy instead of service strategy to aid welfare recipients, and planned new community development under a national growth policy. This combination of centralization and decentralization also facilitated the impounding of federal funds earmarked for projects he opposed and other less-than-positive features of New Federalism, such as the attempt by federal and state agencies to cooperate in the systematic (and often extralegal) surveillance or harassment of allegedly subversive groups or individuals.[46]

Since the objective of Nixon's New Federalism was to circumvent the bureaucracy in Washington by increasing the power of the White House, implementation of this policy naturally alienated a large portion of the federal bureaucracy.[47] At the same time no aspect of Nixon's New Federalism represented a decline in presidential power in relation to the states, local communities, or other countries. Instead, in almost every instance specific agencies or departments within the federal bureaucracy, such as the Office of Economic Opportunity (OEO) and the State Department, were weakened to enhance presidential interests. Leonard Garment, the only liberal Democrat to serve on the Nixon White House's legal staff, correctly observed that the "central paradox of the Nixon administration was that in order to reduce *federal* power, it was first necessary to increase *presidential* power." Or as Nixon more bluntly described this paradox to me: "Bringing power to the White House [was necessary] in order to dish it out."[48]

In a very abstract sense Nixon's diplomatic policies were also a form of New Federalism. They, too, were based on the realization that national and international community had to be pursued and local or regional cultural diversity honored at the same time. They, too, tried to accommodate centralized and decentralized loci of power. Thus although the Nixon administration emphasized the importance of state and local jurisidiction within the United States, it also espoused a dispersed concept of international relations under a "pentagonal," or Five Power, approach to foreign policy. Likewise, the Nixon Doctrine, proclaimed in July 1969, was a strategy of devolution designed to maintain U.S. commitments abroad at reduced costs. "Domestic revenue-sharing was like the Nixon doctrine abroad," the president told Theodore White in a March 1973 interview. "The American government helps, but local governments have got to do it on their own." Thus, Nixon's domestic New Federalism has been appropriately referred to as "national localism," while his diplomatic New Federalism can be considered an example of "regional globalism."[49]

Just as domestic relationships were linked in an overarching federal pattern (some requiring top-down, others bottom-up approaches), so linkage became an essential concept in Nixon's geopolitical design. For example, arbitrary covert or overt actions by any of the five major powers in the Middle East or in the Third

World would automatically affect superpower relationships; yet small nations within any particular major power's sphere of influence could not independently play off the superpowers against each other and expect any outside help from any of those five powers. Thus, linkage would inhibit and contain conflict among the "Big Five," similar to the way in which federalism channels potential conflict between national and state spheres of power.

The major differences in the application of Nixon's New Federalism at home and abroad are quite evident: the term was not used to describe foreign affairs; domestically the policy *appeared* less successful because no single domestic adviser emerged with the influence, prestige, or gusto that Henry Kissinger brought to the conduct of foreign policy; and the unpopularity of the Vietnam war effort hampered Nixon's ability to influence Congress on certain domestic reform issues more than it hampered his foreign policy initiatives, which he could often set in motion unilaterally.

Cognitive and Administrative Style

To the general corporatist and New Federalist framework of his presidency, Nixon brought particular cognitive and administrative styles. However, it is an exaggeration to say: "While every modern president had made use of administrative powers as often as he could, the Nixon White House was unique in relying solely upon them."[50] Nixon submitted extensive domestic programs to Congress during his first administration, although admittedly the intent of some of these New Federalist reforms was to redistribute power away from Congress and the Washington bureaucracy.

Nixon may indeed have "brought Watergate with him from Whittier to Washington,"[51] but like most other alliterations this one is more entertaining than enlightening when it comes to explaining his approach to the age-old dilemma of heads of state: how first to devise policy and then to manage implementation despite the existence of an entrenched, though in many cases talented and capable, bureaucracy. Thus, although his particular psychological makeup does occasionally throw light on his actions in highly charged situations, it is more constructive to evaluate Nixon's presidency in terms of his attempts to restructure the executive branch of government so that both *policy-making* and its *implementation* would be protected from bureaucratic and legislative sabotage.

The terms *formalistic, competitive,* and *collegial* are commonly used to describe the basic cognitive models of management employed by modern presidents.[52] Interestingly, all presidents since Hoover have exhibited only these three cognitively related management styles while in office. According to Alexander George and others, Nixon opted for "the formalistic model characterized by an orderly policy-making structure . . . one that provides well-defined procedures, hierarchial lines of communication, and a structured staff system." Among other things, the formalistic model discourages open personal conflict in the policy-making process.[53]

Regardless of the terminology used, it is clear that Nixon preferred a management style that ostensibly "depoliticized and rationalized the formal policy-making process completely."[54] Practitioners of this approach to decision making tend to minimize the importance of human error or moral considerations. When error in judgments resulted in illegal actions, Nixon did not recognize them for what they were because he had long before become inured to the "underside" or the "mini-Watergates" of American politics. In other words, Watergate was an accident waiting to happen because of the increasingly semiconstitutional nature of the modern U.S. presidency in the Cold War era and because of what I have described elsewhere as Nixon's aprincipledness.[55]

Illegal and unconstitutional presidential behavior did not begin or end with Nixon. Since 1945 it has fluctuated with the degree of an administration's hot or cold warriorism. There is nothing endemically cyclical about his fluctuation. In general, presidents have tended to make mistakes in judgment following landslide elections and at the end of wars because they have found it hard to adjust to normal, rather than wartime, exercise of power. The increasingly arbitrary or "willful behavior" of recent American presidents also reflects a disturbing international phenomenon among heads of state—of whom Nixon was but one national example. Worldwide it has been referred to as "gangsterism."[56] This tendency among modern leaders to ignore constitutional or legislative restrictions when it suits their convictions on particular issues is a more serious latent problem, at least for democratic nations, than the often discussed one of the self- or staff-imposed insulation of top government officials. It was certainly true in Nixon's mishandling of the Watergate coverup, and again more recently in the Iran-Contra affair.

Obviously every president requires a certain amount of isolation and privacy, regardless of his cognitive characteristics and personality. This need for isolation stems from the very magnitude of the

job and the resonsibilities of dealing with "the chaos and complexity
of the modern world—wars, assassinations, wealth amid poverty . . . and . . . the ways in which the Presidency has had to evolve
to deal with these conditions."[57] Although liberals in particular criticized Nixon for allowing his staff to isolate him, case studies of
some of his major decisions show that this did not generally happen.
Options abounded, especially on domestic issues,[58] but Nixon's awkward, stiff, and very private personal style never attracted much
empathy for the problems he faced.

In fact, Nixon's personality and body language irked his opponents
as much as, if not more than, did the specific policies he finally
adopted. Even if he had tried to relax and be more spontaneous (as
indeed he has become since retirement from public office), such a
change in persona might have caused him as much trouble with the
press and public as did his stereotypical aloofness and propensity
for delegating to his staff matters concerning interpersonal conflicts
and unpleasant announcements. According to Dan Rather, Nixon
was "not synchronized . . . he studied how to use gestures . . . [but] was
always what we call on television two frames too late . . . there was
an unnaturalness about him." John Lindsay once described him as
looking like a "walking box of short circuits."[59] Having succeeded
a president who had let everything "hang out," including his gall
bladder scar, Nixon reacted to Johnson's uninhibited and emotional
presidential image by becoming even more uptight and less spontaneous in public than he was before becoming president. "The worst
thing you can do in this job," Nixon has told me and others over
the years, "is to let up," that is, reveal his true feelings.[60]

Because Richard Nixon would not have "let up," he may have
"ended up delegating emotions as well as work" to his staff, "thus
creating an atmosphere in the White House in which extra-legal
activities, once tacitly approved by the president, may well have
encouraged his aides to begin approving their own extra-legal activities, about which Nixon himself may or may not have always known
the details."[61] Certainly this kind of delegation was more prevalent
during the 1972 campaign than in any of Nixon's previous campaigns
for public office. None of the Watergate-related reforms enacted by
1975 effectively addressed the problem of presidential isolation resulting from excessive delegation of presidential power to unelected,
often anonymous individuals who are not responsible to the electorate or Congress. As a result, there is currently little indication

that the isolation of beleaguered presidents who are excessively concerned about leaks has diminished since 1974.

Nixon's first and most enduring bureaucratic reforms occurred in
the realm of foreign policy when, as president-elect, he ordered the
restructuring of the National Security Council. Although Nixon also
instituted many reforms affecting domestic bureaucratic structures,
he did not attempt the most controversial of these, the "supersec-
retary" concept, until the beginning of his second term. All his
recommendations for reorganizing the executive branch followed
the suggestions of the Ash Council. In other words, none represented
whimsical or "fascistic" actions, as was claimed after the Watergate
débacle, although their mode of implementation left a lot to be
desired.[62]

Richard Nixon's mania for establishing orderly procedures appears
to have been rooted less in what some have claimed to be a compulsive desire to avoid personal confrontation than it was in his
"preoccupation with the technology of management."[63] Therefore,
from the beginning of his first term a tendency existed for process
to become policy, for organizational reform to become a substitute
for more substantive considerations, and for effectiveness to become
more important than morality or constitutionality. These rigid, organizational expectations so characteristic of the Nixon administration did occasionally isolate the president from opposing points
of view; but, more important, they produced, according to A. James
Reichley, a "results at any price approach"[64] or, at the very least,
unrealistic expectations about the effectiveness of structural reform
and the ability of even a wartime president to justify everything in
the name of national security. Nixon realized that the executive
branch's capacity for coherent planning had been weakened over the
years by increasingly powerful local or regional interests. Therefore,
after initiating a formalistic governing style, he systematically attempted to gain control of segments of the federal bureaucracy. At
the same time he and his advisers endlessly pondered how to disperse
to the states power over issues that did not require federal standards
and how to combat subversives inside and outside government.

These two issues had little in common; nonetheless, they became
perversely linked beginning in the 1960s (and, some would claim,
reemerged in the 1980s). This linkage led to increased cooperation
among the FBI, the CIA, and urban or state intelligence units, which
then forged links to monitor first the civil rights and then the antiwar

movements. Nixon was prevented by J. Edgar Hoover from implementing an elaborate scheme (the "Houston Plan") for coordinating all counterintelligence agencies from the army, navy, air force, CIA, and FBI into an Interagency Group on Domestic Intelligence and Internal Security.[65] Temporarily thwarted, Nixon began intensive use of the special domestic unit "Operation CHAOS," established by the Johnson administration for monitoring whether antiwar groups were financed by foreign enemies. Subsequently the Nixon administration initiated surveillance of domestic antiwar and other protest groups through a variety of extralegal means. At one level this was an attempt to channel what was perceived to be waning anticommunism (prompted in part by the Nixon administration's rapprochement with China and détente with the USSR) into a broad mainstream cultural campaign aimed at alleged internal subversion.[66]

All the President's Men

Even in the best of times, but particularly in times of transition, presidential policies seldom reflect only the ideas or principles of the president. They are, instead, the collective product of his aides and various divisions of the executive branch. After a series of private interviews with Nixon and with many of those who influenced policy under him, I have come to an understanding of his presidency and administrative style that is based primarily on neither his personality nor his political ethics, but on Nixon's ability as a crisis manager and on the contributions of his closest advisers. These men, more than Nixon's own individual psyche or morality, determined the substantive agenda he pursued in domestic and foreign policy. Those who advised Nixon on major issues (not usually on political dirty tricks or criminal activities, although occasionally there was an overlap) fall into two categories: the "freethinking" outsiders who brainstormed with the president about new ideas and comprehensive programs, and the "political-broker" insiders who worked to draft and implement his legislative and administrative priorities. Of all Nixon's major advisers, only Henry Kissinger developed the ability to play both roles.

Following Nixon's election in 1968 the momentum for change in most domestic and foreign affairs came from such freethinking outsiders as Robert Finch, Richard Nathan, Daniel Patrick Moynihan, Henry Kissinger, and, later, John Connally. All of these men appealed to Nixon's preference for bold action, and none except Robert Finch had been closely associated with him before he became president. During the first administration Moynihan and Kissinger influenced certain crucial details about, but not usually the broad outlines of, domestic and foreign policies by supporting ideas based on the concept of linkage. During his first two years in office Nixon embarked on a systematic course of risk taking in both foreign and domestic policy that attempted to reverse traditional American positions on government organization, the idea of a guaranteed annual income (which he preferred to call a negative income tax), environmental considerations, revenue sharing (including block grants), the value of the dollar, the bombing of Cambodia, rapprochement with China, and détente with the USSR.

The impact of the freethinking outsiders on Nixonian policies is easy to trace. Moynihan, Finch, and Nathan greatly influenced specific legislation on welfare; Kissinger carried out the president's foreign policy, initially as national security adviser and later as secretary of state; and Connally, whom Nixon appointed secretary of the treasury in 1971, almost single-handedly talked the president into both wage and price controls and devaluation of the dollar. Connally also played a crucial role in two of Nixon's most important environmental decisions, the creation of the Environmental Protection Agency and of the Department of Natural Resources—both against the wishes of the farm bloc. Perhaps of all these advisers, Nixon was most impressed by Connally, whom he had wanted for his vice-president in 1968, when Connally was still a Democrat and governor of Texas. Nixon apparently hoped that Connally would succeed him in 1976. "Only three men in America understand the use of power," Nixon confided to Arthur Burns. "I do. John does. And," he grudgingly added, "I guess Nelson [Rockefeller] does."[67]

Nonetheless, the political-broker insiders—gray flannel types such as John Ehrlichman and H. R. Haldeman, the president's two closest aides; Arthur Burns, counselor to the president and later head of the Federal Reserve Board; Melvin Laird, secretary of defense; George Shultz, secretary of labor and later head of the Office of Management and Budget; and businessman Roy Ash, chair of PACEO—increasingly gained ascendancy over the freethinking outsiders, and as a result Nixon's plans to reorganize became more corporate in nature and more central to his thinking. For example, after Nixon created the Urban Affairs Council with its nine subcommittees, he found that advocates of opposing welfare plans were bypassing the newly established structure and appealing directly to him for intercession.

Under such circumstances he quickly learned to appreciate the mediating talents of such political-broker types as Ehrlichman, Shultz, and Laird. Consequently, in Nixon's first months in office these three became dominant insiders on domestic policy, while Haldeman and Ash concentrated on organizational matters.[68]

Ehrlichman, his assistant Egil (Bud) Krogh, John Whitaker (who served first as Nixon's cabinet secretary and later as under secretary of the Interior Department), and Whitaker's assistant Christopher DeMuth substantially influenced both Nixon's ideas and the content of his environmental legislation. Ehrlichman also became an essential conduit in the process of implementing the Ash Council's recommendations on government reorganization, while Arthur Burns emerged as an unexpected champion of revenue sharing within the administration. Shultz confined his advice largely to behind-the-scenes economics and labor issues but proved surprisingly influential on such highly visible social policy questions as welfare and desegregation.[69] Before Kissinger's ascendancy, Laird could be seen brokering on a wide variety of topics from foreign policy to the volunteer army, revenue sharing, government reorganization, and Vietnamization. If there is a single underestimated, understudied influential figure in the first Nixon administration, it is the most diffident of the political-broker insiders, Melvin Laird—one of the few key persons who has not written his memoirs.

Nixon once told me that he thought the "mark of a leader is whether he gives history a nudge."[70] There is no doubt that he nudged history as president, but in ways that he did not anticipate. Whether relying on freethinking outsiders or honest broker insiders, he essentially took the initiative and made many of his own decisions, particularly in foreign affairs. Although he and his closest advisers will undoubtedly continue to disagree on who influenced whom the most, Richard Nixon came to the Oval Office with innovative diplomatic ideas that cannot be claimed even by Kissinger. And to the dismay of many liberals and conservatives in Congress, Nixon also rapidly moved into domestic reform, often on the advice of young, liberal Republicans, but without the fanfare that accompanied most of his foreign policy initiatives. Given the fact that Nixon remains the only president since 1849 to have been elected without his party's having gained a majority in either house of Congress, his historical "nudges" in both foreign and domestic matters are truly impressive in retrospect.

The White House as State Department

One of the most basic decisions every modern president must make is whether to assign the primary role in foreign policy-making to his secretary of state or to his special assistant for national security. If he chooses the latter he will try to centralize and manage foreign policy formulation from the White House rather than from the State Department. Since President Truman's creation of the National Security Council in 1947 but especially since 1960, there has been unremitting contention for power and influence between secretaries of state and the special foreign policy advisers in charge of the NSC staff. At the same time a less evident battle has also raged over whether and how to separate policy formulation from operational or implementing functions. Often these disputes have stemmed as much from the cognitive style of the particular president as from substantive arguments between the secretary of state and national security adviser.[71]

Shortly after Nixon and Kissinger began working together in the fall of 1968, they created the "first full White House–dominant system for the management of foreign policy by reorganizing the NSC."[72] That Nixon intended the White House to function as the State Deparment cannot be doubted. In the first months of his administration, when former Republican National Committee chairman Leonard Hall asked the president how he was getting along with the State Department, Nixon pointed in the direction of the Oval Office and said, "There's the State Department."[73]

Nowhere did the centralized corporate presidency of Richard Nixon manifest itself as a closed system more clearly than in this two-man domination of U.S. foreign policy. In theory the new "Nixinger" system made the NSC the principal foreign policy forum within the White House, assigning the secretary of state responsibility for the execution of presidential decisions resulting from NSC discussions. In practice Nixon's and Kissinger's personal management of foreign policy merged policy formulation and operational functions inside and outside the NSC system. This remains the greatest strength (and weakness) of the Nixonian structural legacy for conducting diplomacy, as the 1987 Iran-Contra hearings demonstrated. Ultimately, even this "system of closed policy-making is limited by the limits of Presidential power at home."[74] Thus, in foreign as well as in domestic matters Nixon found that it was not enough to take

advantage of the lack of a national consensus; it was also necessary
to rebuild consensus, if for no other reason than to have national
support when policies went badly awry.

In March and April 1969 the restructured NSC reached two important but quite dissimilar decisions: one, to bomb selected North
Vietnamese sanctuaries in Cambodia, using a devious double-
bookkeeping method; the other, not to overreact to the shooting
down of an American EC-121 spy plane with thirty-one men aboard.
The former has been generally castigated by the press and public,
while the latter has been generally praised. Yet it is unlikely that
one was a mistake of the NSC system and the other not. The in-
congruity between the two decisions can best be explained by the
amount of private consultation that occurred between Nixon and
Kissinger rather than by any inherent flaw in the NSC system itself.[75]

Because the EC-121 incident occurred unexpectedly, the two men
had little or no time to consult with each other. The Cambodian
sanctuary situation, on the other hand, was inherited from the Johnson administration. Nixon and Kissinger had discussed the problem
several times before the North Vietnamese launched a small-scale
offensive in February 1969. Thus the decision to bomb the sanctuaries was not made in a crisis atmosphere. Basically, it represented
a policy based on the exaggerated expectation that North Vietnam
could be cajoled into being more reasonable in its peace demands
through a combination of bombings, improved U.S. relations with
China, Vietnamization, and unilateral withdrawal. This expectation
was never realized. In the end, after four more years of war, the
United States accepted essentially the same terms the Vietcong had
offered in 1969.[76]

Yet the bombing of Cambodia was one of the few truly covert
foreign policy undertakings of the Nixon administration that received *full* NSC consideration, even though it was after the fact.
Most of the other covert actions bypassed the NSC. This fact is the
most significant aspect of Nixon's foreign policy-making and his
most important legacy to subsequent administrations: *when a decision did not depend primarily on the civilian or military bureaucracy for implementation, the NSC was ignored, whether the action
was covert or not; the NSC was utilized primarily when the covert
or overt policy required bureaucratic support.* The NSC system was
not used as a forum for presenting options to the president by which
to decide the policies of Vietnamization, the Nixon Doctrine, the
secret Kissinger negotiations with North Vietnam, Nixon's New

Economic Policy, the intervention in Chile that culminated in Allende's overthrow, or the planning of Nixon's historic trip to China to redirect our Asian policy in relation to the Soviet Union. All of these were presented to the NSC, if at all, as *faits accomplis*. Indeed, one might ask when the NSC system *was* used. During Nixon's first year as president the NSC decided to begin the secret bombing of Cambodia and to respond to the EC-121 incident. Later in his administration it played a role in a number of other decisions, including the attempt to keep Taiwan in the United Nations with a "two China" policy, the incursions into Cambodia and Laos, the détente agreements with the Soviet Union, Middle Eastern policy before the 1973 Yom Kippur War, and policy in Angola and southern Africa in general.[77]

Although no definitive evaluation of the NSC can be made without access to material that remains classified, it appears that the relationship between certain NSC and non-NSC decisions is crucial to an understanding of how the system actually worked in the formulation of some foreign policies. For example, the carefully guarded secret decision to bomb Cambodia has to be viewed in relation to actions that did not arise from NSC debates but were undertaken around the same time. Whether they realized it or not, the Joint Chiefs of Staff (who had been requesting permission to bomb enemy sanctuaries in Cambodia since 1966) had more bargaining power on this issue under Nixon because he had unilaterally taken actions with which the JCS were not entirely pleased, such as turning the bulk of the fighting and management of the war over to the South Vietnamese, the unilateral withdrawal of American troops from Vietnam, and stepped-up negotiations with the Vietcong in Paris.[78]

Instead of continuing to lament the existence of the NSC under Nixon (and his successors), it is time to begin to reexamine how it operated in specific incidents. The NSC has been an easy target for critics of the "Nixinger" foreign policies, but in reality it is only the symbol of a much more complex corporate reorganizational process. In the final analysis, the NSC or any other government agency is only as good as the people who staff it, and no amount of tinkering or reorganization will change this all-important personnel factor.

If trade-offs and bargaining within the NSC rather than irrational two-man decisions produced both the infamous secret bombing of Cambodia and the measured response to the EC-121 incident, what is one to make of the much-publicized "madman theory" and its relationship or relevance to Nixon's formulation of foreign policy?

Many journalists and historians have assumed that Nixon regularly threatened to act like an anticommunist madman in order to achieve his foreign policy objectives. Nixon's preference for risk taking and his general inclination to act on issues presented as crises lend themselves to such an interpretation. However, few of his major foreign policies were products of a "crisis syndrome," idiosyncratic as they may appear in retrospect.

Conventional wisdom on the origin of the madman theory is relatively simple to trace. In 1978 H. R. Haldeman claimed in *The Ends of Power* that Nixon used the term one day during the 1968 campaign when they "were walking along a foggy beach after a long day of speechwriting." According to Haldeman's account, Nixon was ruminating about how he would end the war in Vietnam during his first year in office, just as Eisenhower had ended the war in Korea; namely, by covertly threatening to use nuclear bombs. At one point Nixon allegedly turned to Haldeman and said: "I call it the madman theory, Bob. I want the North Vietnamese to believe I've reached the point where I might do *anything* to stop the war. We'll just slip the word to them that, 'for God's sake, you know Nixon is obsessed about communism. We can't restrain him when he's angry—and he has his hand on the nuclear button'—and Ho Chi Minh himself will be in Paris in two days begging for peace.'"[79]

When I asked Nixon about this often-quoted statement, he said that he had seldom talked with Haldeman about substantive foreign policy matters and certainly did not remember using the term *madman theory*. He indicated that had he discussed the concept or principle of threatening to use excessive force, it would have been with others in connection with employing Kissinger in the role of the "good messenger" to play off against his own well-known anticommunist views when negotiating with communist nations.[80] I can find no other documented attribution for the madman theory.

More than likely the term originated with Kissinger, not with Nixon. As early as 1959 Daniel Ellsberg gave two lectures in Kissinger's Harvard seminar "The Political Uses of Madness." Ellsberg used Hitler as a specific example of the successful "conscious political use of irrational military threats," and in general told Kissinger's class that such strategy was reckless and irresponsible. Although there is some indication in Kissinger's earliest books that he accepted such an approach as diplomatically feasible, there is no confirmation of his authorship of the theory in his memoirs. To date, only Haldeman, among either Kissinger's or Nixon's closest aides, has indicated any knowledge of the president's use of the term or concept in relation to the use of nuclear weapons in Vietnam, Cambodia, or Laos. If anything, the handling of the EC-121 incident demonstrates that Kissinger, rather than Nixon, personally supported the madman theory.[81]

In retrospect, one of the most unfortunate decisions Richard Nixon made during his first administration was to appoint Henry Kissinger head of the National Security Council—potentially the most influential position within the White House. This opinion, however, is not shared by either Nixon or his top advisers, one of whom insisted to me that "the care and feeding of Henry" was worth all the paranoia, backbiting, leaking, rumor mongering and general self-aggrandizement that Kissinger brought to the White House.[82] Yet most of the early wiretaps and much of Nixon's obsession with covert actions during his first year in office can be attributed at first to Kissinger's ingratiating presence, and later to his direct influence; for Kissinger's personality traits matched, rather than complemented, the most negative ones of the president. The combination of these two men, though occasionally resulting in dazzling foreign policy achievements, also had a dark, devious underside from which only one of them walked away unscathed.

Foreign Policy Scorecard

It was clearly in Nixon's psychic and political self-interest to end the war in Vietnam as soon as possible. Although he came to office committed to negotiate a quick settlement, he ended up prolonging the conflict. As a result, he could never build the domestic consensus he needed to continue the escalated air and ground war (even with dramatically reduced U.S. troop involvement) and to ensure passage of some of his domestic programs. For Nixon (and Kissinger) Vietnam became a symbol of influence in the Third World that, in turn, was but one part of their geopolitical approach to international relations. Thus the war in Southeast Asia had to be settled as soon as possible so as not to endanger other elements of Nixonian diplomatic and domestic policy.[83]

Instead, the president allowed his secretary of state to become egocentrically involved in secret negotiations with the North Vietnamese from August 4, 1969, to January 25, 1972 (when they were made public). As a result, the terms finally reached in 1973 were only marginally better than those rejected in 1969. The advantage gained from Hanoi's agreement to allow President Nguyen Van Thieu to remain in power in return for allowing North Vietnamese troops to remain in South Vietnam can hardly offset the additional loss of twenty thousand American lives during this three-year period—especially given the inherent weaknesses of the Saigon government by 1973. On the tenth anniversary of the peace treaty ending the war in Vietnam, Nixon admitted to me that "Kissinger believed more in the power of negotiation than I did." He also said that he "would not have temporized as long" with the negotiating process had he not been "needlessly" concerned with what the Soviets and Chinese might think if the United States pulled out of Vietnam precipitately.[84] Because Nixon saw no way in 1969 to end the war quickly except through overt massive bombing attacks, which the public demonstrated in 1970 and 1971 it would not tolerate, there was neither peace nor honor in Vietnam by the time that war was finally concluded on January 27, 1973; and in the interim he made matters worse by secretly bombing Cambodia.

The delayed ending to the war in Vietnam not only cast a shadow on all Nixon's other foreign policy efforts but also established secrecy, wiretapping, and capricious personal diplomacy as standard operational procedures in the conduct of foreign policy that ultimately carried over into domestic affairs. Despite often duplicitous and arbitrary actions, even Nixon's strongest critics often credit him with an unusual number of foreign policy successes.

Although fewer of his foreign policy decisions were reached in a crisis atmosphere than his domestic ones, Nixon's diplomatic legacy is weaker than he and many others have maintained.[85] For example, the pursuit of "peace and honor" in Vietnam failed; his Middle Eastern policy because of Kissinger's shuttling ended up more show than substance; his Third World policy (outside of Vietnam and attempts to undermine the government of Allende in Chile) were nearly nonexistent; détente with the USSR soon foundered under his successors; and the Nixon Doctrine has not prevented use of U.S. troops abroad. Only rapprochement with China remains untarnished by time because it laid the foundation for recognition, even though he failed to achieve a "two China" policy in the United Nations. This summary is not meant to discredit Richard Nixon as a foreign policy expert both during and after his presidency. It is a reminder that the lasting and positive results of his diplomacy may be fading faster than some aspects of his domestic policies.

Outflanking Liberals on Domestic Reform

Presidents traditionally achieve their domestic objectives through legislation, appeals in the mass media, and administrative actions. During his first administration Nixon offered Congress extensive domestic legislation, most of which aimed at redistributing federal power away from Congress and the bureaucracy. When he encountered difficulty obtaining passage of these programs, he resorted more and more to reform by administrative fiat, especially at the beginning of his second term. All Nixonian domestic reforms were rhetorically linked under the rubric of the New Federalism. Most competed for attention with his well-known interest in foreign affairs. Most involved a degree of the boldness he thought necessary for a successful presidency. Most increased federal regulation of nondistributive public policies. Most were made possible in part because he was a wartime Republican president who took advantage of acting in the Disraeli tradition of enlightened conservatism. Most offended liberals (as well as many conservatives), especially when it came to implementing certain controversial policies with legislation. Many were also undertaken in a crisis atmosphere, which on occasion was manufactured by individual members of Nixon's staff to ensure his attention and action.

In some instances, as political scientist Paul J. Halpern has noted, Nixon's long-standing liberal opponents in Congress "never even bothered to get the facts straight" about these legislative and administrative innovations; the very people who, according to Daniel Moynihan, formed the "natural constituency" for most of Nixon's domestic policies refused to support his programs.[86] It may well have been that many liberals simply could not believe that Nixon would ever do the right thing except for the wrong reason. Thus they seldom took the time to try to determine whether any of his efforts to make the 1970s a decade of reform were legitimate, however politically motivated.[87] Additionally, such partisan opposition made Nixon all the more willing to reorganize the executive branch of government with or without congressional approval.

My own interviews with Nixon and his own (and others') recent attempts to rehabilitate his reputation indicate that Nixon thinks he will outlive the obloquy of Watergate because of his foreign policy initiatives—not because of his domestic policies.[88] Ultimately, however, domestic reform and his attempts at comprehensive reorganization of the executive branch may become the standard by which the Nixon presidency is judged.

Environmental Policy

Although Nixon's aides cite his environmental legislation as one of his major domestic achievements, it was not high on his personal list of federal priorities, despite polls showing its growing importance as a national issue.[89] White House central files released in 1986 clearly reveal that John Erhlichman was initially instrumental in shaping the president's views on enironmental matters and conveying a sense of crisis about them. Most ideas were filtered through him to Nixon. In fact Ehrlichman, whose particular expertise was in land-use policies, has been described by one forest conservation specialist as "the most effective environmentalist since Gifford Pinchot."[90] Ehrlichman and John Whitaker put Nixon ahead of Congress on environmental issues, especially with respect to his use of the permit authority in the Refuse Act of 1899 to begin to clean up water supplies before Congress passed any "comprehensive water pollution enforcement plan."[91]

"Just keep me out of trouble on environmental issues," Nixon reportedly told Ehrlichman.[92] This proved impossible because Congress ignored Nixon's recommended ceilings when it finally passed (over his veto) the Federal Water Pollution Control Act amendments of 1972. Both Ehrlichman and Whitaker agreed then and later that it was "budget-busting" legislation designed to embarrass the president on a popular issue in an election year. Statistics later showed that the money appropriated could not be spent fast enough to achieve the legislation's stated goals. The actual annual expenditures in the first years after passage approximated those originally proposed by Nixon's staff.[93]

Revamping Welfare

Throughout the 1968 presidential campaign Nixon's own views on welfare remained highly unfocused.[94] But once in the Oval Office he set an unexpectedly fast pace on the issue. On January 15, 1969, he demanded an investigation by top aides into a newspaper allegation of corruption in New York City's Human Resources Administration. Nixon's extraordinary welfare legislation originated in a very circuitous fashion with two low-level Democratic holdovers from the Johnson administration, Worth Bateman and James Lyday.

These two bureaucrats fortuitously exercised more influence on Robert Finch, Nixon's first secretary of health, education and welfare, than they had been able to on John W. Gardner and Wilbur J. Cohn, Johnson's two appointees. Finch was primarily responsible for obtaining Nixon's approval of what eventually became known as the Family Assistance Program (FAP).

If FAP had succeeded in Congress it would have changed the emphasis of American welfare from providing services to providing income; thus it would have replaced the Aid to Families with Dependent Children (AFOC) program, whose payments varied widely from state to state. FAP called for anywhere from $1,600 (initially proposed in 1969) to $2,500 (proposed in 1971) for a family of four. States were expected to supplement this amount, and in addition all able-bodied heads of recipient families (except mothers with preschool children) would be required to "accept work or training." However, if a parent refused to accept work or training, only his or her payment would be withheld. In essence, FAP unconditionally guaranteed children an annual income and would have tripled the number of children then being aided by AFDC.[95]

A fundamental switch from services to income payments proved to be too much for congressional liberals and conservatives alike, and they formed a strange alliance to vote it down. Ironically, FAP's final defeat in the Senate led to some very impressive examples of incremental legislation that might not have been passed had it not been for the original boldness of FAP. For example, Supplementary Security Income, approved on October 17, 1972, constituted a guaranteed annual income for the aged, blind, and disabled.[96]

The demise of FAP also led Nixon to support uniform application of the food stamp program across the United States, better health insurance programs for low-income families, and an automatic cost-of-living adjustment for Social Security recipients to help them cope with inflation. In every budget for which his administration was responsible—that is, from fiscal 1971 through fiscal 1975—spending on all human resource programs exceeded spending for defense for the first time since World War II. A sevenfold increase in funding for social services under Nixon made him (not Johnson) the "last of the big spenders" on domestic programs.[97]

Reluctant Civil Rights Achievements

Perhaps the domestic area in which Watergate has most dimmed or skewed our memories of the Nixon years is civil rights. We naturally tend to remember that during his presidency Nixon deliberately violated the civil rights of some of those who opposed his policies or were suspected of leaking information. Nixon has always correctly denied that he was a conservative on civil rights, and indeed his record on this issue, as on so many others, reveals as much political expediency as it does philosophical commitment. By 1968 there was strong southern support for his candidacy. Consequently, during his campaign he implied that if elected he would slow down enforcement of federal school desegregation policies.[98]

Enforcement had already been painfully sluggish since the 1954 *Brown v. Board of Education* decision. By 1968 only 20 percent of black children in the South attended predominantly white schools, and none of this progress had occurred under Eisenhower or Kennedy. Moreover, the most dramatic improvement under Johnson's administration did not take place until 1968, because HEW deadlines for desegregating southern schools had been postponed four times since the passage of the 1964 Civil Rights Act. By the spring of 1968, however, a few lower court rulings, and finally the Supreme Court decision in *Green v. Board of Education*, no longer allowed any president the luxury of arguing that freedom-of-choice plans were adequate for rooting out racial discrimination, or that de facto segregation caused by residential patterns was not as unconstitutional as *de jure* segregation brought about by state or local laws.[99]

Despite the real national crisis that existed over school desegregation, Nixon was not prepared to go beyond what he thought the decision in *Brown* had mandated, because he believed that de facto segregation could not be ended through busing or cutting off funds from school districts. Nine days after Nixon's inauguration, his administration had to decide whether to honor an HEW-initiated cutoff of funds to five southern school districts, originally scheduled to take place in the fall of 1968 but delayed until January 29, 1969. On that day Secretary Finch confirmed the cutoff but also announced that the school districts could claim funds retroactively if they complied with HEW guidelines within sixty days.[100] This offer represented a change from the most recent set of HEW guidelines, developed in March 1968, which Johnson had never formally endorsed by signing.

At the heart of the debate over various HEW guidelines in the last half of the 1960s were two issues: whether the intent of the Civil Rights Act of 1964 had been simply to provide freedom of choice or actually to compel integration in schools; and whether freedom-of-choice agreements negotiated by HEW or lawsuits brought by the Department of Justice were the most effective ways of achieving desegregation. Under the Johnson administration the HEW approach, based on bringing recalcitrant school districts into compliance by cutting off federal funding, had prevailed. Nixon, on the other hand, argued in his First Inaugural that the "laws have caught up with our consciences" and insisted that it was now necessary "to give life to what is in the law."[101] Accordingly, he changed the emphasis in the enforcement of school desegration from HEW compliance agreements to Justice Department actions—a legal procedure that proved very controversial in 1969 and 1970, but one that is standard now.[102]

Nixon has been justifiably criticized by civil rights advocates for employing delaying tactics in the South, and particularly for not endorsing busing to enforce school desegregation in the North after the April 20, 1971, Supreme Court decision in *Swann v. Charlotte-Mecklenburg Board of Education*.[103] Despite the bitter battle in Congress and between Congress and the executive branch after *Swann*, the Nixon administration's statistical record on school desegregation is impressive. In 1968, 68 percent of all black children in the South and 40 percent in the nation as a whole attended all-black schools. By the end of 1972, 8 percent of southern black children attended all-black schools, and a little less than 12 percent nationwide.[104] A comparison of budget outlays is equally revealing. President Nixon spent $911 million on civil rights activities, including $75 million for civil rights enforcement in fiscal 1969. The Nixon administration's budget for fiscal 1973 called for $2.6 billion in total civil rights outlays, of which $602 million was earmarked for enforcement through a substantially strengthened Equal Employment Opportunity Commission.[105] Nixon supported the civil rights goals of American Indians and women with less reluctance than he did school desegregation because these groups did not pose a major political problem for him and he had no similar legal reservations about how the law should be applied to them.

Mixing Economics and Politics

Nixon spent an inordinate amount of time on domestic and foreign economic matters. Nowhere did he appear to reverse himself more on views he had held before becoming president (or at least on views others attributed to him), and nowhere was his aprincipled pragmatism more evident. Nixon's failure to obtain more revenue through tax reform legislation in 1969, together with rising unemployment and inflation rates in 1970, precipitated an effort (in response to a perceived crisis) to balance U.S. domestic concerns through wage and price controls and international ones through devaluation of the dollar. This vehicle was the New Economic Policy, dramatically announced on August 15, 1971, at the end of a secret Camp David meeting with sixteen economic advisers. Largely as a result of Treasury Secretary Connally's influence, Nixon agreed that if foreign countries continued to demand ever-increasing amounts of gold for the U.S. dollars they held, the United States would go off the gold standard but would at the same time impose wage and price controls to curb inflation. The NEP perfectly reflected the "grand gesture" Connally thought the president should make on economic problems, and the August 15 television broadcast dramatized economic issues that most Americans, seldom anticipating long-range consequences, found boring.[106]

When he was not trying to preempt Congress on regulatory issues, Nixon proposed deregulation based on free-market assumptions that were more traditionally in keeping with conservative Republicanism. The administration ended the draft in the name of economic freedom and recommended deregulation of the production of food crops, tariff and other barriers to international trade, and interest rates paid by various financial institutions. Except for wage and price controls and the devaluation of the dollar, none of these actions was justified in the name of crisis management. In general, however, political considerations made Nixon more liberal on domestic economic matters, confounding both his supporters and his opponents.

Nixon attributes his interest in international economics to the encouragement of John Foster Dulles and his desire as vice-president in the 1950s to create a Foreign Economic Council. Failing in this, he has said that his travels abroad in the 1950s only confirmed his belief that foreign leaders understood economics better than did American leaders, and he was determined to remedy this situation as president. Nixon faced two obstacles in this effort: Kissinger (because "international economics was not Henry's bag"), and State Department officials who saw "economic policy as government to government," which limited their diplomatic view of the world and made them so suspicious or cynical (or both) about the private sector that they refused to promote international commerce to the degree that Nixon thought they should. "Unlike the ignoramuses I encountered among economic officers at various embassies in the 1950s and 1960s," Nixon told me, "I wanted to bring economics to the foreign service."[107]

Because of Nixon's own interest in and knowledge of international trade, he attempted as president to rationalize the formulation of foreign economic policy. After 1962, when he was out of public office and practicing law in New York, he had specialized in international economics and multinational corporations—definitely not Henry Kissinger's areas of expertise. In part because they were not a "team" on foreign economic policy and in part because Nixon bypassed the NSC almost entirely in formulating his New Economic Policy, Nixon relied not on his national security adviser but on other free-thinking outsiders when formulating foreign economic policy.

Next to John Connally, Nixon was most impressed with the economic views of Peter G. Peterson, who, after starting out in 1971 as a White House adviser on international economic affairs, became secretary of commerce in January 1972. Although Connally and Peterson appeared to agree on such early foreign economic initiatives as the NEP and the "get tough" policy toward Third World countries that nationalized U.S. companies abroad, as secretary of commerce Peterson ultimately proved much more sophisticated and sensitive than the secretary of the treasury about the United States' changed economic role in the world. In a December 27, 1971, position paper defending Nixon's NEP, Peterson remarked that the new global situation in which the United States found itself demanded "shared leadership, shared responsibility, and shared burdens . . . The reform of the international monetary systems." he said, must fully recognize and be solidly rooted in "the growing reality of a genuinely interdependent and increasingly competitive world economy whose goal is mutual, shared prosperity—not artificial, temporary advantage." At no point did Peterson believe, as Connally apparently did, that "the simple realignment of exchange rates" would adequately address the economic realignment problems facing the international economy.[108]

In 1971 Nixon succeeded in establishing an entirely new cabinet-level Council on International Economic Policy (CIEP), headed by Peterson. This was not so much a reorganization of functions as it was an alternative to fill an existing void in the federal structure and to provide "clear top-level focus on international economic issues and to achieve consistency between international and domestic economic policy."[109] For a variety of reasons—not the least of which was Kissinger's general lack of interest in, and disdain for, the unglamorous aspects of international economics—the CIEP faltered and finally failed after Nixon left office. Its demise seems to have been hastened by Kissinger's recommendation to the Congressional Commission on Organization of Foreign Policy that it be eliminated, despite the fact that others, including Peterson, testified on its behalf. The CIEP was subsequently merged with the Office of the Special Trade Representative.[110]

Even with Nixon's impressive foreign and domestic record, it cannot be said that he would have succeeded as a managerial or administrative president had Watergate not occurred. Entrenched federal bureaucracies are not easily controlled or divested of power even with the best policy-oriented management strategies. That his foreign policy management seems more successful is also no surprise: diplomatic bureaucracies are smaller, more responsive, and easier to control than their domestic counterparts. Moreover, public concern (except for Vietnam) remained minimal as usual, and individual presidential foreign policy initiatives are more likely to be remembered and to appear effective than domestic ones. Nonetheless, the real importance of Nixon's presidency may well come to rest not on Watergate or foreign policy, but on his attempts to restructure the executive branch along functional lines, to bring order to the federal bureaucracy, and to achieve lasting domestic reform. The degree to which those Nixonian administrative tactics that were legal and ethical (and most of them were) became consciously or unconsciously the model for his successors in the Oval Office will determine his final place in history.

Although Nixon's corporate presidency remains publicly discredited, much of it has been privately preserved. Perhaps this is an indication that in exceptional cases presidential effectiveness can transcend popular (and scholarly) disapproval.[111] What Nixon lacked in charisma and honesty, he may in the long run make up for with his phoenixlike ability to survive disaster. Nixon has repeatedly said: "No politician is dead until he admits it."[112] It is perhaps an ironic commentary on the state of the modern presidency that Richard Nixon's management style and substantive foreign and domestic achievements look better and better when compared with those of his immediate successors in the Oval Office.

7

GERALD R. FORD

A Healing Presidency

Roger B. Porter

Gerald R. Ford was in many respects a unique president. He was unelected as either vice-president or president. Never before had a vice-president succeeded to the presidency on the resignation of his predecessor. Ford had never even run for national or statewide office; his electoral constituency was confined to the Fifth District of Michigan.

Most vice-presidents who have succeeded to the presidency have had strong incentives to continue both the policies and personnel of their predecessor. Gerald Ford, though a remarkably loyal vice-president, particularly given the circumstances of his brief tenure and the Watergate scandal that had engulfed the Nixon presidency, maintained a discreet distance between himself and the White House.

Ford entered the Oval Office when the political fabric of the country was frayed, respect for the institution of the presidency greatly diminished, and the nation's economy and foreign relations in disarray. From May through July 1974 the wholesale price index (the equivalent of today's producer price index) rose at an annual rate of 37 percent. The unemployment rate, though below 6 percent, was also rising. In general the economy suffered from what economists had come to call stagflation.

In reflecting on that period, Henry Kissinger recalls the "hysterical summer of 1974":

I have never doubted that history will rate Richard M. Nixon as an important President. But that was not the mood when

Gerald Ford took over. The Presidency was in a shambles. The last cabinet meeting of the Nixon Administration had ended in as close to open rebellion as the American system of government can produce. The balance between the Executive and Legislative branches was shifting dramatically to a point where the basic authority of the Presidency was in question. Foreign policy, which depends crucially on Presidential authority and national consensus, had to be conducted against the permanent risk of catastrophe.[1]

Ford's situation as vice-president, with a president claiming his innocence and steadfastly resisting impeachment or resignation, precluded much planning or even discussion of how he would manage the presidency if he were to succeed to the office. As a result, the circumstances in which the presidency was thrust upon him were probably as difficult as those facing Abraham Lincoln and Franklin Roosevelt.

A president's leadership has many dimensions. This chapter concentrates on two aspects of Gerald Ford's leadership that affect every presidency. The first is his handling of the transition to the Oval Office, his use of symbolic actions to shape perceptions and influence expectations. Every president's initial steps are important in establishing a climate and environment for the course of an administration. First perceptions are often lasting. During the transition to power, many discover the importance of seemingly small and simple things. The second aspect is Ford's organization of his administration's internal policy development processes, with particular emphasis on his decision-making habits and style.

Transition and Leadership

The principal transition problem facing Gerald Ford in August 1974 was different from that of a newly elected president. He had no electoral mandate to point to or campaign promises to keep. He was free from the debts normally accumulated by successful candidates. His central task was to achieve a balance between two competing demands: the need to provide stability and to hasten recovery from the wrenching events of the previous year and a half; and the need to differentiate, to distance, to strike a new path, and to provide a new beginning. How he went about putting his own stamp on the presidency would prove crucial and revealing.

Establishing a New Team

Although Ford may well have anticipated for months that the president might not complete his term, and thus that he would succeed him, he could hardly have foreseen the rush of events in early August that culminated in Richard Nixon's resignation speech to the nation on Thursday evening, August 8, 1974. Unknown to him, his close friend and former law partner, Philip Buchen, at the time a member of his vice-presidential staff, had given some preliminary thought to a transition. On Friday morning, Buchen and former congressman John Byrnes reviewed with Ford a four-page document that among other things laid out the difficulty of his task: "You must walk a delicate line between compassion and consideration for the former President's staff and the rapid assertion of your personal control over the executive branch."[2]

That day, Ford publicly announced a four-member transition team: Donald Rumsfeld, U.S. ambassador to NATO; former Pennsylvania governor William Scranton; Secretary of the Interior Rogers Morton; and Jack Marsh, a senior aide on his vice-presidential staff.[3] All had served with him in the House of Representatives and were individuals whose advice he had consistently sought and trusted. Wishing to avoid the potential for a dual-track system and a de facto "second White House," the transition team worked quickly. Its members met with the cabinet department and agency heads and others to gather sentiment about how Ford should organize his White House. The team's formal report to the president, completed within two weeks, emphasized the need to elevate the roles of department and ageny officials and to reduce the perceived dominant role of the White House staff. Although they avoided recommending specific personnel changes, members of the transition team and others offered Ford much informal advice on this crucial topic. Some urged him to clean house and quickly demonstrate that a new team was in place in key foreign and domestic policy positions. Others were less insistent on sweeping changes and emphasized the value of continuity. The advice on one matter, however, was remarkably uniform: Ford must establish a presidency distinctive from that of his predecessor. Quick action was politically preferable.

In perhaps the most crucial area of the transition, personnel, Ford placed a high priority on continuity and stability. As early as August 21, Ford signaled his intention to seek election to a full term,[4] but he made personnel changes gradually, accommodating the interests and careers of the people involved. By December he was able to claim that a new White House team and a new cabinet were essentially in place.[5] Ford adopted this incrementalist approach in part because of the people involved and his concern for their careers, but also because it was consistent with his objective of a healing presidency.

Although most people elsewhere in the country were oblivious to this drama, many in the Washington community were aware of the tension that had existed during the last months of the Nixon administration between the White House staff and the vice-president's staff. The strong feelings intensified as Nixon's position deteriorated. Ford recalls: "There was also conflict between our respective staffs. The middle-echelon people who worked under Haig seemed to resent the fact that I had gone through the confirmation process so easily, and they were determined to make life as difficult as possible for me and my assistants. We had trouble securing office space in the EOB [Old Executive Office Building], procuring desks and furniture and hiring sufficient staff . . . the atmosphere became ugly indeed."[6]

Once Ford became president he sought to smooth relations between the two staffs but was faced with open friction between his own former vice-presidential chief of staff, Robert Hartmann, and Nixon's White House chief of staff, Alexander Haig. Ultimately, although Ford was fond of Haig and considered him absolutely loyal, he recognized that it was time for Haig to move on, largely because he possessed a "Nixon image." Without a change at the top of the White House staff, it would be impossible to create a new beginning for his administration.[7] Nevertheless, Ford effected the transition of Haig to his next assignment as NATO commander, and of other White House staff to their next jobs, as gracefully as possible:

> Although I wanted people to perceive that there was a big difference between the Nixon and Ford Administrations, I didn't think that a Stalin-like purge was the way to go about it. Besides, there were people on the White House staff who had nothing to do with Watergate. For me to have fired them all would have tarred them with the Nixon brush. If I kept them on for a while, they could return to private life and be identified with the new President. That was the only fair thing to do, so I made the decision to proceed gradually. Some of the people I didn't want on the White House staff had already left of their

own accord. The others, I told Haig, would have to be gone by January 1.[8]

He used a similar incrementalist approach in making changes in his cabinet. Within months, seven of the eleven cabinet departments had a new secretary. Not only did these changes occur gradually, but the people Ford selected for his cabinet were chosen principally for their competence and independence. Given Ford's twenty-five years of service in the House of Representatives, it is striking that he did not fill more of these senior administration posts with other political officials.

The two reservoirs from which he drew were academia and law. His first cabinet appointment, replacing former senator William Saxbe as attorney general, was Edward H. Levi, former dean of the University of Chicago Law School and at the time president of the university. His choice for Secretary of Health, Education and Welfare was David Mathews, a registered Democrat and president of the University of Alabama. John T. Dunlop, Lamont University Professor at Harvard University and former dean of Harvard's Faculty of Arts and Sciences, was his choice for secretary of labor. All had solid reputations in the academic world and considerable administrative experience. None was considered partisan.

From the legal profession, he chose Carla A. Hills as secretary of housing and urban development, William T. Coleman, Jr., as secretary of transportation, and Elliot Richardson as secretary of commerce. Although all three of these departments are known to have strong constituencies, each of Ford's choices was a consequence not of constituency ties but of his conviction that they would be independent, able administrators. Of the three, only Elliot Richardson had run for public office. But it was Richardson's record as the secretary of three other cabinet departments that recommended him to Ford. Ford retained Henry Kissinger at State, William Simon at Treasury, Earl Butz at Agriculture, and, for over a year, James Schlesinger at Defense. At Interior, he appointed former Wyoming governor Stan Hathaway, who resigned soon thereafter for health reasons. Hathaway was replaced by Thomas Kleppe, a two-term former congressman who for the previous four and a half years had served as the head of the Small Business Administration. Ford recalls that his nomination of Carla Hills "caused an immediate howl of protest from the interest groups over which HUD had jurisdiction. They complained about Carla's lack of expertise in the industry and urged

me to select a realtor, home builder, or city planner. I saw her lack
of expertise as a plus. It was far better to pick someone from the
outside who would assimilate the necessary information and then
decide the issues on their merits."⁹

Two qualities above all others drove Ford's selections of White
House staff and senior administration officials: competence and
compatibility. In describing his approach to his personnel decisions,
Ford observed: "Mr. Nixon had a number of very competent people.
There was no need for me to just throw people out across the board.
I gradually made my own selections of people who fitted my style.
Rumsfeld for Schlesinger was probably the best example."¹⁰

Ford's style—patient, deliberative, measured—was influenced by
his sense of comfortableness. It was lack of comfortableness that
prompted his most highly publicized personnel changes in late October 1975, the so-called Halloween Massacre. The central figure in
this chain of personnel changes was Secretary of Defense James
Schlesinger.

From his first days in the Oval Office, if not before, Ford was wary
of Schlesinger. Events associated with the last days of the Nixon
administration caused him to question Schlesinger's integrity:

> In the full wake of Nixon's resignation, the newspapers were
> full of bizarre stories about his conduct in the final days. Some
> of them indicated that Schlesinger was so concerned about Nix-
> on's mental stability that he had taken steps to make sure that
> the President couldn't give orders to the Armed Services uni-
> laterally. The story made me furious because I was assured no
> such measures had been taken. I talked to Haig about it, and
> we concluded that it had been leaked deliberately from the
> highest level of the Pentagon. That made me madder still. Haig
> was present when Schlesinger walked into the Oval Office.
> "Jim," I said, "I'm damn disturbed by these rumors about what
> was done in the Pentagon during the last days of the Nixon
> Administration. Obviously, they come from the top, and I want
> the situation straightened out right away." Schlesinger didn't
> admit that he had been the source of the leak, but the significant
> thing was that the leaks did stop, at least for a while. As Pres-
> ident, that was the first run-in I had with Schlesinger. I hoped
> it would be the last, but I suspected otherwise.¹¹

During the next year Ford included Schlesinger in the deliberations
on many key foreign policy decisions and often took his advice.¹²

Although Ford often rejected Schlesinger's recommendations, it was comfortableness rather than policy differences that drove Ford's dismissal of Schlesinger.

> There were still some six thousand Americans in and around Saigon, and in that first week of April, Defense Secretary Schlesinger asked me to start evacuating them immediately. He repeated his request almost daily. Kissinger and I opposed so precipitous a withdrawal. (Later, I learned that Schlesinger had ordered the flight of empty or near-empty planes in and out of Saigon—just to establish for the record, I suspected, that it would not be his fault if we failed to remove all our people.)[13]

Perhaps two factors more than any others played a prominent role in Ford's decision to replace his secretary of defense. One was Schlesinger's style in meetings. Repeatedly, it conveyed aloofness, detachment, and an air of intellectual superiority. Not least, it clashed consistently with the style of his secretary of state. Policy differences were not only tolerated but accepted as normal. Friction stemming from personality characteristics was not welcome.

Second was the matter of independence. Ford valued team players. He liked collegiality. Though rarely immersing himself in all the details of implementing a decision, he was far from a detached decision maker. He liked to feel, and to be, involved in shaping his administration's policies. Moreover, Ford had a special interest in defense matters stemming from his long experience as a member of the Armed Services Subcommittee of the House Appropriations Committee. But Schlesinger rarely consulted with Ford on what Schlesinger considered to be Department of Defense issues (in sharp contrast to his successor, Donald Rumsfeld).

Many have speculated about what or who precipitated the changes announced on November 3, 1975.[14] Ford's desire for a change at Defense was the catalyst.

> All these changes were my ideas; nobody came up with them other than myself. I had decided that we wanted to make the change in Defense. I wanted my own man over there in place of Jim Schlesinger. And there was no one closer to me who could do the job than Don Rumsfeld. That was a perfect switch. And I felt secure because I could move Dick Cheney up . . . with [his] twelve to eighteen months of experience to be chief of staff.

Schlesinger and Kissinger never got along. I was never comfortable [with] their never-ending tension . . . And that continuing argument between the two was not constructive, because
there were undertones that disrupted. The only way for me to
get rid of that was to make a change; and I obviously had more
confidence in Kissinger than I did in Schlesinger.[15]

Despite the nearness of the primary campaign for the 1976 Republican nomination, Ford consciously eschewed politically motivated considerations in his selection of senior members of his
administration. In his quest for competent people with whom he
felt comfortable and who would function as a team, he could not
bring to bear the unifying element of having fought a successful
campaign or the personal obligations normally associated with such
an effort. Instead, he reached out well beyond the world he knew
best as a twenty-five-year veteran of the House of Representatives
to try to reassure the country about the institution of the presidency.

Accentuating the Positive

While Ford sought to reassure the country through continuity and
stability he also undertook a series of specific actions to emphasize
the positive aspects of his approach to the presidency. He let actions
rather than rhetoric remind the nation of the differences between
him and his predecessor; others could—and would—articulate the
difference.

The day he learned he would become president, Ford told his
friend Senate Minority Leader Hugh Scott that "accessibility and
openness" would be hallmarks of his administration.[16] Three days
later, Ford held a reception for the members of his former vice-
presidential staff. The staff had their pictures taken with the President and Mrs. Ford and then were invited to go upstairs and tour
the family living quarters, an invitation unprecedented in the previous administration.

Many of the trappings of the so-called Imperial Presidency were
removed. For certain occasions the Marine Band was instructed to
replace "Hail to the Chief" or "Ruffles and Flourishes" with the
Michigan fight song. Within days the number of White House staff
on the A Transportation List, providing officials with portal-to-
portal service, was reduced from 26 to 13. Within weeks the size of
the White House staff was reduced by 10 percent, from 540 to 485.

Ford directed Haig "to make sure that the Oval Office was swept clean of all electronic listening devices."[17]

There were many cosmetic changes. Of the portraits in the Cabinet Room, Eisenhower was retained, but Theodore Roosevelt and Woodrow Wilson were replaced with Abraham Lincoln and Harry Truman.[18] The living quarters in the White House were referred to as "the residence" rather than as "the Mansion." The name of the president's plane was restored to Air Force One.[19] After being sworn in, the new president went to the White House Press Room to introduce his new press secretary, Gerald TerHorst. Taken individually, the changes were modest. Viewed in the aggregate, they demonstrated to a symbol-conscious Washington the reality of a new openness.

After three days in office Ford declared to a joint session of Congress that "inflation is domestic enemy number one" and accepted the recommendation of Senate Resolution 363 for a White House summit conference on the economy. The Conference on Inflation included a series of preparatory meetings dealing with specific sectors of the economy, held at various locations around the country.[20] Ford attended the preparatory sessions in Washington with labor leaders and a bipartisan group of economists; he also attended most of the two-day final conference.

Ford sought to demonstrate his openness through numerous meetings with groups of governors, mayors, and county officials. He held a long meeting with AFL-CIO president George Meany; invited Jesse Jackson, Vernon Jordan, and other black leaders to a Cabinet Room meeting; discussed the Equal Rights Amendment with thirteen congresswomen; and met with the Congressional Black Caucus. The White House Office of Public Liaison invited the leaders and representatives of scores of groups and associations to the White House for meetings with senior White House officials, both to explain administration policies and to hear their concerns. There was a sustained effort to replace the image of an isolated and insulated White House with the image of a White House with its doors open.

Symbolic actions and shifts in style and tone were accompanied by shifts in policy. Perhaps more than any other event, the Vietnam war had divided the country and affected the relationship between young Americans and their government. Ford determined to try to heal the wounds even before U.S. involvement was ended. Within days of taking office, Secretary of Defense Schlesinger suggested moving to deal with 50,000 draft evaders and deserters from the

Vietnam war. Ford consulted a few friends and advisers—his three
sons, former secretary of defense Melvin Laird, Robert Hartmann,
Jack Marsh, Philip Buchen, and Alexander Haig. He settled on a
conditional approach in which the draft evaders and deserters could
"earn" amnesty. Marsh, whom Ford trusted with the most delicate
assignments, was instructed to work with the Departments of Justice and Defense and the Veterans Administration to refine the proposal.

Ford moved quickly and announced the program on August 19
before the most challenging of audiences, the seventy-fifth annual
convention of the Veterans of Foreign Wars in Chicago. This decision
was not preceded by full or elaborate deliberations. His decision
appears to have been driven not only by compassion but also by its
symbolic value in helping to put the recent past behind the nation.[21]

Ford's second dramatic and symbolic act was his full and uncon-
ditional pardon of Richard Nixon on September 8. Because of the
sensitivity of the issue, he consulted only his closest advisers—
Kissinger, Haig, Buchen, Hartmann, and Marsh.

Ford seems to have been motivated partly by a desire to accelerate
final resolution of the Watergate issue, which he was informed could
remain in the courts for months or even years. But perhaps equally
powerful was his desire to dispose of the issue of Nixon's fate, which
consumed the major share of attention at his early press conferences.
He spent countless hours dealing with the legal questions surrounding the disposition of the Nixon tapes and papers. The strain imposed
by this issue, added to the urgency of the nation's economic problems, probably influenced both the timing and content of the pardon.
In his memoir Ford describes his feelings after signing the proclamation: "Finally it was done. It was an unbelievable lifting of a
burden from my shoulders. I felt certain that I had made the right
decision, and I was confident that I could now proceed without being
harassed by Nixon or his problems any more. I thought I could
concentrate 100 percent of my time on the overwhelming problems
that faced both me and the country."[22] However, whether from too
circumscribed a decision-making process, a misreading of public
sentiment, or wishful thinking, Ford "had failed to anticipate . . . the
vehemence of the hostile reaction to my decision."[23] The pardon
put an end to the nation's honeymoon with its new chief executive.
Ford's popularity in the public opinion polls plummeted from a
favorable rating of 71 percent to 49 percent. For many Americans,

this single act overwhelmed the aura of openness, accessibility, and candor that he had so successfully begun to establish.

Even this selective survey of Ford's symbolic actions during the first months of his administration reveals how important symbols are to a presidency. They help set the tone and shape the environment that condition the parameters within which the president can move to shape opinion and policy. After much reflection over many years, and despite acknowledging the likelihood that his pardon of Nixon severely damaged his prospects for election in 1976, Ford remains convinced that it was the right decision for the country, and for him. He feels the same way about his decision to move gradually and incrementally on personnel changes, contrary to the urging of some of his closest advisers to make a clear break with his predecessor's administration.

Ford's actions on some issues and inaction on others can perhaps best be explained by his overriding desire to convey to the nation a sense that he approached "things in a sensible and pragmatic way." Above all, he sought to cool "the passions of the times" and to keep "a steady, firm, and consistent course."[24]

Organization and Style

White House Organization

Understandably, Ford was somewhat wary, at least initially, of the notion of a White House chief of staff. An open White House and an accessible president were major imperatives in his quest to restore the presidency. A chief of staff might, as in the case of Richard Nixon, be used as an intermediary or filter between the president and others. Ford viewed Nixon as someone who "abhorred details, and rather enjoyed pushing them off on subordinates. And that, it seemed to me, was one of the several reasons he had come to this point of having to resign."[25]

The first transition memorandum from Philip Buchen and John Byrnes, which Ford reviewed and approved the morning of August 9, stated: "We share your view that there should be no Chief of Staff, especially at the outset. However, there should be someone who could rapidly and efficiently organize the new staff organization, but who will not be perceived [as being] nor be eager to be Chief of Staff."[26]

During his first weeks in office Ford "was determined to be my own chief of staff."[27] He recalls that his transition team concurred with his "spokes of the wheel" approach, which permitted several senior White House aides independent and virtually unrestricted access to him. The principal virtue of the spokes-of-the-wheel concept is that it projected an aura of openness and accessibility, a perception that was essential to Ford's desire to establish the distinctive characteristics of his administration. Moreover, it also emphasized the president's personal role in assuming control of the executive branch.

The spokes-of-the-wheel experiment, however, was short-lived and only partially implemented. On the afternoon of August 9, shortly after the swearing in ceremony, Robert Hartmann, Ford's vice-presidential chief of staff, moved himself into the office adjacent to the Oval Office formerly occupied by Nixon's personal secretary, Rosemary Woods. A short passageway and door connected the two offices, providing Hartmann with virtually unrestricted access to the president, a source of unending irritation to Alexander Haig.

Initially, Haig continued to operate as chief of staff in somewhat the same way he had for Nixon, seeing the president at the beginning and end of each day, overseeing the scheduling of the president's time and the flow of paper to him, and chairing the morning White House senior staff meeting. Throughout these early weeks, however, Hartmann, Marsh, Buchen, and others had much greater access to the president than had existed during the Nixon-Haig era.

Within a month Ford, though convinced of Haig's competence and loyalty, recognized the necessity for him to move on, in part to signal unmistakably that this was a new administration. On September 21 he called Donald Rumsfeld, who had flown from Brussels to Illinois to attend his father's funeral. The following day, a Sunday afternoon, they discussed White House organization for an hour and a half in the Oval Office.[28]

The president persuaded Rumsfeld to join the White House Staff as assistant to the president, but only after agreeing that the spokes-of-the-wheel concept required a substantial modification. Although a select number of senior White House aides would continue to have direct access to the president, Rumsfeld would be "first among equals" and have responsibility for coordinating their activities.

In December the White House released an organization chart. It showed nine individuals with a direct reporting relationship to the president. Four had responsibility for policy areas: James Lynn (assistant to the president for management and budget), Henry Kissinger (assistant to the president for national security), William Seidman (assistant to the president for economic affairs), and James Cannon (assistant to the president for domestic affairs). Four had responsibility for major functions within the White House: Philip Buchen (counsel to the president), Ronald Nessen (press secretary to the president), Jack Marsh (counselor to the president), and Robert Hartmann (counselor to the president). Legislative affairs and public liaison reported through Marsh, speechwriting and research through Hartmann. The ninth person on the chart with a reporting relationship to the president, identified as coordinator, was Donald Rumsfeld. Rumsfeld, Buchen, Marsh, and Hartmann were given cabinet rank. Kissinger and Lynn also had cabinet rank in their positions as secretary of state and director of the Office of Management and Budget.

Reporting through Rumsfeld as White House coordinator were the three principal conduits of control in the White House: the Scheduling Office, the Staff Secretary's Office (controlling the flow of paper to the president), and the Personnel Office. Although Rumsfeld operated as de facto chief of staff from the outset, he did not formally assume the title, largely for symbolic purposes. Throughout its existence, the Ford administration retained its emphasis on a nonimperial White House.

If there was a single book that most influenced Ford's thinking about the kind of White House he wanted, it was George Reedy's grim and pessimistic monograph, *The Twilight of the Presidency.* Ford drew two main lessons from Reedy's depressing account, which was based in large part on his experiences in Lyndon Johnson's White House. The first lesson was that the president must take care to avoid being isolated and losing touch with the rest of the government and with the country. The second was that the president must steer clear of aides whose principal interest lies in advancing their own position, who behave as courtiers, and who would resist confronting the president with unpleasant realities. Reedy was particularly unenthusiastic about placing the young and the untested in positions of influence in the White House.

Ford never made age a criterion for appointment, but although he provided many opportunities and much encouragement for the youngest members of his staff, the average age of his senior White House aides was higher than that of any administration since Eisenhower.

Ford did not want to be isolated, but he had little interest in personally managing his staff. He later reflected:

I believe a president has to have a chief of staff who is an expert manager and one who does not seek on his own a high identity—in fact, one who purposely avoids that. That individual has to coordinate everything that transpires in the West Wing of the White House and the Oval Office. At the same time, he must keep responsible contact and relationships with the cabinet officers, commission heads, etc. If you don't have that kind of person, I don't think the president's job can be well done.

A president, himself, cannot look into the day-to-day management of the West Wing of the White House or the Oval Office. He cannot—because there isn't time—have all of the relationships and contacts with departments, agencies, and commissions. So, the president, if he has that kind of a manager, then can have sufficient time to analyze issues and to decide how his leadership should be projected to the public. He's free from the minutiae.[29]

Indeed, the quality Ford seemed most attracted to in his chief of staff was efficiency. He was not looking for an alter ego or a super confidant. He wanted an "expert manager."[30]

White House–Departmental Relations

Ford accepted the prevailing conventional wisdom that a powerful and overbearing White House staff had contributed heavily to the difficulties of the Nixon administration. This perspective formed the basis for his view of the most appropriate relationship of his White House staff and department and agency heads:

In the Nixon years, the Cabinet departments and agencies had lost power and influence to such White House appendages as the Domestic Council, the Office of Management and Budget, and the Council on International Economic Policy. That tended to destroy one of the foundations of our form of government. A Watergate was made possible by a strong chief of staff and ambitious White House aides who were more powerful than members of the Cabinet but who had little or no practical political experience or judgment. I wanted to reverse the trend and restore authority to my Cabinet. White House aides with authority are necessary, but I didn't think they had the right to browbeat the departments and agencies. Nor did they have the right to make policy decisions. I decided to give my Cabinet members a lot more control.[31]

The flow of power and influence between the White House and Executive Office staffs and departments and agencies changes over the course of any administration along with shifts in personalities and policy imperatives. How much more control departmental officials in the Ford administration had than their counterparts in the Nixon administration is difficult to determine with precision. What is clear is that Ford created a new environment for White House–departmental relations and that his cabinet officers felt much more involved in his policy development processes. Ford recognized that departmental tugs and ties are inevitable for any departmental official:

The members of my cabinet had views on what their department ought to project, but I don't think they were so enthusiastic or such strong zealots that they undercut the presidency. We had people in the cabinet who, in a policy decision process, would take a position and argue it very strongly. But if my decision was contrary, those cabinet officers who had opposed my decision would not go out and be advocates contrary to the president's point of view. Bill Simon, on more than one occasion, argued for a different point of view, and then when I made a decision that was opposite, still didn't go out and undercut my position.[32]

Ford's view of cabinet officers as able administrators and presidential advisers, operating comfortably in both roles, conditioned his selections. "After we made those very basic changes, I assembled the kind of cabinet, the kind of management, that I would institute if I were starting fresh today . . . the . . . cabinet we had . . . was diverse, loyal, knowledgeable, articulate."[33]

Decision-Making Style

Ford's quarter-century of experience in Congress contributed to his placing a high value on collecting and weighing the opinions and advice of "experts." He referred to his White House chief of staff as an expert manager. In announcing a shift in his economic policy to the Business Council on December 11, 1974, he declared: "I intend to keep my experts working over the holidays, translating into specifics a number of new or alternative measures to augment and update the economic package that I will place before the Congress within the next two months."[34] And in characterizing his presidential leadership style, he began with the concept of assembling experts:

> My style was assembling the best possible experts in their designated fields [so that] the president [would get] the finest advice and counsel. If a president has that kind of advice, the odds are that he'll make a good decision, and good decisions make good leadership. Leadership, in my opinion, is based on results. If you have the right kind of people giving you advice, the odds are that you'll make good decisions. If you make good decisions, you'll get results. And leadership is the product of results.[35]

Ford's other formative experience was his legal training. His own description of his "rules" for decision making reflect this approach:

> They were: (1) have no special confidants within the Cabinet; (2) listen, don't confide; (3) don't get involved in any jurisdictional rivalries; (4) have confidants outside the Cabinet from whom advice can be solicited; (5) don't get mired down in detail— handle the broad policy decisions and leave management and program implementation to the department heads; (6) move aggressively on all fronts toward resolution and decision; (7) look at all proposals as if you're going to have to be the advocate who sells them to the public at large; and (8) finally, encourage dissent before a final decision is made.[36]

Ford applied these rules with remarkable consistency. The format for his policy-making meetings remained constant. He would call on the official with primary responsibility for the issue to begin the discussion. After this initial presentation, he would call on others for their views until all who wished to speak had explained their positions. Frequently an individual's presentation would be punctuated by questions or comments from the president or other participants. Ford then generally asked a series of questions distilled from reading the paper he would have received the day before and from listening to the discussion. Sometimes the questions sought to clarify his understanding of an alternative or an argument. Sometimes he fashioned a new alternative and asked for his adviser's reaction to it. Broad participation characterized the meetings; rarely did a single person or viewpoint dominate the discussion. As Ford exlained his style:

> In the main, I believed that in an NSC meeting or an Economic Policy Board meeting, those who felt strongly should state their positions, and they would oftentimes be different. I enjoyed that kind of exchange because it broadened my knowledge; it helped me refine the issue. To me, that is the proper way for a president to get the full benefit of bright, dedicated people. I like that kind of free exchange within an administration . . . I would seldom make a decision right there.
>
> After the meeting was over, I would either take the option papers that were presented and look them over in the quiet of the Oval Office or would take some notes I might have made as the debate went on. On some occasions I would maybe talk to Don Rumsfeld, when he was my chief of staff, or Dick Cheney, when he was the chief of staff. But in the main, it would be a decision process that I would almost exclusively do by myself.[37]

This combination of a written report and a meeting provided Ford with both the discipline of tightly drafted memorandums and the nuances conveyed in spirited discussions.

Most presidents receive the kind of advice they seek. The pattern of advice to a president is extraordinarily responsive to the signals he sends about what he would like. As president, Ford got essentially what he wanted because of the climate he created. One senior adviser described Ford's style of decision making:

> He knows how to listen to Simon or Usery . . . how to get from them what he needs to know. I have seen him change his mind during the course of a meeting, but he rarely revealed which way he was leaning.
>
> I think he is the kind of person who plays a good poker hand . . . He consciously, I think, goes in with what seems to be an open mind. You can't guess what he wants—that's good. It not only encourages debate, but it encourages people to be prepared with factual arguments. He welcomes these differing points of view. I don't know of anybody whom I feel more comfortable disagreeing with . . . He wants to have a range of viewpoints. It is my judgment that it would offend him if he

thought you were trying to guess what he wanted. He doesn't like yes men.[38]

The tone in these meetings did not constrain those who disagreed with a dominant view, at least in terms of their relationship with the president. According to one senior White House staffer:

The combination of the meetings, the paper flow and the President's style, his willingness to listen to debates and arguments and never to reduce an individual's access because he had disagreed with him on his last decision, really made the system function fairly smoothly . . . you were always free to argue and debate and take the other side, sometimes to disagree very strongly, and he would make his decision and you were perfectly free to go back in two hours later and do it all over again on some other issue if you felt strongly about it. And his personality was such that that never seemed to bother him. He never let disagreements over policy or arguments in any way lead him to change the degree of access that a particular individual had to him.[39]

Finally, Ford periodically reached outside his circle of proximate advisers. His "kitchen cabinet" was a diverse group of invariably candid yet constructive old friends, most of whom had served on Ford's transition team. They included Bryce Harlow, Melvin Laird, William Scranton, John Byrnes, David Packard, and William Whyte. Sometimes they would meet alone with the president; sometimes they were joined by a small group of White House aides: Donald Rumsfeld, Jack Marsh, Robert Hartmann, Richard Cheney, Rogers Morton, and William Seidman. Ford's meetings with his kitchen cabinet evey six to eight weeks provided him with a reality check on specific policy proposals under consideration within his administration as well as with a sense of the mood of the country as seen from outside Washington.

Ford also created the President's Labor-Management Committee, composed of eight senior business leaders and eight labor leaders, with John T. Dunlop as its coordinator. He regularly sought their advice on a broad range of economic policy issues and received their support for many of his policy initiatives. Ford subsequently recruited Dunlop to join his administration full time as secretary of labor.[40]

Gerald Ford's congressional experience significantly shaped his decision-making style and habits. His reaching for "experts," his patience in listening to competing arguments and asking probing questions, his interest in a broad array of subjects, and his interest in testing how his decision would play outside the White House and in Congress reflected the experience he had accumulated for a quarter of a century in the House of Representatives.

Executive Branch Policy Development

Policy Development Models

It is commonplace to observe that presidents employ different styles in the ways they gather information, organize their staff and advice, and seek to provide initiative, energy, and direction to their administration. Some scholars have sought to develop various categories for presidential character and presidential styles.

The implication usually is that individual presidents can be classified by a single character type or style. Such characterizations tend to simplify but obscure two important features or differences in a president's approach to making decisions. First, it is possible, even probable, that a president's decision-making approach will evolve over time. Sometimes these changes are modest and almost imperceptible; other times the changes are striking. Second, a president may employ multiple approaches simultaneously in different policy areas. Rather than indicate uncertainty or confusion, a pattern of varying approaches may reflect an effort to match a decision-making approach with three crucial factors: his level of interest in the policy area; the strengths, limitations, and personalities of his principal advisers in the policy area; and the particular policy priorities, needs, and objectives at the time.

There is an almost infinite variety of approaches that presidents have used in developing policies. Three of the more frequently employed models are adhocracy, centralized management, and multiple advocacy.[41]

Adhocracy shapes policy primarily on a case-by-case basis. As an issue emerges or a problem is identified, an official or group of officials is given responsibility for managing it and advising the president. Task forces or working groups may be created to help develop and assess alternatives. When the issue is resolved, the groups which have been brought together to deal with the problem are disbanded. Adhocracy can involve thorough staff work and analysis or relatively little of it. What it lacks is a stable set of officials who are collectively responsible for a broad policy area over time.

Centralized management concentrates responsibility for policy development among a few people, usually with heavy reliance on relatively large and influential staff resources in the Executive Office of the president. It may involve delegating much authority to one person or relying primarily on one or a very few officials for advice in shaping policy over a broad area. A variant of this model is delegating primary responsibility for issues or problems in a particular area to a "policy czar."

Multiple advocacy, like centralized management, involves managing an entire policy area rather than concentrating on individual issues. Unlike centralized management, it is more collegial and consciously includes department and agency officials in the deliberations over broad areas of policy. Those with responsibility for managing this collegial process are White House–based, functioning as policy managers or honest brokers rather than as advocates.

Characterizing how any presidency manages particular areas is difficult and subject to competing interpretations. Although the distinctions were rarely clear-cut or definitive, an examination of Gerald Ford's decision-making approach suggests that although his general decision-making habits remained consistent across policy areas, he adopted different approaches for decision making in national security policy, domestic policy, and economic policy. Moreover, these differences reflected his personal interest in the subject matter, the qualities and characteristics of the individual advisers he selected, the priority he attached to the policy area, the policy demands he faced, and the policy objectives he sought to pursue.

For much of his administration, policy development on national security issues resembled a variant of centralized management. Decision making with respect to most domestic policy issues most closely resembled a form of adhocracy. His economic policy machinery was a conscious effort to reflect multiple advocacy.

National Security Policy

Gerald Ford assumed the presidency with a great deal of confidence on national security and foreign policy matters. He had traveled abroad extensively, served on the House Foreign Operations Appropriations Subcommittee, and "was confident that [he] knew as much about foreign policy as any member of Congress."[42] Moreover, he found foreign policy issues genuinely fascinating.

He inherited a set of national security policy-making arrangements in which the White House and the National Security Council staff had played a central role. From the outset of his administration, Nixon had used a greatly expanded National Security Council staff under his assistant to the president for national security affairs, Henry Kissinger, to shape and develop foreign policy within the White House. Kissinger's dominant role was evident when he was appointed secretary of state in 1973 while retaining his position as White House national security adviser.

In August 1974 Ford was concerned about the need for stability and continuity in foreign affairs, and he was also extremely fond of Kissinger, who had briefed him every week during Ford's eight months as vice-president. Ford was deeply impressed with Kissinger's intelligence, his pragmatism, his strategic approach to policy, and his success as a diplomat.[43]

Within hours after learning that he would definitely occupy the Oval Office, Ford telephoned Kissinger to tell him that he wished him to remain as secretary of state and to assure him that he was confident they could work well and effectively together.[44] That evening, after Nixon's resignation speech, Ford spoke briefly to the press in the driveway of his Alexandria, Virginia, home. He made only one reference to personnel in his new administration; Henry Kissinger had agreed to remain as secretary of state.

Over time, their relationship deepened into mutual admiration. Their views on most issues coincided and their personalities meshed. They developed a close working relationship that both treasured. They immediately began meeting every day for at least half an hour, and for much longer when major decisions were pending. Their respective contributions to U.S. foreign policy are difficult to determine. According to Kissinger, "Gerald Ford was involved in great detail at every stage of decision-making. And he insisted that all relevant members of his administration be heard without ceding a veto to anyone. I was surely influential, but the final decision as well as its shaping throughout the process was emphatically Gerald Ford's."[45]

From time to time, Ford rejected Kissinger's advice. Despite Kissinger's objections, Ford signed a compromise continuing appropriations resolution in October 1974 that required a cutoff of military aid to Turkey but permitted the president to delay the ban until December 10.[46] The following spring, as the situation in Vietnam deteriorated rapidly, Ford rejected Kissinger's urging to give a "go down with the flags flying" speech blaming Congress almost exclusively for the debacle in Southeast Asia.[47] But for the most part, Kissinger's influence was pervasive. Even on foreign economic policy issues, in which Kissinger readily and repeatedly acknowledged he had little expertise, his voice and views were influential.

Ford waited for over a year before initiating his sweeping national security reorganization in November 1975. In addition to the personnel changes at Defense and the CIA, Ford gave Kissinger's NSC position to the latter's deputy, Brent Scowcroft. This move appeared to reduce the concentration of power in a single adviser and the dominance of a White House–based apparatus. Ford insisted that it did not represent a demotion for Kissinger and did not diminish his influence. As Ford later explained:

> I had always questioned the organizational structure of having a secretary of state also be head of the NSC. The NSC organization in the White House was set up in 1947 by legislation. The purpose was to give to the president a group of highly competent people, very knowledgeable individuals who would analyze for the president, independently, recommendations for policy from State, from Defense, and from the CIA . . .
> It was never, in my judgment—and I think the statute was clear—expected to be an operational unit. Therefore . . . [to have] the secretary of state also heading up the NSC . . . seemed to be in conflict with the basic purposes of the NSC. So, I convinced Henry that it was no downgrading of his responsibilities as the secretary of state.[48]

The new organizational arrangement fit more comfortably into Ford's conception of the proper formal role of the NSC staff. The impact on policy was modest, however, largely because it left undisturbed the close working relationship between Ford and Kissinger. Ford acknowledged that "on foreign policy, from beginning to end, Henry Kissinger was the principal adviser."[49]

Domestic Policy

On domestic policy Ford tried an arrangment that was novel in both theory and practice, delegating responsibility to the vice-president.

The idea may have come from a discussion with his transition team, at least one of whose members raised the question of whether the presidency was too large a job for one person. More likely the idea sprang from three factors: Ford's own experience as vice-president that the office had much unrealized potential; his regard for Nelson Rockefeller's experience in dealing with domestic policy issues; and Ford's sense that his own expertise and comparative advantage were elsewhere. He reflected:

> I wanted my vice-president to have some specific operational responsibilities. Nelson Rockefeller had lots and lots of experience as governor of New York. He was interested in domestic issues; so it was very logical for me to turn that duty over to him and to the Domestic Council. My personal area of expertise in the Congress was on military policy and foreign policy. So, with Nelson Rockefeller on board, it was a logical and understandable thing for me to give him domestic policy, which permitted me to concentrate on the other.[50]

Ford's interest in giving Rockefeller a large role in shaping the administration's domestic legislative program seemed genuine, but it soon ran into two obstacles. The first was organizational. Rockefeller wanted James Cannon to be executive director of the Domestic Council and "to organize the council as an autonomous unit that reported directly to him." Donald Rumsfeld, who had been given responsibility for coordinating all White House activities, viewed the prospect of an autonomous unit outside the White House structure he administered as unacceptable and bound to lead to confusion. After a few tense meetings, Ford agreed that Cannon would serve as executive director of the Domestic Council staff and that Rockefeller would "be in charge of domestic policy."[51] The papers for the president, however, would have to flow through the normal White House staffing system under Rumsfeld's supervision.

For over a year Rockefeller remained convinced that Rumsfeld was intent on undermining the arrangement and diminishing the vice-president's role. On November 3, 1975, the White House released a letter from Rockefeller to Ford indicating that he did not want to be considered as a candidate for vice-president in the 1976 election.

A second, equally formidable obstacle was Ford's decision, announced in his January 1975 State of the Union Address, to oppose any new federal domestic spending programs. This far-reaching constraint was the result of a series of fiscal and budget policy decisions made in late December and early January to deal with the staggering economy. It made undertaking a comprehensive domestic program difficult.

The Domestic Council never met as a body. Jim Cannon, executive director of the Domestic Council staff, remained a close confidant of Rockefeller but also developed a good working relationship with other senior White House officials and functioned as a part of the White House staff. Rockefeller was able to push through only one major policy proposal—an Energy Resources Finance Corporation, to provide loans and loan guarantees to energy development projects—over the objection of most of the president's economic policy advisers. For the most part, the Domestic Council staff spent its time handling sensitive issues on a case-by-case basis.

In comparing the domestic policy and economic policy arrangements in the Ford White House, one senior official observed:

> The EPB [Economic Policy Board] really did get good attendance. You got people from each of the relevant agencies coming each time . . . My experience with the Domestic Council was that it was more ad hoc. You would have a particular issue and a certain group was called: another issue and another group was called . . . Very often . . . even when we were discussing the same issue, attendance would vary . . . The EPB was regular not only in terms of attendance but [also in terms of] times for meetings. It . . . also [had] regular meetings with the President.[52]

The effort to delegate responsibility for domestic policy formulation and the prohibition on new spending made the ad hoc development of domestic policy almost inevitable.

Economic Policy

It was in the area of economic policy that Ford made what he described as "the most important institutional innovation of my administration."[53] Though initially reluctant to make changes in his foreign policy-making apparatus, he used economic policy to demonstrate symbolically that in his administration departments and agencies would exercise a larger role and the White House staff a smaller one.

Ford's transition team strongly recommended restoring the participation of cabinet members in the presidential decision-making

process, moving the chairmanship for the most important and prestigious interagency groups out of the White House, and avoiding
"isolation of the President by providing a flow of information, access
to the president, and a span of control that can be handled while
still allowing time for reflection, and an orderly but inclusive
decision making process."[54] But the report stopped short of
recommending a massive reorganization of the host of economic
policy-making entities that had accumulated during the previous
administration. It did not even raise as an alternative the creation
of a single entity for coordinating all economic policy. It was silent
on what role the White House should play in coordinating economic
policy. It recommended eliminating the Office of the Counselor to
the President for Economic Affairs but did not discuss how its functions should be absorbed or how the various interagency councils
should relate to each other and to the president.

During his first weeks in office Ford met frequently with his senior
economic advisers. He also met with Kenneth Rush, counsellor to
the president for economic affairs, who would soon depart for the
post of U.S. ambassador to France, and with Bill Seidman, his principal economic adviser on his vice-presidential staff, to discuss organizational matters and the upcoming Conference on Inflation. But
it was to Alexander Haig that he turned with a request for a paper
outlining the organizational alternatives for meeting the twin needs
of bringing cabinet officers to the fore and coordinating economic
policy decisions at the highest levels.

Initially Ford was inclined to divide the responsibilities between
Seidman and Treasury Secretary William Simon, making Simon the
spokesman and Seidman the operator of the coordinating mechanism. But Haig persuaded Ford that one person had to be in charge.
They agreed that the one person should be Simon. Characteristically
determined not to become enmeshed in the details, Ford gave Simon
and Seidman the task of formulating a workable arrangement for a
new economic policy entity. He approved the option tying "Simon
and Seidman together as one unit where Simon is the key economic
adviser, and Seidman, under Simon's direction, provides the coordination of policy development and implementation."[55]

Simon and Seidman came back with a much more expansive and
far-reaching concept. A new entity, to be named the President's
Economic Policy Board, would replace all the existing cabinet-level
interagency machinery. Nonstatutory councils and committees would
be abolished; the statutory ones would have Simon as chairman and

Seidman as vice-chairman but would in practice operate under the aegis of the EPB.

The EPB became *the* formal vehicle for conveying economic policy advice to the president. The board was truly collegial and incredibly active: during Ford's administration it held 520 meetings at the cabinet level—an average of almost five a week—and it met nearly 100 times with the president. Without question, it was the most sustained, comprehensive, and successful collegial attempt to advise a president on economic policy matters.

The EPB's operation with Simon as chairman and Seidman as process manager and honest broker fit Ford's style perfectly. He enjoyed the give-and-take of its meetings and seeing the interaction of his advisers. He was comfortable with its major figures: Simon (Treasury), Alan Greenspan (Council of Economic Advisers), Jim Lynn (OMB), John Dunlop (Labor), Elliot Richardson (Commerce), Kissinger (State), Arthur Burns (Federal Reserve), and Seidman. However, the sheer volume of advice that Ford received through the EPB did not prevent him from obtaining less formal counsel on various economic issues. Two individuals outside his immediate White House staff played especially important roles:

> Alan [Greenspan] used to drift into the Oval Office, and he and I would talk very confidentially. I would pick his brains, and he would make suggestions. His advice on economic policy was invaluable.
>
> Arthur Burns, on a very infrequent basis, would stop by. Very informally, we would talk about what the Fed was doing and what we were doing, because both he and I wanted our monetary and fiscal policies to be going on the same track. It was a relationship that was priceless for the coordination of policy.[56]

People who had served in previous administrations were struck by Ford's operating style and by the manner in which the Economic Policy Board conducted its business. One cabinet member who had held senior positions in two previous administrations had the "impression . . . that the involvement of people in the processes of economic decision making was broader and fairer in [the Ford] administration than [in] any other I know about. I felt that a very conscious effort was made to insure that anybody who wanted to be heard or to be present or ought to be informed that a meeting was being held, was invited."[57]

Another senior official, who had also served in Nixon's administration, reflected: "It was the first time in anybody's memory where you had everyone, including those on the periphery of economic issues, involved in the discussions."[58]

One participant with a quarter-century of experience in the executive branch contrasted the EPB with earlier arrangements:

There are several different modes in White House organization. One involves a presidential style in which the President says: "Don't bring me disagreements and inter-agency problems. You guys solve them." One example was Eisenhower. The result was lowest common denominator solutions. We had the NSC and the Operations Coordination Board, the Psychological Strategy Board, and a whole number of other things. We worked through papers and they were ground down until when we finished up they were nothing.

The other style involves the President saying: "Don't try to resolve things among the agencies. Bring me your problems." This was essentially the Lyndon Johnson approach. And then you have no incentive to resolve issues among the agencies. The premium is on getting to the president. That's where it's going to be resolved. So you take the most extreme position and then fall back at the very end.

The EPB to me represented a middle course. First, there was an effort to resolve things at the agency level, but there was a court of last resort at the same time. You had to calculate that there were only so many times that you were going to get to the President. But there were certain things important enough that you were not going to sacrifice your position to reach an agreement.

I am convinced that you need an institution or forum where you can discuss issues and try to resolve them. You need an honest broker. And you need one other thing, a top guy, the President, who is available and accessible from time to time and prepared to make a decision.

The Tin Agreement illustrates what I mean by how the EPB worked. In our interagency meetings we resolved some of the issues, but the basic issue of do we join the Tin Agreement or not join the agreement was unresolved until we took it to the president. We laid out the case and ultimately the president made the decision.[59]

By assigning responsibility to his economic advisers collectively, Ford communicated to his top officials a sense of shared responsibility for economic policy, transcending their specific departmental or agency assignments. As one participant observed: "going to the EPB you had a better recognition that you were only part of a bigger picture."[60]

Not all economic policy issues and decisions were developed by the Economic Policy Board. The most notable decision generated outside the formal system was the October 1975 tax reduction proposal. During July, August, and September 1975, Donald Rumsfeld and his deputy, Richard Cheney, met frequently with CEA Chairman Alan Greenspan, OMB Director Jim Lynn, and Lynn's deputy, Paul O'Neill, to discuss possible tax reduction initiatives and budget strategies. The number of participants was small to preserve confidentiality. In late September and early October, after the fundamental decision to propose a major tax reduction and spending initiative was made, the EPB was involved in refining the details of the proposal.

For the most part, however, a managed multiple advocacy process characterized Ford's economic policy-making arrangements. In a policy area that demanded a great deal of his time and energy, it was an approach that enabled him to use his economic experts effectively. Although some advisers were clearly more influential than others, Ford never developed the same kind of relationship with another individual that he did with Henry Kissinger in shaping foreign policy. It was a consciously collegial enterprise.

One of the most important tasks facing any president in our system of divided powers is his leadership of the executive branch and his use of the resources at his most immediate disposal in shaping policies and developing initiatives. A wide variety of approaches are available to a president; selecting from among them is both challenging and important. In determining the ways in which he will receive advice and make decisions, the president must take into consideration his own interest in the subject matter, the strengths and limitations of his advisers, the policy demands he must address, and his policy objectives.

As a decision maker, Gerald Ford was both open and accessible. Yet within the broad context of this style he shaped his foreign, domestic, and economic policies in distinctly different ways. His use of a variant of centralized management in shaping foreign policy stemmed not only from the compelling case to be made for confidentiality in many foreign policy decisions, but also from his unique relationship with Henry Kissinger. His ad hoc approach to most domestic policy decisions rested both on his interest in delegating much responsibility in this area to his vice-president and on his early decision to support no new domestic spending programs. He had little interest in a continuing interagency apparatus that would raise large numbers of possible initiatives for his decision. The stagflation that he inherited compelled him to devote much time and energy to economic policy. In this area his personal style and the strengths and limitations of his individual advisers combined to make a multiple advocacy approach both natural and desirable.

Gerald Ford assumed office under some of the most difficult circumstances any president has ever faced. He had no electoral mandate to which he could repair. He confronted a nation in many respects both frustrated and disillusioned. In retrospect his policy accomplishments in both foreign and economic policy appear even more remarkable than they seemed at the time. He was defeated in 1976 in one of the closest presidential elections in our history.

During his relatively short tenure in office, Ford demonstrated that healing the nation's wounds from Vietnam and Watergate took priority over his own political fortunes. He left to future presidents a legacy of remarkable skill not only in building morale within the executive branch but also in adopting decision-making approaches in the major areas of federal policy that skillfully took into account the strengths of the team he had assembled and the policy realities he had to address.

8

JIMMY CARTER

The Politics of Public Goods

Erwin C. Hargrove

There are two ingredients essential for effective presidential leadership. The first is the range of manipulative skills pertaining to presidential "power": creating bargaining coalitions, establishing authority over subordinates, keeping potential opponents off balance, ensuring alternative sources of information and advice, and, in general, making the most of the institutional levers available to win influence with other holders of power.[1] It is generally accepted among students of the office that sensitivity to the inherent politics of policy-making is important for a successful presidency and that a lack of sensitivity helps explain poor performance. The second ingredient is public leadership, or, more specifically, the abilities to define the policy dilemmas facing the nation in terms of an emerging historical situation and to suggest solutions that win widespread support. The clearest example in our history is Lincoln's articulation of the terms of union and the need to preserve it. But every president must match a policy agenda to the perceived necessities of the time and create political support for that agenda.[2]

The two ingredients of effectiveness are complementary. Widespread support for a president's definition of the historical situation provides a general political resource for specific initiatives and strengthens the hand of the power broker. Without such a broad underpinning of support, manipulative skill may end in unproductive maneuvering and failure, as in Franklin Roosevelt's largely unsuccessful second term. By the same token, effective public leadership needs to be bolstered by skillful management of political actors and processes.

Timing is crucial to effective presidential leadership: the problems of an era must match the chief executive's insights and skills if he is to enjoy political support. Political leaders may adapt their policy appeals and leadership strategies to historical situations to a degree, but there are limits to such flexibility. A successful presidency is more likely to come from a good match between the president and the hour.

Jimmy Carter is widely thought to have been an ineffective or unsuccessful president, but for reasons that vary greatly according to the analysis. Some critics charge him with ineptness, a failure to understand the world of power.[3] Others draw a picture of a presidency so weakened by the fragmentation of political parties, the democratization of Congress, and public skepticism about leadership and authority that skill virtually became irrelevant.[4] The question to be asked about Carter as president is whether he made the most of his opportunities. Personal skill must be assessed in relation to the historical context and the political resources available to a president. A careful analysis must weigh both skill and opportunity as ingredients of effectiveness. In Carter's case they seem to have reinforced each other both positively—as in his storming of the nomination process and subsequent election—and negatively, as when his seeming ineptitude in office was matched by adverse events such as the hostage crisis. In still other achievements, such as the Camp David treaties, skill may have been an independent factor. And lack of skill may also explain some of Carter's failures, quite apart from events or context, as in the initial overloading of Congress with legislative proposals from the White House. All of this must be sorted out.

Carter is difficult to evaluate as a president because his rise was so quick and dramatic and his fall, though not as quick, was clearly a stunning failure. How could a president who entered office with such a personal victory in 1976 have been so clearly rejected by the voters in 1980? Most answers to this question have been too quick to blame Carter himself and have failed to relate skill to context.

This chapter discusses Carter's political personality, including his style of authority and his beliefs about politics and policy; suggests that Carter believed himself to be entering the White House in a position of strength and that he moved confidently to put his stamp on government and policy; analyzes his leadership in domestic and foreign policy in terms of both the clash between presidential expectations and available political support and the role of skill or

ineptness; considers whether Carter's skill influenced his effectiveness—could he have been a more skillful version of himself, and, if
so, would it have mattered?—and explains his achievements and
failures in terms of the conjunction of skill and opportunity.

Political Personality

Politics and Leadership

After his presidency Carter reflected on his leadership style: "I had
a different way of governing . . . than had been the case with my
predecessors . . . I was a southerner, a born-again Christian, a Baptist,
a newcomer. Very few of the members of Congress, or members of
the major lobbying groups, or the distinguished former Democratic
leaders had played much of a role in my election." And he elaborated:
"As an engineer and as a Governor I was more inclined to move
rapidly and without equivocation and without the . . . interminable
consultations . . . that are inherent, I think, in someone who has a
more legislative attitude, or psyche, or training or experience."[5]

Carter's first political success was to defeat a fraudulent attempt
by local politicians to deny his election to the Georgia senate. He
thus entered politics as an outsider. This feeling of distance was
reinforced by exposure to his fellow senators, whom he found to be
extraordinarily committed to the service of their favorite interest
groups.[6]

According to his own account, Carter developed the idea that the
proper responsibility of the elected official was to be the voice of
the unorganized citizen and all the citizens who made up the general
public.[7] This insight led him to invent a strategy of policy leadership.
He developed and introduced "comprehensive solutions" to problems of education, health, the organization of administrative bodies,
and energy conservation because "in the absence of clear or comprehensive issues, it is simply not possible to marshal the interest
of the general public, and under such circumstances legislators often
respond to the quiet and professional pressure of lobbyists."[8] To his
mind only policy ideas that promised root-and-branch remedies would
have such public appeal. It followed that he would eschew the standard practice of building coalitions behind proposals and instead
preach the gospel of "public goods." Carter's success as governor
convinced him that this deliberate strategy of political leadership
was an effective one. According to a White House aide who was also

with him in Georgia, "he viewed himself as having successfully imposed comprehensive solutions in areas ranging from reform of education [to] reorganizing the state's administrative agencies. He viewed himself as having put those characters in Georgia legislature into shape by having big concepts.[9]

This commitment to comprehensiveness pervaded Carter's leadership strategy in the White House. Another of his assistants there recalls: "Everything that he did in his presidency, except for those things that swamped us for the moment, tended to be efforts in the long term, particularly if you look at energy, which was something in which there was not great political outcry in 1977 to do something about . . . That's why he so much insisted on leaving politics out of the calculations, as though politics per se would always tend to make these things short-term or incremental."[10]

Did Carter perceive such leadership to be political or nonpolitical? He understood that it was not political in conventional terms. As a non–coalition builder he was comfortable neither with Congress as an institution nor with many of its members, because he did not see either them or their institution as "trustees" for the public interest.[11] He saw himself, as president, as a trustee for the public good. But he hoped to be rewarded politically for his achievements. As he remarked: "We had a very heavy agenda of items that I thought would be beneficial for our country. I can tell you with complete candor that we didn't assess the adverse political consequences of pursuing these goals . . . I didn't think it was particularly foolhardy. I thought eventually our good efforts would be recognized and our achievements would be adequate to justify my reelection. But I was not under any misapprehension about the adverse consequences of . . . getting involved with the Middle East when everybody else had had little success or moving toward the Panama Canal treaties."[12]

In his own eyes, then, he was a political leader who would assert the public interest. One aide recalls: "we used to always joke that the worst way to convince the President to go along with your position was to say that this would help [him] politically, because . . . he wanted to be a different type of President. He was elected somehow to be a different kind of President. He was running against the sort of system of inside deals and so forth. He saw himself above that system . . . He seemed to like sometimes going against the grain to do what was right."[13]

Carter often rejected advice to time policy initiative prudently from a political standpoint. Advisers suggested that the Panama Canal treaties and the Middle East initiative were second-term issues and bad domestic politics.[14] But he persisted, arguing that he wanted to have some achievements in his first term in case there was not a second.[15] A number of his major achievements, particularly in foreign policy, were on issues that he had been warned against for political reasons.

But as time went on he learned to use political advice and to organize the White House accordingly. From the beginning he had a small group of informal political advisers: Mrs. Carter, Charles Kirbo, Bert Lance, Jody Powell, and Hamilton Jordan. Vice-president Mondale was on the edge of this group.[16] A steady stream of political advice about domestic legislation and economic policy came from Stuart Eizenstat and the White House Domestic Policy Staff, which Eizenstat directed. Eizenstat considered it essential that every adminstration legislative proposal be tested against prevailing opinion in Congress and among the organized Democratic interest groups in Washington.[17] And eventually Hamilton Jordan and Jody Powell began to attend meetings of Carter's national security advisers, not to contribute to policy but to bring political sensitivity to decisions.[18]

Carter's White House assistants suggest that he placed increasing value on political advice as time passed. A domestic policy aide describes the change: "He tended to worry much more in the last couple of years about what the public reaction would be and what the political impact would be. Early on, he was very much 'I only want to know what the right thing to do is. I only want to know what the best policy is and I'll worry about the politics of it later. You give me the best policy.' Later on those kinds of bravado statements tended to disappear and he wanted to know what he could pass, what we could get through, what did this committee chairman want, what did this interest group want. That was a function of worrying more about reelection as we got closer to it."[19]

Carter learned to accept second best in order to have policy achievements on his record. And he permitted politics to shape policy development. But he seems never to have been inventive in devising strategies of political appeal and persuasion for major policy initiatives. Rather, politics seems to have entered into his considerations most often when it was time to devise an acceptable fallback position after the comprehensive approach had failed. This was true in energy, welfare reform, education, and much else. Carter's clear preference was to favor public goods leadership.

There is another puzzle here. Leadership in behalf of public goods requires public, popular leadership, which appeals over the heads of interest groups and legislators. Yet this was not really Carter's style. He was very good as a campaigner in making general moral appeals and asking people to trust him, but as president he focused his energies on decision making rather than on public leadership. Other aspects of Carter's political personality provide possible clues to this puzzle.

Beliefs and Values

Carter is a legatee of the vanished tradition of southern progressivism. Southern progressives were middle class, drawn from the professions and commerce, and advocates of economic development and social reform to protect the weak and unfortunate. They opposed machine politics, political corruption, and unethical business practices and preached the gospel of efficient, honest government. There was an absence of emotion in their politics and a distrust of demagogues. Good government was to be based on expertise rather than on popular politics.[20]

This was Jimmy Carter's ideology in regard to social and economic policy. He characterized himself as a fiscal conservative and a social liberal. He rose to political office in Georgia as one who combined the goal of serving human needs with the attainment of efficient government—thus the central theme of administrative reorganization during his governorship. Few northern Democrats clearly understood or accepted this balance of values.[21]

In his views on foreign policy, Carter thought of himself as a Wilsonian: he saw the United States as a witness to morality in the relations among nations, particularly in regard to human rights.[22] Yet Carter was not always visibly guided by this general set of principles. When asked to rank his goals by priority he refused, saying that he hoped to achieve them all. He was seen as all trees and no forest.[23] The common criticism of Carter was that he was an engineer lacking a political philosophy. He did have a general philosophy that guided his actions. But he was ambitious to achieve a number of specific goals and therefore did not appear to have clear priorities; and his mind was given to factual analysis of specific problems. This blend of ambition and homework obscured the fact that he had clear principles.

Carter's ambition for policy achievement was derived in part from his religion. He was a New Testament rather than an Old Testament Christian. Southern Baptists believe that with God all things are possible. Carter was an unusual Southern Baptist in his belief that moral transformation could be achieved in politics. But his optimism was derived from his faith. He was not a Calvinist in politics, although there may be traces of Calvinism in his personal character. He preached a gospel of hope.[24]

Carter's strongest cognitive drive was for competence. He took pride in his ability to master difficult problems.[25] He regarded this capacity as a resource for persuasion. Former aides cite numerous instances in which Carter was highly persuasive because he knew more about a problem than anyone else. One example was his solo appearance before the Georgia legislature to defend his reorganization proposals.[26] Sometimes this was a form of showing off that had little to do with persuasiveness. For example, he had to be cautioned not to talk too much during briefings lest he intimidate the experts briefing him.[27]

Carter sought to understand the substance of the problem as such rather than its politics. He was not curious about the history of issues or individuals.[28] He perhaps took too much pride in the fact that he did not, for example, have to turn to his aides for assistance with maps of the Middle East when he was negotiating with Begin and Sadat, but he did see this knowledge as an asset for negotiation.[29]

In Carter there was a congruence among political ideology, religious faith, and cognitive style. He was a unifier and integrator who hoped to achieve ambitious goals by a combination of study and appeal to the public good. This style of leadership presented some problems. Goals within his ideology necessarily had to be balanced against each other, such as fiscal conservatism and social liberalism or simultaneous cooperation and competition between the United States and the Soviet Union. What appeared to many to be ad hoc decision making or even inconsistency, as Carter shifted between seemingly incompatible goals, did not appear so to him. He was continually seeking to integrate opposing themes within his own beliefs. The optimism of his faith and his confidence in study and the "right reason" that it would produce told him that unity and agreement could be achieved.

Style of Authority

A Carter assistant recalls that the president "wanted to have a sense of conquering the office in its every manifestation," with the result that he tried to make too many decisions. It was not only that he sometimes got bogged down in the details of issues but also that he tried to decide too many things himself.[30] Carter believed that the first and most important responsibility of the president was to make intelligent decisions. He was his own chief of staff until the third year of his administration, when Hamilton Jordan was appointed to the position, and he created collegial modes of decision making in which there was lively discussion among small groups of advisers. His favorite meeting was the weekly foreign policy breakfast, at which a small number of advisers could discuss and decide the most important issues.[31]

Carter used White House staff as one might expect a governor to do, as personal assistants. Gubernatorial staffs in most states are legislative and public relations experts who work on visible political issues. They seldom get involved in policy-making with cabinet officers. In the White House, Carter relied greatly on his domestic, economic, and foreign policy aides, but not as potential coordinators and referees among cabinet officers. To have given them such authority would have violated the principle of collegiality.

The strength of this system for decision making was that the president was accessible and informed. The weakness was that the president's desk could become overloaded with incommensurate policy options because he would let everyone contribute recommendations. Staff assistants tried to referee, but Carter gave them only limited authority to do so. A further weakness was that when collegiality broke down, the president would pick and choose among advisers, as he wished, but the world outside saw disarray. Carter always regarded himself as in control, but his insensitivity to his political reputation caused him to tolerate conflict among his associates, sometimes to his own detriment.

Winning the Presidency

Carter conceived the idea of a campaign for the presidency on the theme of moral leadership long before Watergate. He believed the 1972 McGovern campaign had appealed to a real need for moral leadership and hoped to combine that theme with an appeal to competence in the efficient management of government as demonstrated in Georgia.[32] His 1975 autobiography focused on the twin themes of honesty and competence.[33] By this time the events of Watergate had reinforced the call for morality. Carter was most effective when he was running as an individual during the primary campaigns, with his personal appeals for a government as good as its people and with his promise never to lie to the people. As the candidate of the Democratic coalition he almost lost the general election, and this near loss provides clues to problems in his presidency. He appealed to many voters who were not Democrats, but he also confused many Democrats, such as the union leader who said, "I don't know who he is, where he's going or where he's been."[34] From the beginning he went against the prevailing current of Democratic politics. His domestic policy assistants negotiated carefully with the United Auto Workers and the mayors of the big cities on the issues of national health insurance and welfare costs in order to allow Carter latitude on large spending commitments even as he promised action in those areas.[35] But the likelihood of conflict between a fiscally conservative president and the various Democratic constituencies was already apparent. He overcame this problem somewhat by his promises to restore the economy to health through expansionary policies. But even as he and his advisers developed the economic stimulus package after the election, the president-elect began to worry that inflation was his real long-term problem and to think and talk in terms of fiscal restraint.[36] Again, he was potentially pitted against his own coalition.

Carter also made moral appeals central to his foreign policy themes in the 1976 campaign. At this time détente between the United States and the USSR had eroded. Disagreement between the two powers focused on Soviet adventurism in Africa and Asia. Secretary of State Kissinger had sought to respond with U.S. action but was caught between hawks and doves.[37] Carter called for more détente and less force and talked about human rights. But already public opinion was moving toward concern about U.S. vulnerability to Soviet power.[38] As in economic policy, a sea change was under way in foreign affairs. The themes with which Carter won the presidency were no longer appropriate.

Carter entered the White House without strong support from the organized elements of the Democratic coalition, including its congressional members. He had no mandate for the domestic and economic policies he favored, and the context of foreign policy issues was shifting. Yet, like most newly elected presidents, he acted with boldness, as if he had a mandate.

Policy Leadership

Domestic Policy

The repetitive story of Carter's performance on domestic policy—which includes economic and social policy—reveals the programs that were too comprehensive. The effort to steer a middle course between excessive inflation and recession alienated Democrats, who wanted spending, without winning the support of fiscal conservatives. Program proposals packaged in terms of an appeal to public goods in welfare reform, energy, educational organization, and national health insurance likewise failed, for similar reasons, to win supporters. Carter's principal success was with energy policy, but it took four years of hard pushing from the White House to build a coalition for passage of a comprehensive program.

Carter had campaigned on the theme of getting the economy moving and had criticized the Ford administration for tolerating high unemployment levels. After the election his advisers developed a package designed to stimulate the economy, on the assumption that the existing slack would inhibit inflation.[39] However, unlike the Kennedy-Johnson years, when such a strategy had worked, Carter's presidency had been preceded by a period of chronic inflation. There was a risk that recovery would bring inflation. Although Carter had misgivings about the stimulus package as it was being developed, congressional leaders and business and labor groups were exerting very strong pressures for a program.[40] The new president was moving in concert with his political coalition.

But it was not long before Carter made it clear to his party that he would not favor traditional Democratic policies. He withdrew the fifty-dollar tax rebate for each taxpayer that had been included in the stimulus package, after delay in congressional passage of the plan and signs of a recovering economy persuaded him that it was no longer needed.[41] By this time Carter had become convinced that inflation was the real problem, not only for the nation but for himself politically, and he proceeded to tell his cabinet and the congressional leaders so.[42] This shift in thinking early in the administration produced the strategic problem of reconciling economic policy with

political realities with which Carter and his advisers were to grapple
for four years. The central task was to revive the economy without
inflation. Democratic presidents, given who their constituents are,
may find this a difficult task. Both Carter and Kennedy were going
against their party's tendencies. Kennedy had to persuade Democratic congressional leaders that a tax cut combined with deliberate
deficit spending, according to Keynesian theory, was intelligent policy. Many were initially skeptical, as Kennedy himself had been.
But the threat of a "Kennedy recession" and the growing strength
of social reform forces in the Democratic party emboldened Kennedy
to initiate the proposal for a tax cut that passed in 1964.[43] Carter
was fighting against the political legacy of that success in altogether
different economic conditions. He was convinced that the problem
of inflation called for budgetary restraint. But Democrats knew only
the politics of growth. The Great Society programs had been passed
in the meantime, and there was very little political room for maneuver in budget cutting, especially for a president who eventually
decided that defense expenditures should be increased after the post-
Vietnam halt.

There was an additional problem. The underlying inflationary
forces in the economy were so strong that a mistake by government
could not easily be corrected. It was not clear whether economists
knew how to curb inflation without the drastic measures that would
bring a recession.[44] The only strategy available to a Democratic president and his economic advisers was to steer a cautious course between the perils of inflation and recession. Thus for four years Carter
annual budgets shifted from expansionary to contractionary according to whether the immediate problem was thought to be inflation
or recession. Carter's first complete budget, sent to Congress in
January 1978, was expansionary; it increased domestic programs and
requested a tax cut and tax reform. That budget was based on a CEA
report that forecast an economic slowdown in 1978. However, 1978
turned out to be a boom year; the CEA had underestimated the
strength of the economy. Accordingly, the president's budget in January 1979 was much tighter, with a projected deficit of only 30
billion dollars. Yet administration economists were not convinced
that inflation was a serious problem and believed that a tightening
of economic expansion would curb potential inflation.[45]

The January 1979 budget made cuts in Medicare and Social Security aid to state and local governments and proposed an increase
in defense spending. The pattern to be identified later, in the Reagan

years, was already taking shape. The January 1980 budget was an election-year document, containing many good things for Democratic constituencies in health, education, employment, and urban development programs. Total federal spending was also up because of high inflation and high unemployment. Carter and his advisers were hoping to survive a year of high inflation without triggering a recession. However, the inflation rate and Carter's announcement of defense increases after the Soviet invasion of Afghanistan caused national financial markets to decline. The president and his advisers soon rewrote the budget, in concert with Congress, to be much tighter and anti-inflationary.[46] Several of Carter's economic advisers later felt that this budget, combined with selected controls on consumer credit, stimulated the "quickie recession" whose full effects were felt just before the November election. By this time Carter was adamant in pursuit of a balanced budget and rejected the advice of his economists that he recommend a midyear tax cut for business to stave off the recession. During the campaign he ignored possible appeals to Democratic constituencies in favor of the theme of fiscal soundness.[47] In retrospect, Carter administration officials felt that they would have won the economic policy battle had it not been for the OPEC oil price increases in mid-1979, which added several points to the inflation index. Administration economists did not see this new inflation as domestically induced and could not justify action to slow down the economy drastically because of it.[48] But the consequence was that the middle path between inflation and recession became narrow, rocky, and entrenched. Carter entered the 1980 election with inflation and recession to his credit.

Centrist economic advice and centrist political strategies reinforced each other, in both success and failure. And in the process the loyalty of the Democratic constituencies was severely strained. One example will suffice. At the beginning of the midterm Democratic national convention in Memphis in the fall of 1978, word had leaked out that OMB was going to bring in a very tight budget for January. Speaker after speaker at the convention lambasted the Carter administration for abandoning the historic social reform mission of the Democratic party and opposed any cuts in social programs.[49] The gap between Kennedy and Democratic liberals, on the one side, and Republican critics of a spending president, on the other, had begun to widen and would continue to do so until November 1980.

The dilemmas of microeconomic policy choices revealed Carter's political problems even more painfully. Carter's fiscal conservatism and his dislike of interest groups were in conflict with his leadership of the Democratic coalition, which made many inflationary demands on government. The president's strategy was to scale down such demands and yet retain allegiance. But that strategy put him on the defensive. White House domestic policy advisers considered it very important to keep labor, farmers, teachers, environmentalists, and other Democratic groups on Carter's side, but each of these felt that only half a loaf was offered. Carter was reluctant to take rhetorical credit for spending programs and seemed to take pleasure in denying benefits. His preference was clear: restrain spending in order to keep budgets down and to fight inflation. But he experienced countervailing pressure from fellow Democratics. His attempts to stand firm were undermined by cabinet officers, members of Congress, and even his own aides. He usually ended up compromising, with no one happy.[50]

These examples do not make it clear whether the Carter administration contributed to the inflation that hurt it politically in 1980, nor do they explain who voted against Carter and why. What is apparent is that Jimmy Carter and his economic advisers pursued a policy of steering a narrow path between inflation and recession. It was a rational policy on both economic and political grounds. What alternatives were there for a Democratic president? The short-term political costs required alienating organized Democratic groups. The long-term political gamble was that the economy would be kept in balance. That gamble did not pay off for Carter.

The Carter administration's social policy initiatives clearly demonstrated the president's search for public goods. Realizing that the Democratic coalition needed to move to the political center, he wished to rationalize and consolidate existing social programs and administer them more efficiently, and thus broaden political support for his party.[51] However, this political aspiration seems to have been less salient than the strong predisposition for comprehensive packaging that Carter brought to policy development. Three scenarios resulted. Two illustrate the strengths and weaknesses of public goods politics: comprehensive proposals either attracted constituencies and were passed into law or failed because constituency support was lacking. Welfare reform and national health insurance failed; but civil service and regulatory reform were successes, as was the energy policy in the long run. The third scenario occurred when comprehensive proposals were scaled back in order to win legislative passage.

The urban policy package and the creation of the Department of Education illustrate this approach.

Welfare reform and national health insurance revealed contrasting sides of the same dilemma. There was a dearth of constituencies in the first case and a conflict among constituencies in the second. But in neither case could a Carter constituency be constructed. The appeal of a comprehensive policy fell between stools. As governor of Georgia, Carter had decided that the national welfare system was inequitable and inefficient and was on record as favoring a national program with uniform payments across the states and strong work incentives.[52] When told by the income security transition team that incremental changes in the existing AFDC system would most easily get through Congress, the president-elect replied that he would fulfill his promise of a comprehensive bill. Carter charged Joseph Califano, secretary of HEW, with producing a bill that would provide a nationally uniform welfare system, including public employment for the employable, at no greater cost than the existing system.[53] Eventually HEW and the Department of Labor developed a compromise bill that stayed within the financial guidelines only because it made tenuous assumptions about cost savings in other programs as a result of welfare reform. Evidently Califano never took seriously the president's admonition to stay within existing costs because he did not believe that a uniform system could do so. But Carter's repeated messages to Califano that payment levels were too high reveals his seriousness.[54] The key member of the White House Domestic Policy Staff assigned to the problem believes that Carter wanted welfare reform as a conservative issue.[55] It was to establish the tone of the president's social policies. But there was no constituency in Congress for that approach. The conservatives opposed welfare reform, and the liberals wanted more of it than Carter would give. The bill did not get out of committee, in part because of competition from energy, Social Security, and tax reform legislation. The passage of Proposition 13 in California in 1978 killed any prospect of approval. A scaled-down version met with no more success.[56]

National health insurance was not an issue with which Carter the candidate had had much experience. During the campaign he had spoken out for the principle of a universal national health insurance program in order to win an endorsement from the United Auto Workers, but his total commitment in terms of costs and timing was qualified.[57] Such a program would be expensive and clashed

with the campaign theme of a balanced budget. As a result, in his
first year as president Carter felt his way on national health insurance between competing factions within his administration and among
congressional Democrats. Carter's economic advisers opposed any
plan, fearing its inflationary effects, while his social policy advisers,
including Califano, argued the need to keep the commitment. Senator Edward Kennedy and the AFL-CIO were pushing hard for a
program of total coverage that would probably require heavy administrative controls to keep costs down; but there was limited
congressional support for such a program. Carter spent considerable
time and effort trying in vain to win Kennedy's support for a general
plan that would be introduced in phases according to estimates of
cost. The political rivalry between the two men was reinforced by
the widening division among Democrats over the administration's
"conservatism." By the time Carter presented a set of general principles for a health insurance program, in May 1979, it was too late
for congressional action. Carter could have sided with Kennedy and
the unions on a losing cause. Or he could have come out early for
a modest proposal in the hope of winning centrist support in Congress. He might also have delayed the issue until a second term. His
hesitancy reflected his uncertainty of success with any of those
options because of divisions within the Democratic administration
and coalition. Carter wanted to avoid a political fight with Kennedy,
but ultimately his concern about inflation was stronger. Moreover,
it was too late to develop a constituency.[58]

Regulatory reform, most notably airline deregulation at the Civil
Aeronautics Board, and civil service reform through the leadership
of the Civil Service Commission were two notable public goods
achievements that had widespread political support. The opposition
of the airline industry was no match for the arguments, widely
accepted by both Democrats and Republicans, that consumers would
benefit from greater competition. Civil service reform was more
difficult, but Virginia's and Maryland's congressional spokesmen for
federal bureaucrats were too few to block action. The president also
had the able leadership of Alfred Kahn and Alan Campbell, experienced professionals who knew how to work with Congress.

The passage of the energy program, in two installments, demonstrated the great difficulty of constructing a political coalition in
behalf of a public good. The energy problem was Carter's kind of
issue: the shortage of fuel and dependence upon oil imports was a

national problem, and yet the local, regional, and private interests represented in Congress had been unable to formulate a policy despite requests by two previous presidents. The policy had to integrate oil, natural gas, coal, and nuclear power and thus overcome narrow interests, and it could not be developed as a solely partisan matter.[59] How could Carter resist such a challenge?

The administration's 1977 bill had 113 interlocking provisions that the president demanded Congress consider as one package. It included a gasoline tax, a tax on inefficient cars, a crude oil tax, conservation measures, federal regulation of intrastate natural gas, and inducements for industry to use more coal and tax credits for solar development. According to one presidential aide, the bill was "vintage Jimmy Carter" in that it required Congress to comply with the president's determination of the public good. In his April appeal to the American people Carter called the bill the "moral equivalent of war."[60]

The subsequent story is well known. House speaker Tip O'Neill created an Ad Hoc Select Committee on Energy to coordinate the work of the five committees responsible for energy bills, and this tight management resulted in House passage in the first session. In the Senate, however, rivalry among committees and open conflict between producing and consuming states delayed passage because of controversy over natural gas deregulation, which Carter opposed. A bill was finally passed at the end of the second session when Carter gave way on deregulation. It had been a much longer and tougher fight than he had envisioned.[61]

But the passage of the program did not resolve all the problems. Price controls on oil were scheduled to be lifted in June 1979 in accordance with a 1975 law. Carter's response was to ask Congress for a windfall profits tax to recapture part of escalating oil company revenues. A bill to promote synthetic fuel development was moving along in Congress, and Carter appropriated it as part of his program. But progress was slow, and when the president returned from a July trip to Japan to find his standing in opinion polls at a new low, he staged the dramatic meetings with national leaders at Camp David to evaluate his administration. The culmination was a televised speech to the nation in which Carter cited governmental failure to face the energy problem in a disciplined way as the symbol of a national inability to unite to face problems. The public goods president had found the perfect vehicle for the kind of appeal he liked to make. Carter urged Congress to act quickly on a number of energy measures, and, although in fact it moved slowly, most of the bills were passed in 1980.[62]

Carter would have liked to design all initiatives as comprehensive programs, but sometimes he settled for incremental changes in return for some political success, as in the cases of the urban package and the creation of the Department of Education. It is likely that welfare reform and national health insurance proposals would have been more successful had they been introduced early as incremental changes in existing programs.

Carter entered the presidency without a plan for urban policy and asked Patricia Harris, secretary of Housing and Urban Development, to conduct a comprehensive review of existing programs and make recommendations for an administration policy. Harris found it difficult to develop proposals in the interdepartmental task force assembled for that purpose and turned to Stuart Eizenstat, director of the White House Domestic Policy Staff, for help. In the meantime, Carter had directed that any program should ask for no new money and should give strong roles to the states and private institutions. The program that eventually emerged was not comprehensive but a collection of specific ideas, such as an urban development bank and an employment tax credit. The *New York Times* described it as "as much political as substantive," adding that "it had a little something for everybody . . . Ultimately the plan was shaped greatly by lobbying, from mayors, governors, neighborhood advocates, businessmen and federal bureaucrats."[63] Carter gave the Democratic constituencies a measure of what each wanted, and thereby sacrificed any opportunity for a comprehensive program. He may never have wished anything more than a consolidation of existing programs.

Carter did want a Department of Education that was something more than a holding company for the National Education Association. The Presidential Reorganization Project (PRP) initially presented him with an idea for a comprehensive Department of Education and Human Development that would combine the Office of Education, then in HEW, with many of the social welfare agencies from the same department; all programs directed toward children would be brought together. However, Eizenstat and other political advisers warned that such a plan was politically unfeasible, and Carter acquiesced, asking only for as comprehensive a department as possible. When the PRP came back with a fairly narrow, constituency-based proposal, the president insisted that congressional testimony be rewritten to broaden the departmental base; as a result, programs such as Indian schools, Head Start, Department of Defense overseas schools, and the school lunch program were included in the new department. After prolonged conflict in Congress the Office of Education emerged in a still larger form. Carter's domestic policy advisers had been right about the politics of passage.[64]

It would be too easy to say that the search for public goods through comprehensive program proposals was quixotic because constituencies would be lacking. This was indeed the case in regard to issues characterized by long-standing political divisions, such as welfare reform and national health insurance; there was no evidence that bargaining coalitions could be constructed to produce majorities. But under some circumstances the public goods approach was a gamble that could work. It worked in regard to deregulation, civil service reform, and energy policy because the general political climate was sufficiently congenial that conceptions of the public interest could be articulated and recognized.

It is doubtful that Carter's reluctance to give the whole loaf to various Democratic constituencies in either economic or social policy hurt him with the majority of voters. It surely did hurt him within the Democratic party, as was evidenced in the Kennedy race for the presidential nomination. The greatest irony was that the administration lost the fight against inflation. Carter had known from the beginning that failure would be punished. The external shock of OPEC price increases in 1979 hurt the administration. One could hardly blame Carter for that. But, aside from the OPEC actions, it was politically difficult for a Democratic president to impose fiscal discipline.

Foreign Policy

Carter brought to the presidency a world view that might be called Wilsonian in the high value it placed on cooperation among nations to secure human rights, and to achieve peace. He hoped for cooperation between the United States and the USSR as an antidote to continuing competition and hoped to reduce U.S. defense commitments and restore the American role of moral leadership throughout the world in behalf of human rights. He also brought a determination personally to address long-standing, unresolved problems such as the Panama Canal and the Middle Eastern conflict. This was the same public goods approach as his attack on comparable domestic problems. Cyrus Vance writes that in such cases "Carter did what he thought American interests and values demanded even though he was keenly aware of the political risks."[65]

Foreign policy problems permitted Carter to use his strengths as a problem solver.[66] His four major achievements—the Panama Canal treaties, the normalization of U.S. relations with China, the Camp David agreement between Egypt and Israel, and the negotiation of the Salt II treaty with the Soviet Union—were to a great extent personal achievements. There is ample evidence in the accounts of participants that Carter took these initiatives against the advice of prudent counselors. These advisers told him that the canal treaty was a second-term issue and that he would earn very little political credit at home from a Middle East agreement, cautioned him not to let an agreement with China complicate SALT, and urged him to seek a renewal of the arms reduction agreement achieved by President Ford at Vladivostok in 1974.[67] He took none of this advice. In every case except the tie with China, he underestimated the difficulty of the problem and admitted it to himself and others. But such an awareness only made him redouble his efforts. In the case of SALT, he complicated his problem by sending Secretary of State Vance to Moscow in April 1977 with an overly ambitious proposal for arms reductions that went far beyond the terms of Vladivostok and compounded the error by discussing the proposal publicly before it was made privately. The results were delay and rejection. But he was also capable of presenting an accord in the most favorable public light, as at Camp David, even though it fell far short of a comprehensive agreement.[68] These four cases reveal Carter characteristics already apparent in his domestic policy initatives: ambition, naïveté, tenacity in the search for root-and-branch solutions, and a willingness to settle eventually for second best and to put the best possible face on it.

The central story in U.S.-Soviet relations in the Carter years was the collapse of détente, which left Carter without a policy toward the Soviet Union. Richard Nixon and Henry Kissinger had assumed that the inducements of arms reductions and liberalized trade with the United States would cause the Soviets to desist from Third World adventures. The assumption was mistaken. Kissinger, as Ford's secretary of state, moved to check Soviet interventions in Africa, the Middle East, and Southeast Asia but found himself caught in the crossfire between Republican conservatives opposed to détente and Democratic liberals hostile to U.S. interventions in Angola and other contested areas.[69] Carter and Secretary of State Vance adhered for three years to the hope that détente could be revived. His public rhetoric on foreign policy was based not on Cold War themes but on his hopes for peace, stability, and human rights. The greater influence of National Security Adviser Zbigniew Brzezinski over policy in the final year was largely a consequence of Carter's response to the Soviet invasion of Afghanistan, which forced him to withdraw the SALT II treaty from Senate consideration, and to the dramatic crisis in Iran, which reinforced Brzezinski's long-standing plea for greater attention to Middle Eastern security issues.

But at the end Carter stood before the American people without a policy. The fall of the Shah, the seizure and holding of American hostages in Iran, and the Soviet action in Afghanistan were events beyond his control even though he suffered politically because of them. The more crucial political difficulty was that Carter had created high expectations that could not be fulfilled. The erosion of détente that was under way when he entered the Oval Office eventually overtook his presidency. The public had been leery of American action abroad during the Kissinger period, but during the Carter years the public became increasingly concerned about American weakness in the world, a theme that Ronald Reagan was to dwell on in his campaign.[70] Had Carter possessed a more realistic understanding of power politics he might have been able to prepare public opinion for the failures and events beyond his control that undermined his foreign policy. But then he would not have been Jimmy Carter, and it is possible that he would have not have attempted the successes he did achieve.

The same pattern appears in all policy areas. Major successes were in large part personal achievements by the president. The Carter administration lacked the support of a strong domestic partisan coalition, and appeals to public interest and to a diffuse public had uneven results. The major strategic conceptions undergirding economic and foreign policy were overtaken by events, to some degree because those conceptions were incomplete and not flexible enough to anticipate and interpret conflicts or reversals. The thinness of strategic thinking was in part Carter's fault and in part reflected the historical context, which he could not control. A final assessment of the extent of Carter's responsibility for the fate of his presidency must depend upon an analysis of his skill in the conduct of the presidential office.

Skill in Office

An analysis of Carter's personal skill as a leader within the context of the prevailing political environment must determine whether his skill—or ineptness—affected outcomes, whether the environment at times overwhelmed his skill, and whether Carter might have changed the environment. How did Carter develop policy positions and sell them to others? His record reflects how well—or badly— he performed the integrally related roles of manager of policy development within the administration, political persuader of both Congress and the public, and diplomat.

Policy Development

Accounts of policy development in each of the major policy areas reveal a president who made discrete decisions according to his conclusions about the facts and the merits of issues, and on the basis of homework and discussion. This could be said of any president, but chief executives differ in the degree to which they factor political considerations into policy-making. Carter focused first on finding the correct solution and only then turned his attention to political persuasion.

Presidents make relatively few major economic decisions each year, and the advisory process is highly institutionalized.[71] The Council of Economic Advisers, OMB, and the Treasury dominate macro policy and act as the president's agent with the departments on micro policy issues. Carter accepted this loose but structured system for presidential advice and addressed issues as they came through it. Nothing in particular about the structure of the decision-making system appears to have influenced his major economic decisions. The unremitting theme was his effort to keep spending down in order to combat inflation while keeping Democratic interest groups at least partially content. The zigzag character of his decisions demonstrates that these goals were probably incompatible. A more consistent or decisive economic policy-making process would have shown single-minded intellectual and political conceptions on the part of the president and his advisers. President Reagan, for example, imposed a consistent set of ideas and political strategies on economic policy at the outset, but his values and his political opportunities were different from those of Carter. The loose collegiality of the Carter process gave way to greater hierarchy under Reagan with the

White House staff and OMB setting economic policy. The comparison suggests that decision-making processes reflect policy purposes as much as they influence them.[72] Studies of presidential decision making that assume that the process influences the actual results may be incomplete. It is just as likely that the character of the process, as shaped by the president, is a manifestation of his policy goals. Thus a president with strong, clear goals may seek less discussion, as the Reagan example suggests. Carter's desire to balance competing goals explains the iterative discussion and decision process described here.

Social policy-making was even looser in structure than economic policy because of the great number of actors. The Domestic Policy Staff was not empowered by the president to arbitrate among departments but only to act as a broker, to try to work out agreements, and to clarify options for presidential decision. Carter made decisions, after full analysis and discussion, issue by issue in serial fashion. There seems to have been minimal calculation about the relation of one issue to another. For example, welfare reform was sent to the congressional finance committees at a time when they were already overloaded with administration proposals on energy and tax reform.[73] Again, as with economic policy, the policy development process reflected Carter's belief in policymaking through problem solving relatively independently of politics. A policy development process guided by a few central conceptions of political strategy would presumably have been organized differently, again perhaps with greater centralization.

National security decision making was a collegial process with the president at the center. He regarded both the secretary of state and the White House assistant for national security as advisers to him and as complementary to each other in both their personalities and institutions. Thus, Carter saw Vance as a man of judgment, balance, and perspective and the State Department as a repository of historical memory rather than as an innovator of ideas. Carter liked Brzezinski's liveliness of mind and exposition and regarded the NSC staff as a resource for the development of fresh ideas. Carter thought of Brzezinski not as a neutral "custodian" for the development of policy options within the administration but rather as a personal adviser with views of his own. Disagreement between Vance and Brzezinski therefore did not bother Carter because he, Carter, would make the decisions.[74] Foreign policy decision making on the central issues of U.S.-Soviet relations had an ad hoc, serial quality not unlike decisions on economic and welfare policy. Although observers often explained decisions in terms of the relative influence of Vance or Brzezinski as clear differences emerged and Carter appeared to be caught in between, the decisions usually reflected Carter's own judgments of proper action as he assessed the merits of specific arguments. For example, the president's speech at Annapolis in June 1978, in which he both urged cooperation with the Russians and warned about the possible U.S. response to Soviet adventurism, was not, in his mind, a splicing of Vance's and Brzezinski's views. Carter was stating his own views.[75] The structure of the decision-making process thus appears to have been a manifestation of Carter's belief that foreign policy should be made through problem solving. He was playing to his understanding of his strengths.

In all three policy areas Carter liked small, loose, collegial decision-making structures in which he could hear diverse viewpoints and shift his weight, decision by decision. The emphasis was more on specific decisions than on creating the organizational capability for long-term strategic action in accordance with a few overriding principles. The balancing of principles took place in Carter's head. This kind of decision making reflected Carter's relative minimal attention to priority setting or strategic thinking and action.

There were perennial complaints within the administration itself about this way of doing things. The president would not give sufficient policy guidance to prevent turf fights among subordinates, the authority of White House staff to settle internal administration disputes was too limited, and consequently too many choices went to the president.[76] These were real problems. They made it difficult to achieve policy agreement within the administration. Carter was himself impatient with protracted disagreement. He liked diversity of opinion but not the bureaucratic politics that went with it. But it was not possible to have diversity without conflict.

Leadership of Congress

Carter organized his congressional relations to suit his own style of leadership in the same way that he organized executive decision making. His central assumption was that the president is a trustee for the public interest and should not permit himself or his staff to be drawn into the legislative bargaining games in which organized interests are predominant. This had been his leadership style as governor, and it was the theme of his campaign for the presidency.

He was going to ask Washington to do business in a different way. Accordingly, he developed his legislative agenda in 1977—including the energy program, welfare reform, and the defiance of Congress on water projects—and sent it to Congress with minimal consultation with congressional leaders. The economic stimulus package was an exception, but it was a more traditional Democratic program about which the president had mixed feelings. Although much of the first year's program eventually passed, the manner in which it was presented created a legacy of bad feeling between White House and Congress that lasted for four years.[77]

The White House learned the lesson. Carter asked Vice-President Mondale to chair a legislative group that would establish priorities and optimal timing for new bills. The president also gave greater authority to Stuart Eizenstat and the Domestic Policy Staff to coordinate policy development by the departments and to sound Congress and interest groups about the political feasibility of administration ideas.[78]

Carter's relations with Congress after the first year revealed the increasing competence of White House lobbying activities in achieving legislative results. But these successes were increasingly marred in the last year by the unraveling of the Democratic coalition and the widespread impression that the president had become the prisoner of events.

In its second session, in 1978, the Ninety-fifth Congress ratified the Panama Canal treaties, airline deregulation, civil service reform, and the natural gas pricing bill that completed the energy package; it also eliminated some of the most egregious pork-barrel public works projects. The bill for hospital cost control failed against very strong political opposition. Perhaps most important, the administration invented the task force device for conducting legislative battle, first in an ad hoc way under Hamilton Jordan's leadership in the Panama treaty fight, and then formally in the creation of the White House Office of Public Liaison under Anne Wexler. The Wexler office compensated for Carter's limitations as a presidential persuader by institutionalizing the persuasion function, not with Congress, but by bringing groups of citizens to the White House for briefings by the president and others on current legislative issues. Close collaboration among Wexler's group, Eizenstat's Domestic Policy Staff, Lloyd Cutler and other foreign policy legislative strategists, and the Congressional Liaison Staff eventually made the Carter White House effective in dealing with Congress.[79]

During Carter's last two years in office, however, this capacity for institutional effectiveness was underutilized because the administration was overtaken by events that disrupted presidential-congressional relations. It took skillful legislative work to bring the Department of Education bill to passage.[80] The second energy package was passed only as a result of dramatic interventions by the president. But the main story is one of unraveling. The conflict between the president and Congress over the budget had become institutionalized since the 1974 passage of congressional budget reform; Carter had simply taken the place of his two predecessors in trying to hold budgets down. As it became apparent that Senator Kennedy was going to run against the president in the primaries, it became more difficult for congressional Democratic leaders to control their majorities. After the U.S. embassy and hostages were seized in Iran in November 1979, Carter entered a final, disastrous legislative year. Although the White House Domestic Policy and Congressional Liaison Staffs felt that they knew their business better than ever before, Carter was absorbed in economic and foreign policy issues. The unresolved hostage problem, the Soviet invasion of Afghanistan and the resulting withdrawal of the SALT II treaty from the Senate, the rising inflation that necessitated a second administration budget in March, and Kennedy's primary victories in New York and California weakened the president greatly in Congress. The most dramatic instance of this weakness was seen in the response to the second budget, which had been carefully negotiated between the White House and the congressional leadership. Carter was determined to have a tax on gasoline, and Congress overrode his veto of a congressional resolution opposing such a tax. The president felt that Congress, and especially his own party, had betrayed an agreement for political reasons.[81]

Legislative support scores for presidents are crude instruments, but by such standards Carter did not do badly. His scores varied little over four years, from a low of 75.1 to a high of 78.3 percent, with an average of 76.4. Carter's four-year average was lower than Johnson's overall 84 percent, but Johnson declined to 78 percent in his last year, when Carter had 77 percent. The big difference lay in Johnson's successful first year and Carter's weak one. Carter's poor start colored his congressional relations for the rest of his administration. His average was just above that of Nixon, who faced a Democratic Congress. But Carter was not unlike Nixon and Ford in going against the wishes of Congress much of the time.[82]

Much of Carter's legislative program became law; he cannot be described as a legislative failure. But Carter did not manage highly conflictual policy issues in a way that held his coalition together or enhanced his reputation with Congress or the public. The legislative and policy successes of the middle years could not save him from apearing not to be in charge when overwhelming events converged in the final year.

Public Leader

Carter was good at selling himself as a person in the 1976 primary campaigns. Allen Otten, a seasoned Washington reporter for the *Wall Street Journal*, regarded him as the "best one-on-one" presidential candidate he had ever seen.[83] But Carter was selling himself as a moral person who would clean up things in Washington, not as someone who would provide issue leadership. Once in the White House he appeared to emphasize decision making as his principal task. His speechwriters recall that Carter seldom met with them to discuss speeches but simply asked for drafts on particular subjects and returned the drafts with corrections if he did not like them; thus speeches were prepared at one step removed from the President.[84] He did not want to give a State of the Union message on his first opportunity to do so in 1978 and had to be persuaded to do it by his staff.[85] When his speechwriters invented the phrase "New Foundation" to characterize his domestic programs for the 1979 State of the Union message, he disavowed it soon afterward at a press conference.[86]

Perhaps he had a realistic perception that formal speeches were not his strength; his several nationally televised talks on the energy problem had little impact on public attitudes. But he did like to speak in arenas in which he could show off his knowledge and competence. One of his assistants recalls that Carter did not like to be outshone by Vance or Brzezinski in knowledgeability on an issue.[87] He especially liked White House briefings of citizens' groups on important legislative issues. He liked town meetings and press conferences for the same reason. Carter entered the presidency with the idea of demystifying it in reaction against the "imperial presidency": "Hail to the Chief" was temporarily banned from presidential appearances; he carried his own luggage; and at his inauguration he and Mrs. Carter walked down Pennsylvania Avenue. Such behavior matched his campaign style, but it seemed to go over less well in the presidency. For example, when the president ran in a six-mile race on a hot Maryland day but failed to finish, an outcome that was vividly televised and widely displayed in newspaper photographs, his effort to present himself as a person rather than as a president seems to have backfired.

In any event, Carter created a public persona of morality rather than one of power. He was perhaps concerned to guard his personal reputation for rectitude more than his professional reputation for political skill. This characteristic was consistent with the way in which he became president, but it posed two drawbacks for his conduct as a public leader. First, he personalized problems of state. For example, in his effort to win freedom for the hostages in Iran it may have been a mistake for him to draw attention to his personal responsibility through frequent meetings with hostages' families and especially through the Rose Garden strategy, in which he stayed out of primary contests with the argument that he was needed in Washington to work on the hostage problem. As the problem failed to go away, Carter became a prisoner in the White House, and the initial public favor that he had received by personalizing the issue turned sour.

Second, Carter frequently failed to calculate the political effects of his public words and actions. He was inclined to present issues in ways that would protect his personal reputation for rectitude. Thus, he publicly revoked the fifty-dollar rebate of the economic stimulus package without warning his own secretary of the treasury or congressional leaders; he disavowed deployment of the neutron bomb in Western Europe even though his secretaries of state and defense had negotiated an agreement with U.S. allies; he announced the terms of a SALT II proposal to the Soviet Union at a United Nations speech before the proposal had been made to Kremlin leaders privately; he called for a homeland for the Palestinians at a town meeting in Massachusetts in the early stages of the search for a Middle Eastern peace agreement, thus making himself vulnerable to domestic Jewish opinion far in advance of negotiations.[88] And he undid the favorable public response to his televised July 1979 speech on the national crisis of civic will, with energy as an illustration, by subsequently firing several cabinet officers.[89]

Carter seemed to fail to understand that a national political leader must establish influence with other power holders by creating images that will win widespread public acceptance. In short, a political leader who would succeed must be political. Public persuasion is not simply a matter of rational argument, as Carter appeared to believe. Policies are most effectively sold when wrapped in larger themes about the American experience to which the public can respond. When he was overtaken by events in his last year, Carter's reactive, case-by-case style of leadership may have given the public the impression that he had lost control. He thought that his policy achievements would speak for themselves and win him political credit, but the public memory is short.

The irony is that a southerner should lack rhetorical skill. This lack could have been a deliberate response to the southern demagogues of his youth, but more likely it reflected his primary vocations as engineer and problem solver. He could be emotional and rhetorical on moral themes in familiar settings, such as black churches, where he knew the cadence and themes and liked the people. But even so, at his best he sold himself, not policies.

The Carter administration, unlike those of Kennedy, Johnson, Nixon, and Reagan, lacked a unifying ideology consistent with emerging trends of politics and history. An administration of ad hoc, serial decisions provided little raw material for presidential rhetoric. His style of leadership matched the few political resources available to him.

Chief Diplomat

At least three of the four big achievements—Panama, China, Camp David, and SALT II—were not the result of Carter's skills alone; the Camp David agreement may be an exception. But his tenacity, capacity for homework, ambition to achieve, and persuasiveness certainly contributed to these successes. Carter believed it important to attack hard problems that, if allowed to fester unresolved, might create even worse future difficulties. He hoped to be rewarded politically for success, but at the outset of each initiative he had no expectation of either success or political benefit. If anything, failure seemed more likely. Carter's sense of duty and his public goods approach to leadership impelled him to try.

Carter chose to pursue the canal treaty, conducted successful negotiations, and persuaded the Senate to ratify what proved to be a politically unpopular measure. By all accounts, his personal role was central to that success, especially in the persuasion of senators. This was no mean achievement given the widespread popular failure to understand and accept the need for a treaty.[90]

Camp David was Carter's greatest personal triumph, although it was Sadat who created the dialogue between Egypt and Israel. Frustrated with the difficulties of getting the two parties together, Carter hit on the novel solution of inviting Begin and Sadat to Camp David. The planning group from the State Department and National Security Council that wrote the background papers for the meeting hoped for agreement on the terms of future discussions. But Carter, who knew that with an election coming his political capital for risk taking was running out and who also hoped for political credit from an agreement, wanted a concrete agreement that both parties would sign. He got it by favoring Begin's position, with Sadat's acquiescence.[91]

The negotiations with China on the normalization of relations proved easier than expected, and it is not clear that Carter's role was crucial. He was so eager to announce the agreement that he risked, against Vance's warning, the possibility that the Soviets would retaliate by delaying the SALT II agreement. The announcement came in early 1979, just before Vance was to meet with Andrei Gromyko in Geneva to put the finishing touches on SALT II; and indeed the Soviets balked and delayed for another six months.[92]

Carter showed the same ambition with his unrealistic initial proposal to the Soviets on SALT. It would have been better to ratify the Ford-Brezhnev 1974 agreement and then move to SALT III, but Carter wanted to put his stamp on policy and was ignorant of the history of the issue and the perennial Soviets' tendency to respond negatively to surprises. However, the president's subsequent demonstration of determination and knowledgeability to Gromyko put the negotiations back on track successfully.[93]

These four achievements reveal Carter's strengths and weaknesses as a diplomat. His ambition and naïveté were two sides of one coin. The same tenacity that sometimes produced success sometimes also made him oblivious to the negative effect of one issue on another.

The revolution in Iran, the fall of the Shah, and Carter's inability to free the hostages are quite sufficient to explain the president's political defeat. Case studies of the fall of the Shah offer ample evidence of the administration's ignorance about events in Iran and of the internal divisions that may have paralyzed a creative response. But there are few convincing prescriptions for what that response should have been.[94] The events were beyond American control. Carter saved the lives of the hostages. His political error was in not distancing himself from the issue; but one might ask if that was possible in a televison age.

General Assessment

To determine whether Carter's skill, or lack of skill, made a difference in his policy achievements and failures and in the political resources available to him, we must first tally his major successes and failures.

The principal successes were legislative achievements in domestic policy (energy, deregulation, civil service reform) and foreign policy (the successful negotiation of the Panama Canal treaties, the agreement with China, Camp David, and SALT II). The principal legislative failures were in domestic policy (welfare reform, national health insurance) and the president's withdrawal of the SALT II treaty from the Senate. The great failures in economic policy were the rise in inflation and the impending recession. The principal foreign policy failures were the fall of the Shah and the hostage crisis. This list does not include all the Carter successes and failures. But the addition of, say, the mixed results of tax reform, the passage of the Alaskan lands bill, and the successful negotiation of multilateral trade relations would not alter the proportions of success and failure.

The legislative successes in domestic and foreign policy (energy and Panama being the chief examples) were the result of Carter's vision and tenacity. His legislative failures in domestic policy such as welfare reform and national health insurance reflect the same style. The withdrawal of the SALT treaty was a response to Afghanistan. Carter's ineptness with Congress in the first year probably hurt his reputation in Washington, and perhaps with the public, more than it damaged his legislative program in subsequent years. He might have had welfare reform and health insurance had he introduced scaled-down, incrementalist measures at the outset; but both issues carried such political hazards that this seems unlikely.

Carter's management of economic policy is hard to assess. The zigs and zags of alternately fighting recession and then inflation were unsettling to the financial community. But Carter was caught in the fact that high inflation cannot be reduced except through recession. Neither economic science or Democratic politics provided an answer for his problem.

Carter's personal skills contributed to his major foreign policy achievements, especially the canal treaties and Camp David. His principal failure was in Iran, and it is not clear whether alternative courses of action, either to save the Shah or free the hostages, would have proved viable. It is difficult to argue that any American administration could have done anything to prevent the Soviet invasion of Afghanistan, thus dooming the SALT II treaty in the Senate.

Carter made a great mistake when in early 1977 he proposed to the Soviets major cuts in arms reductions far beyond the agreement negotiated by President Ford. His ignorance and unrealistic ambition showed clearly. Had the more modest version of SALT II been negotiated and ratified in 1977, and the canal treaties negotiated but not sent to Congress until the next year, Carter might have built stronger support in Congress and with the public to help him when things later went awry.

The most telling criticism against Carter as president is that he did not calculate the political consequences of action beforehand and thus often squandered limited political resources.[95] The example of SALT II illustrates this point. He should have given more careful consideration to the chances for measures such as welfare reform. Carter would not have been required to offer only incremental proposals; public goods policy was good politics in many cases (energy, deregulation, civil service reform). He attempted to do too much too soon in both domestic and foreign policy. As a result, he suffered more failures than was necessary. It is doubtful that he could have achieved more major successes had he been a better political strategist.

A more conventional Democratic president, who would have worked better with the Democratic coalition in and out of Congress, might have achieved a few more domestic policy successes, such as the urban package and the Department of Education, and perhaps a greater contribution to inflation from the domestic budget. But a more conventional, politically more astute president might have lacked Carter's boldness, which was the distinctive feature of his presidency and which accounts for his major successes in domestic and foreign policy.

Carter's greatest deficiency as president and as a political leader was his inability to establish a bond with the public. It is not enough to make intelligent decisions. The public wants a president who is in command of his office and of events, or who at least appears to be in command. Carter seemed oblivious to such appearances. He could not accept the fact that often the public cannot tell the difference between appearance and reality. In his last frustrating year he had no capital with public opinion because he had not created a public persona that might have provided such capital. But it would have been difficult for any president to overcome inflation and the hostage crisis. In the political environment that constrained the president in 1980, skill was irrelevant.

9

RONALD REAGAN

The Primacy of Rhetoric

FDR, Kennedy, and Teddy Roosevelt loved the
Office of the Presidency and the bully pulpit it
afforded them. And so do I.

— Ronald Reagan, 1984

There is hardly any human action, however
particular it may be, that does not originate in
some very general idea men have conceived of
the Deity, of his relation to mankind, of the
nature of their own souls, and of their duties to
their fellow creatures. Nor can anything prevent
these ideas from being the common spring from
which all the rest emanates.

— Alexis de Tocqueville, 1840

William K. Muir, Jr.

There are many perils in writing about an incumbent president, but
most of them stem from the fact that readers approach the topic
defensively. The cause of this is that a chief executive still in office
is still powerful; even if he has not wrought havoc, he may yet do
so. We therefore tend to read his half-told story with a prudence
unnecessary when studying the exploits of someone who no longer
grasps the dagger of authority. This defensive skepticism is useful
to us, and we may even spice it with anger when an incumbent
comes from a political party not our own and has engaged, as all
presidents must, in the thrust-and-parry of partisan debate.

I understand this reaction. As a reader, I have felt such annoyance
myself. In the early presidency of Jimmy Carter, the slightest praise

caused me such deep chagrin that my fourteen-year-old daughter
composed "To Dad on Father's Day, 1977":

> It's time to face the facts
> Now that election time is done:
> Although the race was very close,
> *Jimmy Carter won.*
> At first you'll hold a grudge, I'm sure,
> But soon you should come through.
> Have *some* pity for the guy—
> He's a father too!
> You may be Republican,
> And he a Democrat.
> You, skinny from working hard,
> He, a little fat.
> Because of this I'm sure you are
> Of him not very fond,
> But still again, I must repeat,
> You share *one* common bond!
> Happy Father's Day!

I repeat my daughter's plea in hopes that the reader will value
this essay less as an account of President Reagan and more as a way
of looking at the presidential job. If you find its particular political
or historical assertions upsetting, pretend you are really reading, not
about Ronald Reagan, but about FDR, or Ike, or whatever other
president appeals to you. It is all right with me if you discount my
admiration for the specifics of the Reagan presidency in order to get
to the general point of the essay.

One of the presidential powers is to speak. It is a unique constitutional power, for the president does not have to share it with any
other branch of government. His messages to the people do not have
to be authorized by Congress, nor upheld by the Supreme Court,
nor executed by the bureaucracy. This independent rhetorical power
is central to the presidency, and a prime responsibility of every chief
executive is to use it well and, through language, to clarify the
fundamental and animating ideas that free people carry in their heads
and that give purpose to their actions. The person who sits in the
Oval Office has the duty to replenish what Tocqueville called "the
common spring from which all the rest emanates.'" If a president

fails to execute this rhetorical power, he will be a failed president, and the country will be steeped in confusion. If he does it well, the nation and its people will be vigorous and good. That is the point of this essay: Philosophical ideas have human consequences, and presidents best govern with philosophy.

The Rhetoric of Human Liberty

The key to the Reagan administration is its rhetorical character. It was organized to achieve a moral revolution—moral in the sense of affecting the character-shaping ideas of the American people, a revolution in the sense of returning the nation to its moral starting point.

Above all other objectives Reagan sought to mold the fundamental axioms on which Americans premised their lives.[2] He used the presidency to speak to the basic questions of what constituted the self-interest of free men and women, their responsibilities to one another, and (most fundamental of all) their very nature. He set out to define a philosophy of freedom, to distinguish it from a philosophy of equality, and to plant it in the soul of the nation.

Virtually all of Reagan's domestic policy achievements either ended in that moral goal or proceeded from it. The cuts in the federal budget, the domestic and international stabilization of the dollar, the reduction of income tax rates, "revenue-neutral" tax reform, the increase in volunteerism, the reforms in social policy, the emphasis on excellence in education and the insistence on infusing moral values into school curricula, the withdrawal of government from some of its former regulatory and fiscal responsibilities, the adherence to free trade and resistance to protectionism—all became part of the president's agenda because they reinforced his moral objectives.

Reagan's primary instrument to shape America's morals was rhetoric, and any effort to describe his administration must focus on the rhetorical presidency—the words he spoke, the institutions that transmitted them, and the difference they made to state and nation.

When Ronald Wilson Reagan was elected president in 1980, from the perspective of history the 235 million Americans then living were well fed, well housed, and well educated.[3] And they thought of themselves as free. They could marry whom they wanted, if another free person would accept them. They could work where they wanted, if other people were willing to pay for their services. They could travel wherever they wished, if anyone would give them hospitality once they got there. They could persuade others on any matters they believed in, if anyone wished to listen. They could worship freely, if their God found their faith or good works acceptable. And they could associate with whomever they chose, if anybody else cared to be associated with them.

In short, Americans were free on condition—on condition that they were willing, and able, to please. The central rule of the game was that they had to reciprocate, had to help others in order to get their help. Exchange was the latticework of a free society, the condition that maintained it. The marketplace, of course, epitomized this voluntary give-and-take, but the norm of reciprocity pervaded every aspect of society.[4]

This contingent aspect of a free society affected Americans profoundly. On the one hand, it made them care about one another and cultivate the habit of empathy; for if freedom required pleasing others, it was necessary to know what it was that pleased them.[5] A free society entangled the individual in the affairs and aspirations of his neighbors. But, on the other hand, because the free life was conditional it was mentally and emotionally exhausting. Occasional disappointment, despair, and loneliness were inescapable aspects of the free life.

Consider the following assessment of American freedom. In the spring of 1986 several Soviet educators visited the United States to observe at a dozen first-rank high schools. Afterward the chief of the delegation commented on the way American students were encouraged to think for themselves. What struck him most forcibly was the heavy responsibility the students assumed for their own work: there was virtually no "mothering" by their teachers. His next remark was instructive: "Of course, you have to do this because you train them for a tougher life," where they must be more "competitive." In the Soviet Union, he said, "We live in an environment that takes care of us from the cradle to the grave, and we tend to be dependent on one another." Then, speaking of the American students, he added, "Their self-reliance is something that we should have more of."[6]

A free people had trouble appreciating—or admitting—just how "tough" life was in a self-reliant society. Because of the general diffusion of wealth and comfort, Americans tended to belittle their own hardihood out of belief, as the ironic verse in *Porgy and Bess* goes, that "the living is easy." In fact the opposite was true. Modern times complicated moral life. The one thing that cars, abundant energy, and high technology made easier was the assumption of additional personal responsibilities. In earlier days, when an individual could not use television to view starving people, travel fifteen hundred miles to care for an ailing parent, or telephone someone almost anywhere in the world, his obligations seemed less extensive.[7]

Moreover, because of its conditional character, the self-reliant life was filled with occasions to fail—to be divorced, go broke, be lonely or degraded or overcommitted. A century and a half ago Tocqueville warned that individuals inhabiting a free society would feel "powerless" in the face of forces much larger than their independent and solitary selves.[8] As a result, the men and women constituting a free society were highly susceptible to a sense of personal inadequacy.

Attention had to be paid to the vulnerabilities of freedom. Somehow, individuals had to be strengthened with understanding, a sense of life's meaningfulness, and the knowledge of how to cope with their common frailty. Otherwise, things fell apart.

And things did fall apart during the troubled year of 1967. In that year the writer Joan Didion visited the "hippie" community in the Haight-Ashbury area of San Francisco, where she saw with horror the ignorance, the wretchedness, and the loveless estrangement of its young inhabitants:

> We were seeing the desperate attempt of a handful of pathetically unequipped children to create a community in a social vacuum. Once we had seen these children, we could no longer overlook the vacuum, no longer pretend that the society's atomization could be reversed. This was not a traditional generational rebellion. At some point between 1945 and 1967 we had somehow neglected to tell these children the rules of the game we happened to be playing. Maybe we had stopped believing in the rules ourselves, maybe we were having a failure of nerve about the game. Maybe there were just too few people around to do the telling. These were children who grew up cut loose from the web of cousins and great-aunts and family doctors and lifelong neighbors who had traditionally suggested and enforced the society's values. They are children who have moved around a lot, *San Jose, Chula Vista, here.* They are less in rebellion against the society than ignorant of it, able only to feed back

certain of its most publicized self-doubts, *Vietnam, Saran Wrap, diet pills, the Bomb.*

They feed back exactly what is given them. Because they do not believe in words—words are for "typeheads" . . . and a thought which needs words is just one more of those ego trips—their only proficient vocabulary is in the society's platitudes. As it happens I am still committed to the idea that the ability to think for oneself depends upon one's mastery of the language, and I am not optimistic about children who will settle for saying, to indicate that their mother and father do not live together, that they come from "a broken home." They are sixteen, fifteen, fourteen years old, younger all the time, an army of children waiting to be given the words.[9]

The lost flower children of the 1960s had never been told "the rules of the game," had never been encouraged to develop the "nerve" to try to be valuable to others, and had not been trained in the arts of association absolutely necessary to cope with what Didion calls "society's atomization." These lessons, she wrote with sadness, "had somehow [been] neglected"—"at some point between 1945 and 1967."

At other points in our history they had not been neglected. The community made sure that all persons belonging to it heard and mastered the language and the values of self-government. In the seventeenth century, in the first English settlements on the American continent, the New Englanders dealt communally with the self-doubts that lurked in their souls. The weekly sermon was a part of their civic life, supplying them with the meaning of freedom, educating them in "the rules of the game," and enveloping their communities in "the web" of a common sense of things.

Ever since, the sermon, along with the pulpit from which it was delivered, has signified the indispensable part ideas play in keeping a free people from falling apart and into despair. No reader of *The Scarlet Letter* can forget Nathaniel Hawthorne's description of the resonance of the language of the Reverend Mr. Dimmesdale. Herman Melville, in *Moby-Dick's* powerful opening image, likened the preacher's pulpit to the prow of the ship of state. In a more secular age Theodore Roosevelt conceived of the presidency as giving him a "bully pulpit" from which to do the very things Didion said must not be left neglected: "to create a community," to suggest "the society's values," to provide the language that nurtures "the ability to think for oneself," to challenge the "most publicized" platitudes of the day, to anticipate the individual's self-doubts and give meaning to the battle to overcome them.

By 1980 nothing had happened to diminish the significance of the community sermon. If anything, the need had become more compelling because the attacks on freedom had become more insistent.

"In the beginning was the Word," wrote St. John. Words made thought possible; thought clarified intention; intention directed the energies of the self-reliant individual. In a free society any man who would lead others had to engage their motives by the effective use of language—by what was called rhetoric.

To what should the rhetoric of leadership speak? According to Tocqueville, "there is hardly any human action . . . that does not originate" in our personal solutions to three questions: What are our "duties to [our] fellow creatures"? What is "the nature of [our] own souls"? and What is the meaning of life (that is, what "Deity" do we adopt, and what is "his relation to mankind")?[10] To these three central human issues—how to relate to others, what affects the course of human events, and what constitutes a significant life— President Reagan, in the exercise of his rhetorical power, gave these clear and consistent answers:

1. The central feature of a free society—its very definition, so to speak—is not the competition among individuals, but the voluntary and reciprocating association between them.

2. Human nature has never been pure and never perfectible: it has always consisted of a divided self, with hate and love inextricably and permanently intermixed. Every individual, of whatever culture or status, is marked with the capacity for cruelty and the free will to overcome the countless temptations to hate and hurt.

3. The ethical measure of man is not the actual consequences of his actions, but his efforts to resist his worse, and uphold his better, self; that is, what matters about an individual is not his material, but his spiritual, achievement.

These three notions—partnership, human imperfection, and spiritual dignity—justified the Reagan domestic and foreign programs, synchronized the personnel of the administration, and inspired the nation. In combination, they constituted the moral revolution of the Reagan years.

For each of these three ideas, I want to take up two questions.

First, what were the competing and antecedent notions with which they clashed? Second, how did the president present them?

Idea 1: The central feature of a free society—its very definition, so to speak—is not the competition among individuals, but the voluntary and reciprocating association between them.

Not long ago Peggy Noonan, a presidential speechwriter, said of the rhetorical craft: "The likening of one thing to another is a way of trying to convey a realistic picture of what is going on and calling for the need to face up to it."[11] She was explaining why Reagan's story-telling and analogical gifts were important. Metaphor—likening the unfamiliar to something concretely understood—was crucial to a president's influence as leader. If a president's rhetorical task is, in Joan Didion's words, "to tell [Americans] the rules of the game we happened to be playing," that is, if his job as chief executive is to provide definition of the situation, that definition has to be metaphorical. Metaphor is required to make society understandable even to the youngest and least experienced Americans. What Reagan had to do was originate a fundamental metaphor, one that would make sense of all the other metaphors a free people resort to in their daily lives. Moreover, it would have to challenge the currently prevailing metaphor and vanquish it.

The dominant metaphor when Reagan entered the White House in 1981 was that life was a footrace: "You do not take a person who for years had been hobbled by chains and liberate him, bring him to the starting line of a race, and then say, 'You are free to compete with all the others,' and still justly believe that you have been completely fair."[12] These words were spoken by Lyndon Johnson on the issue of civil rights at the Howard University commencement in 1965. The speech committed the American presidency to achieving "not just equality as a right and a theory, but equality as a fact and as a result."[13]

The metaphor of the footrace had quickly seized the imagination of the American society and remained unchallenged during the administrations of Nixon, Ford, and Carter, presidencies that paid virtually no attention to matters of rhetoric. It would be hard to overstate how rich in implication it was. If life was a "race" and if it was not "completely fair" to all who had to "compete" in it, then it was necessary for someone to adjust the "starting line" and provide a head start for those who "for years" had run in "chains." Furthermore, it could even be argued that, if removing the chains and giving a head start did not achieve equality "as a fact," if despite help life's losers continued to lose, the fault was not in them, but in "you," the American people. The metaphor made thinkable the remedy of handicapping those who had never run in shackles before. Hobbling the fastest would be "fair" because the rules of the race were that none of the contestants should get to the finish line before the hindmost, the slowest of the slow.

The metaphor implied still more. Existence was a life-and-death competition of all against all—a virtual civil war.[14] The speed and strength and intelligence of one American worked to the disadvantage of other Americans. The government was the handicapper-in-charge; its proper job was to discriminate, to encourage some and impede others, not in proportion to their character, but inversely to their material success. And, finally, the image of the footrace signified that equality, "as a fact and as a result," was in the saddle of events.

As Garry Wills, the classicist-turned-commentator, has observed, "the metaphor is a mess."[15] If the results of a race are fixed, why run it? Is the competition a meaningless exercise, designed by government to exhaust human energies pointlessly? Where does the race begin, how long is it, and when will a competitor know it is over? Why is there only one race, and who is in it? All these questions, and countless more, were left unanswered. Little wonder that many Americans, like the flower children described by Joan Didion, were confused by "the rules of the game," if the rules were as senseless as these appeared. If life was truly a never-ending sprint for the finish line, it was proper that society stay in a state of "atomization." After all, every schoolboy knows that collaboration between contestants would be out of keeping with the very purpose of a race. Nonetheless, the metaphor became the platitude of the times.

To defuse Johnson's metaphor, a president had to develop an alternative. For Reagan, "partnership" became that alternative.[16] The metaphor of partnership supplied American individualism with a social context. It implied a basis for cooperation, contrived initially on self-interest but fortified by gratitude and mutual respect. Partnership was voluntary, its roots set in the constitutional right to assemble and the frontier habits of moving on. It stood for the primacy of personal freedom as powerfully as Johnson's race metaphor represented the primacy of equality.

The metaphor of partnership had less invasive and less expansive implications than intimate national metaphors such as "house" or "family" (Lincoln: "a house divided"; FDR: "a new deal" in the household's ongoing pinochle game). It also provided a consoling contrast to the image of the solitary, self-absorbed long-distance runner.

And, most important of all, partnership instructed a society in what to do when trouble struck. "Team up," it said; "the strength and wisdom of others are advantages, not threats." Association was the secret of a free society, and the secret of association was exchange, give-and-take, giving fair weight. Partnership made the critical distinction between self-reliance and self-sufficiency. A self-reliant person handled his problems by sharing them with others and later returning the favor. He did not have to bear his burdens all by himself. And that was the central rule of the game.

Partnership became the logo of the Reagan administration. The word was stamped on its laws (the Job Training Partnership Act), imprinted on its programs (the Private Sector–Public School Partnership, the Child Safety Partnership, Public Private Partnerships for Fair Housing), and proclaimed in its messages: "Farm and city people have long been partners in economic and social progress. Without farms to provide food and fiber, cities would be barren; without the products and services of cities, farms would be primitive."[17]

The president's own elaborations on the theme of partnership were perpetual and comprehensive. They were sometimes folksy and at times exquisite. Consider the image of the mountaineers, a part of his address to the Japanese Diet on November 11, 1983. One can hardly conceive a political image more intricately spun, as he spoke of the intertwined destinies of Japan and the United States.

Our two nations may spring from separate pasts, we may live at opposite sides of the earth, but we have been brought together by our indomitable spirit of determination, our love of liberty, and devotion to progress. We are like climbers who begin their ascent from opposite ends of the mountain. The harder we try, the higher we climb, and the closer we come together—until that moment we reach the peak and we are as one.

It happened last month. One American and two Japanese groups began climbing Mount Everest—the Japanese from the side of Nepal and the Americans from the side of Tibet. The conditions were so difficult and dangerous that before it ended two Japanese climbers tragically lost their lives. But before that tragedy, those brave climbers all met and shook hands just under the summit. And then, together, they climbed to the top to share that magnificent moment of triumph.

Good and dear friends of Japan, if those mountaineers could join hands at the top of the world, imagine how high our combined 350 million citizens can climb, if all of us work together as powerful partners for the cause of good.[18]

The metaphor of the mountaineers would remind its audience of several features of partnerships. Partners do not have to be uniform nor conform to a single way of doing things (they can have "opposite" starting points and negotiate different terrain). Their very differences combine to strengthen the partnership beyond a mere aggregate of the efforts of its individual members; the unique strength of one partner can compensate for the frailties and limits of others. Nor does partnership preclude the existence of civilized competition between partners. This last quality of partnership was the central subject of a toast the president offered to Prime Minister Suzuki at a state dinner in 1981:

We have become principal trading partners and chief competitors. There's a legend in Japan about two villages separated by a river, and on moonlight nights a man from one town would come out and sing. And his voice would resound farther and farther, floating out across the river. And then it happened one night another voice was heard, and the second was fully as rich as the first. And when the original singer heard it, he realized he was faced with a strong rival, and he sang and sang at the top of his voice. And the singing grew more and more beautiful as each singer found depths to his talent that he hadn't known were there.

Well, Japan and America are like those singers. We each seek great achievements, and the standards we set for each other are marks of excellence. And yet we do not exhaust ourselves in the contest, but rather pursue our respective goals as friends and allies.[19]

In this beautifully elaborated tale, the singers found new "depths" to their talent because the friendly rivalry supported each of them in their aspirations to achieve. Because their contest was subject to reasonable traditions and rules agreed to by both sides, it did not wear them down and "exhaust" them. Stimulated by the competition, they tested their talents and improved them beyond previous "marks of excellence." The common experience of each doing his best ripened into mutual respect, which in turn perfected the basis for becoming true "friends and allies"—genuine "partners."

Once a free society was defined as partnership and not as brute competition, the meaning of all things changed. Free enterprise, for example, came to be seen, not as greed and conquest, but as institutionalized cooperation between supplier and customer. In the light of the partnership metaphor, it became clear how markets fostered habits of empathy and excellence in those who participated.

Changing the dominant metaphor from competitive race to teamwork was of transcendent importance to a nation whose citizenry was free to act on the basis of what it thought. The change in thinking transfigured reality, much as if the filters in front of Americans' eyes were replaced so as to soften colors that had previously been exaggerated and to bring into prominence objects that had once scarcely been seen.

Idea 2: Human nature has never been pure and never perfectible; it has always consisted of a divided self, with hate and love inextricably and permanently intermixed. Every individual, of whatever culture or status, is marked with the capacity for cruelty and the free will to overcome the countless temptations to hate and hurt.

In 1979 the author Richard Reeves journeyed through America, talking with more than 180 newspaper publishers, academics, lawyers, community leaders, writers, policemen, clergy, pollsters, and politicians. Repeatedly he was told, "The old values are being destroyed."[20] When he asked what was destroying them, the usual answer was "Freud." Reeves called on Harvard sociologist David Reisman, who had "written perceptively about the impact of Freud and psychology in general on American behavior and ethics," for an explanation. According to Reeves, Reisman said: " 'Let it all hang out' and other idiocies have been elevated to values by the popularizers of psychology . . . When Freud appeared, we didn't have the intellectual ballast to deal with his ideas. We went overboard from the beginning. So it would be more correct to say that it was not Freud, but misinterpretations of Freud, which have had profound impact in the United States."[21]

Reeves observes:

the suggestion that people somehow were not responsible for
their own behavior, that they were somehow controlled by mysterious forces—unconscious or psychological (or sexual!) forces
in the analysis of Sigmund Freud, and economic imperatives in
the analysis of Karl Marx . . . had essentially been absorbed into
the experiences and character of Americans . . .The personality
for this mélange of ideas, information and disinformation, "values" and "life styles" was the Viennese doctor with a goatee
and pince-nez glasses, "Freud."[22]

The American misinterpretation of Freud, the idea "that people
somehow were not responsible for their own behavior, that they
were somehow controlled by mysterious forces," threatened to destroy those "old values" that had once been passed down by (in Joan
Didion's phrase) "the web of cousins and great-aunts and family
doctors and lifelong neighbors."

Freud's "science" of human nature, with its trinity of id, ego,
and superego, was radically opposed to the religious trinity of sin,
soul, and conscience. The conscience was kind; the superego tended
to "cruelty." The conscience served to guide the pilgrim forward to
a better future; the superego pointed mankind backward to his primitive and childish ways. Sin was purposeful and knowing injury to
another; the id was naive, blameless, and unintelligent, knowing
"no values, no good and evil, no morality." The defeat of sin led to
the greater glory of man; defeat of the id's untamed passions transformed the individual into a social conformist. The soul was healed
and redeemed by serving others; the ego was damaged and wasted
by civilization.[23]

Freud viewed religion as "a really serious enemy" because it inspired men to pursue unrealistic ethical standards, consoled them
when things backfired as a result, and caused them to refuse "to
submit to the inevitable."[24] Men could never be masters of their
own futures; personal freedom was an illusion. "Dark, unfeeling,
and unloving powers determine human destiny."[25] Thus Freud dismissed the difference between matters of circumstance and matters
of choice; erased—or at least allowed others to erase—the distinction between the mindless forces of nature and intentional assaults
by one human upon another's freedom, the purposeful choices to
bully, enslave, and murder; and minimized the significance of having
one's freedom taken away.

Most important, from the perspective of Reagan's rhetoric, along with individual responsibility, Freud—his American misinterpreters—threw out the closely related traditional notion of evil, of intentional and unnecessary injury to the freedom of another. With the denial that men were free, the notion of evil became an anachronism and dropped from the moral vernacular. Its disappearance, however, left what Joan Didion called a "vacuum," and it constituted a semantic loss of great importance. It left men silent in the face of human oppression.

Ronald Reagan sought to restore the traditional notion of evil to popular discourse. He wanted to galvanize the assumption that individuals were responsible for their decisions to harm others. The very word *evil* affirmed man's moral freedom, and it was this moral freedom of will that gave man his dignity and justified his primacy over the state.

On March 8, 1983, the president paid a brief visit to Orlando, Florida. In between remarks to a group of educators and an appearance at a Republican fundraiser, he squeezed in a talk to the National Association of Evangelicals, a convention of 2,000 politically moderate Baptists and Methodists. Of all the speeches the president was to make in his two terms, none was more important in rhetorical terms. It became known as the "evil empire" speech, but it was much more than a reference to a popular movie. It was about the larger notion of evil — about man's choice to do, or refrain from doing, purposeful and unnecessary injury to the freedom of others.

The climax of the talk began: "we must never forget that no government schemes are going to perfect man. We know that living in this world means dealing with what philosophers call the phenomenology of evil, or, as theologians would put it, the doctrine of sin. There is sin and evil in the world, and we're enjoined by Scripture and the Lord Jesus to oppose it with all our might."[26] Reagan then spoke of the recurring presence of evil in American life:

Our nation, too, has a legacy of evil with which it must deal. The glory of this land has been its capacity for transcending the moral evils of our past. For example, the long struggle of minority citizens for equal rights, once a source of disunity and civil war, is now a point of pride for all Americans. We must never go back. There is no room for racism, anti-Semitism, or other forms of ethnic and racial hatred in this country. I know that you've been horrified, as have I, by the resurgence of some hate groups in our midst. The commandment given us is clear and simple: "Thou shalt love thy neighbor as thyself."[27]

Groups that focused the "hate" of their members so as to injure others were, in a word, "evil," and they should be denounced as such and opposed "with all our might."

He then talked of the Soviet regime and its systematic preaching of hatred and aggression in the name of "class war."

During my first press conference as President, in answer to a direct question, I pointed out that, as good Marxist-Leninists, the Soviet leaders have openly and publicly declared that the only morality they recognized is that which will further their cause, which is world revolution. I think I should point out I was only quoting Lenin, their guiding spirit, who said in 1920 that they repudiate all morality that proceeds from supernatural ideas—that's their name for religion—or ideas that are outside class conceptions. Morality is entirely subordinate to the interests of class war. And everything is moral that is necessary for the annihilation of the old, exploiting social order and for uniting the proletariat.[28]

In simple terms the president was saying that the Soviets were a hate group and their leaders instruments who functioned to incite and "focus" the hateful impulses of their adherents.

let us be aware that while they preach the supremacy of the state, declare its omnipotence over individual man, and predict its eventual domination over all peoples on the Earth, they are *the focus of evil* [italics added] in the modern world. It was C. S. Lewis who, in his unforgettable *Screwtape Letters*, wrote: "The greatest evil is not done now in those sordid 'dens of crime' that Dickens loved to paint. It is not even done in concentration and labor camps. In those we see its final result. But it is conceived and ordered (moved, seconded, carried, and minuted) in clean, carpeted, warmed, and well-lighted offices, by quiet men with white collars and cut fingernails and smooth-shaven cheeks who do not need to raise their voice."[29]

What is the proper reaction to these quiet practitioners of evil, who would of their own will crush the moral freedom of others? The president responded: "if history teaches anything, it teaches that simple-minded appeasement or wishful thinking about our adversaries is folly. It means the betrayal of our past, the squandering of our freedom. So I urge you to speak out against those who would place the United States in a position of military and moral inferiority."[30]

He then summarized his two major points. First, he reiterated the religious understanding of human nature—that it is not perfectible, that there exist in the soul of every man "aggressive impulses," and that "the temptation of pride" to deny them weakens the very strength necessary to struggle with them:

> You know, I've always believed that old Screwtape reserved his best efforts for those of you in the church. So, in your discussions of the nuclear freeze proposals, I urge you to beware the temptation of pride—the temptation of blithely declaring yourselves above it all and labeling both sides equally at fault, to ignore the fact of history and the aggressive impulses of an evil empire, to simply call the arms race a giant misunderstanding and thereby remove yourself from the struggle between right and wrong and good and evil.[31]

Second, he spoke to the folly of ignoring the individual's moral freedom to choose to struggle against the impulse to hate and hurt.

> The real crisis we face today is a spiritual one; at root, it is a test of moral will and faith. Whittaker Chambers, the man whose own religious conversion made him a witness to one of the terrible traumas of our time, the Hiss-Chambers case, wrote that the crisis of the Western world exists to the degree in which the West is indifferent to God, the degree to which it collaborates in Communism's attempt to make man stand alone without God. And then he said, "for Marxism-Leninism is actually the second oldest faith, first proclaimed in the Garden of Eden with the words of temptation, 'Ye shall be as gods.' The Western World can answer this challenge," he wrote, "but only provided that its faith in God and the freedom He enjoins is as great as communism's faith in Man." I believe we shall rise to the challenge. I believe that communism is another sad, bizarre chapter in human history whose last pages even now are being written. I believe this because the source of our strength in the quest for human freedom is not material, but spiritual. And because it knows no limitation, it must terrify and ulti-

mately triumph over those who would enslave their fellow man.[32]

The "evil empire" speech directly addressed the issues raised by the misinterpreted Freud: Did men have to "submit to" the "dark, unfeeling, and unloving" facts of slavery, racism, anti-Semitism, the concentration camps, and the gulag, or did they have the moral freedom to oppose those evils? Was mankind's only way to avoid bloody anarchy the meek submission to state-imposed enslavement, or was history writ large with the successful struggles of free people to "deal with"—to defeat—hatred and cruelty? Was the injunction to stop hating "unrealistic," or had it inspired men to be better than their worst impulses? Were totalitarian rulers who glamorized evil and focussed the impulses to hate and destroy really destined to dominate, or did they, by pandering to men's evil impulses, leave their citizenry unfit for anything but enslavement and their country enervated and enfeebled?

The president had voiced these ideas, and in much the same words, before. On May 9, 1982, he had called the Soviet Union "a huge empire ruled by an elite that holds all power and privilege."[33] And speaking before the British Parliament on June 8, 1982, he had asked: "we see totalitarian forces in the world who seek subversion and conflict around the globe to further their barbarous assault on the human spirit. What, then, is our course? Must civilization perish in a hail of fiery atoms? Must freedom wither in a quiet, deadening accommodation with totalitarian evil?"[34] But the words *empire* and *evil* did not then explode into the American consciousness as they did in the Orlando speech. In a recent interview, presidential speechwriter Tony Dolan explained why: "The phrase 'evil empire' had originally been in the British Parliament speech, and it was there to the last minute, when some of the boys took it out. But I kept coming back to it, and eventually I wore them down, and when it appeared in the Evangelicals speech, they said, 'So what? It's an unimportant speech to an unimportant constituency.' and the rest is history."[35]

"The boys" were those members of the president's staff who Dolan felt had no understanding of the rhetorical presidency, the kind who thought "that what governing is about are meetings, conferences, phone calls, rules and decisions." They were the ones who failed to understand Dolan's first principle, that "ideas are the stuff of politics . . . the great moving forces of history."

Dolan continued by talking about how the "evil empire" phrase originated:

> In the Orlando speech the president used the phrase "focus of evil," and he talked about America's legacy of evil—anti-Semitism, hate groups, and we are enjoined by our beliefs and the Lord to deal with that legacy.
>
> I was writing the focus of evil line, but then I needed a follow-up in the next paragraph. So I used the phrase "evil empire." I must say I heartily welcomed the reaction, that it was likened to *Star Wars*. Some even called it the Darth Vader speech. But why was the movie *Star Wars* so popular? Because it was a fantasy which did what Bruno Bettelheim says fantasy performs: it is a healthy expression of reality. Kids know there is evil in the world, and no matter how many nice words we use to buffer ourselves from that insight, the reality is that there's evil, and that it has to be fought against.

Dolan went on: "The point is that in the free world we acknowledge our shortcomings, and seek to do our best the next time, to do better. In the Soviet Union they say their shortcomings are part of the revolutionary process and try to justify them. Reagan made that point a long time before he became president...I often say that writing speeches for this president is writing some things he has already said and giving them back to him to say again."

Dolan, who as a newspaper journalist had won a Pulitzer Prize for his articles about organized crime in Connecticut, called the term *evil empire* "a semantic infiltration."

> The secret is to give the world a cliché, a semantic infiltration. Now and forever the Soviet Union is an evil empire . . . . The Soviet Union itself can't let go of it. It torments them; so they say it themselves. I found that also with the Mafia in Connecticut. The human conscience is such that evil acts bother people, and I've found that if you let the bad guys talk, they'll get preoccupied with trying to rebut it, and in the end they concede it. You know, the Soviet Union knows the importance of words. That's why they have coined phrases like "Wars of National Liberation" and "People's Republics." The "evil empire" is one of the few semantic victories the West has won . . . In history it has always been thus. It was Churchill's rhetoric

which made a difference in the World War. People respond to the truth. With "evil empire," people said, "That's right. Cut out all the bull. The emperor has no clothes." Who was it that said "brood of vipers"? Christ. He did the same thing, with those hypocritical scribes. He just did it.

Then Dolan talked of the institutional forces within the presidency itself that moved an incumbent president to speak of such profound subjects as the sinful nature of man and the moral effect of political systems on character. According to Dolan, the office itself impelled its occupant to instruct a confused world why liberal democracy was morally superior to totalitarianism.

I think [the president's] notions about the importance of democracy and its use in making the world prosperous and peaceful were inchoate, were latent. But when you go to the world and you urge on the expansion of democracies, the importance of holding elections, you think about the reasons justifying what you urge. It was the British Parliament speech where he first promoted democratic elections as possible and useful throughout the world.

Dolan spoke admiringly of his boss, who had used the presidential pulpit to such powerful effect:

People say that the president is The Great Communicator. He's not. He's The Great Rhetorician. He uses words. He uses logic. There is substance in every paragraph. His arguments flow from one point to the next. And he uses anecdotes and statistics to back them up. He has a philosophy. He develops it. And he adheres to it. As I said, the Reagan speechwriters' major function is to plagiarize the president's old speeches and give them back to him to say.

Idea 3: The ethical measure of man is not the actual consequences of his actions, but his efforts to resist his worse, and uphold his better, self; that is, what matters about an individual is not his material, but his spiritual, achievement.

American philosophy was early identified with the notions of pragmatism. In 1840, for example, Alexis de Tocqueville described Americans' way of thinking as "to accept tradition only as a means of information, and existing facts only as a lesson to be used in doing otherwise and doing better . . . to tend to results without being bound by means."[36]

Skepticism in the service of progress—what has been called pragmatism—promoted inquiry and technological improvement. But as a system of ethics—as a set of standards by which the individual answers the two pressing questions "What should I do?" and "What have I counted for?"—it imposed a standard at once vague and heartlessly severe. Pragmatism admonished an individual to do "better," but it specified neither what "better" was nor the cost of achieving it. Pragmatism's severity arose from its primary emphasis on results. That did not preclude pragmatic philosophers such as John Dewey from evaluating the honesty of the means by which results were obtained.[37] But by its silence on the subject of failure, pragmatism— or at least the vulgarized version that would predictably arise in a society with a well-developed "taste for well-being"[38]—dismissed the importance of well-intentioned effort that failed; people who did not achieve results did not count. Good intentions, brave efforts, sincerity, tough odds became irrelevant in moral assessment. Pragmatism insisted on asking, "Did the individual *do* better?" not "Did he *try* to do better?"

There was much to be said for the pragmatic standard in certain areas of human activity. No one testified more eloquently to its propriety than the German scholar Max Weber (1856-1920) when, toward the end of his life, he discussed the proper ethical standards to be applied to those who entered politics. The politician had only two choices: either he could live by an "ethic of principle," whereby motives would be the proper measure of his political acts; or he could choose an "ethic of responsibility," a consequentialist or results-oriented philosophy.[39] In the realm of politics, Weber insisted, the only possible standard was the consequentialist one. "He who lets himself in for politics, that is, for power and force as means, contracts with diabolical powers, and for his action it is *not* true that good can follow only from good and evil only from evil, but that often the opposite is true. Anyone who fails to see this is a political infant."[40]

The holocausts, the gulags, the slaughters of innocents that have afflicted our century have convinced many that Weber was right. It seemed to defy moral sense to exonerate the perpetrators of such horrors because of their proclamations of a higher motive, nor to exculpate those who failed to resist because of a personal fastidiousness about using force to deter cruelty. Weber seemed correct in holding those who had voluntarily assumed authority to an ethical standard based on results.

But it was too severe a standard by which to measure the lives of ordinary persons. Pragmatism ignored the fact that individuals who (unlike Weber's politician) lacked "force and power as means" lived in a contingent world, one in which their own efforts could not guarantee successful outcomes. Even though a mother's child did not turn out well, a sense of human decency required an ethical standard that honored a mother who cared (and denied honor to one who did not).

Moreover, a pragmatic ethic would imply, in a world of limited material achievement, a moral inegalitarianism. If results were the only things that mattered in the ethical realm, there would be only an elite few to honor and a mass of moral no-accounts.

Consider Willie Loman, in Arthur Miller's *Death of a Salesman.* He worked unremittingly. He was a good neighbor and a good husband. He raised two sons as best he knew how. He hurt no one intentionally or without remorse. He never stole. He paid his debts. Willie Loman was a decent man. Yet when he took his own moral measure, he found himself worthless. "A man must count for something," he cried, but he had no results to count.[41] On his pragmatic scale, all the kindnesses, all the good humor, all the struggles against temptation to cheat or hate or quit, all the spiritual decency of the man were simply irrelevant.

But they did count. Morally they had to count in a society in which free men had no choice but to be self-reliant. There had to be a moral marker that would accord respect for decency, regardless of the results it produced. There had to be dignity for courage, honesty, and love, for persevering, for prevailing in the battle for one's soul. There had to be a gauge of the spirit of man.

Reagan confronted the failed results of his own best efforts—the unexpected downturn of the economy in 1982, the destruction of the marine barracks in Beirut in 1983, the tragedy of the space shuttle Challenger in 1986, the confusion of the Iran-Contra affair in 1987—and shared them with the American public. We watched him and learned from him. We learned what he really valued as we never could have learned in times of prosperity. He signified in his reactions that the human spirit was what counted, and thus repelled the pervasive tendency to live by a pragmatic ethic. He transformed the way Americans measured themselves, and he enlarged their self-respect.

Not always, but often with astonishing effect, Reagan used the bully pulpit, not to hide failure, but to redeem it with spiritual meaning. For example, in April 1984, when presidential candidates might be expected to consolidate their hard-core supporters and focus on the national good fortune, the Baptist Fundamentalists met in Washington for their annual convention. The White House staff expected the president to speak on social issues of concern to the Baptist leadership, such as abortion, pornography, and school prayer bans.

President Reagan, however, had other plans. He had earlier received a letter from a Marine Corps chaplain, Lieutenant Commander Arnold Resnicoff, who had been on duty the morning in October 1983 when terrorists destroyed the barracks of the American marines posted to Lebanon to keep the peace there. The chaplain was a rabbi, and he described with vividness both the devastation and the marines' reaction to it. The president had forwarded the letter to his speechwriting department with a note asking them to write a few introductory remarks to it. He was planning to read the entire letter to the Baptist Fundamentalists.[42] No one on Reagan's staff thought the letter appropriate to the occasion, and several members registered their objections. The audience would be expecting a different topic, one closer to their concerns. Besides, the letter was about one of the administration's failures; it would only call to mind a disappointing policy, one that was best kept out of the public's mind.

Nonetheless, the president insisted, and it was done. He read the entire letter at the Baptist gathering, and by conventional standards the speech was no great triumph. Unquestionably the subject took the Fundamentalists by surprise. The applause appeared restrained; hecklers in the audience upset the pacing of the delivery; and the press coverage was indifferent.

But consider the effect of the final three paragraphs of Rabbi Resnicoff's letter on the 2,000 clergy whose responsibility it was to speak from their pulpits to the ethical concerns of their own congregations.

That October day in Beirut I saw men reach heroic heights— indeed, heights of physical endurance and courage, to be sure, but heights of sacrifice, of compassion, of kindness, and of simple human decency as well, and even if the admission might bring a blush to the cheeks of a few marines, heights of love.

Long ago the rabbis offered one interpretation of the Biblical verse which tells us that we're created in the image of God. It does not refer to physical likeness, they explained, but to spiritual potential. We have within us the power to reflect as God's creatures the highest values of our creator. As God is forgiving and merciful, so can we be; as He is caring and kind, so must we strive to be; as He is filled with love, so must we be.

Because of the actions I witnessed during that hell in Beirut, I glimpsed at least a fleeting image of heaven, for in the hearts and hands of men who chose to act as brothers, I glimpsed God's hand as well. I did not stand alone to face a world forsaken by God. I felt I was part of one created with infinite care and wonderful awesome potential.[43]

Amid memories of carnage and failed policy, the president led his audience to contemplate "the highest values of our creator." In reading the letter he magnified ten thousand fold the effects of the lesson the rabbi had to teach: Free men and women had to deal with circumstance not always of their own choosing, but it was up to them whether they would react with cowardice or courage, with decency or despair, with love or bitterness. That was how free persons took control of their own destinies.

Ordinary men and women understood that message—farmers struggling to keep their farms, families coping with a troubled member, jobless wondering whether they could learn new skills and start again, isolated folk frightened to live in their crime-ridden neighborhoods, individuals degraded by smart alecks. They knew that they could measure up on the scale of values they shared with their president. If battling the temptation to quit, to hate, and to hurt was the spiritual result that counted, then they, too, could stand proud and tall—and find new depths to their courage.

Moral Institutions

Moral institutions—organizations that propagate systems of ideas—are the least visible, and perhaps the least appreciated, of our national institutions. President Reagan enlisted the assistance of an existing moral institution and also created another, secondary one to educate the American democracy in his ideas of human liberty.

In its ideal form a moral institution has six components:

1. A written text, undeniable, virtually unchangeable, and abstract. The text provides the institution with continuity, mental discipline, and comprehensive application to a broad and ever-changing variety of human undertakings.

2. An authoritative center, or chief exegete, with the final say in resolving conflicting interpretations of the abstractions of the text.

3. A school to prepare a community of disciples to spread the word of the text by applying it to the practices and circumstances of the outside world. Education of carriers of the word is continuous in order to increase their ranks and replace the dead and the tired.

4. A means of continuously supervising the disciples, keeping their commitment alive and unambiguous to the institution and the text and ensuring that they speak out vigorously, frequently, and with one voice.

5. A system of two-way communication between disciples in the field and the authoritative center. Because the disciples come into direct contact with specific worldly problems, the center must allow them some indirect influence over interpretation of the text, or risk demoralization. Furthermore, a genuinely two-way communications system permits a moral institution to modify its doctrines gradually, decreasing the chances of deep schism and nurturing consensus, a sense of participation, and great energy throughout the institution.

6. Least important is a set of symbols to distinguish adherents from outsiders. The symbols fortify a sense of identification—a feeling among the individual members of a common destiny with the institution.[44]

The United States after World War II was dominated by two moral institutions. Each possessed all or most of the six critical components of propagation described above.

The law was foremost.[45] Its major text was the U.S. Constitution, and the Supreme Court its chief exegete. The central tenet of the law's doctrine was ably condensed in a 1937 opinion by Justice Benjamin Nathan Cardozo: "the law has been guided by a robust common sense which assumes the freedom of the will as a working hypothesis in the solution of its problems."[46] The more than half-million lawyers throughout the nation were the law's disciples.[47] Trained in more than 175 law schools in the reading of the text and its written and precedent-setting interpretations, they constituted a vast army of individuals virtually uniform in their commitment to the major tenets of their legal faith.[48] The disciplinary structures of the law—lower court judges and bar associations—were firmly institutionalized, capable of dispensing powerful sanctions to punish the heretic and reward the adherent. The commentary apparatus, joining center and disciples in two-way communication of facts and values, was unexcelled. Lawyers and judges were professionally compelled to read one another's official correspondence, and there was a vital network of law journals, professional meetings, and continuing education of bench and bar to maintain connections. Finally, through titles, symbols, and ceremony, the members of the legal fraternity were publicly singled out from those not trained in law.

Religion was nearly as effective as the law.[49] Catholicism, Judaism, and Protestantism, the mainstream religions of the United States, shared a common text, the Bible. Theological schools were in place, and more than 300,000 trained clergy were dispersed to virtually every locality in the nation.[50]

Finally, religion had a host of disciplinary rules and sanctioning bodies, a rich network of commentary, and the symbols of the cross of Christianity and the Star of David. Religion's weakness as a moral institution was the lack of a chief exegete to resolve arguments over interpretation of the biblical text. The various sects approached abortion, pacifism, and commerce differently, and the discord of the clergy on these matters contrasted with the greater unity of the legal profession. No doubt the force of religion was lessened by such factionalism, but habits of comity and consultation within the clerical community helped fortify agreement on matters of fundamental doctrine.

In other nations one might have detected different institutional bases for sustaining the centering notions of a culture—labor unions, the army, the civil bureaucracy, disciplined political parties, the universities, even the profession of science. But in the United States none equaled the force of law and religion in propagating moral ideas.

It might appear that the media—especially television and the movies—constituted not only a primary, but *the* primary, moral institution. On examination, however, the claim proves dubious. Consider the variety of voices with which the media spoke (they lacked an authoritative center). Moreover, media lacked a text to provide continuity and comprehensiveness of application, and the schooling and disciplining of journalists were delegated to the control of external forces (for example, the law of libel was administered by lawyers). The media, being diverse and organizationally undisciplined, reflected cultural ideas propagated elsewhere and spoke without the singleness of sentiment by which a primary moral institution attains dominance. Perhaps that was why the writer and sometime journalist Henry Adams called the American media "an inferior pulpit."[51]

America's elementary and secondary schools were another inferior pulpit. Although the public schools might rightly claim to have inculcated the virtue of tolerance in schoolchildren, that very tolerance had undermined the school system as an idea-propagating institution. To be effective in formulating the core ideas to which disciples committed themselves, a moral institution must be neither confusing nor equivocal.

Much the same weakness afflicted capitalism. Despite the availability of a text to expound (Adam Smith's *Wealth of Nations*), early American capitalism had relied on the law for the schooling and disciplining of its followers. When the law ceased to play its one-sided role as advocate for free enterprise, capitalism was enfeebled. In modern times large individual firms such as IBM and the telephone companies disciplined their employees' thinking in one respect or another, but their doctrines were highly particularized to the workplace and lacked the comprehensive application of a primary moral text.[52]

A president with rhetorical purposes had to piggyback his message on one of the established moral institutions. No president normally had the length of tenure nor the manpower to organize, and penetrate the society with, a pervasive network of his own. Wartime was the obvious exception to that rule, for as commander in chief the president headed the military, a moral organization of great effectiveness and size. No doubt much of Lincoln's moral ascendancy stemmed from that fact, as did FDR's.[53] But in the 1980s the president had to borrow an existing network in order to have a profound impact on Americans. The stronger—that is, the more mentally disciplined, the more numerous, the more fervent—the moral institution with which he allied himself, the better off he was from a rhetorical point of view. An institution such as the media or the public schools, which spoke equivocally and without continuity or context, lacked precisely those qualities by which a president could penetrate public consciousness.

The president's choice of allies among existing moral institutions was limited by another factor. If he wanted to use for his own purposes an organization's text, exegetics, schooling, discipline, and commentary, he had to be useful in return. He had to be willing to fortify respect for the organization's doctrines, galvanize its disciples, and vest its commentaries with importance. This he could not possibly do if his own general ideas directly contradicted the established organization's.

Law and religion, then, were the two candidates for the president to use. But each posed serious obstacles to his collaboration with them. The doctrine of rule of law maintained judicial independence from presidential encroachment on the spokesmen of the law. The only acceptable means of penetrating the moral institution of the law was by appointments to the federal judiciary. But an appreciable amount of time would have to pass before he could fill a large number of vacancies and his appointees would begin to write opinions and commentaries that would affect the discipline.

Religion was also buffered against the president's effort to affect it. The principle of separation of church and state deprived him even of the appointive power he enjoyed over the law. Nonetheless, Reagan turned to religion because of the congruence between his emphasis on character and religion's central preoccupation with individual meaning. The alliance was also abetted by its convenience: there were so many occasions to collaborate. For example, a presidential speechwriter, Peter Robinson, talking about some remarks he had prepared for Reagan to deliver to the National Association of Evangelicals in March 1984, recalled:

> I spent quite a lot of time on how important religion was in this country—in the nation's founding, the pilgrim fathers, mentioned in the Declaration of Independence. It is from Him that Americans derive their rights. Religion legitimates our system of government. The United States political philosophy stands at the intersection of religion and politics. Lincoln said as much in his Second Inaugural. What he says, when one comes down to it, is that there was one overarching issue, could men own other men? And the religious answer, not the economic answer, not the material answer, was No . . . I developed that theme, discussing the Civil War and the civil rights movement, quoting Martin Luther King, who led what was, after all, a religious movement.[54]

By "the United States political philosophy," Robinson meant the moral revolution the president was seeking to bring about.

There was common ground occupied by the president and the clergy. Both were entrusted to answer that haunting question, what good did it do mortals to try? Both had repeatedly to speak about death to their audiences. The frequent obligation to commemorate dead Americans in a funeral oration compelled the president to speak of the meaning of death in the context of life. Was there life after death? Did the effects of personal honesty and love and decency abide beyond a man's lifetime? In contrast, did barbarity and greed, the evil of men, vanish as soon as there was no longer cause to fear their perpetrators? When Reagan addressed these existential questions, the religious community, especially the clergy, listened intently and willingly. It was in their interest to listen for and reinforce the president's funeral messages.

A significant share of Reagan's rhetoric was devoted to religious discourse. In five of his first six years in office, funeral orations and speeches made directly to religious audiences made up nearly 10 percent of his prepared remarks. For example, those eulogized in funeral orations in 1984 included Princess Grace of Monaco, President Harry Truman, Senator Henry Jackson, Vice-President Hubert Humphrey, Terence Cardinal Cooke, and American servicemen who had died in Normandy, Vietnam and Grenada. The religious audiences included the National Religious Broadcasters, the Baptist Fundamentalists, the National Association of Evanglicals, the New York State Federation of Catholic School Parents, B'nai B'rith, and Re-

Religious discourse of President Reagan, 1981–1986

Year	Prepared remarks[a]	Speeches to religious audiences	Funeral orations	Percentage religious discourse
1981	160	1	11	7.5
1982	245	10	11	8.5
1983	282	8	14	7.8
1984	334	10	16	7.8
1985	210	6	14	9.5
1986	257	1	5	2.3

a. Does not include remarks prepared for visits by foreign leaders and for journalists' interviews and press conferences.

publicans at an ecumenical prayer breakfast at the party's national convention.

The effect of this collaboration "at the intersection of religion and politics" was to make the president's philosophy—and the rhetoric in which he expressed it—both more coherent and more restrained. To harmonize his political outlook of personal responsibility and productivity with his religious philosophy stressing brotherhood and charity, the president made connections that he had not made before, either as governor of California or as presidential candidate. Harmonizing his message of human liberty with basic religious needs neither distorted nor diverted his notions; on the contrary, it regulated them and purified them of their earlier excesses. In return, his message galvanized the members of the religious community. Thus, religion became the president's primary pulpit.

But a president with rhetorical objectives must avoid complete dependence on a moral institution he cannot dominate. Reagan therefore undertook to build a secondary pulpit, one in which he could personally oversee the instruction and supervision of his followers, in case events deprived him of the collaboration of the primary moral institution. He also realized that a secondary moral institution could be used to influence, not public opinion, but the thinking of administration officials; it could serve as an intragovernment pulpit.

A moral institution, even a secondary one, must have a text. Reagan's was the speech sometimes called "A Time for Choosing" but referred to by his speechwriters simply as "The Speech."[55] It was the repository of Reagan's prepresidential views. Delivered to a nationwide television audience on October 27, 1964, and repeated in whole or in part countless times since, "The Speech" consisted of a single, abstract idea, universal in application. The idea was that centrally administered government tended to weaken a free people's character. By overregulation and fiscal overindulgence, distant government demoralized and enervated its citizenry. According to "The Speech," federal runaway bureaucracy stripped people of their will to be self-reliant and their capacity for self-government. By spreading "bounties, donations, and benefits," a centralized administration first lightened, and then assumed, the "responsibility for our own destinies." And its nitpicking and unreasonable restraints made flaccid the society's sense of responsible self-restraint. As a result the people lost not only a feeling of pride in their own accomplishment but even a desire for accomplishment. "The Speech" elaborated the idea comprehensively to explain why craftsmen lost pleasure in their work, business managers countenanced inefficiencies, farmers planted unwanted crops, engineers built unnecessary projects, parents separated and left their children, city officials laid waste decent neighborhoods, bureaucrats expanded their dominions excessively, courts turned a blind eye to the erosion of civil liberties, and citizens grew frightened to speak up against runaway government. In short, the central state, by acting "outside its legitimate function," transformed a hardy people into weaklings lacking self-respect.

Reagan's speechwriting department—the half-dozen men and women who prepared the more than half a million words the president spoke annually—was the chief exegete, providing the authoritative interpretation of the text. They knew "The Speech" virtually by heart. It was the focus of their art. They saw their job as one of elaborating on its core idea and applying it in new situations. Chief speechwriter Ben Elliott described his typical preparations: "What I personally did to sound like Reagan was to spend the three weeks before I went to work for him reading all his speeches and making these sheaves of notes—on war, on blacks, on rhetoric, on economy. And I just absorbed his way of expressing things."[56] He also absorbed the ideas the president expressed.

Speechwriter Al Meyer called the text and his department's interpretation of it "the conscience of the presidency."

The president has a set of objectives and wants to move things in that direction. This compound [the White House and the Old Executive Office Building] consists of the crucial people who keep and maintain a handle on that direction, and if they don't do it, no one else will. Can you imagine: Who in the Department of Education would submit a budget of zero dollars for the next year? The place is full of career government officials, good ones, people who believe in what they're doing, and they're not going to eliminate themselves . . . the direction to do that has to be in this compound. The conscience of the presidency is in this compound and in the political levels of the Executive Branch. This president makes the federal government get smaller, and it's in the interest of the Department of Education and all the rest to make it bigger. And if you do not have a conscience, it will get bigger.[57]

"The conscience of the presidency"—the text and its public interpretations—was published in *The Compilation of Presidential Doc-*

uments, a government periodical established in 1965. Each issue, typically about fifty pages long and minutely and cumulatively indexed for easy retrieval, contained everything the president had said or written in the preceding seven days. Like the "advance sheets" that inform judges and lawyers of the latest judicial precedents, *Presidential Documents* kept each of the federal departments abreast of the latest presidential word.

But who were the disciples engaged in spreading the word? How were they trained in its meaning, committed to its dispersion, and disciplined by its force? The answers are the president's cabinet and the way he used it.

The cabinet has long been a problematic institution, one constantly engaged in the bootless task of finding a function.[58] Typically, all the posts except State, Defense, Treasury, and Justice have been lonely and invisible. Surrounded by career employees, separated by city blocks from the president himself, beset by importunate congressional committees and necessitous clients, isolated from the inner workings of their own agencies, department heads have tended to resign soon after their appointment or to fill their time by undertaking a pet project of their own.

Reagan transformed the fifteen members of his cabinet into willing evangelists who carried the word to the specialized bureaucracies and their clienteles. To discipline and maintain their loyalty, the president and the counselor to the president, Edwin Meese, created seven cabinet councils, each dealing with a broad subject area.[59] Each council was composed of half a dozen cabinet members, Meese, the president, Chief of Staff Jim Baker, and Vice-President George Bush. Each council was charged with identifying problems and designing acceptable solutions to them.

The sheer number of the councils made excessive demands on their members' time and in his second term Reagan reduced them to three. But for the purposes of building a moral institution within the presidency, they functioned precisely as intended. First, they made the secretaries' lives interesting. For example, the secretary of agriculture was able to leave the day-to-day complications of the agricultural sector and join with colleagues on the Cabinet Council on Commerce and Trade to think about trade relations in general.

Second, the cabinet council structure schooled and disciplined the secretaries in the president's principles. They met under the direct tutelage of the president, confronted urgent and complicated problems, and had to make responsible judgments. As happens at such times, they found abstract principles useful in alleviating the confusion of dazzling, disorganized fact. In applying a few central principles on which they could agree—and that meant the president's principles—they found it easier to make difficult decisions. The cumulative exercises of applying principle to practice emboldened them, built their confidence in the president's fundamental doctrine, and acquainted them with its implications.

The department heads took these comfortable ideas back to their agencies, used them to justify programs to recalcitrant employees, and answered reporters' questions in their terms. They went to the public, not to be taught what was wrong, but to teach the president's definition of what was wrong. Their daily exercise in principled thinking built solidarity among them and equipped them to speak with a uniformity of voice that resembled the way lower court judges spoke in constitutional terms.

Jayne Gallagher, principal speechwriter and public affairs officer for the Department of Housing and Urban Development, provided one illustration of how this training in articulate principle at the White House affected the bureaucracies.

> Public presentation is the major function of the head of an agency . . . The secretary of HUD has to explain what it is we are doing and why. That is, he has to present the great overview of the department. He has fifteen assistant secretaries to do the laundry lists [that is, to talk about the details of programs]. But a cabinet officer's responsibility is to talk about philosophy, and the methods and goals within that philosophy. In a nutshell, [Secretary] Sam Pierce's philosophy, the department's philosophy, is—to take the words right out of the president's mouth— to do more with less. And we have.[60]

After speaking of HUD's achievements, she articulated the department's philosophy. "We don't assume that poor people should be poor their whole lives. We don't believe that. Poor people have just as much ambition for themselves and their children as any middle-class family you can find." She was expressing the president's basic and frequently repeated axiom that class made no difference.

Gallagher talked about the congressional opposition to this notion.

> That philosophy causes Secretary Pierce a great deal of grief on the Hill. Congressman Henry Gonzales is ready to assault Sec-

retary Pierce, and there are people who have a philosophical mind-set which was described by Mr. [Patrick] Moynihan in his book: There is a segment of people who make their money off the poor, and if there were to be no more poor, they wouldn't have anything to do. Our programs are working and . . . stem from the philosophy of this administration.

After describing a couple of HUD innovations to encourage self-help, Gallagher came back to the uses of philosophy:

We had a problem in New Orleans, and there was an ugly situation building up. People were afraid that their homes were going to be demolished, and they would have no place to live. We sent four assistant secretaries down there to work with Mayor Moreal. And they solved it. We suggested that the New Orleans Public Housing Authority put out a flyer to all the tenants of public housing to explain to them what was happening and that there would be no demolition of their houses. But New Orleans objected. They had never put out a flyer to New Orleans tenants before, and it might raise suspicions. Can you imagine, never having put out any explanations in the entire history of the Authority? Geez!

Secretary Pierce is beginning to enjoy the bully pulpit since he's starting to talk big ideas.

There was the moral dynamic of discipleship: the creation of a philosophy of freedom, building the secretary's agreement with it, recurrent schooling, recurrent practice by the secretary in expressing it, serious and recurrent challenges to exercise his application of it, and the dispersal of his example to the assistant secretaries so that they, too, could carry the word into places as different as the halls of Congress and the streets of New Orleans. Gallagher called this process of moral change "to theme an agency."

One other reason for the success of Reagan's secondary pulpit was the existence of an institutionalized means of commentary that permitted ever-widening circles of adherents to discuss the president's text and argue its proper interpretation with the chief exegetes, the speechwriters. The means of commentary consisted in part of a network of conservative journals such as *The Public Interest, Commentary, The Conservative Digest, The National Review, Human Events,* the *Wall Street Journal,* and *The New Republic.* But of even greater importance was the "administration's" news-

paper.[61] Begun in the second year of the Reagan administration and
financed by Korean businessmen (all members of the Reverend Sun
Myung Moon's Unification Church), the *Washington Times* opened
its columns to dozens of eloquent and experienced conservatives. It
had a small circulation (about 100,000) that masked its importance.
Virtually all the spokesmen of the Reagan administration read it,
especially its three pages of "Commentary." In the *Washington Times*
scores of philosophers, columnists, economists, generals, historians,
political scientists, White House staff, cabinet secretaries, and leaders from the bureaucracy and Congress daily debated the appropriate
ways to apply the president's philosophy. Here, in the liveliest forum
in town, the president's words were quoted, discussed, controverted,
and reinforced. Ideas from one column would be discussed in someone else's column the next week and sooner or later would appear
in some official's speech. Its daily appearance stirred an abundance
of controversy within the presidency. The dialogue built a philosophical solidarity that produced courage in the president's disciples.

Liberty and Equality

Reagan taught from both his primary and his secondary pulpits. He
spoke both to the people and to the members of his administration.
One key to his success was the harmony between the ideas transmitted at the two levels. The administration theme, that centralized
government weakened the hearts and nerve of the citizenry, had as
its predicate the same ideas that constituted the popular sermon:
that human nature was a divided nature, evil impulse struggling
with good; that the ethical measure of human worth was spiritual,
signifying the victory within of good over evil; and that a society
predicated on private exchange fortified the individual in his spiritual battle. Reciprocity provided countless tiny compulsions to please
others; a welfare society robbed the individual of those demands to
reciprocate that supported him in his inner battle with his worse
side.

The rhetorical strategy worked precisely because it was effected
on two levels. The message from the primary pulpit reduced people's
expectations of government, and the message from the secondary
pulpit justified to the bureaucracy its reduced role.

Effecting a moral revolution within two presidential terms was a
task of enormous difficulty, especially in peacetime. The president
faced serious obstacles. The ceaseless repetition of doctrine was

personally fatiguing. And he had to be blessed with good fortune; some degree of national prosperity, over which a president had only the most marginal control, had to coincide with his efforts. Yet despite these odds, Reagan's moral revolution appears to have succeeded. The moral institution of religion has been filled with lively commentary and emboldened in contesting nihilistic doctrines. At the same time, the moral institution of the law has been steadily peopled with Reagan judges—men and women who have gone to school on Reagan notions and who find in the law's historic axioms of personal responsibility a strong moral reasonance. Their judicial opinions, now being quoted in legal periodicals, reprinted in law school textbooks, and repeated by editorial writers, constitute the education of a coming generation of political leaders.

Two general ideas vie to dominate the American mind. One is freedom, the other equality. The former requires all citizens to take personal responsibility for their actions and expects much in the way of personal skills, human understanding, and individual courage. The latter speaks of collective responsibility and expects the state to vanquish the deficiencies of those who constitute the society under its sway. Freedom gives scope to human flaws and virtue; equality diminishes the expression of both.

One hundred and fifty years ago Tocqueville noted this rivalry of political philosophies and observed the human willingness to surrender personal liberty for equality unless educated otherwise:

> There exists . . . in the human heart a depraved taste for equality, which impels the weak to attempt to lower the powerful to their own level and reduces men to prefer equality in slavery to inequality with freedom. Not that those nations whose social condition is democratic naturally despise liberty; on the contrary, they have an instinctive love of it. But liberty is not the chief and constant object of their desires; equality is their idol; they make rapid and sudden efforts to obtain liberty and, if they miss their aim, resign themselves to their disappointment; but nothing can satisfy them without equality, and they would rather perish than lose it.[62]

The central event of American political life has been the rivalry between liberty and equality, between self-government and paternalistic government, between the contingency of the free life and the certitudes of the submissive one. If human liberty is to prevail as "the chief and constant object" of Americans' desires, it must have a powerful champion. To the president in his bully pulpit falls the task of fortifying the meaning of moral freedom and the spiritual importance of being masters of our own souls.[63] It is he who has to educate the democracy, to tell the language of freedom with all the eloquence and statesmanship at his command, and to replenish "the common [philosophical] spring from which all the rest emanates." Ronald Reagan has executed that responsibility with exceptional skill.[64]

10

NINE PRESIDENTS

In Search of
A Modern Presidency

Fred I. Greenstein

In borrowing the title of this chapter from Pirandello, I do not mean to confuse the president's task with that of the political analyst. Presidents are immersed in day-to-day politics and policy-making. Only a few have devoted much effort to reflecting self-consciously about the conduct of the modern presidency.

The presidents whose leadership is reviewed in the previous nine chapters searched for ways to discharge their duty less through cerebration than through their actions in the political arena. Responding to and at times shaping events, they created the evolving modern presidency. Studied chronologically in terms of their impact on their successors, they enable us to trace and explain the evolution. Studied comparatively, they illuminate the possibilities of and limits on presidential leadership. The account in this chapter is explicitly chronological but only implicitly comparative: rather than applying the same categories to each presidency, it traces how the categories, precepts, and other lore bearing on presidential leadership arose out of and were repeatedly reshaped by the American political experience. The discussion draws on the nine preceding chapters but does not summarize them; the analysis is my own.

Three presidents served during the first half of the fifty-six years between the 1932 and 1988 elections; six during the second half. The first section of the chapter discusses in detail the formative period of the Roosevelt, Truman, and Eisenhower presidencies, during which a striking transition from the traditional to the modern presidency occurred and came to be taken for granted. That only three presidents served for so long undoubtedly contributed to the transformation of the presidency into its expanded modern form. The second section identifies certain descriptive and prescriptive assumptions about presidential leadership that had come to be widely accepted by 1960, and then traces subsequent shifts in these assumptions as the presidency came to be viewed in dizzying succession as regnant, imperial, imperiled, and restored to its authority, foreshadowing the discussion, in the third and final section, of the six presidencies of what might be called the mature phase of the modern era—those of Kennedy through Reagan. During this later period the presidency seemed often to be in rapid transformation. A backward look, however, reveals a slow evolution within a context of broad continuity and highly instructive variation.

The Formative Period

The emergence of the physical and symbolic defining characteristics of the modern presidency is evident in the several city blocks surrounding 1600 Pennsylvania Avenue.[1] William Hopkins, who began working as the White House stenographer under Hoover in 1931 and went on to become executive clerk, holding his White House position until his retirement in the Nixon years, remembers that he shook hands with President Hoover the year before going to work in the White House. Hoover still found it possible to carry on the leisurely nineteenth-century New Year's Day tradition of personally greeting any person who cared to join the reception line leading into the White House.[2]

In Hoover's time, the presidency had not become so central a symbol for public emotions and aspirations that elaborate procedures for protecting the White House from potentially dangerous intruders were deemed necessary. The White House of our time is surrounded by a high, electronically sensitized fence; its gates are locked and carefully guarded; and the fence extends across West Executive Avenue to the ornate Old Executive Office Building, creating a two-block presidential compound. In Hoover's time a lower, unelectrified fence surrounded only the White House, and its gates stood open. Anyone walking east of the White House from what was then the site of the State, Navy, and War Departments customarily did so by strolling across the White House grounds.

Moreover, when Hoover was president, the West Wing of the White House had sufficient space to accommodate the modest presidential staff. The bureaucracy of the modern presidency now occupies not only the building across the street from the West Wing, but also a red-brick, high-rise New Executive Office Building on 17th Street. Extensions of the presidency are to be found in many other nearby buildings, including the Georgian-façade edifices facing Lafayette Square.

Roosevelt: The Breakthrough

The first stage in the transformation that accounted for these physical changes was an almost overnight rise in expectations about the appropriate duties of the chief executive. This resulted from the convergence of a deep national (and later international) crisis with the accession and long incumbency of perhaps the most giftedly entrepreneurial president in American history, Franklin D. Roosevelt. Nothing was inevitable about the appearance in 1933 of innovative presidential leadership. FDR's nomination in 1932 had not been a sure thing. As Leuchtenburg reminds us, President-elect Roosevelt barely escaped assassination. It is impossible to believe that the next in succession, Vice-President-elect John Nance Garner, would have produced the massive change in policies and practices that occurred under Roosevelt's leadership. One can argue that even under Garner or the various other presidential contenders of the time, including a reelected Hoover, social conditions would have fostered demands for strong leadership.[3] But the outcome of these demands might well have been some form of indigenous dictatorship, such as that described in Sinclair Lewis's novel *It Can't Happen Here*. Crisis was a necessary rather than a sufficient condition for the modern presidency that began to evolve under Roosevelt. The crisis of the 1930s had other consequences in other nations.

The premodern historical record—especially the record of the nineteenth century—contains countless examples of congressional antipathy to mere suggestions by the president that particular legislation be enacted.[4] During the early years of the republic, it was widely held that even the veto could not legitimately be used as an expression of policy preference by the chief executive.[5] FDR promptly established the practice of advocating, backing, and engaging in the politics of winning support for legislation. By the end of his long tenure, presidential legislative activism had come to be taken for granted, if not universally approved.

This activism began within four days of Roosevelt's taking office. The relentless succession of legislative enactments passed by the special session of Congress during the Hundred Days from noon on March 9, to 1:00 A.M. on June 15, 1933—including such major policy departures as the banking act, the securities act, the Civilian Conservation Corps, and the National Industrial Recovery Administration—was appropriately viewed as the result of Roosevelt's leadership. In some cases his leadership involved bringing about the enactment of programs which had long been on the public political agenda, such as the Tennessee Valley Authority, but which needed the impetus of the Hundred Days legislative campaign to achieve approval. In one case—that of the Federal Deposit Insurance Corporation— Roosevelt received praise for passage of a program that he personally opposed but acceded to after realizing it had too much congressional support to be defeated.[6]

That FDR was given credit for the initiatives of others illustrates the tendency during his administration for people to think increasingly of the president as a symbol for the government. One way to deal with the increasing complexity of government was to personify it. Even before Congress could convene, as the nationally broadcast inaugural ceremony proceeded the chief executive was almost instantly transformed from a remote, seemingly inert entity to a vivid focal point of national attention. FDR's confident comportment; the high oratory of his inaugural speech, with its grave warning that he would request war powers over the economy if Congress failed to act; his ebullience; the decisiveness of the next day's "bank holiday" executive order—all of this elicited an overwhelmingly favorable public response to the new president. As William Hopkins, who was then in the White House correspondence section, remembers: "President Roosevelt was getting about as much mail a day as President Hoover received in a week. The mail started coming in by the truckload. They couldn't even get the envelopes open."[7]

Significantly, the volume of presidential mail has never tapered off. Contemporary estimates are that the president receives over a million letters annually.[8] Roosevelt evidently was able to wed his own great powers of personal communication to the general sense of national urgency, channeling what had hitherto been a static patriotic sentiment—American veneration of the great presidents of the past—into a dynamic component of the incumbent's role. In initiating this characteristic of the modern presidency, he undoubtedly enhanced his ability and that of his successors to muster public support in times of perceived national crisis. But he also undoubtedly established unrealistic and even contradictory standards by which citizens tend to judge both the personal virtue of presidents and their ability to solve the typically controversial social and political problems that arise during their administrations.

FDR also accustomed the nation to expect that the president would be aided by a battery of policy advisers and implementers. At first these aides were officially on the payrolls of diverse non–White House agencies or commuted from their academic or other posts, but were unofficially "the President's men."[9] Best remembered now is the sequence of scholarly braintrusters who advised FDR as governor of New York and early in his first term as president; then of the lawyers who drafted and politicked for the next stage of New Deal legislation; and finally of Harry Hopkins, who served as wartime presidential surrogate in international diplomacy.

Politically attentive Americans tend to regard unofficial presidential advising—such as Jackson's Kitchen Cabinet and Colonel Edward House in Wilson's administration—with suspicious fascination. The fascination derives from the titillation of identifying the "real" powers behind the throne. The suspicion arises from the fear of illegitimate, legally irresponsible power—an especially strong concern in a polity in which so many of the political actors are lawyers inclined to invoke constitutional principles, even in debates over matter-of-fact interest-group conflicts.

In any case, in the fishbowl context of American politics gray eminences do not remain gray for long. Two of the leading young lawyers who were Roosevelt's principal agents during the so-called Second New Deal, Thomas Corcoran and Benjamin Cohen, were pictured on the cover of *Time* magazine. This visibility of the unofficial aides who were essential to maintaining FDR's momentum as policy initiator threatened the legitimacy of his leadership. To the degree that such aides upstaged him, they also detracted from his centrality as a symbol of national leadership. These costs of using visible unofficial advisers must have contributed to Roosevelt's interest in procedures that would provide the presidency with aides who *were* official but *were not* conspicuous.

Just such a corps of aides was proposed in the 1937 recommendations of the Brownlow Committee, the committee on administration of the federal government appointed by Roosevelt. Arguing that because of the mushrooming responsibilities of the executive branch, "the President needs help," the Brownlow Committee proposed the creation of an Executive Office of the President, including a White House Office staffed by skilled, energetic aides with "a passion for anonymity." After extensive political bargaining, the Reorganization Act of 1939 was passed and implemented by executive order.[10]

Roosevelt's shift from exclusive use of behind-the-scenes advisers to use of a staff authorized by statute is recorded in the *United States Government Manual* released in October 1939. Listed immediately following the page identifying the president of the United States is what continues to be the umbrella heading under which presidential agencies are grouped—the Executive Office of the President (EOP). The White House Office (WHO) is listed next. (In October 1939 there were only three WHO aides; by the 1970s and 1980s, there were more than fifty.)[11]

Each *Manual* since 1939 has listed next the Bureau of the Budget (after 1970, the Office of Management and Budget). BOB/OMB has consistently been the second most influential Executive Office appendage. The BOB had been established as a presidential agency in 1921, after a decade of efficiency-minded lobbying by "good government" reformers who sought to substitute a consolidated and centrally cleared executive budget for the disaggregated requests submitted to Congress by individual agencies until then. Before the passage of the 1939 Reorganization Act, however, the bureau was not a policy-framing body, but a bookkeeping agency—lodged in the Treasury Department building—that sought to achieve mechanical economies in budgetary requests through exercises of parsimony in some cases as picayune as saving paperclips and pencil stubs.

After the Reorganization Act the bureau received a new director, Harold D. Smith, who was both passionately anonymous and assiduously devoted to building an organization of gifted public administrators who would have a continuing responsibility to the presidency, no matter who served in the office. Smith's unpublished diary and the memoirs of Washington insiders of that period make it clear that he privately assumed an active, invariably diffident, advisory relationship with President Roosevelt.[12] The bureau itself was moved in 1939 from the Treasury Department building to office space in the frequently renamed building directly across the street from the West Wing of the White House. Smith continued to have similar regular conferences with Truman during his first year as president. So zealous was Smith for anonymity that the bureau was rarely discussed in the press, and during his tenure as director Smith's name appeared only twice—and then in neutral contexts—in the *New York Times Index*.

Because the great changes between 1933 and 1945 in expectations about the magnitude, impact, and nature of the presidency were the outcome of both the political climate during Roosevelt's time in office and FDR's highly personal style, "the modern presidency" did not *have* to continue in the wake of FDR's death. Roosevelt's personality-centered presidency might simply have been one of the many transitory highs in the recurring cycle of presidential passivity and activism, such as the intense but brief legislative activism of the early Wilson administration. Roosevelt's monopoly of political attention and his capacity to arouse public feeling were reminscent of the visibility and appeal of his cousin, Theodore Roosevelt. His use of emergency powers in response to crisis had strong precedents in the Lincoln administration. Therefore, when Roosevelt died, when World War II ended, and when a virtual unknown—widely perceived as a "little man"—succeeded him, there was reason to expect, fear, or hope that, much as in the Wilson–Harding transition, the presidency would again move from center stage in national government to the wings. But that did not happen.

Truman: Institutionalization

Truman's impact on public policies was uneven; his impact on the modern presidency as an institution was profound. Under Truman, the presidency did in fact continue to be central in national politics. There was, however, a shift from the ad hoc, personally stimulated policy initiatives of Roosevelt to the methodical development of policy by Truman in concert with WHO and BOB staff members and other public officials. This shift is aptly described by Max Weber's phrase "the routinization of *charisma.*"

As tattered and imprecise as the term *charisma* has come to be, it cannot be stretched to describe Truman's leadership, especially the flat, halting public communications of his first eighteen months in office. Truman's initial Gallup poll rating of 87 percent—the highest single rating in a half-century of presidential approval polls— merely expressed national mourning for FDR and sympathy for the lot of the president who faced what obviously was going to be the monumental task of attempting to succeed Roosevelt; it was not an assessment of Harry S. Truman. After that, Truman's performance as president frequently garnered more disapproving than approving poll responses. This was in part an effect of the unsettled political times over which Truman presided. (Roosevelt, like Lincoln, died before it was necessary to face the kinds of problems that arise in the aftermath of wars—problems that are almost certain to erode presidential popularity.) But Truman's perceived substantive and palpable rhetorical shortcomings as a national leader also contributed to his endemically low popularity. Moreover, he had the added burden that would have fallen to any successor of Roosevelt (and perhaps to Roosevelt himself had he survived his fourth term)—that of living up to the standard FDR had set during the depression and the war as an inspirer of public confidence. (A similar burden was to weigh on John F. Kennedy's successors, most notably, as Berman shows, on Lyndon Johnson.)

Whatever his inspirational inadequacies, Truman was no back-to-normalcy Harding. This was evident as early as September 1945, when in a twenty-one-point reconversion message he anticipated the major themes of what soon evolved into the Fair Deal program.[13] Truman also was not the inexperienced "failed haberdasher" his critics alleged him to be. From his chairmanship of a major wartime investigating committee that scrutinized the performance of "home front" activities and from his service on the Senate Appropriations Committee, he had over a decade of experience that had made him expert in the operations and policies of the federal government. Moreover, before his election to the Senate, his extensive experience as a county administrator and his omnivorous reading had left him well furnished with political knowledge, skills, and ideals.

There are harbingers of the future president in the handful of documents that the Truman Presidential Library has been able to salvage from Truman's years in local government. Some of them, in which he methodically accounts for county revenues and expenditures and proposes reforms, anticipate Truman's exceptionally close work with his BOB staff in examining the many policy issues that quickly fell into the bailiwick of that agency. Early speeches to patriotic and other civic groups presage many aspects of his presidential leadership—speeches extolling the centrality of the president in the constitutional system; praising decisive, manly, and moral leaders, including great presidents;[14] and conceiving of social processes as the outcome of the triumph of good leaders over poor ones.[15]

Truman's impact as institutionalizer of the modern presidency is clear from the differences between his and Roosevelt's ways of using the Bureau of the Budget. During the Roosevelt years Harold Smith repeatedly expressed concern in his diary that he would fail to build a continuing staff agency that could serve successive presidencies. So incorrigibly informal was Roosevelt's way of operating that he often treated Smith simply as if he were another of Roosevelt's many unofficial advisers rather than the head of a statutory presidential staff agency. Smith worried that the agency he was staffing with the most promising administrators he could find would be compromised institutionally by FDR's continuing impulse to use the director as a mediator among feuding departments and wartime agencies. He was distressed, as he put it, about being used as Roosevelt's "Mr. Fixit."

Under Truman both the bureau and its director became an integral part of the presidency. During Smith's holdover period and the tenure of his exceptionally able successor, James Webb, the bureau rapidly became the central coordinating institution for framing and formalizing annual presentations of what came to be called "the program of the president." Truman was a direct party to the soon taken-for-granted expanded role of the Bureau of the Budget of compiling the program of the president, the enlargement of the White House Office staff, and the conversion of that staff into a team that met daily with him, dividing a workload far exceeding the capacity of the traditional presidency. By 1947 the efforts of the White House staff and of the Bureau of the Budget were closely coordinated as a result of Truman's, Smith's, and Webb's efforts.

From time to time BOB aides, especially if they developed strong Fair Deal political convictions, "crossed the street" and became White House aides. Meanwhile the bureau continued to develop its joint roles of helping the president to frame his policy program and examining policy proposals both for consistency with the overall outlines of that program and for technical feasibility. During Truman's first two years in office the bureau likewise began, as a standard procedure, to examine all departmental appropriations requests for consistency with the president's program. Even more important (and less probable, given the title of the agency), the bureau became centrally involved in the legislative process. It became a regular BOB duty to clear and coordinate all legislative requests originating within federal departments, to help draft legislation emanating from the White House, and to clear and draft executive orders—all in the name of an explicitly stated criterion: the program of the president. The BOB also continued to perform a function acquired in the late 1930s—review and clearance with other relevant agencies of all congressional enactments with a view to recommending whether they be signed or vetoed.

The annual BOB compilation of proposed legislation and the final budget document provide the basis for what has become the obligatory mode of commencing and setting the policy-making agenda of each political year—a State of the Union message, backed up by draft legislation. Delivered by the president with dignified republican ceremony to a joint session of Congress and other assembled dignitaries, the contemporary State of the Union message enunciates the general outlines of the president's program, as well as containing traditional rhetoric and pronouncements about current national conditions and future prospects.

The State of the Union message is one of three major presidential communications that go to Congress each January. The second is the budget document itself, accompanied by the budget message and the *Budget in Brief*, complete with graphic illustrations. The third is the *Report of the President's Council of Economic Advisers* (CEA). The CEA, established in the Employment Act of 1946, is one of two permanent accretions to the Executive Office during the Truman years. The chairman of Truman's first council had wanted the annual report to be an independent assessment of the economy not coordinated with the political emphasis of the overall presidential program. This view of the role of the CEA did not prevail, however. The council soon became part of the president's team, and its report and the other two January messages quickly became complementary presentations of the same program. (On one occasion in the 1980s a CEA chief, Martin Feldstein, departed from this norm; Reagan administration spokesmen immediately disparaged and disavowed the economic report.)

A second statutory body, the National Security Council (NSC), grew out of the legislation that brought about the unification of the armed forces. Initially the NSC was conceived of by many congressmen who had supported unification as a potential check on presidents' autonomy in their role as commander in chief. Truman, however, "domesticated" the NSC as well as the CEA. Ever since his administration, these and numerous more transient EOP agencies have been institutional underpinnings of the modern presidency.

Just as the professional staff of the BOB acquired some of the qualities of those British civil servants who perennially aid the executive, whatever party is in power, so the president's January communications have become roughly akin to the messages to new British parliamentary sessions, ghostwritten by the government in power for delivery by the monarch. But American presidents face one of the most vigorously autonomous legislatures in any parliamentary democracy. Hence their messages only help set the terms of the next legislative session's political debate, whereas the proposals voiced by the British monarch are almost invariably enacted into law. The many legislative defeats Truman received from the Seventy-ninth through Eighty-second Congresses illustrate how a presidential program may be consistently blocked by an opposition coalition. The amount of Truman's Fair Deal domestic program that was enacted was unimpressive, although, as Hamby notes, his administration was reasonably successful in the Eighty-first Congress. And it was remarkably successful in assembling a sufficiently large bipartisan foreign policy coalition to authorize the Truman Doctrine, the Marshall Plan, and other postwar reconstruction and Cold War initiatives.

Truman was also responsible not merely for initiating but also for carrying through policy-making in areas included in the expanded domain of independent presidential action. Among the most consequential exercises of executive initiative by this believer in a presidency with substantial autonomous powers were the decision to use atomic weapons at the end of World War II, the decision to commit American troops to Korea, and the executive order integrating the military. Many of Truman's autonomous decisions were politically costly, including some that reflected his commitment to maintaining the independent powers of the presidency—for example, the steel seizure and the recalling of General MacArthur.

Despite stalemate in domestic policy-making, his low general popularity, and the political costliness of some of his decisions, Truman's continuing executive assertiveness accustomed all but the most conservative national political actors to look at the president as the main framer of the agenda for public debate—even when much of the debate involved castigation of his proposals. Truman, like Roosevelt, was not singly responsible for the changes in the presidency that occurred during his years in office. Key advisers such as Smith and Webb were also influential. Moreover, Truman was operating in an environment of big government, the welfare state, and American international involvement that inevitably tended to place major responsibilities on the executive branch. Nevertheless, like Roosevelt, Truman himself does emphatically seem to have been a major independent influence on the shape of the modern presidency. Not everyone in the postwar period was convinced that the welfare state should continue or that the United States should maintain its international commitments. Conservatives of both parties felt that the New Deal welfare innovations should be repealed or cut back. Conservative isolationists and left-leaning supporters of Henry Wallace's 1948 Progressive party, from wholly different motives, opposed American involvement in the international arena. After World War II some democracies failed to acquire assertive, stable executive leadership. The French Fourth Republic is an obvious example. What, then, was to be expected of the evolving "center stage" presidency when Truman was succeeded by a president who was widely perceived as a believer in his newly adopted party's claim that the balance of political leadership should be redirected toward Congress?

Eisenhower: Ratification

When the Republicans returned to power in 1953 and the institutional changes and role expectations of the modern presidency were not fundamentally altered, the Great Divide had been crossed. Drawing on his long military exposure to staff work, Eisenhower arranged for a White House Office that was more formally organized and larger than Truman's, rather than diminished in size and importance. At least in the official scheme of things, the Eisenhower White House was an organizational hierarchy. Directly under the presidential apex was a chief of staff—for the first six years, the zealous Sherman Adams. Assigned a title that signaled his preeminence, *the* assistant to the president, Adams was listed first in the *United States Government Manual.* Other White House aides were enumerated in an indented list that visually conveyed their subordination to Adams. Adams's counterpart in foreign affairs—again for the first six years— was Secretary of State John Foster Dulles.

We know from a variety of sources, including the recently opened confidential files of the president's personal secretary, that Eisenhower was far from being a mere puppet of Adams and Dulles. He was intimately involved in national security policy-making and had multiple sources of information about domestic as well as foreign affairs. Indeed, his innovations in the use of formal machinery for planning and coordinating policy were complemented by his alert, close management of the informal policy-making process. However, as a domestic political conservative without a strong desire to innovate except in modest, incremental ways, Eisenhower does seem to have deputized Adams and his associates to attend to a variety of policy issues that would have received extensive personal attention by Truman himself. He also used Adams as a framer of alternatives in circumstances in which Truman would have canvassed alternatives on his own.

Eisenhower took two other steps toward formalizing cabinet and NSC procedures. He held regular cabinet meetings, in which policy papers solicited from the executive agencies by a cabinet secretariat were discussed, although, as in other presidencies, the cabinet was not a decision-making body. And he employed a National Security Council policy planning procedure through which the weekly NSC meeting debates were sharpened by the use of prepared papers that crystallized the policy positions on which individuals and entities in the executive branch agreed and disagreed and through which implementation of the policies that the president enunciated after hearing NSC deliberations was systematically planned.

Although Eisenhower's formal White House organization was supplemented by informal proceedings, the informal procedures were not publicized at the time, perhaps because Eisenhower played up the head-of-state side of presidential leadership, deliberately obscuring the president's close involvement in his administration's *realpolitik*.[16] Therefore, by the end of the 1950s Eisenhower's NSC procedure and other routines he had instituted came to be regarded as unproductive mechanical rituals. In fact the formal meetings of the cabinet and NSC were genuine forums, hammering out policy plans and helping the president to arrive at decisions after hearing contending points of view. The decisions themselves, however, were made by the president and key associates in informal meetings in the Oval Office.

Eisenhower also helped ratify the modern, institutionalized presidency by establishing the first White House legislative liaison office, staffed by a skilled lobbying team headed by retired major general Wilton P. Persons, a veteran cultivator of Capitol Hill who had handled Eisenhower's congressional relations when the latter served first as chief of staff of the army and then as NATO commander. General Persons' staff consisted of comparably experienced professionals who took it for granted that their purpose was to advance a presidential program.

Above all, under Eisenhower there continued to *be* a president's program. Throughout his two terms, Eisenhower proved to be a presidentialist—that is, a defender of the accrued responsibilities of the modern presidency at both the policy and the symbolic levels. At the policy level, for example, Eisenhower immediately became intensely active in the campaign that successfully defeated the Bricker Amendment, which would have made presidential executive agreements with other nations subject to Senate ratification. At the symbolic level, he drew on his long-standing public credit as the most popular figure to emerge from World War II in order to maintain a remarkably consistent high level of prestige and popularity with the electorate, even when Washington insiders derided him for his seeming lack of political skill and knowledge.

A further and especially consequential aspect of the Eisenhower presidency was his continued use of the institutional resource that makes it possible to have a program of the president—the Bureau of the Budget. Eisenhower's first bureau director, Joseph Dodge, became attuned to the bureau's procedures before assuming office, taking advantage of Truman's offer of interelection "internships" for Eisenhower appointees. Dodge quickly recognized the high quality of the bureau's senior personnel and their readiness to shift from shaping a Truman program to shaping an Eisenhower program. Although there was no first-year Eisenhower legislative program, in 1953 the BOB staff routinely sent out requests for proposed legislation to all federal agencies, just as it had done since the mid-1940s. Before the year was over it became evident that an Eisenhower program would be submitted to Congress in January 1954. By the time Eisenhower left office, the practice of submitting a presidential program to Congress had become routine.

In August 1956 Eisenhower's secretary, Ann Whitman, replied to an inquiry from Milton Eisenhower as to how the president's workload might be reduced. Her letter suggests how a modern president, working in a tightly staffed White House, allocated his energies. Later presidents would allocate their energies differently, making less use of formal arrangements and maintaining a greater balance of attention to domestic and foreign policy. But all of their schedules reflected a presidency whose demands had expanded exponentially.

Mrs. Whitman produced this breakdown of Eisenhower's time:

Regular Weekly Meetings:

1. The National Security Council seems to be the most time-consuming, from the standpoint of number of hours *in* the actual meeting, the briefing before the meeting that has seemed to become a routine, and the time that the President must give, occasionally, to be sure that the meetings reflect exactly the decisions reached . . . [Mrs. Whitman thought that frequently the president was already well informed on the substance of national security policy and therefore did not need the briefings and meetings for his own information. She observed that "he himself complains that he knows every word of the presentations as they are to be made. However, he feels that to maintain the interest and attention of every member of the NSC, he must sit through each meeting."]

2. The Cabinet meetings are not usually so long as NSC, but the President feels in some instances that to fill out an agenda, items are included that are not necessarily of the caliber that should come before the Cabinet . . .

3. The Press Conferences. These meetings are preceded by a half to three-quarter hour briefing by staff members. [Mrs. Whitman felt that in most cases Eisenhower was already sufficiently informed to meet the press without briefings, but added that "the meetings do serve the purpose of letting him know how various members of the staff are thinking."]

4. Legislative Leaders Meetings. When the Congress is in session, these are held weekly but do not last, on the average, more than an hour and a half and only about five minutes' preparation is required.

5. The President has a weekly meeting with the Secretary of Defense.

6. The President usually has a half-hour meeting with [economic advisers] Dr. [Gabriel] Hauge and Dr. [Arthur] Burns. I think he finds these meetings valuable and do not believe the sessions are unduly prolonged.

Mrs. Whitman also noted that the president had a half-hour daily intelligence briefing from Colonel Andrew Goodpaster, and she listed roughly a dozen categories of "other items that occupy his time," some of them taking up very little time (such as independent agencies), some of them involving time-consuming ceremonial duties (receiving ambassadors, meeting dignitaries and civic groups, state dinners, and signatures), and others involving policy and intermittently consuming much time. The latter included the State Department ("meetings with the Secretary are irregular, based upon the urgency of the particular crisis of the moment"); additional defense matters ("here is a great time-consuming area . . . I can't always see why some of the inter-Service problems cannot be resolved before they come to the President"); "other Cabinet matters" ("The President is available at all times to any Cabinet member for consultation"); "personnel, appointments, domestic matters" ("My general impression is that all such items have been pretty well digested [by Sherman Adams] before they reach the President, and that only his final judgment is required"); and speeches ("The President spends a great deal of time personally on his speeches, but I don't think that routine can ever be changed. I think only by the process of editing and reworking does the speech become truly his own—and I think the hours—and I guess he spends twenty to thirty on each major speech—are inevitable").[17]

Assessments of the Modern Presidency

The Lore of the Formative Period: Neustadt's Analysis as Prism

By the end of the Eisenhower years scholars and other observers of American politics had reached a number of conclusions about the qualities and characteristics of the modern presidency, and about the circumstances that make presidential leadership more or less successful. A 1960 book by former Truman White House aide Richard Neustadt, *Presidential Power: The Politics of Leadership*,[18] crystallized much of this lore. It therefore provides an excellent prism through which to view how the presidency was interpreted by sophisticated observers at the end of its formative period and how interpretations shifted in response to the vicissitudes of subsequent presidencies.

A central part of Neustadt's analysis is his contrast of both Truman's feisty but unpopular performance and Eisenhower's seemingly flaccid but popular performance with Roosevelt's skilled presidential leadership. As the son of a New Deal official, Neustadt absorbed the political discourse, memoirs, and early biographies that portrayed Franklin Roosevelt as the exemplar of a successful modern president. Like most of the liberals and centrists who produce the bulk of the commentary on the presidency, he was sympathetic to Roosevelt's reformist social policies and internationalist foreign policies. And no one who had lived through the Great Depression and World War II would have been unaware of Roosevelt's extraordinary capacity to rally the American people.

Neustadt's emphasis on skill, however, led him to discuss FDR not in terms of his policies and public appeal, but rather in terms of his skills at maneuvering in "The Washington Community"— the key political actors throughout the nation and abroad as well as in the capital whom the president must influence in order to bring about his policy aims. The Roosevelt who is Neustadt's model of an effective president is a sophisticated, tough, political operator. He is powerful because he cares about and cultivates power; because he is attuned to what it takes to have an impact on his political environment; and because he is exceptionally well informed about that environment.

To Neustadt, a core source of Roosevelt's success was the set of practices that drove many of Roosevelt's associates to distraction: his propensity to set different people to work on the same or over-lapping assignments, sometimes deliberately encouraging them to compete for the presidential ear. The sparks that were struck by staff competition provided Roosevelt with political illumination. And because Roosevelt was so deeply steeped in knowledge of politics and policy he could ensure that *his* priorities and not those of his associates shaped his leadership.

Neustadt's explanation of Roosevelt's skill and influence follows from his comparison of Roosevelt's attributes and practices with those of Truman and Eisenhower. It was all too evident that Neustadt's own former boss had not been a master of political maneuver. Truman lacked Roosevelt's vigilant instinct to measure his actions in terms of how they would advance his capacity to put his personal imprint on politics and policy. He did not have Roosevelt's un-questioned sense of being suited for the presidency—a sense that it was as natural for *him* to be president as for fish to swim and birds to fly. Moreover, Truman was impatient of "squabbling New Deal-ers." He would have rejected the notion that an administration's infighting can advance the president's capacity to lead.

But, Neustadt argued, despite Truman's non-Rooseveltian style and assumptions, he had compensating qualities that, as it were, inadvertently led him to approximate key elements of Roosevelt's approach to leadership. Although Truman did not seek *personal* power, he subscribed to the constitutional principle that a strong, forceful presidency is a necessary force in the political system. Thus, Truman could grant that he had no better *individual* qualification to be president than millions of other Americans, but still be confident that *as president* he was required—not just entitled—to act decisively and with dispatch. And, although Truman deplored disorderly administration, his unpretentiousness and congenital informality, nurtured in the backslapping worlds of Missouri courthouse politics and Capitol Hill, led him to override his impulse to be a tidy administrator, kept him in touch with the eddies of politics, and enabled him to stay on top in his administration.

For Neustadt, as for most other presidency watchers at the time, Eisenhower was a pole apart from Roosevelt, exemplifying the obverse of effective presidential leadership. Apparent signs of Eisenhower's flawed leadership included his seeming detachment from the fine points of current Washington politicking and policy debate, his use of a chief of staff, and his extensive reliance on formal procedure. Eisenhower seemed to be a figurehead president, who had delegated to subordinates and committees the tasks that enable a president to put his stamp on the policy agenda.

This image of Eisenhower and of the shortcomings of employing formal policy-making machinery and a staff hierarchy in the White House Office was magnified by the policy debates and political position-taking that were under way when Neustadt was writing. The 1957 Soviet success in launching the first satellite stimulated heated debate over whether administration lassitude had produced a "missile gap." The missile gap debate converged with a continuing controversy over Eisenhower's emphasis on holding down military spending in order to maintain a strong economy. Criticisms of this stance commonly assumed that the president's "mechanistic" NSC policy-planning procedures had led to a foreign policy that was not sufficiently responsive to Cold War requirements. The apparent evidence was the administration's unwillingness to build more missiles and develop conventional military forces with a capacity to fight "brushfire wars" in the developing nations.

In 1960 this criticism of Eisenhower's *modus operandi* found one of its most influential forums in the hearings conducted by Senator Henry Jackson on national security policy-making procedures. Neustadt, a sometime adviser to the Jackson Committee, was asked to write a memorandum suggesting to President-elect Kennedy a strategy for organizing the presidency. Kennedy wound up including *Presidential Power* in his omnivorous reading. For a while Washington gossip had it that the spirited, flexible, "vigorous" Kennedy leadership style stemmed from the president's reading of Neustadt.[19]

Presidential Power, however, simply clarifies and defends the conception of good presidential leadership that was then current—that of an informal, Rooseveltian conduct of the presidency that contrasted with current perceptions of Eisenhower's operating manner. Neustadt's analysis justified a leadership style congenial to Kennedy, a restless, quick-witted, energetic former legislator who had never administered large organizations and had no reason to expect formal policy machinery to produce anything but red tape.

An additional line of reasoning that runs through *Presidential Power* was congenial to Kennedy and also to most contemporary analysts of the presidency, including the authors of the standard American government textbooks. Part of this rationale is essentially empirical and continues to be widely accepted: that the presidency is *the* central institution of the political system and that a strong, energetic president is necessary to make the system work. Part is normative and became anachronistic before the 1960s were over: that a president's policies are the best indicator American politics provides of the public interest. This reasoning led to two conclusions: first, political and social checks that restrain American presidents are impediments to making good public policy; second, analysts of the presidency need to be concerned not with what presidents can legitimately do within the constitutional order, but rather with how to enhance presidential influence on policy.

Lore Collides with Events: Changes in the Reputation of the Presidency

Why did Neustadt and most other serious political analysts contend that by virtue of being the chief executive, the president is a better judge than other political actors of the public interest? How could intelligent and learned observers embrace a view that within a decade became absurd, if not a lapse in judgment?

The rationale was often stated in terms of the structure of the political system, but the underlying motive for expecting good policies to emerge when presidents are strong rested more in the commentators' policy preferences than in their diagnoses of political structure. The structural diagnosis stressed the president's nationwide constituency and the requirement, built into his job, that he think about policy in national and even global terms. In contrast, the argument continued, legislators think and act in ways that reflect their districts. The sum of district views, exacerbated by the tendency for safe-district members of Congress—most of whom were conservative until the late 1960s—to monopolize control of committees, made Congress a cracked mirror, a distorted reflection of national will and needs.

The proponents of this thesis appear to have been influenced less by the compelling logic of their diagnosis of structure than by the policy records of the first three modern presidents. Roosevelt and Truman advocated more liberal domestic policies than were favored by the dominant coalitions in Congress, and Eisenhower favored more liberal policies than did congressional Republicans. Roosevelt, Truman, and Eisenhower pressed skeptical congressional majorities to approve a more internationalist foreign policy than the legislators otherwise would have backed. Since the writers themselves favored the policies of presidents, it was easy for them to accept uncritically the thesis that, because of the way the political system is constituted, what presidents view as good policy is likely to be good for the country.[20]

Belief in the propositions that (1) presidents are the best institutional interpreters of the public interest and (2) their power should be augmented soon declined. By 1988 there were no less than four new prevailing sets of assumptions about the merits of the presidency. They form a convenient preface to a discussion of the impact and lessons of the leadership of the six chief executives who served after the formative period of the modern presidency.

1. The presidency regnant. From the early to mid-1960s, commentators on the presidency who wanted to see the office strengthened and who felt that the president is the natural source of good policy rejoiced. In the 1960 campaign, Kennedy asserted that he rejected a "restricted concept of the president." The president, he maintained, should "place himself in the very thick of the fight" and "be prepared to exercise the fullest powers of his office—all that are specified and some that are not."[21]

In domestic policy, Kennedy was able to get only modest legislative results from the coalition of conservative Democrats and Republicans that dominated Capitol Hill. Nevertheless, Kennedy's New Frontier legislative program reflected an obvious, if at times cautious, restatement and expansion of the New Deal–Fair Deal agenda. Kennedy's liberal policy proposals contributed to his general image as a forceful presidential activist. So did the high oratory of his inaugural address and his virtuoso performances in the new medium of the live, televised presidential press conference. More substantive contributions to the impression of a president committed to activism—and sometimes getting results—were Kennedy's public confrontation with the steel industry, which resulted in the rollback of an industry price increase, and, far more significant, his forceful action in the Cuban missile crisis, which led to withdrawal of the missiles the USSR had surreptitiously installed in Cuba.

Kennedy's main contribution to the belief that a regnant presidency was having a good effect on public policy came after and as a result of his death. The national grief caused by the assassination and the posthumous idealization of Kennedy, and therefore of the policies he had been seeking to bring about, were capitalized on by Johnson and contributed to a burst of legislative activity by the hitherto stalemated Eighty-eighth Congress. Johnson made broad appeals designed to rally the nation and also politicked extensively, using the ability and knowledge that had made him a gifted congressional leader to gain passage of such legislation as the Civil Rights Act of 1964 and the War on Poverty program. Moreover, after his landslide victory over the outspokenly conservative Goldwater, Johnson took advantage of the temporary liberal Democratic majority in the Eighty-ninth Congress to press successfully for enactment of liberal domestic legislation that had been blocked for the previous three decades. Even more than Kennedy, he seemed to personify the standards set forth by Neustadt for good presidential leadership.

2. *The imperial presidency.* The jagged sequence of decline in Lyndon Johnson's Gallup poll approval ratings (Figure 1) captures the fate of Johnson's support by both the general public and many of the very political observers and commentators who had called for and then praised a more influential presidency. Throughout 1965 the torrent of Great Society legislation was accompanied by a deliberately downplayed, incremental increase in U.S. military commitments designed to prevent communist victory in South Vietnam. During that year the number of American troops in Vietnam increased from 23,000 to 185,000, and the troop mission evolved from advising to direct combat and systematic bombing of North Vietnam.

War protest was a minor theme in the politics of 1965, but throughout the rest of Johnson's elected term, troop levels mounted (reaching half a million in 1968) and Johnson's public backing plunged. Among the public at large, Johnson had critics who felt he had not

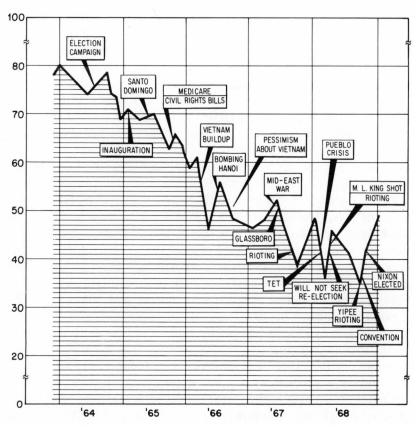

Figure 1. Public approval ratings of Lyndon B. Johnson (Source: *Gallup Opinion Index*, October–November 1980, p. 25).

prosecuted the war aggressively enough, as well as critics who favored withdrawal from the conflict. The latter view, however, was far more prevalent among most writers on the presidency, just as it was, on the campuses of the most prestigious colleges and universities, the scenes of increasing antiwar protest. Writers on the presidency and other shapers of political discourse, such as the growing bloc of congressional doves, argued that the war was wrong, or at any rate not in the national interest; that it was being prolonged and expanded as a result of Johnson's misguided commitment to Cold War dogma; and that in initiating and escalating it Johnson had abused, or at least used unwisely, the powers of the presidency.

In 1973 Arthur M. Schlesinger, Jr., one of the most eloquent longstanding defenders of the merits of strong presidential leadership in his biographies of Jackson, Roosevelt, and Kennedy, performed a seeming about-face with a book whose title—*The Imperial Presidency*—provided a label for the next widely accepted view of the nature of presidential leadership.[22] Written primarily in response to Johnson's escalation of the Vietnam conflict and Nixon's prolongation of it through his first four years in office, Schlesinger's book appeared late in 1973, when public support of President Nixon had begun to plunge (Figure 2).

In January 1973 there was a popular settlement in Southeast Asia, and American troops were withdrawn from Vietnam. Soon, however, the nation was being regaled with almost daily televised disclosures of abuse of White House power. From the spring of 1973 until after Nixon resigned in August 1974, the mess of Watergate strengthened the conclusion many political commentators had already reached in response to the Vietnam morass: that the presidential power is subject to imperial abuse.

3. *The imperiled presidency.* Throughout the rest of the 1970s the view that presidential power had become excessive began to be displaced by the notion that presidential power had become distressingly reduced. One political figure who understandably advanced the alliterative thesis that the presidency had become "imperiled, not imperial" was Gerald Ford, the first president to be defeated at the polls since Herbert Hoover.[23] Replacing Nixon in a glow of goodwill and favorable publicity, Ford promptly pardoned his predecessor. His initially high approval rating plummeted. During his first six months in office, his public support level declined from somewhat over 70 percent to under 40.

Ford's presidency, the shortest in the twentieth century, faced

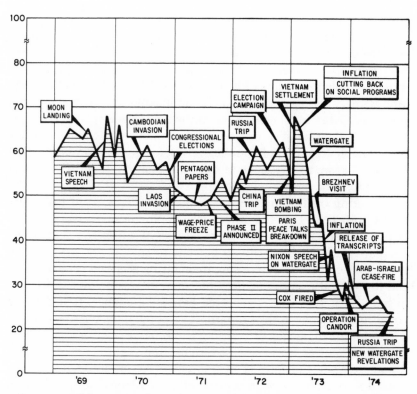

Figure 2. Public approval ratings of Richard M. Nixon (Source: *Gallup Opinion Index*, October–November 1980, p. 21).

problems of building a compatible White House staff and cabinet from Nixon administration holdovers, Ford's Washington and Michigan congressional district associates, and new personnel. Like earlier presidents, Ford received the blame for economic problems that were in no obvious way of his making. He had barely developed the interestingly variegated system for managing his presidency that Porter describes in Chapter 8 when the new, primary-based, media-driven nominating system that had been developing since the late 1960s enabled a popular Republican rival, former California governor Ronald Reagan, to challenge him for nomination. It is little wonder that he lost the general election.

Reflecting on the presidency in the late 1970s, Ford had every reason to believe that the office was slipping into receivership. His experience and others' demonstrated its volatility. His successor's popularity eroded from the 70 percent to the 50 percent range in 1977. Twice in 1978, Carter's approval rating was a mere 39 percent; and for several months in 1979 his support was below 30 percent. In his fourth year Carter repeated Ford's experience, first facing a powerful challenge in the primaries by a popular opponent—Senator Edward Kennedy—and then losing the general election.

4. *Presidential power restored?* In his first year in office President Ronald Reagan transformed an ambiguous victory into what he succeeded remarkably well in representing as a landslide mandate. In contrast to Carter, Reagan was able to advance a winning legislative program. Unlike Carter or Ford, he was renominated without opposition and reelected handily. Among the nine modern presidents, he was matched only by Roosevelt and Kennedy in his capacity to communicate effectively and easily to the general public. From the beginning of his first term until the Iran-Contra disclosures in his second, Reagan and his associates conveyed the impression that a strong, effective, popular leader had restored the presidency to prominence in the political system.

By the 1980s, however, the assumption that the position of the chief executive in the American political system virtually guaranteed that he would advocate "good" policies was a thing of the past. Any political observer who had operated during the 1960s and 1970s would have had personal experience of disapproving some of the policies and performance of one or more presidents. The observer would also have come to reject assumptions about the inherent strength or weakness of the presidency. By then the modern presidency was reaching a stage in which its major properties were changing only slowly. Moreover, the number of disrupted or single-term administrations had provided evidence for more subtle assessments than those captured in such labels as the regnant, imperial, imperiled or restored presidency.

Lessons of the Later Modern Presidency

Even the one president in American history who served more than two terms, Franklin Roosevelt, was something of a bird of passage in the Washington community compared with senior legislators, Supreme Court justices, and longtime civil servants, lobbyists, and Washington lawyers. After 1960 it became increasingly evident to presidents, as well as to those with whom they must deal, that a president's capacity to have an impact is compromised by the brevity of his time in office. The obvious strategy for those who oppose presidential initiatives is obstruction and delay. For presidents, who need to reserve much of the third and fourth years of their first term for renomination and reelection politics and who face a national policy-making system that can readily stalemate their efforts, there is a strong temptation to move rapidly after election, even when this may mean advancing policies that have not been adequately studied. Presidential turnover also fosters discontinuity in public policy as newcomers learn their jobs. And when presidents know that they have a short time to get results, they are tempted to take executive action that goes beyond the formal or informal norms of the political system.

As poor a bargain as the short presidency may be for the American people and political system, the high turnover in presidents has increased scholars' understanding of the short- and long-run effects of the presidents' operating styles and other characteristics of presidents and their principal associates. Each new presidency expands the observation points available for assessing the circumstances that make presidential leadership more or less effective. In addition, the post-1960 presidencies have had consequences for the presidency itself that are of continuing importance.

Kennedy and His Legacy

Twenty years after his assassination, national surveys of the general public showed that Americans regarded Kennedy as the best of the modern presidents.[24] Scholarly assessments, however, by no means match this public adulation. Some analysts view him as a gifted leader who applied intelligence, open-mindedness, and pragmatic dedication to problem solving; for others he has been, in Brauer's words, "a sitting duck for demythologizing." Critics have characterized Kennedy as a leader with more panache than substance, a Cold Warrior who significantly increased the nation's Vietnam entanglement, and a nuclear risk taker.[25]

Public views of Kennedy, however, continue to partake of the posthumous idealization that started with the outburst of spontaneous grief occasioned by the death in office of any president, and magnified by the shock of assassination and loss of a magnetic young leader whose media presence had been both engaging and inspirational.[26] The political information that reaches most Americans— including the many who have no memories of the living Kennedy— does not include revisionist biographies of presidents. It does include such continuing evocations of the idealized JFK as the prime-time television news reports in 1987, on what would have been Kennedy's seventieth birthday. On that occasion, as before, the networks showed film clips displaying Kennedy's engaging wit in press conferences and his inspirational inaugural address; in this and in other ways they reinforced the sense that from January 1961 through November 1963 the nation had a truly great president.

It may be that idealizations of a past president contribute to a public political psychology that holds later presidents to sterner tests of performance by raising expectations about what can be accomplished through presidential leadership. That expectations can exceed perceptions of presidential performance is clear from a Gallup survey conducted in October 1979. When asked if the incumbent president, Jimmy Carter, could solve the contemporary problem they considered to be most pressing, only 30 percent of a national sample said "yes." When asked if the problem was one that could be solved by a president, if the right one were available, 59 percent said "yes."[27] The survey, of course, does not show that public memories of Kennedy contribute to such expectations. Indeed there may be no conclusive way to ascertain whether assessments of Kennedy's virtues have had any consequences for other aspects of public political thinking. There is abundant evidence that politicians who followed Kennedy have been influenced by his legacy of what Hargrove calls the public (in contrast to the governmental) face of presidential leadership.

The real John F. Kennedy (not to speak of his idealized memory)

set standards for effective public appeal that no subsequent president, at least until Ronald Reagan, could meet. Successors competed
with his elusive ghost at a time when doing so became more difficult.
Since the 1960s, the primary medium for reporting public affairs in
general and the presidency in particular has changed from print to
television news, and from television news that essentially relayed
presidents' messages to interpretative television news that seeks
dramatic story lines and effective "news bites." Today, if a president
and his aides cannot present presidential policies in ways that trans-
late into favorable news narratives, the networks create their own
dramatic portrayals, sometimes focusing on the president's shortcomings.[28]

In the presidencies since Kennedy's, it is not surprising to find
increasingly professionalized speechwriting staffs and more use of
media consultants, market research, and other techniques designed
to help the president "play in Peoria." There also has been a continuation of Kennedy's practice of holding live press conferences, a
practice which has not fostered clarity in the enunciation of public
policy, and which every successor, including Reagan, has had difficulty using effectively but has felt he could not halt.[29]

Paradoxically, the massive efforts to expand and reinforce the
personal visibility of presidents since the early 1960s have coincided
with repeated slides in public support. As has often been suggested,
one likely factor in such slides is presidents' inability to live up to
the expectations aroused by their own rhetoric.

Kennedy's approach to rallying the public had more enduring consequences for the presidency than did his leadership style in the
Executive Office of the President and elsewhere in the Washington
community. But his White House operating style provides important
insight into the approach to presidential leadership that, by the end
of the Eisenhower years, observers such as Neustadt had come to
expect to be particularly productive.

Kennedy practiced what scholars have characterized as the collegial variant of Roosevelt's competitive approach to consulting and
working with his associates.[30] He did not incite feuds among associates as Roosevelt had, but did open himself to widely diverse information and advocacy. He avoided such formal offices and
arrangements as a chief of staff or an NSC staff system. Instead, he
relied on informal give-and-take for advice and information. The
resulting ferment undoubtedly fostered creativity. The Peace Corps,
which remains an international asset, was instituted early in Ken-

nedy's first year in office, an imaginative exemplification of his demand that Americans ask what they could do for their country, not what it could do for them. Early in 1961 too, Kennedy set in motion a program based on the literal, as well as figurative, high aspirations of putting a man on the moon before the end of the decade. This proposal, which appears to have been triggered by a search for an issue that would restore the lost sense of momentum after the Bay of Pigs disaster, was not delayed or aborted as a result of deliberations by Eisenhoweresque (formal) study groups. In this instance it is not clear that Kennedy-style spontaneity contributed to good policy. After the initial success of project Apollo, which landed a man on the moon, manned exploration of the solar system was discontinued. It may well be that if the pros and cons of Apollo and the alternative of unmanned exploration had been weighed, the project would not have been undertaken and resources would have been channeled into more productive ways of advancing the national space effort.[31]

Kennedy's Executive Office operating methods departed most dramatically from those of Eisenhower's in the area of foreign affairs. Almost immediately after taking office, he abolished the elaborate agenda-setting and implementation-planning procedures used by Eisenhower for studying basic foreign policy problems and coordinating his foreign policy team. This had not been a Neustadt recommendation. It was of a piece with a number of actions taken in the glow of Kennedy's first weeks in office that seemed almost to be exuberant exercises in government by press release.

There was no close media attention to Kennedy's changes in national security machinery, but the handful of newspapers that cover Washington closely did take note of the general informality of his White House operations, including his return to the Roosevelt and Truman tradition of being his own White House coordinator. When, on August 17, Cuban exiles landed with U.S. aid at Cuba's Bay of Pigs in a disastrously misguided mission, commentators who had been refreshed by the easy Kennedy style quickly turned on him for sloppy leadership.

Kennedy's response to the Bay of Pigs was to seek a means of avoiding similar mistakes. Characteristically, he looked not to machinery, but to men; not to formal cures, but to more effective informal activity. He asked his longtime aide and alter ego, Theodore Sorensen and his brother Robert to play active roles as skeptics and problem-solving generalists in crisis management situations. One result was that both men were important actors in the intense secret deliberations during the Cuban missile crisis the next year, and both contributed to the shift from the initial presumption that an air strike on the Soviet missile sites in Cuba was necessary to the final decision to announce a blockade and permit the Soviet Union to disengage, avoiding a military confrontation that might have escalated into a nuclear exchange. As with the Apollo project, the overall quality of the "Cuba II" decisions and decision making remains a matter of controversy, in part because much of the key documentation necessary to study virtually all presidential national security policy since the mid-1950s remains classified.[32]

One important area of Kennedy's foreign policy decision making—the process through which Kennedy established military force levels—has been closely studied through interviews and therefore is well understood despite the unavailability of key documents.[33] The evidence suggests flawed performance. The existence of a missile gap was an article of Democratic faith in the 1960 campaign. But once in office, Kennedy immediately had access to U-2 surveillance data showing that Soviet missile development was far behind that of the United States. Defense Secretary Robert S. McNamara acknowledged as much in a background news conference soon after the administration took office. Kennedy himself avoided the issue for most of the year. Despite the absence of a Soviet missile threat and, evidently, largely in response to pressures from the military and out of the momentum of campaign promises, the Kennedy administration presided over a missile buildup that by the time of the president's death vastly exceeded the Soviet force levels. This buildup, in turn, almost certainly contributed to the Soviet buildup over the next decade, and eventually to the "window of vulnerability" debate that prompted first the Carter and then the Reagan administrations to continue the upward spiral of nuclear arms.

Kennedy's informal, collegial approach to decision making continued in the Johnson presidency, though with somewhat different "atmospherics." This style did not become a permanent feature in the operation of the presidency. An aspect of Kennedy leadership that has endured is personalization of the White House staff. Apart from Sherman Adams, virtually none of the Eisenhower White House aides were covered in the press. Even Adams's successor after 1958 as the assistant to the president had the lowest of profiles outside the Washington community.

Many of Kennedy's aides, however, like much of the rest of the glittering Kennedy presidency, were deemed newsworthy. The long-run significance for the presidency of the changing role of White House aides in the Kennedy years is not just their visibility, but, more important, the tendency of White House staff to become policy enunciators and advocates. Here the most significant innovator was White House Assistant for National Security McGeorge Bundy. Bundy came to receive billing in the media as a surrogate secretary of state, possibly more influential in policy-making than the actual secretary of state, Dean Rusk. In the centrifugal executive branch that the separation of powers fosters in the United States, independently powerful White House national security advisers have periodically contributed to muddled foreign policy-making and to conflicts or, at a minimum, lack of cooperation between secretaries of state and such White House aides as Henry Kissinger in the Nixon adminis-tration, Zbigniew Brzezinski in the Carter administration, and John Poindexter in the Reagan administration. A further cost has been a reduction in presidents' ability to make good use of the specialized advice and support available from State Department foreign policy professionals.[34]

Lyndon B. Johnson: Executive Role, Legislative Style

Like Kennedy and Truman, Lyndon B. Johnson brought to the pres-idency the political reflexes of a senator. Truman was what old-time legislators called a "workhorse"; he acquired close internal knowl-edge of government operations as an assiduous member of the Ap-propriations Committee. He became visible almost accidentally as a result of his performance on a widely publicized workhorse as-signment—chairing an acclaimed committee mandated to identify waste in military spending. Senators with the traditional aversion of some senior legislators to headline grabbing would have labeled Kennedy a "show horse." He was one of the senators whose efforts were not directed toward creating and enacting legislation but in-stead to engaging in national policy discourse.

    Johnson was neither a committee-room workhorse nor a show horse whose reuptation came from the attention he received for making public policy pronouncements. Indeed, he often reserved stating his position until immediately before a roll call. He was the quintessential broker. He brought to the White House what many presidency watchers of the time thought of as the attributes most necessary for presidential success—a fierce will to put his own brand on political outcomes, and extraordinary skill and experience in traversing the Washington policy-making labyrinth.

The attributes that made Johnson a successful legislator during his ten years as Senate Democratic leader served him well during the widely admired initial year of his presidency. He was the catalyst in the second session of the Eighty-eighth Congress for passage of Kennedy's stalemated civil rights legislation. He seized upon speech-writer Richard Goodwin's facile suggestion that his program be called the Great Society and, capitalizing on an inchoate Kennedy study group proposal for a War on Poverty, attached the label of the Kennedy program to a billion-dollar mixture of existing and new welfare programs, and saw it through to enactment. In the 1964 election he managed to occupy all but the most conservative space in the spectrum of American politics, conducting a campaign against his Republican opponent that gained him both a landslide victory and the first Congress since 1936 with a secure majority of liberal Democrats.

Johnson's gifts as a legislative broker were central to his widely acclaimed 1965 domestic policy successes: the unprecedented procession of Great Society enactments, including Medicare, aid to education, voting rights, and aid to Appalachia and cities. Moreover, during his first two years in office Johnson expanded his political repertoire beyond bargaining and coalition building. His confident comportment and decisive actions after the Kennedy assassination restored national confidence. His addresses in support of the Great Society programs and civil rights were inspirational evocations of national aspirations.

Early in 1965, in a speech on Vietnam at Johns Hopkins University, Johnson even struck a successful inspirational Great Society note, calling on both sides to cease combat and enjoy the benefits of an American-funded Mekong River Development, fashioned after the Tennessee Valley Authority. But behind the rhetoric he remained a political broker. Johnson's aide Bill Moyers reports that after giving the speech, the president told an associate: "Old Ho can't turn that down." Moyers' wry afterthought was that, "If Ho Chi Minh had been George Meany, Lyndon Johnson would have had a deal."[35]

The decision-making mode by which, in 1965, Johnson led the nation from advising to fighting in Vietnam and increased the troop level there ninefold was of a piece with his legislative style. Throughout that year he never made his administration's overall aims in

Vietnam clear, except in the most general terms. (Very probably they were never clear to him.) Both within his circle of advisers and in the larger national political arena, he resolved substantive disagreements over radically different conceptions of the national interest and proposals for action by engineering compromises that commanded short-run support. The Johnson administration's process of deliberation on Southeast Asia policy was informal and flexible, but unhappily so. Hard questions—"How much military force would the United States invest?" "For how long?" "At what economic and political cost?" "With what likely payoff?"—were never asked.[36]

Pragmatic decision making such as Johnson's, in which policy dilemmas are worked out by compromise and by increments, were codified—and represented as inevitable, and perhaps therefore desirable—in such scholarly analyses of the period as Charles E. Lindblom's influential essay, "The Science of Muddling Through."[37] Muddling through and brokered policy-making under Johnson's leadership, however, enmeshed the nation in a war in Asia.

In the short-term 1965 context, Johnson's Vietnam policy was politically brilliant. At the time, he had widespread public approval for his foreign policy. Even on campuses, protestors were a small minority. But short-term brilliance in initiating a presidential policy is different from brilliance in bringing about the enactment of a law. When a law is on the books the legislative leader can turn to new business. With troops in Vietnam, Johnson's business had just begun. Before it ended, the political base of his leadership was destroyed.

Muddling through and splitting the difference between fundamentally different policy options affected another outcome of the Johnson presidency. Johnson persisted in seeking the support of the increasing demands of both the war and the Great Society while resisting tax increases. The result was wage and price inflation that continued long after he left office.[38]

By the end of the Johnson administration several seeming verities about conduct of the modern presidency had been undermined by events.

1. The president's political skill and will to shape events no longer seemed per se desirable.

2. The premise that informal management of presidential decision making would in itself enhance creativity by fostering

flexibility and well-advised presidential choices was no longer supportable without major qualifications.

3. The very notion of what constitutes political success in presidential leadership had to be rethought. Johnson's Vietnam policy had been a political success in the short run. Presidential success, it became evident, must also be assessed in terms of long-term political consequences and the workability and desirability of presidential policy, not just in terms of the president's ability to bring about his policy aims.

There were other enduring effects on the presidency of the Johnson leadership and the Johnson years, some of them extensions of developments that began under Kennedy.

Reduced influence of senior civil servants. Within the Executive Office of the President, initiation of domestic policy shifted from the civil service career professionals in the Bureau of the Budget to the president's White House office aides. The policy activism of the two presidents who served from January 1961 to January 1969 was inconsistent with letting domestic proposals emerge methodically through the executive branch agencies, undergoing screening and clarification in the Bureau of the Budget. The BOB legislative clearance procedures were slow and tempered the impulse to innovate. More and more, policies began to be invented by the politically appointed policy advocates in the West Wing, who were geared to respond rapidly to presidential instructions. White House domestic policy invention and initiation became institutionalized. Johnson assigned former Defense Department aide Joseph Califano the task of generating and assessing new domestic policy proposals. He encouraged Califano's policy team to barnstorm the country on task force visits with policy specialists, such as academic social scientists, searching for new and challenging proposals for the president's domestic policy program. Califano's group was the precursor of the Domestic Policy Council, established by President Nixon, and the domestic policy staffs that have continued to be a feature of later administrations.

On the other side of West Executive Avenue from the West Wing, the longtime institutional policy analysis professionals of the Executive Office—the senior Budget Bureau aides—languished, if they were not coopted into Califano's operations. Some BOB veterans argue that because the Great Society programs had not been evaluated by neutrally competent professionals in advance of enactment, they were prone to go awry in the field. That argument has never been systematically assessed. It is certain, however, that the professionals in the "permanent government," whether in the Executive Office of the President or in the agencies, declined in influence.[39]

High-profile legislative leadership. By the end of the Johnson years, the low-profile White House legislative liaison machinery instituted by Eisenhower had become a visible component of the White House Office. Kennedy's liaison chief, Lawrence O'Brien, remained through the Johnson presidency, although he nominally became postmaster general. In contrast to the efforts of Eisenhower's envoys to the other end of Pensylvania Avenue, O'Brien's lobbying was widely covered by the press. Both Johnson and Kennedy also frequently encouraged admiring press accounts of their own personal skill in exercising influence throughout the Washington community, as well as in Congress. In doing so they acted consistently with the precept of Neustadt and others for whom Roosevelt's leadership is exemplary— that effective presidents must develop their professional reputation in the thrust-and-parry of policy-making. The tradeoff was that they lost their capacity to play the part of a politically transcendent chief of state on occasions calling for political unity.

Restraints on presidential initiatives. By the time Johnson left office, American politics was becoming even more intractable for presidential leadership than it had been in the 1940s and 1950s, when most academic commentators yearned for a stronger presidency. The trends included growing opposition to unilateral use of presidential power, which, after Watergate, was to lead to presidency-curbing legislation, increased public cynicism about the merits of presidential policy proposals, and greater press inclination to challenge presidential assertions and proposals.

A changed presidential nominating system. The last two years of Johnson's presidency left the Democratic party so divided over Vietnam that its 1968 nominating convention in Chicago was ravaged by acrimony in the convention hall and, on the streets, bloody confrontations between antiwar protestors and Mayor Richard Daley's police force. Vice-President Humphrey was nominated for president without having contested a primary, but he was unable to distance himself from Johnson's Vietnam policy. (His most powerful opponent, Robert Kennedy, had been assassinated on the night of the California primary.) The legitimacy of the 1968 nomination was manifestly flawed. Party activists set about to change the nominating rules to make the conventions more representative. Inadvertently they set in motion forces that induced a majority of states to shift from selecting presidential nominating convention delegates by councils of party activists to a practice that up to that time had been used in a minority of states—direct primary elections of delegates bound in advance to support a particular presidential candidate.[40]

This party-weakening departure has had profound consequences for the presidency. Presidents and legislators have become independent entrepreneurs, establishing their own constituencies. As a result they are less likely to be members of common alliances with state and local party leaders that encourage cooperative policy-making. Under the new system it is also likely that a first-term president will have to campaign for renomination. The prolonged, arduous nominating campaign forces presidents to shift their focus from the politics of governing to those of nominating, and thus reduces the president's impact on policy-making. The changed process also has the potential of enabling a political unknown, who may not have the skills required for national policy-making, to be nominated. This, many political observers argue, occurred in 1976, when the Democrats nominated Jimmy Carter. As of late 1975 Carter had only 2.5 percent approval among Democratic party identifiers and very little support among party activists. He profited from the new arrangements, which made it possible for political unknowns to break out of large candidate fields in the early primaries, take a strong lead, and win the nomination.

Richard M. Nixon: The Administrative Presidency

Presidents who enter the White House after their party has been out of office for some time understandably suspect the loyalty of the federal employees who served their predecessors. So it was with Roosevelt, Eisenhower, and Kennedy. So it came to be with Nixon. As Hoff-Wilson suggest, Nixon's belief that civil servants were seeking to thwart his program was not solely a result of his chronic tendency to distrust the motives and goodwill of other political actors. Her analysis is consistent with that of a group of scholars who discovered striking differences between Nixon's views and those of the civil servants who administered his programs, concluding that "even paranoids have enemies."[41] Moreover, Nixon and his associates were acutely aware of the tendency of heretical civil servants to subvert the views of a new administration's political appointees, enlisting them in alliances against the administration's policies.

Nixon's response, during his first term, to bureaucratic subversion was to increase the size of the White House staff and to populate it with Nixon loyalists. He used a hierarchical mode of organizing the Executive Office of the Presidency, similar to the arrangements that had prevailed during Eisenhower's administration and shifted policy-making from the agencies to the EOP.

Then, early in his second term, he sought to move his proven loyalists into the departments and to consolidate leadership of the departments through a "supercabinet" consisting of a small number of reliable secretaries who would implement his policies. He abandoned his plan when the Watergate scandals began to unfold, but his proposal anticipated President Reagan's successful use of appointments as a systematic means of making and enforcing administration policy.[42]

After an initial shakedown period Nixon settled into working practices that gave his chief of staff, H. R. Haldeman, and his policy chief, John Ehrlichman, even more comprehensive responsibility as the gatekeepers of domestic policy information and options than Eisenhower had Sherman Adams. In foreign policy, Nixon's equivalent to John Foster Dulles was his assistant for national security affairs, Henry Kissinger. Unlike Dulles, however, Kissinger was a White House aide, unconfirmed by the Senate and responsible only to the president. Dulles, as secretary of state, had been able to draw on the full resources of his department. Kissinger, in line with the general Nixon approach of centralizing national policy-making in the White House, built a National Security Council staff of unprecedented size.[43] So marginal was the Department of State in Nixon administration foreign policy-making that Secretary of State William Rogers was not even informed in advance of the administration's most innovative foreign affairs departure—the opening to China.

Unfavorable perceptions of Nixon's use of Haldeman and Ehrlichman and of Kissinger's role in the White House made Presidents Ford and Carter shun such practices. Nixon's two immediate successors were careful to avoid even the appearance of running their White House in a strictly hierarchical manner and of seeking to impose strict policy uniformity on their appointees to the executive branch. But an important residue of Nixon's effort to enhance the president's ability to shape policy by politicizing presidential administration of the executive branch endured. In the aftermath of a study by a commission headed by Litton Industries president Roy Ash, Nixon recommended and Congress accepted Reorganization Plan No. 2, which went into effect July 1, 1970, transforming the Bureau of the Budget into the Office of Management and Budget (OMB). The OMB has a layer of presidentially appointed assistant directors for policy between the director and the senior civil servants who led this political entity when it was the BOB. Nixon also treated his OMB directors more as White House advisers than as administrators of a staff of presidential civil servants whose purpose was to provide the presidency with "institutional memory" and dispassionate policy analysis. No doubt the BOB's capacity to be dispassionate has been idealized by veterans of the Smith–Webb era, when the Budget Bureau first became actively linked to the presidency. Nevertheless, the OMB is a fundamentally different institution from the BOB. Terms such as "passionate anonymity" and "neutral competence," which well characterize Harold Smith's conduct of the Bureau of the Budget under Roosevelt and Truman, could scarcely be less appropriate for describing the intensely visible, politically combative role played by Reagan's OMB director David Stockman.[44]

Another obvious source of conflict that Nixon had to anticipate was Congress. He was the first twentieth-century president to be elected without a majority of his own party in Congress. Nixon's response to obstacles to his leadership was to construe presidential prerogative broadly. The rapprochement with China was a Nixon initiative that received accolades. But his use of his power as commander in chief to order military incursions into and secret bombing of Cambodia aroused major protest. So did his sweeping application of presidential discretion not to spend appropriated funds. Presidents since at least Jefferson's time have sometimes chosen not to spend funds appropriated by Congress, in the interest of preventing waste and inefficiency. Nixon, however, was prepared to impound funds— as in his effort to disempower the Office of Economic Opportunity— to contravene congressional intent. Indeed, after he was refused a major reorganization of the executive branch, he let it be known that he would conduct his duties *as if* a reorganization of departments into larger entities headed by a supercabinet had been approved.

Early in 1973 it seemed that unilateral centralization of presidential power was a *fait accompli*. This was the conclusion of an authoritative-sounding front-page *New York Times* series by John Hebers.[45] The impact of these articles had barely sunk in, however, when the revelations before Senator Sam Ervin's "Watergate committee" began. By the end of April the president had accepted the resignations of H. R. Haldeman and John Ehrlichman. The sequence of disintegration thereafter is well known: the discovery that there were White House tapes of illegal actions and a coverup; the release of an incomplete but still damaging initial set of tapes; "the Saturday night massacre," in which Nixon fired the two top Justice Department officials when they said they would not deny information to the Watergate special prosecutor; the Supreme Court action forcing release of further tapes that showed that the president had known all along of the coverup; finally, Nixon's resignation in the face of certain impeachment by the House and conviction by the Senate.

The putative "lessons" and consequences of Watergate and of Nixon's leadership style in general are too numerous even to catalogue, but three stand out.

First, many political observers concluded that Nixon's failure to prevent the politically damaging wrongdoing of White House aides validated what had been a widely accepted truism in the early lore of the modern presidency: "The president needs to be his own chief of staff."[46] Nixon, the argument went, had been so reliant on his "Berlin Wall" of Haldeman and Ehrlichman that he had been blinded to the need to forbid such unproductive, politically dangerous, and otherwise inappropriate practices as the "dirty tricks" that culminated in the burglary of the Democratic National Committee headquarters. A corollary was that the White House staff had been allowed to become so large that it was no longer controllable by the president and his top assistants, and therefore was an encumbrance rather than an aid to presidential leadership.[47]

Second, the Nixon experience provided perspective on another aphorism about presidential leadership: "Presidents are better able to lead through persuasion than through command."[48] The refutation was straightforward. Nixon had found it unnecessary to engage in persuasion in order to open relations with China, order bombing of Cambodia, or impound funds. But heavy-handed use of command also contributed to his fall. The willingness of Congress to take the extraordinary step of removing a president was in part a response to Nixon's continuing failure to use persuasion to win congressional support and to his repeated efforts to circumvent Congress. In short, presidential capacity to exercise unilateral power had been underestimated, but it remained true that a president who relied heavily on command powers might have to pay major penalties.

Third, as a result of the general alteration in views about the presidency that ensued from the experiences of Vietnam and Watergate, Congress enacted a seemingly formidable array of presidency-curbing legislation. Most of these laws have not been tested definitively and, in any event, have had only marginal effects on presidential practices. All told, however, the new legislation is a warning against presidential imperialism. Certainly if the new laws had been in force in the past, many historic acts of presidential initiative would have had to be carried out with more systematic attention to obtaining congressional support.[49] Here are some of the major enactments:

After fifty-three years during which BOB/OMB had existed as an agency wholly in the president's preserve, in 1973 the OMB director and deputy directors for the first time became subject to congressional confirmation (P.L. 93–250, 88 Stat. 11, 1974).

The Impoundment Control Act of 1974 (Title X of P.L. 93–344) requires that if a president does not want to expend appropriated funds he must report "recission" to Congress. He may *defer* spending funds unless one house of Congress votes disapproval. Recissions must be approved by both houses within forty-five days.

The Case Act, passed in 1972 (P.L. 92–403), requires that all executive agreements with foreign powers be reported to Congress.

The War Powers Resolution of 1973 (P.L. 93–148) requires the president to consult with Congress "in every possible instance" before committing troops to combat and to submit a report on his action to Congress, and makes it necessary for Congress, unless physically unable to meet, to authorize the military action.

Two Modern Presidents Who Met Electoral Defeat

The political styles and careers of Gerald Ford and Jimmy Carter were fundmentally different. Ford was an experienced Washington veteran with well-established political beliefs tempered by a legislative leader's capacity for compromise. He began remarkably quickly to unlearn his ad hoc congressional work habits and find an operating mode more suitable to the demands of the presidency. Carter seemed to revel in his lack of Washington roots and to identify himself less with his brief Georgia governorship than with his nonpolitical experience as a businessman-engineer who had achieved success by mastery of detailed knowledge and use of rationalized operating procedures. He appeared to be highly reluctant to adapt this style to the demands of the presidency.

As different as they were in style, both provide remarkably similar illustrations of how powerfully media practices have affected the capacity or incapacity of presidents to have a political impact. Immediately after becoming president, each was portrayed glowingly. During this initial cult-of-personality period, the focus was on endearingly unpretentious personal qualities. Ford managed to get in a healthy swim at the end of the day and toasted his own English muffins in the morning. Carter carried his own baggage. Rather than riding in a motorcade, he walked with his wife and daughter down Pennsylvania Avenue from Capitol Hill to the White House after being inaugurated.

Inevitably, what then became newsworthy was the president's clay feet. Ford's standing crumbled rapidly after he pardoned Nixon in September 1974. He remained newsworthy as a personality, but he was caricatured as a slow-witted, uncoordinated bumbler. Carter's press coverage and Gallup poll support took longer to become negative. Still, the very means he and his media advisers employed to build his personal support were also susceptible to derision—for example, a fireside television address is remembered less for its content than for the president's ostentatiously informal garb, a cardigan sweater. Before the end of his first year as president, Carter's legislative program was stalemated. His friend and OMB director, Bert Lance, had to resign because of controversial earlier banking practices. Although the media continued to depict Carter in personal terms, accounts now stressed not his folksiness, but his unpresidential diminutiveness. He came to be portrayed as a man who literally as well as figuratively lacked stature and was dwarfed by his responsibilities. Despite the brevity of their tenure, both presidents provide perspective on the potential for, and limits on, leadership in the modern presidency.

Gerald Ford's post-Watergate leadership. In the wake of the bad press that Nixon's centralized White House advising system received, Ford initially rejected employing a chief of staff and deliberately resumed the earlier presidential practice of personally coordinating top aides. For Ford, the results were lack of coordination and decisions made on the basis of imperfect information and incomplete advice. There is reason to believe, for example, that the decision to pardon Nixon was made with little consultation—that Ford had not reflected on the political implications of a pardon for which Washington and public opinion were unprepared. He recalls that "after six months I did find that a President needs one person who at least coordinates such as the president's assistant for national security affairs, the head of the Domestic Policy Council, the head of the Economic Policy Board, et cetera."[50] For his chief of staff he turned to former congressman and Nixon cabinet member Donald Rumsfeld and, after Rumsfeld became defense secretary, to Richard Cheney.

Unlike Haldeman and Ehrlichman in the Nixon presidency, Rumsfeld and Cheney were never reputed to be Berlin Walls. Working for an open, flexible president who had spent his career in the camaraderie of Congress, Ford's chiefs of staff helped him to organize his activities, set priorities, and assure himself of exposure to a wide range of advice and information. They could not and did not seal him off. In contrast to other modern presidents, who tended either to work through a limited number of staff intermediaries or to work collegially with aides, Ford's practice varied. At one pole, his economic advising was deliberately structured so that all relevant government actors could argue their cases in Ford's presence before his Economic Policy Board (EPB). The EPB had a staff mechanism that fostered regular consultation. Issues were clarified and policy differences sharpened at the staff level. Ford then participated freely in give-and-take EPB meetings, making decisions in the context of what Porter describes as rigorous multiple advocacy, in contrast to mere ad hoc exchanges of views.[51]

At the other pole, foreign relations retained a hierarchical advisory pattern. Ford respected Henry Kissinger's statecraft and also was confident of his foreign policy views. He did not feel the need for a broad forum. Kissinger had been named secretary of state late in Nixon's presidency but retained his White House status as assistant for national security into the Ford presidency. After a year Ford appointed a low-profile foreign policy professional, Brent Scowcroft, to the White House position, keeping Kissinger as secretary of state, but continued to draw principally on Kissinger for advice on foreign affairs.

Ford's presidency also demonstrated the sturdiness of the venerable separation of powers. In the November 1974 election the Democratic majority in Congress was swollen by forty-four in the House and three in the Senate. Ford neither rigidified nor became passive.

Although he had some positive legislative success in tax cutting and deregulation, his most striking impact was negative. Casting his veto almost as if it were the 436th congressional vote, he rejected sixty-one congressional enactments, mostly spending bills, and was upheld forty-nine times.

In foreign affairs, Ford was unfazed by the Vietnam legacy and the War Powers Act. He did not consult with Congress when he deployed military force in May 1975 to recover the merchant ship *Mayaguez* and its crew, after they had been seized by Cambodia. On the other hand, Congress displayed its own counterforce capacity. Rather than defer to Ford as commander in chief, Congress curbed him on a number of his most urgent proposals: request for emergency aid of the disintegrating forces of South Vietnam, a plea to lift an embargo on aid to Turkey, and a request for aid to the enemies of the Marxist force in Angola.

Jimmy Carter: Washington Outsider in the White House. A major lesson of the Carter presidency arises from events that occurred *before* he took office as a consequence of the new presidential nomination system. Carter was the paradigmatic unemployed millionaire who could concentrate single-mindedly on winning support well before the beginning of the formal delegate selection process. He and his strategists made many visits to Iowa, building a personal following in the year before that state conducted its neighborhood delegate selection caucuses. As the first event of the presidential nomination season, the Iowa caucuses receive intense attention, even though the Iowans who meet in local schoolrooms and firehouses to choose delegates are a tiny, unrepresentative fraction of the national Democratic electorate.

More Iowa caucus votes went to uncommitted delegates than to Carter supporters, but he was judged by the media to have done "surprisingly" well in a large Democratic field, drawing heavily on the Iowans he had cultivated while the other Democratic candidates were busy at their duties in Washington. Much of the surprise came simply from his initial lack of visibility. In the week between the Iowa caucuses and the equally publicized New Hampshire primary, the suddenly newsworthy Carter appeared on national talk shows. Evening television news broadcasts emphasized his "post-Watergate" style. And he made the covers of the weekly newsmagazines. In the New Hampshire primary the media judged him the winner because he got the largest single bloc of delegates. There was little attention to the fact that he had taken far more conservative stands on issues than had the other candidates in a field of outspoken liberals. Carter, the outsider, assailing the Washington community, won the nomination and scraped through in the general election.[52]

Arriving in Washington without experience and suspicious of the mores of federal-level politics, Carter would have been predictably deficient in making the system get results even if he had not resisted Washington's political folkways. He compounded his problems by staffing his White House with equally provincial veterans of his campaign team. And he set the stage for White House–cabinet conflict by appointing cabinet secretaries with far different perspectives from those of his immediate aides: Washington veterans with long-standing policy commitments such as Joseph Califano (Health, Education and Welfare), James Schesinger (Energy), Harold Brown (Defense), and Patricia Roberts Harris (Housing and Urban Development). He chose as secretary of state another Washington veteran, the pragmatic Cyrus Vance. Ignoring the Ford precedent of using a dispassionate manager of the policy process as a White House assistant for national security affairs, Carter gave the position to a foreign policy intellectual whose intense anti-Soviet convictions fated him to clash with the more pragmatic Vance—Zbigniew Brzezinski. At the time, some political commentators suggested that Carter might have been better off deploying the veterans in the White House, where they would have his ear, and the outsiders in the cabinet. But Hargrove's interview-based account suggests that, whatever the advisory constellation, Carter would have been determined to be his own policy synthesizer and political strategist.

Carter's problems arose both from lack of knowledge of Washington politics and from his misplaced confidence that he already knew how to proceed. He had acquired a fascination with zero-base budgeting, the politically innocent notion that one can treat each government program as if it has no previous momentum, constituency, or history, examining it and its appropriations afresh.[53] What Hargrove calls Carter's public goods approach to devising comprehensive policy proposals proved in general to be an invitation to reinvent less adequate versions of the wheel. Thus, in his already overloaded first year, Carter insisted that his aides devise *de novo* what proved to be a politically and practically unworkable proposal to reform the system for providing welfare support. This project absorbed enormous amounts of time, and the outcome was neither enactment of comprehensive reform nor piecemeal amelioration of the shortcomings of existing arrangements.[54]

By denying conventional political wisdom, Carter quickly acquired what had been once Eisenhower's reputation—that of the
least politically skilled modern president. Like Eisenhower, Carter
may someday be judged more favorably; at the time he left office
his reputation had no place to go but up. Any Carter revisionism,
however, will probably concern itself more with his political skills.

The relationship between the Carter White House and Congress
provides particularly rich illustrations of the problems to be encountered by an apolitical, or even, as Carter often seemed to be,
antipolitical, president. There was a solid Democratic majority in
both houses of Congress. Yet Carter quickly antagonized the party
leaders. He did so in small but symbolically meaningful ways, such
as relegating the Speaker of the House to a back-row seat at the
inaugural celebration. He erred fundamentally by bombarding Congress with too many legislative proposals for it to handle, many of
them complex; by setting no priorities among proposals; and by
overloading key committees, such as House Ways and Means, with
requests. In general, both the amenities and the grand strategy of
Carter's congressional liaison were handled ineptly. Carter himself
was a workaholic, spending many hours alone poring over and mas-
tering the details of proposed policies. But in doing so he neglected
the personal discourse and negotiations that would have enabled
him to enlist the support of those who were necessary to enact and
implement his policies.

Periodically, such aspects of Carter's style as his extraordinary
energy and determination and his keen mind for detail worked to
his advantage. During his second year in office he took the lead in
intense personal persuasion of individual senators in order to win
ratification of the treaties necessary to prepare the way for yielding
American control of the Panama Canal.[55] And his thirteen-day exercise in personal diplomacy with Egyptian president Anwar Sadat
and Israeli prime minister Menachim Begin led to the first rapprochement between an Arab nation and Israel.[56]

A number of familiar hazards of modern presidential leadership
were evident in the Carter presidency: blurred foreign policy, resulting from conflict between the White House national security
assistant and the secretary of state;[57] tension between White House
staff and cabinet aides; and disorganization within the White House
staff. In the wake of a 1979 cabinet shuffle, Carter appointed his
chief political aide, Hamilton Jordan, as official chief of staff, but
there is no evidence that this had a significant effect on White House

operations. The most fundamental lesson of the Carter experience seems to have been validation of perhaps the least controversial proposition in the lore of the modern presidency: whatever else his qualities, the president needs to be a working politician who can work with or otherwise win over the Washington community.

A "Reagan Revolution"?

Ronald Reagan also came to Washington presenting himself as an outsider, and even won reelection four years later by portraying himself as an everyday American who happened to be in Washington to transform misguided public policies. In fact Reagan took on and to Washington politics with gusto.

It is a mistake to think that because he spent much of his adult life as a motion picture actor Ronald Reagan has been apolitical. Reagan had a strong spectator's interest in politics and held broadly conceived views on public affairs from at least the early 1930s. A Democrat and four-time Roosevelt voter, by the late 1930s he was active first in motion picture union politics, then in campaigning for Democratic candidates. As late as 1950 he campaigned for the California Democratic slate and therefore against Republican senatorial candidate Richard Nixon. As president of the film actors' union, he engaged directly in extensive collective bargaining, an experience with solid parallels to the political bargaining in which he participated years later in public office. At this time he also began nurturing his anticommunism, participating in the early Cold War struggles over Communist party influence in trade unions.

Reagan became a successful lecturer on the virtues of free enterprise, a skilled conservative campaign orator, and a two-term governor of the largest state in the nation. By the time he was president, he had become a political professional, whatever his protestations to the contrary. Of the nine modern presidents, he was most explicit in proclaiming a distinct ideological stance. Whatever the actual philosophical underpinnings of Reagan's beliefs, it is clear, as William Muir asserts, that Reagan wanted to bring about a fundamental shift in the policies to which the majority of the nation's leaders had committed themselves. Yet Reagan's anti-Washington stance was the obverse of Carter's. Rather than being repulsed by the requirements of political bargaining to ingratiate oneself with other politicians and to apeal to the larger public, Reagan embraced them in the happy warrior fashion of the president who first captured his imagination, FDR. Because Reagan had been outspokenly conservative for many years, his victory in 1980 was widely interpreted in terms of the title of Rowland Evans and Robert Novak's instant analysis: "The Reagan Revolution."[58] In fact the 1980 vote did not reflect broad endorsement of Reagan's general political philosophy.[59] Rather, Reagan as politician-salesman transformed a nonmandate into something that more closely resembled the genuine item—*after the election.*

Reagan carried most states but won only 51 percent of the popular vote. More Democratic than Republican votes were cast for the Senate. The Republican votes happened to be concentrated in states where they made a difference. Polling showed no major change in basic public attitudes in 1980 and made it clear that voters were unhappy with both major party candidates and the independent candidate, John Anderson. More a rejection of Carter than an endorsement of Reagan, the 1980 vote appears to have been what Stanley Kelley, Jr., calls a "lesser of two evils election."[60]

As if they could have been deliberately created as antitheses by a political novelist, Reagan and Carter had diametrically opposite first years in office. Indeed, Reagan's aide and associate Edwin Meese III reports that Reagan's advisers carefully studied Carter's errors and deliberately crafted a first-year strategy aimed to go right where Carter had gone wrong.[61] Thus, in contrast to Carter's bewildering flood of legislative proposals, "the economy was Reagan's first, second, and third priority."[62] Staffing the White House and OMB with veterans of earlier Republican administrations, Reagan conducted a legislative campaign matched only by that of Lyndon Johnson's first elected year in the extent to which it redirected national policy. It achieved this effect as a result of two bold legislative enactments: a three-year tax cut based on supply-side economic doctrine and a major reduction in domestic spending.

Press reports of the internal organization of the Reagan presidency stress disagreements and feuding. So do early memoirs, such as those of former secretary of state Alexander Haig and OMB director David Stockman.[63] The troika of top White House aides in Reagan's first term, James Baker III, Edwin Meese III, and Michael Deaver, were commonly depicted as being at odds. The chief of staff of the first two years of Reagan's second term, Donald Regan, was described as jealously seeking to choke off other aides' access to the president. OMB Director David Stockman and Secretary of State Alexander Haig seemed sometimes to be in business on their own. Haig's successor, George Shultz, and Defense Secretary Caspar Weinberger carried on a barely concealed feud. And none of Reagan's several assistants for national security was successful in fostering a process through which the principal foreign policymakers spoke with one voice.

There is no evidence that Reagan, like Roosevelt, deliberately fostered disagreements among his associates in order to increase his own information and options. In his first term, competiton within his White House staff may have had this inadvertent result; at any rate it contributed to the effectiveness of White House staff work in the domestic sphere. That Reagan did not deliberately create a competitive advising system as a way of increasing his power and effectiveness is evinced by his failure to derive policy-making advantage from the conflicts he tolerated among his foreign policymaking associates and by what appears to have been his unreflecting acquiescence to the shift in his second term from using a politically sophisticated White House triumvirate to relying on a single aide who was neither Washington-wise nor disposed to provide the president with a sense of the diversity of views within his team. Indeed, when confronted with the Tower Commission report on the Iran-Contra fiasco, Reagan finally parted with the aide in question, former Merrill Lynch chief and treasury secretary Donald Regan. Asked by the Tower Commission investigators whether the president had been forewarned of the inevitable political costs of an arms-for-hostages exchange with Iran, Regan's reply, a mixed stock market and golfing metaphor, bespoke an approach to staffing that is ill suited to preserving the chief executive's options: "The President was told," he acknowledged, "but by no means was it really teed up for him what the downside risk would be as far as American public opinion was concerned."[64]

Ronald Reagan, however, succeeded in general in bringing skilled operatives to his administration. Few members of the Washington community appear ever to have been more effective than James Baker III, whether based in the White House as in Reagan's first term, or in the Treasury Department as in his second. The political campaign that led to passage of the 1981 tax and spending cuts was based on a high-powered combination of cultivating Congress and stimulating pressure from constituencies. Moreover, for sheer professionalism the Reagan White House's use of media specialists, legislative liaison experts, and the dedicated staff of speechwriters that Muir discusses will be a model for future presidencies. When the staffing has been bad, it has been horrid. But much remains worthy of emulation in Reagan's approach of setting forth broad principles, enlisting skilled aides, and harnessing both his own communication skills and his aides' understanding of Washington politics in order to advance his policies.

The Reagan presidency's approach to *designing* policies, however, does not seem likely to be a model for future presidencies. Lyndon Johnson had similar defects as sponsor of a sound policy, skillfully leading the country into an ill-conceived war. The Johnson and Reagan experiences show that the exclusive interest in presidential skill by writers who had only the formative period of the modern presidency to work with is insufficient. Presidents need also to be able to evaluate policies and anticipate their consequences.

The well-known unintended consequence of reducing revenues in 1981 was a skyrocketing federal deficit. Both in his interviews with William Greider and in his 1986 memoir, David Stockman asserts what was apparent to most economists. There was no evidence for Reagan's article of faith, derived from supply-side economic theory, that a tax cut would increase savings and other investment, stimulating economic growth and therefore revenues. Stockman acknowledged that he had been a party to understating the magnitude of the deficit that would, under any plausible assumptions, have resulted from the tax cut. No one anticipated the recession that compounded the effect of the flawed estimates.[65]

An inadvertent consequence of the ballooning deficit (interpreted by some Reagan critics as a deliberate means of discouraging spending programs) was a state of affairs that contributed to making what has been inaccurately called the Reagan Revolution a real transformation in American policy and political discourse. Orthodox Democratic domestic policy is to seek new programs and therefore the necessary funding for them. In the 1980s, however, proposals to increase domestic spending went out of style. Reductions in spending (and, among those who had the courage to seek new taxes, finding new revenues) became the priority.

As his second term proceeded, defense spending, which Reagan had considered untouchable, was the target of cuts. Even as the administration's defense spending requests were being cut back, however, Reagan continued another of his policy emphases: his willingness to project U.S. military influence abroad in, for example, Latin America and the Middle East. Moreover, he was prepared to reclaim presidential prerogative as commander in chief. Thus he chose not to view the War Powers Resolution as a major restraint in the 1986 bombing of Libya: he consulted with legislators only two hours before the aircraft already in the air from their English bases struck their targets.

Military affairs was just one of the areas in which Reagan resumed the trend, begun in the Nixon presidency, toward "the administrative presidency."[66] It can be said that Nixon and Reagan had the courage to act on what once were the convictions of liberals, taking it for granted that the president should use whatever power he can muster, including power to administer programs, to shape policy. Reagan used the power of appointment aggressively. Despite controversies over the executive decisions of particular administrators, such as Interior Secretary James Watt, Reagan in general was able to staff executive branch agencies with administrators who assiduously used their official position to advance the administration's aims, making potent use of executive orders and discretionary policy implementation. Early studies, such as those by Richard Nathan of welfare policy and by Michael Kraft and Norman Vig of environmental policy, show substantial success in changing the direction of policy.[67]

This is not to say that the Reagan administration invariably got what it wanted. After 1981, for example, administration budget and other proposals were repeatedly scrapped or rewritten by Congress.[68] But despite such defeats, Reagan persisted in pressing for results. Indeed, as what David Stockman calls a "terminal optimist," Reagan regularly treated what seemed from the Washington perspective to be defeats as mere setbacks in skirmishes.[69] Setbacks are less likely to disempower a president if he continues to give the impression of being on the march—as Reagan sought to even while the Iran-Contra investigation proceeded on Capitol Hill—and if palpably objective events such as recession or war that affect citizens directly do not occur. Several of the modern presidents bore their responsibilities like crosses. Others, including Reagan for most of his presidency, were able to maintain control of the national political agenda, in part by concrete accomplishments, but also by exuding confidence and self-assurance.

Continuity and Change

Two centuries after the founding fathers agreed upon the sketchy characterization of an American presidency in Article 2 of the Constitution, the presidency continues to resemble its blueprint in a number of important ways. At the same time the expanded modern presidency that began to take shape in 1933 has become firmly institutionalized and is undergoing its own evolution.

The separation of powers is the element in the Constitution that remains most recognizable. A James Madison ushered into the Iran-Contra hearings would have no difficulty recognizing that his legacy had endured. Power is not concentrated in one branch of government. The branches check one another. A resurrected Madison would also quickly find much other recent evidence: Gerald Ford's persistence in vetoing appropriations bills, Carter's need to invest laborious effort in currying congressional support for the Panama Canal treaties, and Reagan's need, after his first year in office, to retreat to a bargaining relationship with Congress in budgetary politics.

Two other traditional legacies to the modern presidency are more implicit than explicit. They are the vagueness, and therefore openness to specification by the president and his politically significant others, of the description of the presidency in the Constitution, and the condensation into one role of what most democracies that emerged in the nineteenth and twentieth centuries divide between two roles, an ecumenical head of state and a partisan national political leader.

The lack of detailed specification of presidential powers and the Delphic references to "the executive power" and to the power to make treaties, appoint ambassadors and "other officers," and be commander in chief have provided license for extensive independent presidential action since the early days of the republic. In the premodern presidency the most significant examples of presidential policy-making initiative were in foreign affairs and national security, including instances (the Whiskey Rebellion, the Pullman strike) in which national force was used to quell domestic unrest. There are obvious parallels beyond mere geography between Thomas Jefferson's dispatch of marines against the Barbary pirates and Ronald Reagan's authorization of an air strike against the government of Muammar Qaddafi. But there is a difference: Reagan's action was part of a pattern. The United States has become a major global actor, and day-to-day foreign policy-making is orchestrated from the White House. The vagueness of the statement "the executive power shall reside in the President of the United States of America" has made it simpler to justify the expansion since 1930 of executive policy-making capacity, which is one of the defining characteristics of the modern presidency.

The continuing significance of a unitary executive who is both head of state and political leader would have struck more of a familiar chord to George Washington than to James Madison. In his presidency, Washington was intensely preoccupied with constructing precedents that would enable a republican president to maintain the legitimacy of a successful monarch. In the modern presidency there has been continuing evidence of the importance and complexity for presidential leadership of the combination of regal and republican responsibility. Jimmy Carter came to regret his impulse to dispense with the playing of "Hail to the Chief" and other monarchical trappings of the presidency. For a time during the Watergate inquiries, Richard Nixon seemed secure against impeachment because much of the public and Congress assumed that to be deemed guilty of "high crimes and misdemeanors," the head of state would have to have done something far more grievous than break a law, much less advance an unpopular policy. Then the status of the American· president as a transcendent head of state turned to Nixon's disadvantage. When it became demonstrable that, despite repeated denials, he had lied, even his most committed supporters defected. Citizens and even public officials in other nations continue to be bewildered that a national leader should be forced to leave office for what seems to them a normal act of political expediency, but for Americans Nixon's behavior was evidence that their chief executive had character defects that made him unworthy of representng their nation.

The four major changes that, beginning in 1933, produced the modern presidency—increased unilateral policy-making capacity, centrality in national agenda setting, far greater visibility, and acquisition of a presidential bureaucracy—remain central elements of the presidency and of presidential leadership in the final decades of the century. Although the increasing capacity of presidents to make policy by personal initiative builds on premodern precedents, especially in foreign policy-making, modern chief executives have the capacity to take far more momentous initiatives, given the nation's superpower status and the explosion in the technology available for foreign and national security actions.

A convenient way to get a sense of how executive policy initiatives—some of them direct orders by the president, but most of them actions by lower-level functionaries—have mushroomed is to thumb through the many volumes of the *Federal Register*. The executive orders and other administrative pronouncements printed there have the same effect as the laws and other rules that emerge from Congress and are compiled in *Statutes at Large.* An irony of the expanded presidency of the modern era is that Congress has not grown weaker. It continues to put its stamp on important legislation. But the legislation then needs to be implemented by the executive branch, and therefore further empowers the president.

The second transformation of the president's job, the shift from being reactive to setting the agenda for Washington policy-making, is a well-established component of the modern presidency. Ronald Reagan's control over the policy-making agenda in 1981 was as certain as Franklin Roosevelt's in the Hundred Days. Reagan employed the institutionalized mechanisms of the BOB/OMB that took shape under Truman. Reagan's inability to dictate the budget after 1981 did not totally change matters. In each year since, his budget was the point of departure for bargaining on Capitol Hill and between the branches. In his second term, Reagan chose what seemed to be the quixotic objective of reforming the tax code. To engage in a major overhaul of that amalgam of provisions linked to countless vocal constituencies was to enter a serpent's nest. Tax change seemed likely to be politically costly and might trigger unanticipated, unwanted economic consequences. Nevertheless, once the president promoted this issue, packaging it appealingly as "tax simplification," legislators felt it necessary to hold hearings, draft legislation, and subject themselves to the pleas of lobbyists. The Democrats concluded that it would be politically costly to oppose simplification and sought to make the issue their own. The outcome: a comprehensive tax change was enacted.[70]

The third modern change in the presidency—the quantum increase in the visibility of presidents that began with Roosevelt's 1933 inaugural address—stems from both the profound consequences presidential action can have in the contemporary era and expanding communications technology. Roosevelt was heard over radio and seen through newsreels. Eisenhower was the first president to employ a White House television consultant. Kennedy was the first gifted television president. Reagan innovated further, using state-of-the-art techniques to make himself a ubiquitous media presence. During Reagan's tenure it came to appear that "going public" had replaced bargaining among Washington actors as the engine of presidential leadership.[71]

Changes in the party system also contributed to the impulse of presidents to increase their visibility and to seek to influence other

Washington policymakers by going over their heads to their constituents. Neither an unskilled Carter nor a skilled Reagan could have produced the kind of easy, backchannel conflict resolution that occurred, for example, in the concluding negotiations through which Eisenhower and congressional leaders arrived at agreement on the final details of the Civil Rights Act of 1957.

In August 1957, the issue standing in the way of passage of that act was a provision permitting federal judges to administer fines and prison sentences to state officials who deprived citizens of their voting rights. If such cases were to have been decided not by judges, but rather by the lily-white southern juries of the time, there would have been no effective sanction against southern officials who ignored the act's provisions. Through the efforts of the two Texas power brokers who led the majority Democratic party, Speaker Sam Rayburn and Senate Majority Leader Lyndon Johnson, a group of swing congressmen had been won over to the provision, which finally became law: fines as great as $300 and jail sentences up to forty-five days would be acceptable without the requirement of a trial. Johnson, who considered this a more favorable compromise than he had hoped for, telephoned President Eisenhower and "asked the President to see quietly if his boys would agree to that. The President asked for ten minutes. He called [Republican leaders William Knowland and Joseph Martin] off the floor; both agreed . . . [Eisenhower] called Lyndon Johnson back and said everything was okay. He asked for a little time so the proceedings would be in order, which Lyndon agreed to . . . The President called [his chief of legislative liaison] who was delighted at the compromise."[72]

Such simple exercises in bargaining and vote delivery are no longer feasible. The changes in the political environment that make bargaining more difficult also affect presidential leadership in ways other than disposing him to go public. The authors of a famous 1950 American Political Science Association report advocating stronger, more cohesive political parties (the reverse of what has happened to the party system) worried that, in the absence of partisan bonds that domesticate presidential power by linking it to power centers in Congress and the constituencies, an attenuated party system would favor "a President who exploits skillfully the arts of demagoguery, who uses the whole country as his political backyard, and who does not mind turning into the embodiment of personal government."[73]

Demagoguery, a pejorative characterization of personal appeal to the public, is in the mind of the beholder. Nevertheless, the 1950 report sounds remarkably prophetic of Watergate. The burglary of the Democratic party headquarters, after all, was linked to partisan change. It was not the Democrats' counterparts in the GOP that initiated this action, but a new-style, candidate-centered political action committee—the Committee to Re-Elect the President. The same centrifugal qualities of the political system that encourage presidents to go public rather than bargain, clearly also foster the impulse, most evident in the Nixon and Reagan presidencies, for administrations to outflank the legislative process and accomplish their aims by administrative discretion, that is, by employing command rather than persuasion.

The bureaucracy of the modern presidency—its fourth component—is central to the president's capacity to use, abuse, or lose control over discretionary policy-making. The Executive Office of the President was still embryonic at the end of Roosevelt's twelve years in office. Thereafter the EOP staff and other executive branch personnel at the president's disposal progressively expanded. In the aftermath of Nixon's presidency there were many proposals that, if only to avoid "White House horrors" such as the Watergate break-in, presidential staffs be reduced. Carter's transition team explored this possibility as part of an effort to find ways to rationalize the organization of the federal government. The Carter solution turned out to be a change in appearance, not in reality. It was to reassign some officials who would in the past have been listed as White House aides to such entities as the Domestic Policy Staff and the Office of Administration. The Reagan presidency has been extensively staffed, adding sophisticated specialists in mass communications and political operations to what already had become an increasingly functionally differentiated "presidential branch" of the government.

Students of the presidency appropriately warn us, as Hugh Heclo does in The Illusion of Presidential Government, that it is often misleading to discuss presidencies as if each of their products is a direct consequence of the president's own leadership.[74] Lyndon Johnson's former press secretary, George Reedy, has popularized the view that the expanding staffs of presidents contain and insulate them, preventing them from having independent influence on public affairs.[75] Robert Gallucci, in a study of the role of presidential associates in making United States policy toward Vietnam, characterizes the relationship between presidents and their principal aides by an analogy that leaves more room for the president's initiative: "The president makes . . . policy only in the sense that the customer in a restaurant makes dinner when he orders his food; he chooses from a limited menu prepared for him by the establishment and usually must accept the interpretation of his choice as it is reflected in the execution of his order. That is to say, 'makes' it hardly at all, although those dining with him are likely to hold him responsible if they are made to consume it also."[76]

But even the image of presidents' being constrained to choose from menus that others have created is overstated. The early lore of the modern presidency assessed the leadership skills of presidents in terms of their capacities to control the West Wing equivalents of kitchen help—that is, to make informed judgments about what fare their aides should dish up. By the Nixon era, scholarly thought had identified regularities in the patterns of presidential organizational advising and their effects on the chief executive's capacity to control his aides and employ them to make informed, considered political choices.

Kennedy and Johnson, according to the typology that has been derived from Neustadt's analysis, employed *collegial* systems, fostering give-and-take, imaginativeness, but slackness of policy implementation. Eisenhower and Nixon, with their reliance on chiefs of staff and committee machinery, employed *"formalistic"* procedures, an invitation to unimaginative but orderly presidential leadership. The term *competitive advising* was reserved for FDR's practice of encouraging the palace politics of his associates.[77]

The underlying question that led to this classification remains appropriate: How can presidents make effective use of advice and information in developing, promoting, and implementing policies? But the classification itself does not capture the complexity and variation of advisory practices; nor does it account for the role of the president as shaper and user of his advisory system and as independent actor. Eisenhower and Nixon, for example, used informal as well as formal decision-making procedures. Their camaraderie notwithstanding, the array of aides who served Kennedy had a de facto chief of staff in Theodore Sorenson. By the late 1970s, little was heard of the admonition not to establish lines of command and channels of responsibility within the White House. At a 1986 conference of staff aides from Eisenhower's through Carter's administrations, both the aides themselves and academic participants, notably Richard Neustadt (who after Watergate counseled against the use of a White House chief of staff), held that "even at the irreducible minimum scale, the White House staff needs an administrative head."[78] They also concluded that there is no best way to organize a presidential bureaucracy. Presidential staffs, they agreed, should, or at any rate will, be arranged in a way that fits the president's own style and needs.

It does not, however, follow that presidents and their aides lack choices about how to be more or less successful. A review of the experience of the modern presidencies makes it clear that presidents and their associates have varied in their capacities to respond to and shape the political environments in which they operate. Success and failure have not simply been a result of "luck" and "instinct." Periodically, genuine choices have been made that had real consequences. For example, after a first year in office in which he had personal contact with many advisers, Richard Nixon appears to have cut himself off from pluralistic advisory relationships, and thus to have reduced the diversity of information and advice to which he was exposed. Kennedy and Ford, on the other hand, took steps to profit from unhappy experiences early in their administrations (the Bay of Pigs, the pardon of Ricard Nixon) and to improve the way they worked with their aides.

Leadership in the modern presidency is not carried out by the president alone, but rather by presidents with their associates. It depends therefore on both the president's strengths and weaknesses and on the quality of the aides' support. Four questions follow: Under what circumstances do aides enhance the president's strength? When do they fail to do so? Under what circumstances do they compensate for his weaknesses? When do they exacerbate them?

Presidential leadership, including the complementary roles of the chief executive and his advisers, can be better understood at the end of the Reagan presidency than in the years of Roosevelt, Truman, and Eisenhower. And it will be even better understood in the future. That understanding is not only academic. Though an unlikely savior, more than other mortals the American president can be described in the words of a moving spiritual: "He's got the whole world in his hands."

Contributors

Larry Berman is a political scientist at the University of California, Davis. His books include *The Office of Management and Budget and the Presidency, 1921–1979* (1979), *Planning a Tragedy: The Americanization of the War in Vietnam* (1982), *The New American Presidency* (1987), and *Lyndon Johnson's War: The Road to Stalemate in Vietnam* (1989).

Carl M. Brauer is a historian with The Winthrop Group, Inc., in Cambridge, Massachusetts. His books include *John F. Kennedy and the Second Reconstruction* (1977) and *Presidential Transitions: Eisenhower through Reagan* (1986).

Fred I. Greenstein is a political scientist at Princeton University. His books include *Children and Politics* (1965), *Personality and Politics: Problems of Evidence, Inference and Conceptualization* (1969), *The Hidden-Hand Presidency: Eisenhower as Leader* (1982), and *The Quality of Presidential Decision Making: The Use of Advice and Information in Two Vietnam Crises*, with John Burke (1989).

Alonzo L. Hamby is a historian at Ohio University. His books include *Beyond the New Deal: Harry S. Truman and American Liberalism* (1973), *The Imperial Years: The United States Since 1939* (1976), and *Liberalism and Its Challengers: F.D.R. to Reagan* (1985).

Erwin C. Hargrove is a political scientist at Vanderbilt University. His books include *Presidential Leadership: Personality and Political Style* (1966), *The Power of the Modern Presidency* (1974), *Presidents, Politics, and Policy*, with Michael Nelson (1984), and *Jimmy Carter as President: Leadership and the Politics of the Public Good* (1988).

Joan Hoff-Wilson is a historian at Indiana University and Executive Secretary of the Organization of American Historians. Her books include *American Business and Foreign Policy, 1920–1933* (1971), *Ideology and Economics: United States Relations with the Soviet Union, 1918–1933* (1974), *Herbert Hoover: Forgotten Progressive* (1975), and *Nixon without Watergate: A Presidency Reconsidered* (1990).

William E. Leuchtenburg is a historian at the University of North Carolina, Chapel Hill. His books include *Flood Control Politics* (1953), *The Perils of Prosperity, 1914–1932* (1958), *Franklin D. Roosevelt and the New Deal, 1932–1940* (1963), *A Troubled Feast* (1973), and *In the Shadow of FDR: From Harry Truman to Ronald Reagan* (1983).

William H. Muir, Jr. is a political scientist at the University of California, Berkeley. His books include *Law and Attitude Change* (1967), *Police: Street-corner Politicians* (1977), and *Legislature: California's School for Politics* (1983).

Roger B. Porter is a political scientist at Harvard University. His books include *Presidential Decision Making: The Economic Policy Board* (1980) and *The U.S.–U.S.S.R. Grain Agreement* (1986). He has served in the Ford, Reagan, and Bush White Houses as Special Assistant and Executive Secretary of the President's Economic Policy Board (1974–1977), Deputy Assistant to the President and Director of the White House Office and Policy Development (1981–1985), and Assistant to the President for Economic and Domestic Policy (1989–).

Notes

Introduction

1. Graham T. Allison, *Essence of Decision: Explaining the Cuban Missile Crisis* (Boston: Little, Brown, 1971), p. 1.

2. Jeffrey K. Tulis, *The Rhetorical Presidency* (Princeton: Princeton University Press, 1987).

3. For further discussion of the differences between the traditional and modern presidencies, see the preface to Fred I. Greenstein, Larry Berman, and Alvin Felzenberg, eds., *Evolution of the Modern Presidency: A Bibliographical Survey* (Washington, D.C.: American Enterprise Institute, 1977).

4. Fred I. Greenstein, "What the Presidency means to Americans: Presidential 'Choice' between Elections," in *Choosing the President*, ed. James D. Barber (Englewood Cliffs, N.J.: Prentice-Hall, 1974), pp. 212–247.

5. See the accounts of twentieth-century presidents by James D. Barber in *The Presidential Character: Predicting Performance in the White House* (Englewood Cliffs, N.J.: Prentice-Hall, 1972, 1977, 1985), many of which suggest that the personal qualities of incumbent presidents have important consequences for the course of historical events. For an abstract discussion of the circumstances under which political leaders' personal qualities are likely to have an impact on events, see Fred I. Greenstein, *Personality and Politics: Problems of Evidence, Inference, and Conceptualization* (Princeton: Princeton University Press, 1987).

1. Franklin D. Roosevelt

1. Fred I. Greenstein, "Change and Continuity in the Modern Presidency," in *The New American Political System*, ed. Anthony King (Wash-

ington, D.C.: American Enterprise Institute for Public Policy Research, 1978),
p. 45.

2. Robert Murray and Tim H. Blessing, "The Presidential Performance Study: A Progress Report," *Journal of American History*, 70 (December 1983), 542.

3. Quoted in Joseph E. Kallenbach, *The American Chief Executive:
The Presidency and the Governorship* (New York: Harper & Row, 1966),
p. 266.

4. Carl T. Keller to Albert G. Keller, March 27, 1937, box 21, Sumner-
Keller MSS, Yale University Library. In the same month a former Hoover
official high in the ranks of the Republican party recorded in his diary: "A
congressman said to me this afternoon, 'There is just one thing now, as I
see it, that will save this country from a major disaster, and that is the
death of the President and [John L.] Lewis and Miss [Frances] Perkins. I
consider myself a Christian and I am a Christian but I feel so strongly for
the nation that if I did not have a wife and children and grandchildren who
would feel themselves disgraced I should really make it my business to
shoot as large a proportion of the three as possible, beginning of course,
with the President' "; William R. Castle, Diary, March 19, 1937, Castle
MSS, Houghton Library, Harvard University. See also George Wolfskill and
John A. Hudson, *All but the People: Franklin D. Roosevelt and His Critics,
1933–1939* (New York: Macmillan, 1969).

5. William Manchester, *The Glory and the Dream: A Narrative
History of America, 1932–1972* (Boston: Little, Brown, 1974), p. 166.

6. Caroline Bird, *Invisible Scar* (New York: McKay, 1966), p. 219.

7. Richard Bissell, "Carefree Harvard Days of Three Presidents,"
McCall's, 90 (October 1962), 162. At a memorial service for FDR in 1945,
a schoolteacher allegedly said, "For the first time in twelve years I can raise
my hand and pledge allegiance to the flag"; Clipping from *Seattle Post-
Intelligencer*, April 17, 1945, Naomi Achenbach Benson MSS, box 27, University of Washington.

8. Quoted in James MacGregor Burns, *Roosevelt: The Lion and the
Fox* (New York: Harcourt, Brace, 1956), p. 144.

9. Quoted in Jonathan Daniels, *The Time between the wars: Ar-
mistice to Pearl Harbor* (Garden City, N.Y.: Doubleday, 1966), p. 272. In
1944 Clare Booth Luce called Roosevelt "the only American President who
ever lied us into war because he did not have the political courage to lead
us into it"; quoted in Thomas A. Bailey, *Presidential Greatness: The Image
and the Man from George Washington to the Present* (New York: Appleton-
Century-Crofts, 1966), p. 155.

10. Samuel I. Rosenman, *Working with Roosevelt* (New York: Harper
& Brothers, 1952), pp. 86–87.

11. Barton J. Bernstein, "The New Deal: The Conservative Achieve-

ments of Liberal Reform," in *Towards a New Past: Dissenting Essays in American History* (New York: Pantheon, 1968), p. 265.

12. Noel F. Busch, quoted in Torbjorn Sirevag, "Rooseveltian Ideas and the 1937 Court Fight: A Neglected Factor," *Historian*, 33 (August 1971), 584.

13. C. Herman Pritchett, *The Roosevelt Court: A Study in Judicial Politics and Values, 1933–1947* (New York: Macmillan, 1948), p. 265.

14. Rexford Guy Tugwell, *The Brains Trust* (New York: Viking, 1968), pp. xxi–xxii; idem, "The New Deal: The Rise of Business," part 2, *Western Political Quarterly*, 5 (September 1952), 503; Bernard Sternsher, "Tugwell's Appraisal of F.D.R.," *Western Political Quarterly*, 15 (March 1962), 67–79.

15. An important source on the Twenty-second Amendment is the Records of the National Committee against Limiting the Presidency, Harry S. Truman Library, Independence, Mo.

16. Thomas Paterson, *On Every Front: The Making of the Cold War* (New York: Norton, 1979), p. 31. See also Ralph B. Levering, *The Cold War, 1945–1972* (Arlington Heights, Ill.: Harlan Davidson, 1982), p. 15.

17. Robert A. Divine, *Roosevelt and World War II* (Baltimore: Johns Hopkins Press, 1969), p. 97. See also Robert Dallek, *Franklin D. Roosevelt and American Foreign Policy, 1932–1945* (New York: Oxford University Press, 1979), p. 537. For a more critical estimate see Gaddis Smith, *American Diplomacy during the Second World War, 1941–1945* (New York: Wiley, 1965), pp. 9–10.

18. Isaiah Berlin, "Roosevelt through European Eyes," *Atlantic Monthly*, 196 (July 1955), 67.

19. Carlo Levi, *Christ Stopped at Eboli* (New York: Time, 1947), pp. 123–124.

20. Foster Rhea Dulles, *America's Rise to World Power, 1898–1954* (New York: Harper, 1955), p. 222.

21. Arnold J. Toynbee, *Survey of International Affairs 1931* (London: Oxford University Press, 1932), p. 1. See also Robert H. Ferrell, *American Diplomacy in the Great Depression: Hoover-Stimson Foreign Policy, 1929–1933* (London: Oxford University Press, 1957), pp. 1–2.

22. W. Cameron Forbes, Diary, December 31, 1931, Forbes MSS, Houghton Library, Harvard University.

23. Manchester, *Glory and the Dream*, p. 31. See also Amy Maher to Edward P. Costigan, vertical file 1, Costigan MSS, University of Colorado, Boulder.

24. Robert M. Collins, *The Business Response to Keynes, 1929–1964* (New York: Columbia University Press, 1981); p. 28. See also George Bernard Shaw, *The Political Madhouse in America and Nearer Home* (London: Constable, 1933), p. 27; Louis Taber, Columbia Oral History Collection, Butler Library, Columbia University, p. 259; Willis Van Devanter to Dennis

Flynn, January 18, 1933, vol. 46, Van Devanter MSS, Library of Congress; James Grafton Rogers to Felix Frankfurter, February 1, 1933, box 97, Frankfurter MSS, Library of Congress.

25. *Sales Management*, March 15, 1933, p. 244.

26. Donald Hiss, quoted in Katie Louchheim, ed., *The Making of the New Deal: The Insiders Speak* (Cambridge, Mass.: Harvard University Press, 1983), pp. 41–42.

27. Walter Millis, "The Roosevelt Revolution," *Virginia Quarterly Review*, 9 (October 1933), 481. See also "Hope in the Middle West," *Spectator*, July 14, 1933, p. 44; Emanuel Celler, *You Never Leave Brooklyn* (New York: John Day, 1933), pp. 11–12; Charles H. Trout, *Boston, the Great Depression, and the New Deal* (New York: Oxford University Press, 1977), pp. 124–127.

28. Nicholas Roosevelt to Mrs. J. West Roosevelt, March 22, 1933, ser. 1, box 7, Nicholas Roosevelt MSS, Syracuse University.

29. Hiram Johnson to Katherine Edson, April 20, 1933, box 3, Edson MSS, University of California, Los Angeles. See also Hiram Johnson to J. Earl Langdon, March 15, 1933, Johnson MSS, Bancroft Library, University of California, Berkeley.

30. H. G. L., "We Have a Leader," *Forum*, 89 (April 1933), 193. See also James R. Garfield, Diary, 1933, Garfield MSS, Library of Congress; John W. McCormack, Kennedy Library Oral History, John F. Kennedy Library, Boston; Charles T. Hallinan, "Roosevelt as Europe Sees Him," *Forum*, 89 (June 1933), 348.

31. Rita Halle Kleeman, *Gracious Lady: The Life of Sara Delano Roosevelt* (New York: D. Appleton-Century, 1935), p. 170.

32. David Potter, "Sketches for the Roosevelt Portrait," *Yale Review*, n.s., 39 (September 1949), 46. See also Frances Perkins, Columbia Oral History Collection, 7: 556–557. One of his biographers believes that "the most potent of clues to the innermost workings of his psyche" is "the fact that Franklin Roosevelt was a man of great and evidently remarkably simple religious faith" with "the inward certainty that he was a chosen one of the Almighty, his career a role assigned him by the Author of the Universe"; Kenneth S. Davis, "FDR as a Biographer's Problem," *Key Reporter*, 50 (Autumn 1984), 5.

33. Richard E. Neustadt, *Presidential Power: The Politics of Leadership from FDR to Carter* (New York: Wiley, 1980), p. 119. See also Thomas H. Greer, *What Roosevelt Thought: The Social and Political Ideas of Franklin D. Roosevelt* (East Lansing: Michigan State University Press, 1958), p. 88.

34. Clinton L. Rossiter, *The American Presidency* (New York: Harcourt Brace, 1960), p. 145.

35. Quoted in Editors of Time-Life Books, *This Fabulous Century*, vol. 4 (New York: Time, 1969), 141.

36. T. R. B., "Washington Notes," *New Republic*, November 1, 1933, p. 332.

37. *Time*, June 10, 1940, p. 17.

38. Frank Freidel, *Franklin D. Roosevelt: The Apprenticeship* (Boston: Little, Brown, 1952), p. 5.

39. James Roosevelt and Sidney Shalett, *Affectionately, F.D.R.* (New York: Harcourt, Brace, 1959); Henry Fairlie, "The Voice of Hope," *New Republic*, January 27, 1982, p. 17.

40. Frances Perkins, *The Roosevelt I Knew* (New York: Viking, 1946), p. 164.

41. *The Public Papers and Addresses of Franklin D. Roosevelt*, ed. Samuel I. Rosenman, 13 vols. (New York: Random House, Macmillan, Harper, 1938–50), 7: 302.

42. Rexford G. Tugwell, "The Experimental Roosevelt," *Political Quarterly*, 21 (July–September 1950), 262.

43. *The Secret Diary of Harold L. Ickes*, 3 vols. (New York: Simon and Schuster, 1953–54), 1: 695.

44. Raymond Clapper, Diary, November 16, 1936, Clapper MSS, Library of Congress (hereafter cited as Clapper MSS). More than two years earlier, an elderly Seattle man had written his congressman: "Support Roosevelt to the end in the New Deal. For if it fails, HO, HO, it Will be Just to[o] bad"; W. B. Gordon to Marion Zioncheck [March 1934], box 3, Zioncheck MSS, University of Washington. See, too, John H. Clarke to Newton D. Baker, December 6, 1935, box 60, Baker MSS, Library of Congress; Breckinridge Long, Diary, October 22, 1936, Long MSS, Library of Congress; *Sheffield* (Ala.) *Standard*, February 18, 1936, David Lilienthal Scrapbooks, Lilienthal MSS, Princeton University Library.

45. Dixon Wecter, *The Hero in America* (Ann Arbor: University of Michigan Press, 1963), p. 461.

46. Quoted in Irving Bernstein, *A Caring Society* (Boston: Houghton Mifflin, 1985), p. 307. See also Fillmore H. Sanford, "Leadership Identification and Acceptance," in *Groups, Leadership and Men*, ed. Harold Guetzkow (Pittsburgh: Carnegie Press, 1951), pp. 173–174.

47. Quoted in Edward S. Corwin, *The President, Office and Powers, 1787–1957: History and Analysis of Practice and Opinion* (New York: New York University Press, 1957), p. 273.

48. John Gunther, *Roosevelt in Retrospect* (New York: Harper & Brothers, 1950), p. 135.

49. *Time*, January 15, 1934, p. 13.

50. Leo C. Rosten, *The Washington Correspondents* (New York: Harcourt, Brace, 1937), p. 49. Although Roosevelt gave the impression of nonchalance at his first press conference, Jimmie Byrnes, the South Carolina senator, noted afterward that "his hand was trembling and he was wet with perspiration." The president himself said that before long he was sure to

make some damaging slip. Yet Byrnes added: "I saw he liked the conference and found it immensely stimulating. I think that he found in these verbal challenges a substitute for the competitive sports in which he could no longer take part"; James F. Byrnes, *All in One Lifetime* (New York: Harper, 1958), p. 74.

51. John L. Blair, "The Clark–Coolidge Correspondence and the Election of 1932," *Vermont History*, 34 (April 1966), 111.

52. Rosten, *Washington Correspondents*, pp. 49–50. The correspondent was Henry M. Hyde of the *Baltimore Evening Sun*. Two days earlier Hyde had noted in his diary: "Atmosphere of White House loses all formality; becomes easy and friendly"; Henry Morrow Hyde, Diary, March 6, 1933, Hyde MSS, University of Virginia.

53. For his experience on the *Crimson* see Kenneth S. Davis, *FDR: The Beckoning of Destiny, 1882–1928; A History* (New York: G. P. Putnam's Sons, 1972), pp. 144–148. Reporters did not always agree on the merits of FDR's methods. "Sometimes the 'off-the-record' material is helpful; often it is an embarrassment," wrote a correspondent who admired FDR's press conferences. "Many newspaper writers covering the White House would prefer that this relic of Mr. Roosevelt's days as Governor of New York, when he had a small and intimate audience, were done away with"; Charles W. B. Hurd, "President and Press: A Unique Forum," *New York Times Magazine*, June 9, 1935, p. 3. But others valued off-the-record information. On one occasion a newspaperman said, "Off the record, Mr. President, can you fill us in on what the situation is on that? Personally I am as ignorant as a nincompoop of it all, and if I could get a little background or off the record . . . On inflation and deflation of the dollar and so forth"; Elmer E. Cornwell, Jr., *Presidential Leadership of Public Opinion* (Bloomington: Indiana University Press, 1966), p. 151.

54. Quoted in M. L. Stein, *When Presidents Meet the Press* (New York: Julian Messner, 1969), p. 86. Reporters learned to study FDR's mood. One of them recalled: "If the cigarette in his holder was pointed toward the ceiling and his head was thrown back, the news would be good, from Roosevelt's standpoint. If he was hunched over his desk and the cigarette pointed downward, look out, somebody was going to get hell"; Jack Bell, *The Johnson Treatment* (New York: Harper & Row, 1965), p. 144.

55. Raymond Brandt, quoted in Joseph A. Califano, Jr., *A Presidential Nation* (New York: Norton, 1975), p. 55.

56. Thomas L. Stokes, *Chip off My Shoulder* (Princeton: Princeton University Press, 1940), p. 367.

57. John Dos Passos, "Washington: The Big Tent," *New Republic*, March 14, 1934, p. 123. See also Mark Sullivan to Ray Lyman Wilbur, April 3, 1933, Wilbur MSS, Stanford University Library; Emile Schreiber, "A travers l'Amérique de 1934," *L'Illustration*, August 18, 1934, pp. 504–509.

58. *Literary Digest,* January 5, 1935, p. 6.

59. Raymond Clapper, "Why Reporters Like Roosevelt," *Review of Reviews and World's Work,* June 1934, pp. 15, 17. See also Graham J. White, *FDR and the Press* (Chicago: University of Chicago Press, 1979).

60. Erwin D. Canham, "Democracy's Fifth Wheel," *Literary Digest,* January 5, 1935, p. 6; Douglass Cater, *The Fourth Branch of Government* (Boston: Houghton Mifflin, 1959), pp. 7–17; Elmer E. Cornwell, Jr., "The Presidential Press Conference: A Study in Institutionalization," *Midwest Journal of Political Science,* 4 (November 1960), 370–389.

61. *St. Louis Post-Dispatch,* May 31, 1935; *Baltimore Evening Sun,* May 31, 1935; *Washington Post,* June 1, 2, 1935; James T. Williams to his father, May 31, 1935, Williams MSS, University of South Carolina, Columbia; Edward Keating, Diary, May 31, 1935, Keating MSS, University of Colorado, Boulder (hereafter cited as Keating MSS).

62. Quoted in Robert West, *The Rape of Radio* (New York: Rodin, 1941), pp. 421–422.

63. David Halberstam, *The Powers That Be* (New York: Knopf, 1979), p. 15.

64. Quoted in Wilfred E. Binkley, *President and Congress* (New York: Knopf, 1947), pp. 274–275.

65. William J. Hopkins, Kennedy Library Oral History, p. 6. At a dinner party Roosevelt boasted, "Hoover got 400 letters a day. I get 4000"; Dorothy Thompson, Diary, 1936, Thompson MSS, Syracuse University.

66. Ira R. T. Smith with Joe Alex Morris, *"Dear Mr. President . . . ": The Story of Fifty Years in the White House Mail Room* (New York: Julian Messner, 1949), p. 156. Roosevelt, noted a veteran newspaperman, could not hope to read all the bales of letters of some one hundred each, "but frequently he would order half a dozen bundles sent to his desk. Thus he kept a highly sensitive and extraordinarily long index finger on the public pulse"; Charles Hurd, *The White House, a Biography: The Story of the House, Its Occupants, Its Place in American History* (New York: Harper & Brothers, 1940), p. 306.

67. John C. Donovan, *The Politics of Poverty* (New York: Pegasus, 1967), p. 18.

68. *New Republic,* April 7, 1937, pp. 251–252.

69. Quoted in Richard Harwood and Haynes Johnson, *Lyndon* (New York: Praeger, 1973), p. 36. See also Thomas I. Emerson, Oral history transcript, pp. 1–2, New York State School for Industrial and Labor Relations, Ithaca, N.Y.; William E. Leuchtenburg, *In the Shadow of FDR: From Harry Truman to Ronald Reagan* (Ithaca: Cornell University Press, 1983).

70. John H. Clarke to Franklin D. Roosevelt, September 18, 1937, file 2, folder 17, Clarke MSS, Western Reserve Historical Society, Cleveland.

71. Alf M. Landon to Roy M. Howard, June 13, 1938, box 89, Landon

MSS, Kansas State Historical Society, Topeka; Edward Keating, Diary, November 15, 1936, Keating MSS; Clipping from *Pittsburgh Press*, June 7, 1936, box 71, Mary Van Kleeck MSS, Smith College.

72. Bernard F. Donahoe, *Private Plans and Public Dangers: The Story of FDR's Third Nomination* (Notre Dame, Ind.: University of Notre Dame Press, 1965), pp. 6, 8; Grace Abbott, "My Vote Goes to President Roosevelt," Typescript, Abbott MSS, University of Chicago Library.

73. Quoted in E. Pendleton Herring, "First Session of the 73rd Congress," *American Political Science Review*, 27 (February 1934), 82.

74. Quoted in Robert Rienow and Leona Train Rienow, *The Lonely Quest: The Evolution of Presidential Leadership* (New York: Follett, 1966), pp. 186–187.

75. Arthur M. Schlesinger, Jr., *The Coming of the New Deal* (Boston: Houghton Mifflin, 1959), p. 557.

76. Godfrey Hodgson, *All Things to All Men: The False Promise of the Modern American Presidency* (New York: Simon and Schuster, 1980), p. 60.

77. Wilfred E. Binkley, *The Man in the White House: His Powers and Duties* (Baltimore: Johns Hopkins Press, 1958), p. 180.

78. Harold M. Barger, *The Impossible Presidency: Illusions and Realities of Executive Power* (Glenview, Ill.: Scott, Foresman, 1984), p. 101.

79. Erwin C. Hargrove, *The Power of the Modern Presidency* (Philadelphia: Temple University Press, 1974), p. 53.

80. George C. Robinson, "The Veto Record of Franklin D. Roosevelt," *American Political Science Review*, 36 (February 1942), 76; Samuel and Dorothy Rosenman, *Presidential Style: Some Giants and a Pygmy in the White House* (New York: Harper & Row, 1976), pp. 345–346.

81. George W. Robinson, "Alben Barkley and the 1944 Tax Veto," *Register of the Kentucky Historical Society*, 67 (1969), 197–210; Polly Ann Davis, "Alben W. Barkley's Public Career in 1944," *Filson Club Quarterly*, 51 (April 1977), 144; Leon Henderson, Diary Notes, February 24, 1944, box 36, Henderson MSS, Franklin D. Roosevelt Library, Hyde Park, N.Y.

82. Marcus Cunliffe, *American Presidents and the Presidency* (London: Fontana, 1972), p. 267.

83. Raymond Clapper, "Resentment against the Supreme Court," *Review of Reviews*, 95 (January 1937), 38.

84. Representative Charles Gifford, quoted in *Congressional Record*, 78th Cong., 1st sess., p. 56.

85. *Public Papers of Roosevelt*, 5: 235.

86. Ibid., 7: 14.

87. Bruce Collins, "Federal Power as Contemporary American Dilemma," *The Growth of Federal Power in American History*, ed. Rhodri Jeffreys-Jones and Bruce Collins (De Kalb: Northern Illinois University Press,

1983), p. xiv; V. O. Key, Jr., *The Responsible Electorate* (Cambridge, Mass.: Harvard University Press, 1966), p. 31; Morris Sheppard to H. B. Prother, [misdated] January 3, 1937 [1938], box 118, Morris Sheppard MSS, University of Texas, Austin; "Richard Russell: Georgia Grant," Typescript of Cox Broadcasting Corporation broadcast, February 12, 1970, Richard B. Russell MSS, University of Georgia.

88. André Maurois, *From the New Freedom to the New Frontier* (New York: David McKay, 1962), p. 156.

89. *Public Papers of Roosevelt,* 13: 40–41.

90. Clipping from *Detroit News,* November 7, 1936, Blair Moody Scrapbooks, Moody MSS, Michigan Historical Collections, University of Michigan. One analyst called him the country's "chief economic engineer"; Sidney Hyman, *The American President* (New York: Harper, 1954), pp. 263–264.

91. James MacGregor Burns, *Presidential Government: The Crucible of Leadership* (Boston: Houghton Mifflin, 1966), p. 200.

92. William E. Leuchtenburg, "Franklin D. Roosevelt's Supreme Court 'Packing' Plan," in *Essays on the New Deal,* ed. Harold M. Hollingsworth and William F. Holmes (Austin: University of Texas Press, 1969); Bernard Schwartz, *The Supreme Court: Constitutional Revolution in Retrospect* (New York: Ronald Press, 1957), p. 389; Marriner S. Eccles, *Beckoning Frontiers* (New York: Knopf, 1951), p. 336.

93. Quoted in Eccles, *Beckoning Frontiers,* p. 336.

94. Quoted in Schlesinger, *Coming of the New Deal,* p. 534.

95. Ibid., p. 535.

96. Ibid., p. 528. See also Neustadt, *Presidential Power,* pp. 156–158.

97. Barger, *Impossible Presidency,* p. 205.

98. Neustadt, *Presidential Power,* pp. 115–116.

99. Burns, *Presidential Government,* p. 152.

100. Grant McConnell, *The Modern Presidency,* 2d ed. (New York: St. Martin's Press, 1976), p. 96.

101. Hodgson, *All Things to All Men,* pp. 58–59. One observer noted "national figures using the same washroom, shoulder to shoulder, and pretending not to see each other"; Russell Lord, quoted in Stephen Hess, *Organizing the Presidency* (Washington, D.C.: Brookings Institution, 1976), p. 30.

102. Stanley High, Diary, Oct. 19, 20, 1936, High MSS, Franklin D. Roosevelt Library, Hyde Park, N.Y.

103. Richard E. Neustadt, "Approaches to Staffing the Presidency: Notes on FDR and JFK," *American Political Science Review,* 57 (December 1963), 855.

104. Quoted in Arthur M. Schlesinger, Jr., *The Imperial Presidency* (Boston: Houghton Mifflin, 1973), p. 409.

105. Quoted in Louchheim, *Making of the New Deal*, p. 225.

106. Quoted in Jack Bell, *The Presidency: Office of Power* (Boston: Allyn and Bacon, 1967), p. 26.

107. Raymond Moley, *After Seven Years* (New York: Harper & Brothers, 1939), pp. 128–130.

108. H. L. Mencken, "The New Deal Mentality," *American Mercury*, 38 (May 1936), 4. See also John Frey, Columbia Oral History Collection, p. 572.

109. The best account of blacks in the Roosevelt era is Harvard Sitkoff, *A New Deal for Blacks: The Emergence of Civil Rights as a National Issue, vol. 1: The Depression Decade* (New York: Oxford University Press, 1978).

110. William H. Chafe, *The American Woman: Her Changing Social, Economic, and Political Roles, 1920–1970* (New York: Oxford University Press, 1972), p. 42. See also Susan Ware, "Women and the New Deal," in *Fifty Years Later: The New Deal Evaluated*, ed. Harvard Sitkoff (New York: Knopf, 1945), pp. 113–132.

111. Quoted in William H. Chafe, "Biographical Sketch," in *Without Precedent: The Life and Career of Eleanor Roosevelt*, ed. Joan Hoff-Wilson and Marjorie Lightman (Bloomington: Indiana University Press, 1984), p. 597.

112. Ibid. The columnist was Raymond Clapper. Her activities also elicited widespread criticism. Even before the inauguration a Boston lawyer was already writing in his diary: "Mrs. Roosevelt is to have a weekly meeting with reporters—à la the President! This adds new terrors to the next four years"; George Read Nutter, Diary, Massachusetts Historical Society, Boston.

113. Otis L. Graham, Jr., *Toward a Planned Society: From Roosevelt to Nixon* (New York: Oxford University Press, 1976); Lester G. Seligman and Elmer E. Cornwell, Jr., *New Deal Mosaic: Roosevelt Confers with His National Emergency Council* (Eugene: University of Oregon, 1965); Peri E. Arnold, *Making the Managerial Presidency: Comprehensive Reorganization Planning, 1905–1980* (Princeton: Princeton University Press, 1986); Marion Clawson, *New Deal Planning: The National Resources Planning Board* (Baltimore: Johns Hopkins University Press, 1981); Lester G. Seligman, "Developments in the Presidency and the Conception of Political Leadership," *American Sociological Review*, 20 (December 1955), 706–712.

114. Kallenbach, *American Chief Executive*, p. 256.

115. Luther Gulick, quoted in Rossiter, *American Presidency*, p. 129; Burns, *Presidential Government*, p. 73. See also Barry D. Karl, *Executive Reorganization and Reform in the New Deal* (Cambridge, Mass.: Harvard University Press, 1966).

116. Quoted in Robert E. Sherwood, *Roosevelt and Hopkins: An Intimate History* (New York: Harper & Brothers, 1948), pp. 72–73; see also Charles E. Jacob, *Leadership in the New Deal: The Administrative Chal-*

lenge (Englewood Cliffs, N.J.: Prentice-Hall, 1967), pp. 33–34.

117. Stuart Gerry Brown, *The American Presidency: Leadership, Partisanship, and Popularity* (New York: Macmillan, 1966), p. 46.

118. Stanley High, "The White House is Calling," *Harper's*, 175 (November 1937), 585.

119. Moley, *After Seven Years*, p. 393.

120. J. David Stern, Columbia Oral History Collection.

121. George Creel, *Rebel at Large* (New York: G. P. Putnam's Sons, 1947), p. 293.

122. *Time*, June 10, 1940, p. 17. See also Raymond Clapper, Diary, May 10, 1938, Clapper MSS; Ellen S. Woodward MSS, box 8, Mississippi Department of Archives and History, Jackson.

123. George W. Anderson to Louis D. Brandeis, February 12, 1937, Brandeis MSS, Supreme Court box 19, folder 1, University of Louisville Law Library.

124. Speech by U.S. Senator Alan Cranston, Commonwealth Club, San Francisco, June 15, 1973. The ensuing discussion draws upon my reply to Cranston, published as an op ed piece in the *Los Angeles Times*, September 18, 1973.

125. Raymond Price, *With Nixon* (New York: Viking, 1977), pp. 228–229, 235, 246, 285–286. Maurice Stans has commented: "New developments of recent years are making some of Nixon's actions less discreditable than they were once made to appear. In the House Judiciary hearings in 1974 there was strong contention that he had misused the forces of government agencies for political purposes, by getting them to spy on and punish enemies of his regime, and this became one of the counts of impeachment. It was not publicly known then, but subsequent revelations have established, that Presidential use of the FBI, the CIA, the IRS, and the Postal Service to exercise surveillance over radical and revolutionary groups dangerous to the nation extended at least as far back as Franklin D. Roosevelt. Employing these agencies to target political adversaries was no less common, and in some instances much more frequent and intensive. As author M. Stanton Evans has written, 'In the light of these disclosures it is plain that Nixon, whatever his sins, was hopelessly outclassed in public infamy by the likes of Franklin Roosevelt, John Kennedy, and Lyndon Johnson. Yet it was Nixon who caught and continues to catch the brickbats, while these Democratic heroes have somehow avoided media censure' "; Maurice Stans, *The Terrors of Justice* (New York: Everest House, 1978), pp. 455–456.

126. In 1948 one former FDR cabinet official wrote to another: "I suppose Roosevelt will go down in history a great man, certainly he was a ruthless politician. With it all, he was most attractive personally. In the last analysis, he must have considered himself especially annointed [*sic*]. In my view, when he found what he could do with the radio, he made up

his mind to stay President as long as he lived, if possible, and to take such course from time to time, as seemed most likely to achieve this objective"; Jesse H. Jones to James A. Farley, March 10, 1948, box 7, Jones MSS, Library of Congress. Farley himself later said: "Ickes I thought—I don't want to be profane and won't be. But I met two terrible men in my lifetime, and he was on top of the list. Impossible person. Thought everybody else was honest except Ickes . . . I sat alongside of him for six months without talking to him. Because he would tap my wires and he denied that he tapped them. And I accused him of tapping my wires and those of the President Mr. Roosevelt. And he denied it but I put it right down his throat and insisted that he did"; James A. Farley, Oral history transcript, University of Kentucky. I appreciate the courtesy of Bill Cooper in granting me access to this document.

127. Binkley, *President and Congress*, p. 238.

128. Quoted in Herman Finer, *The Presidency* (Chicago: University of Chicago Press, 1960), p. 78.

129. Edwin S. Corwin and Louis Koenig, *The Presidency Today* (New York: New York University Press, 1956), p. 34.

130. Quoted in Arthur M. Schlesinger, Jr., "Congress and the Making of American Foreign Policy," in *The Presidency Reappraised*, ed. Rexford G. Tugwell and Thomas E. Cronin (New York: Praeger, 1974), pp. 94–95.

131. Binkley, *Man in the White House*, p. 237.

132. *Congressional Record*, 77th Cong., 2d sess., p. 7044.

133. Marcus Cunliffe, *American Presidents and the Presidency* (London: Fontana/Collins, 1972), p. 267.

134. Quoted in Richard Polenberg, *Reorganizing Roosevelt's Government: The Controversy over Executive Reorganization, 1936–1939* (Cambridge, Mass.: Harvard University Press, 1966), p. 27.

135. Emmet Hughes, *The Living Presidency: The Resources and the Dilemmas of the American Presidential Office* (Baltimore: Penguin, 1974), pp. 140–141.

136. Binkley, *President and Congress*, pp. 248–251.

137. Rossiter, *American Presidency*, pp. 149–150.

138. Quoted in ibid., p. 152. Another prominent British official recorded similar thoughts: "On the midnight news last night I hear that Roosevelt is dead. Parliament to-day will adjourn. He should have lived even a few weeks longer, to see the full light of victory in Europe. But he has seen the dawn and, but for him, there would have been no dawn. Only a long darkness for us all; an eternal night for most of us"; Hugh Dalton, Diary, April 13, 1945, Dalton MSS, British Library of Political and Economic Science, London School of Economics and Political Science.

139. Schlesinger, *Imperial Presidency*, p. 409.

140. McConnell, *Modern Presidency*, p. 15.

141. Corwin and Koenig, *Presidency Today*, pp. 86–87.

142. E. S. Corwin, "Some Aspects of the Presidency," *Annals*, 218 (November 1941), 128. Corwin did, though, see two novel aspects: "Roosevelt's consistent championship of the demands of certain groups, especially Agriculture and Labor," and "the dissolving effect" of FDR's legislation on the principles of separation of powers and dual federalism.

143. Forty years later the vitriolic columnist Westbrook Pegler wrote, "It is regrettable that Giuseppe Zangara hit the wrong man when he shot at Roosevelt in Miami"; quoted in Cunliffe, *American Presidents and the Presidency*, p. 147.

144. Greenstein, "Change and Continuity," p. 48. See also Otis L. Graham, Jr., "1933: What Would the 1930s Have Been Like without Franklin Roosevelt?" in *Speculations on American History*, ed. Morton Borden and Otis L. Graham, Jr. (Boston: Little, Brown, 1973), pp. 119–138.

145. Sidney Hook, *The Hero in History: A Study in Limitation and Possibility* (New York: Humanities Press, 1943), pp. 151–183.

146. John Kenneth Galbraith, "Revolution in Our Time: Marx and Lenin; Lloyd George and Roosevelt; John Maynard Keynes," *Bulletin of the American Academy of Arts and Sciences*, 40 (December 1986), 9; "Transcript of Shorthand Notes taken at a Conference of young Liberal Delegates of Caernarvonshire, held in the Guild Hall, Caernarvon, on Saturday afternoon and evening, the 16th of October, 1937," David Lloyd George MSS, G/22/3/12, Beaverbrook Library, London. See also Typescript [1937?], box 9, H. A. L. Fisher MSS, Bodleian Library, Oxford University; R. H. Pear, "The Impact of the New Deal on British Economic and Political Ideas," *Bulletin of the British Association of American Studies*, 4 (August 1962), 24.

147. Christina Stead, *The Man Who Loved Children* (New York: Holt, Rinehart and Winston, 1940), p. 291.

148. H. G. Nicholas, "Roosevelt and Public Opinion," *Fortnightly*, 163 (May 1945), 303.

149. Ibid., p. 304.

150. Califano, *Presidential Nation*, p. 8.

151. Rossiter, *American Presidency*, p. 151.

152. See especially the reservations of Theodore J. Lowi in *The Personal President: Power Invested, Promise Unfullfilled* (Ithaca: Cornell University Press, 1985).

2. Harry S. Truman

1. Major "presidential greatness surveys," including three from the early 1980s, are summarized and discussed in Robert K. Murray and Tim H. Blessing, "The Presidential Performance Study: A Progress Report," *Journal of American History*, 70 (December 1983), 535–555. The Truman quotation at the beginning of the chapter is from Transcripts of Recordings for

a Proposed History of the American Presidency, tape 1, Harry S. Truman Papers, Post-Presidential Files, Harry S. Truman Library, Independence, Mo. (hereafter cited as HSTL).

2. Until recently this debate was conducted roughly along the ideological lines that divided New Left historians from center-liberal scholars. Richard S. Kirkendall, ed., *The Truman Period as a Research Field: A Reappraisal, 1972* (Columbia: University of Missouri Press, 1974), provides a relatively quick and painless introduction to the debate. Some recent writing, however, leads me to believe that it is becoming increasingly difficult to categorize the debate over Truman's capabilities along easily identifiable ideological lines. For William E. Leuchtenburg's contribution see *In the Shadow of FDR: From Harry Truman to Ronald Reagan*, rev. ed. (Ithaca: Cornell University Press, 1985).

3. Bernard Sternsher, "Harry Truman: The Gallup and Roper Polls," in *Popular Images of the President*, ed. William Spragens (Westport, Conn.: Greenwood Press, forthcoming), provides an authoritative summary and analysis of Truman's standing as gauged by the polls. I am indebted to Professor Sternsher for making a copy available to me.

4. See Murray and Blessing, "Presidential Performance," p. 555.

5. David Reisman, *The Lonely Crowd* (New Haven: Yale University Press, 1950); James David Barber, *Presidential Character: Predicting Performance in the White House* (Englewood Cliffs, N.J.: Prentice-Hall, 1972). See also Nan Robertson's interview with Reisman in the *New York Times*, December 14, 1980. One notable exception to the generalization that public figures rarely bare their souls to biographers may be Doris Kearns, *Lyndon Johnson and the American Dream* (New York: Harper & Row, 1976), although even in this case scholars argue whether Ms. Kearns was the fortunate recipient of sincere revelations or the object of yet another LBJ con job.

6. The following paragraphs draw heavily on my own research into Truman's early life. Much of the information in them can be found in Harry S. Truman, *Memoirs, vol. 1: Year of Decisions* (Garden City, N.Y.: Doubleday, 1955), chap. 9; Jonathan Daniels, *Man of Independence* (Philadelphia and New York: J. B. Lippincott, 1950), chaps. 2–5; Alfred Steinberg, *The Man from Missouri* (New York: G. P. Putnam's Sons, 1962), chaps. 2–5.

7. For Truman's use of "deformity," see his July 28, 1949, interview with Jonathan Daniels for *Man of Independence*, copies at HSTL, originals in Jonathan Daniels Papers, Southern Historical Collection, University of North Carolina, Chapel Hill. For "sissy," see Merle Miller, *Plain Speaking* (New York: Berkley, 1973), pp. 31–32.

8. For Truman's Commerce Bank personnel records and those of his brother, see Miscellaneous Historical Documents Collection, files 308, 309, HSTL. They make clear the vivid contrasts between the two brothers.

9. Truman to Bess Wallace, November 19, 1913, HST Papers, Fam-

ily, Business, Personal File, HSTL (hereafter cited as FBP). This and many other letters to Bess Wallace Truman are reproduced in Robert Ferrell, ed., *"Dear Bess"* (New York: Norton, 1983).

10. For this aspect of Truman's career, the Civic Research Institute Papers, Western Historical Manuscripts Collection, University of Missouri, Kansas City, are especially valuable.

11. The Truman quote may be found in an undated handwritten speech (almost certainly the one delivered at Grandview, June 30, 1924), 1924 campaign file, FBP.

12. Pickwick memoranda [c. 1930], Truman Papers, Post-Presidential Files.

13. On Truman's development as a campaigner see Daniels, *Man of Independence*, pp. 168–172; Steinberg, *Man from Missouri*, pp. 114–119.

14. For the Missouri political scene see Richard S. Kirkendall, *A History of Missouri*, vol. 5: *1919 to 1953* (Columbia: University of Missouri Press, 1986), chaps. 3–6; Lyle W. Dorsett, *The Pendergast Machine* (New York: Oxford University Press, 1968), chaps. 6–9; William Reddig, *Tom's Town* (Philadelphia and New York: J.B. Lippincott, 1947), esp. chaps. 3–4.

15. On the family situation see Margaret Truman, *Bess W. Truman* (New York: Macmillan, 1986), chaps. 10–12.

16. Truman, *Memoirs*, 1: chap. 11; Steinberg, *Man from Missouri*, chap. 16.

17. For Truman's army hospital stays, see Medical Records, 1917–55, Harry S. Truman, Army Personnel Records, HSTL.

18. For the negative impression of the "Missouri Gang" on one White House insider, see Eben Ayres Diary, April and May 1945, Ayres Papers, HSTL.

19. Dean G. Acheson, *Present at the Creation* (New York: Norton, 1969), pp. 149–150; Andrew J. Dunar, *The Truman Scandals and the Politics of Morality* (Columbia: University of Missouri Press, 1984). The letter to Hume (December 6, 1950) is reproduced in full in Steinberg, *Man from Missouri*, pp. 394–395.

20. Truman to Bess Wallace, May 12, 1914, FBP; Truman to William Southern, July 8, 1949 (unsent), President's Secretary's File, HSTL (hereafter cited as PSF); Truman to Roy Roberts, June 12, 1950, ibid.

21. For the version of his meeting with Byrnes, see Truman, *Memoirs*, 1: 551–552; for MacArthur see Miller, *Plain Speaking*, pp. 315–318.

22. Truman, "Speech draft re railroad strike" [May 1946], Clark Clifford Papers, HSTL; Truman, Diary, December 11, 1946, and January 27, 1952, PSF.

23. Perhaps the quintessential expression of this negative image is Robert S. Allen and William V. Shannon, *The Truman Merry-Go-Round* (New York: Vanguard, 1950). For the Pulitzer cartoon, see *New York Times*, May 6, 1952.

24. Numerous historians and political scientists have praised this method of administration as the means by which Roosevelt assured himself of a continuous flow of information and guaranteed that he would not be isolated from important decisions. It appears to me, however, that it also led to a high degree of counterproductive confusion and demoralization among those who sought to serve him. Whether its alleged virtues outweighed its vices remains unclear to me, as does the question of whether there were better means of preserving presidential authority.

25. Harold D. Smith, Diary, February 8, 1946, Smith Papers, HSTL. On the administrative side of the Truman presidency, see esp. Francis H. Heller, ed., *The Truman White House: The Administration of the Presidency, 1945–1953* (Lawrence: Regents Press of Kansas, 1980). Richard E. Neustadt's chapter, an excellent summary of the staff situation in the later Truman presidency, is especially valuable.

26. Clifford's achievement seems all the more impressive given the fact that his uncle, Clark McAdams, had been editor of the *St. Louis Post-Dispatch*, a liberal-oriented newspaper that nonetheless had consistently criticized Truman during his senatorial years. Truman loathed the publication, referring to it from time to time as the *St. Louis Post-Disgrace*.

27. Harriman was first an administrative assistant to the president, then director of the Mutual Security Agency. His long friendship with Dean Acheson precluded any significant conflict with the Department of State.

28. Acheson, *Present at the Creation*, pp. 184–185; Walter Millis, ed., *From the Forrestal Diaries* (New York: Viking, 1951), pp. 87 (July 18, 1945), 142 (March 7, 1946); Heller, *Truman White House*, pp. 88–89; Alfred D. Sander, "Truman and the National Security Council, 1945–1947," *Journal of American History*, 59 (September 1972), 369–388; Anna K. Nelson, "The 'Top of Policy Hill': President Eisenhower and the National Security Council," *Diplomatic Hisory*, 7 (Fall 1983), 307–326, esp. 308–310; Harry S. Truman, *Memoirs, vol. 2: Years of Trial and Hope* (Garden City, N.Y.: Doubleday, 1956), pp. 46–60, esp. (for NSC) pp. 59–60.

29. Peri Arnold, *Making the Managerial Presidency* (Princeton: Princeton University Press, 1986), cogently argues against excessive presidential involvement in administrative reorganization on the grounds that it has in effect become a no-win issue likely to offend strategically placed constituencies while failing to generate significant public support. The result, therefore, is to create forces that impede an administration's policy objectives.

30. Truman's World War I letters to Bess Wallace (FBP) provide fascinating evidence of both his attraction to French culture and his determination to belittle it. For the Stalin-Pendergast comment, see Daniels, *Man of Independence*, p. 23; for Truman's Wilsonian internationalism, see, for example, *Public Papers of the Presidents: Harry S. Truman, 1948* (Washington, D.C.: Government Printing Office, 1964), pp. 325, 327, 730, 849; for

TVAs around the world, David E. Lilienthal, *The Journals of David E. Lilienthal*, vol. 2: *The Atomic Energy Years, 1945–1950* (New York: Harper & Row, 1964), p. 475; for totalitarianism see, for example, Truman, Diary, June 7, 1947, Truman Papers, PSF; and Truman's remarks to C. L. Sulzberger (November 4, 1947) in Sulzberger, *A Long Row of Candles* (New York: Macmillan, 1969), p. 364.

31. Truman, *Memoirs*, 1: 120; J. Garry Clifford, "Harry Truman and Peter the Great's Will," *Diplomatic History*, 4 (Fall 1980), 371–385; on China, see Truman to A. E. Weston, April 25, 1951, PSF, and David E. Lilienthal, *The Journals of David E. Lilienthal*, vol. 3: *Venturesome Years, 1950–55* (New York: Harper & Row, 1966), p. 171 (January 31, 1951); on Spain see Memorandum from Truman to Dean Acheson, August 2, 1951, and attached letter, Thomas Harkins to Fred Land, July 25, 1951, Truman Papers, PSF.

32. For Truman's opinion of Stettinius, see Truman to Jonathan Daniels, February 26, 1950 (unsent), PSF; on Byrnes see Truman, *Memoirs*, 1: 546–552; Robert Messer, *The End of an Alliance* (Chapel Hill: University of North Carolina Press, 1982).

33. Truman's reverence for Marshall is well known. Forrest Pogue, *George C. Marshall: Statesman, 1945–1959* (New York: Viking, 1987), provides an authoritative account of their relationship from Marshall's perspective. A voluminous literature exists on the Palestine issue. Robert J. Donovan, *Conflict and Crisis* (New York: Norton, 1977), chaps. 34, 39, provides a solid, balanced, brief account of Truman's role. On the Vinson mission, see Truman's own rationalization in his *Memoirs*, 2: 213–219.

34. On the Acheson-Truman relationship see Acheson, *Present at the Creation*, esp. pt. 3.

35. Quoted in Miller, *Plain Speaking*, p. 285; Roy Jenkins, *Truman* (New York: Harper & Row, 1986), p. 168.

36. Samuel Lubell, *Future of American Politics*, 3d ed., rev. (New York: Harper & Row, 1965), chap. 2.

37. For the administration's attitude toward and liaison with Congress, see Heller, *Truman White House*, pp. 225–231.

38. For general insights into Truman's relations with Congress, see, in additon to Heller, *Truman White House*, Robert J. Donovan's two volumes, *Conflict and Crisis* and *Tumultuous Years* (New York: Norton, 1982); Donald R. McCoy, *The Presidency of Harry S. Truman* (Lawrence: University Press of Kansas, 1984); Richard E. Neustadt, *Presidential Power: The Politics of Leadership* (New York: Wiley, 1960); idem, "Congress and the Fair Deal: A Legislative Balance Sheet," *Public Policy*, 5 (1954), 351–381.

39. Mary Hedge Hinchey, "The Frustration of the New Deal Revival" (Ph.D. diss., University of Missouri, 1965), provides probably the most systematic treatment of politics and congressional relations in 1945 and 1946.

40. Susan Hartmann, *Truman and the 80th Congress* (Columbia: University of Missouri Press, 1971), deals very well with the way Truman used the Congress, but, as is the case with almost all historical studies of presidential-congressional relations, undertakes no exploration of the structure of the Congress itself.

41. David B. Truman, *The Congressional Party* (New York: Wiley, 1959), and Duncan McRae, *Dimensions of Congressional Voting* (Berkeley and Los Angeles: University of California Press, 1958), both attempt an analysis of the Eighty-first Congress. To my mind, neither is fully satisfactory. On Social Security see Arthur J. Altmeyer, *The Formative Years of Social Security* (Madison: University of Wisconsin Press, 1968), chap. 7.

42. On Truman's relations with the Eighty-second Congress, see Alonzo L. Hamby, *Beyond the New Deal: Harry S. Truman and American Liberalism, 1945–1953* (New York: Columbia University Press, 1973), chaps. 19–22.

43. For the 1948 rhetoric see *Public Papers of Truman, 1948.*

44. Sternsher, "Harry Truman: The Gallup and Roper Polls."

3. Dwight D. Eisenhower

1. For an introduction to this literature and a review of earlier writings depreciating Eisenhower's leadership but documenting his popularity, see Mary S. McAuliffe, "Eisenhower the President," *Journal of American History,* 68 (December 1981), 625–632; Fred I. Greenstein, "Eisenhower as an Activist President: A Look at New Evidence," *Political Science Quarterly,* 94 (1979–80), 577–586; idem, *The Hidden-Hand Presidency: Eisenhower as Leader* (New York: Basic Books, 1982); Robert A. Divine, *Eisenhower and the Cold War* (Oxford: Oxford University Press, 1981); Blanche Wiesen Cook, *The Declassified Eisenhower: A Divided Legacy* (Garden City, N.Y.: Doubleday, 1981); Stephen E. Ambrose, *Eisenhower,* vol. 1: *Soldier, General of the Army, President-Elect, 1890–1952,* and vol. 2: *The President* (New York: Simon and Schuster, 1983–84).

2. Murray Kempton, "The Underestimation of Dwight D. Eisenhower," *Esquire,* September 1967, pp. 108ff.; Garry Wills, *Nixon Agonistes: The Crisis of the Self-Made Man* (Boston: Houghton Mifflin, 1969).

3. *The Papers of Dwight David Eisenhower,* 12 vols. to date (Baltimore: Johns Hopkins University Press, 1970–) (hereafter cited as *PDDE*).

4. Theodore White, *In Search of History* (New York: Harper & Row, 1978), p. 347.

5. Richard M. Nixon, *Six Crises* (Garden City, N.Y.: Doubleday, 1962), p. 161.

6. See, for example, Piers Brendon, *Ike: His Life and Times* (New York: Harper & Row, 1986); my review of Brendon's book in "Book World," *Washington Post,* September 7, 1986; and Robert J. McMahon, "Eisenhower

and Third World Nationalism: A Critique of the Revisionists," *Political Science Quarterly*, 101 (1986), 453–473.

7. Richard E. Neustadt, *Presidential Power: The Politics of Leadership* (New York: Wiley, 1960, 1976, 1980). The second and third editions have additions to the subtitle—*with Reflections on Johnson and Nixon* and *from FDR to Carter*, respectively.

8. David Eisenhower, *Eisenhower: At War, 1943–1945* (New York: Random House, 1986).

9. As early as the late 1920s Eisenhower had been employed as deputy to Army Chief of Staff MacArthur, working within sight of the White House on reports to the president and Congress.

10. Dwight D. Eisenhower, Personal Diary, 1935–1966 (hereafter cited as PD), January 1, 1950, Dwight D. Eisenhower Library, Abilene, Kansas (hereafter cited as DDEL).

11. Personal communication, Professor Louis Galambos, Johns Hopkins University.

12. Eisenhower to Paul E. Helms, March 9, 1954, Dwight D. Eisenhower, Diaries Series, DDEL (hereafter cited as DDE).

13. Eisenhower to General George Catlett Marshall, September 20, 1943, *PDDE*, 3: 1439–40.

14. Eisenhower to William Benton, May 1, 1953, DDE.

15. Eisenhower to Henry ("Harry") Luce, August 8, 1960, DDE.

16. Fred E. Fiedler, *Leadership* (New York: General Learning Press, 1951), p. 15; idem, "What Triggers the Person-Situation Interaction in Leadership," in *Personality at the Crossroads: Current Issues in Interactionist Psychology*, ed. David Magnusson and Norman S. Endler (Hillside, N.J.: Lawrence Erlbaum Associates, 1977), pp. 151–163.

17. Eisenhower to Charles Porter, August 7, 1959, Ann Whitman Diary Series, DDE (hereafter cited as AWD).

18. Eisenhower to John S. D. Eisenhower, February 19, 1943, *PDDE*, 2: 996. These remarks suggest that Eisenhower's propensity to make explicit the principles on which he acted did not shackle him to particular courses of action. Andrew J. Goodpaster, Eisenhower's White House defense liaison officer and staff secretary from 1954 to 1961, reports that Eisenhower was able to use his formulations of operating principles to persuade others how to act as well as to clarify his own thinking. "The principles were not always consistent with each other. But his power of selecting the right principle that really had an appeal and using it instrumentally and effectively was part of his method," Remarks at Conference on Leadership in the Modern Presidency, Woodrow Wilson School, Princeton University, April 3, 1987.

19. For a discussion of his specific administrative arrangements see Greenstein, *Hidden-Hand Presidency*, chap. 4.

20. By the 1970s it finally became part of the conventional wisdom of the American presidency that the Executive Office of the President is far

too large and complex for presidents to operate without either a single top White House aide or, at least, a team of aides to help the president control his agenda. The actual term *chief of staff* was not used to designate such chief White House aides as H. R. Haldeman (Nixon), David Rumsfeld (Ford), and Hamilton Jordan (Carter). It first appeared in the *United States Government Manual* in the Reagan administration. See Samuel Kernell and Samuel L. Popkin, eds., *Chief of Staff: Twenty-Five Years of Managing the Presidency* (Berkeley and Los Angeles: University of California Press, 1986).

21. A number of those associated with the Eisenhower national security machinery argue that the policy planning unit that Eisenhower established to address implementation and that Kennedy eliminated (the Operations Coordinating Board of the National Security Council) would have prevented the Bay of Pigs fiasco.

22. Dwight D. Eisenhower, *The White House Years: Mandate for Change, 1953–1956* (Garden City, N.Y.: Doubleday, 1963), p. 114.

23. Eisenhower to Forrestal, February 8, 1948, *PDDE*, 9:2243–44 (hereafter cited as Eisenhower–Forrestal).

24. In describing Eisenhower's way of using his cabinet, I discuss how he rallied his aides in making domestic policy. The same approach applies to his use of the NSC in making foreign policy. Most of the foreign policy record for the 1950s remains classified. Because virtually all domestic policy documents are available, I use domestic policy-making to illuminate both domestic and foreign policy-making.

25. Ann Whitman to Milton Eisenhower, August 28, 1956, Name Series, box 13, DDEL.

26. See John P. Burke, "Political Context and Presidential Influence: A Case Study," *Presidential Studies Quarterly*, 15 (1985), 301–319.

27. January 18, 1954, DDE.

28. Eisenhower–Forrestal.

29. Eisenhower to Milton Eisenhower, November 23, 1954, DDE.

30. Eisenhower to Secretary of Defense, August 2, 1954, DDE.

31. January 5, 1953, PD.

32. Eisenhower to Gabriel Hauge, February 13, 1956, DDE.

33. Eisenhower to Henry ("Harry") Luce, August 8, 1960, DDE.

34. Eisenhower to Walter Bedell Smith, November 14, 1942, *PDDE*, 2: 712.

35. Teletype from Eisenhower (in Denver) to Sherman Adams (at the White House), September 25, 1954, *DDE*.

36. For example, Eisenhower to Charles Wilson, January 27, 1954, DDE.

37. Eisenhower to Herbert Brownell, January 25, 1954, DDE. Years later, when I showed this letter to Mr. Brownell, he immediately characterized it as a reprimand, adding, "That was as far as he ever had to go with me."

38. Eisenhower to General Paul Carroll, September 11, 1953, DDE.

39. Dwight D. Eisenhower, *Waging Peace, 1956–1961* (Garden City, N.Y.: Doubleday, 1965), pp. 681–682.

40. Memorandum for Mr. Rabb, August 12, 1953, DDE.

41. See the many entries for 1954 in James C. Hagerty Diary, DDEL.

42. Telephone log, March 8, 1954, DDE.

43. Eisenhower to General Alfred E. Gruenther, February 26, 1953, Administration Series, DDEL.

44. Eisenhower to General Maxwell D. Taylor, January 2, 1946, *PDDE*, 7: 710.

45. Eisenhower–Forrestal.

46. June 1, 1953, PD.

47. Eisenhower to Robinson, October 22, 1953, DDE.

48. Eisenhower to Oveta Culp Hobby, November 24, 1953, DDE.

49. Eisenhower to Cutler, March 23, 1954, DDE.

50. Eisenhower to General George S. Patton, Jr., April 29, 1944, *PDDE*, 3: 1839–40.

51. For striking insights into Eisenhower's practice of speaking euphemistically about his counterparts (apart from military enemies), compare his circumspect discussions of even his strongest critics and most intractable associates in his World War II memoir, *Crusade in Europe* (Garden City, N.Y.: Doubleday, 1948), with the scholarly account of his private views of his associates during the same period in Stephen Ambrose, *The Supreme Commander: The War Years of General Dwight D. Eisenhower* (Garden City, N.Y.: Doubleday, 1970). The latter is replete with evidence of personal and personality conflicts and how Eisenhower dealt with them. Also see Eisenhower's careful instructions to the publisher of Doubleday that a proposed preface to an English reprinting of *Crusade in Europe* contain no discussion of the debates about the relative merits and effectiveness of different World War II commanders and their plans; Eisenhower to Douglas M. Black, November 9, 1959, DDE.

52. Eisenhower to the Honorable George N. Craig, March 26, 1954, DDE.

53. Eisenhower to Mark Wayne Clark, April 4, 1946, *PDDE*, 7: 982.

54. Eisenhower to Clark, July 3, 1946, *PDDE*, 7: 1172.

55. Dwight D. Eisenhower, *At Ease: Stories I Tell to My Friends* (Garden City, N.Y.: Doubleday, 1967), p. 350.

56. See Robert Griffiths' well-documented account of Eisenhower's centrist mind set, "Dwight D. Eisenhower and the Corporate Commonwealth," *American Historical Review*, 87 (1982), 87–122.

57. Eisenhower to William Phillips, June 5, 1953, DDE.

58. Eisenhower to Nelson Rockefeller, May 5, 1960, DDE.

59. H. Hyman and P. B. Sheatsley, "The Political Appeal of President Eisenhower," *Public Opinion Quarterly*, 17 (1953–54), 443–460.

60. Eisenhower to Harry Cecil Butcher, notes from Eisenhower's diary, December 10, 1942, *PDDE*, 2: 823–824.

61. John Gunther, *Eisenhower: The Man and the Symbol* (New York: Harper and Row, 1952), appendix.

62. Eisenhower to Edgar Newton Eisenhower, September 6, 1944, *PDDE*, 4: 2192–93.

63. Eisenhower to Luce, August 8, 1960, DDE.

64. Eisenhower, *Mandate for Change*, p. 60.

65. John Osborne, "Gabbing with [Bryce] Harlow," *New Republic*, May 13, 1978, pp. 12–14.

66. Eisenhower to Luce, August 8, 1960, DDE.

67. Greenstein, *Hidden-Hand Presidency*, chap 5.

4. John F. Kennedy

1. For a good recent example of the Kennedy assassination literature see Henry Hurt, *Reasonable Doubt: An Investigation into the Assassination of John F. Kennedy* (New York: Holt, Rinehart and Winston, 1985).

2. Kennedy revisionism has come from the left, right, and middle of the political spectrum. Among the most widely read and widely reviewed examples are Peter Collier and David Horowitz, *The Kennedys: An American Drama* (New York: Summit Books, 1984); Garry Wills, *The Kennedy Imprisonment: A Meditation on Power* (Boston: Little, Brown, 1982); Henry Fairlie, *The Kennedy Promise: The Politics of Expectation* (Garden City, N.Y.: Doubleday, 1973); Joan Blair and Clay Blair, Jr., *The Search for JFK* (New York: Berkley, 1976); Herbert S. Parmet, *Jack: The Struggles of John F. Kennedy* (New York: Dial Press, 1980); and *JFK: The Presidency of John F. Kennedy* (New York: Dial Press, 1983); Doris Kearns Goodwin, *The Fitzgeralds and the Kennedys* (New York: Simon and Schuster, 1987).

3. Robert K. Murray and Tim H. Blessing, "The Presidential Performance Study: A Progress Report," *Journal of American History*, 70 (December 1983), 535–555.

4. *Harris Survey*, August 25, 1983, and April 15, 1985; *Wall Street Journal*, June 4, 1987, p. 66; *New York Times*, July 7, 1987, p. 1.

5. Quoted in Theodore C. Sorensen, *Kennedy* (New York: Harper & Row, 1965), p. 22.

6. Arthur M. Schlesinger, Jr., *The Cycles of American History* (Boston: Houghton Mifflin, 1986), pp. 406–418.

7. Quoted in Sorensen, *Kennedy*, p. 219; this section draws heavily upon Carl M. Brauer, *Presidential Transitions: Eisenhower through Reagan* (New York: Oxford University Press, 1986), pp. 61–105.

8. On Kennedy's appointments see Robert Kennedy (by John Bartlow Martin), Robert Lovett, Adam Yarmolinsky, Harris Wofford, Meyer Feldman, Clark Clifford, Chester Bowles, and Richard Bissell, Kennedy Library

Oral Histories, John F. Kennedy Library, Boston (hereafter cited as Kennedy Library); Clark Clifford, Memorandum of conversation with Senator Kennedy, November 30, 1960, reel 1, Clark Clifford Papers, Kennedy Library; Richard Neustadt, "Memorandum on Staffing the President-Elect," October 30, 1960, box 1072, John F. Kennedy Papers, Pre-Presidential, Kennedy Library; Harris Wofford, *Of Kennedys and Kings: Making Sense of the Sixties* (New York: Farrar, Straus and Giroux, 1980), pp. 67–97; Arthur M. Schlesinger, Jr., *Robert Kennedy and His Times* (Boston: Houghton Mifflin, 1978), pp. 244–260, 443–454; Peter Wyden, *Bay of Pigs: The Untold Story* (New York: Simon and Schuster, 1979), pp. 95–96, 98–100, 268–269; Richard Gid Powers, *Secrecy and Power: The Life of J. Edgar Hoover* (New York: Free Press, 1987), pp. 353–383.

9. Sorensen, *Kennedy*, pp. 251–258; David T. Stanley, Dean E. Mann, and Jameson W. Doig, *Men Who Govern: A Biographical Profile of Federal Political Executives* (Washington, D.C.: Brookings Institution, 1967), pp. 24, 130, 132–33.

10. Robert Lovett, Kennedy Library Oral History, p. 20.

11. On Kennedy's political career before 1961, see esp. Parmet, *Jack*; on his approach to personnel and organizations, see the Robert Kennedy (by J. B. Martin), Adam Yarmolinsky, and Harris Wofford, Kennedy Library Oral Histories; Wofford, *Of Kennedys and Kings*, pp. 70–86.

12. Wofford, *Of Kennedys and Kings*, p. 70.

13. On Kennedy's staff see esp. Sorensen, *Kennedy*; Pierre Salinger, *With Kennedy* (Garden City, N.Y.: Doubleday, 1966); Kenneth P. O'Donnell and David F. Powers with Joe McCarthy, *"Johnny, We Hardly Knew Ye": Memories of John Fitzgerald Kennedy* (Boston: Little, Brown, 1972); Mary McGrory, "The Right-Hand Men—Pierre Salinger, Lawrence O'Brien, and Kenneth P. O'Donnell," in *The Kennedy Circle*, ed. Lester Tanzer (Washington, D.C.: Luce, 1961), pp. 75–81; Comments by McGeorge Bundy, Forum on JFK and Public Service, John F. Kennedy School of Government, Cambridge, Mass., May 29, 1987.

14. Salinger, *With Kennedy*, pp. 64–72; Sorensen, *Kennedy*, pp. 258–265; Frederick Dutton and Walt Rostow, Kennedy Library Oral Histories.

15. George Kennan, Walt Rostow, Frederick Dutton, and Charles Bohlen, Kennedy Library Oral Histories; Interview note, Richard E. Neustadt, December 22, 1960, box 3, Laurin L. Henry Papers, Kennedy Library.

16. Schlesinger's *Robert Kennedy and His Times* is an outstanding biography.

17. Gerald T. Rice, *The Bold Experiment: JFK's Peace Corps* (Notre Dame, Ind.: University of Notre Dame Press, 1985), pp. 302–303.

18. Salinger, *With Kennedy*, pp. 81–87; Parmet, *JFK*, pp. 101–130.

19. Sorensen, *Kennedy*, pp. 310–322; Salinger, *With Kennedy*, pp. 84–143; Mary McGrory, Peter Lisagor, George Herman, and Robert Kennedy (by J. B. Martin), Kennedy Library Oral Histories.

20. Benjamin C. Bradlee, *Conversations with Kennedy* (New York: Norton: 1975), pp. 19–20.

21. Quoted in Sorensen, *Kennedy*, p. 323.

22. Salinger, *With Kennedy*, pp. 53–59; Sorensen, *Kennedy*, pp. 322–326.

23. Peter Lisagor, Kennedy Library Oral History; George H. Gallup, *The Gallup Poll: Public Opinion, 1935–1971*, vol. 3 (New York: Random House, 1975), p. 1765.

24. *Public Papers of the Presidents: John F. Kennedy, 1961* (Washington, D.C.: Government Printing Office, 1962), pp. 1–3.

25. James Meredith, *Three Years in Mississippi* (Bloomington: Indiana University Press, 1966), pp. 50–59; Gallup, *Gallup Poll*, 3, p. 1707.

26. Gallup, *Gallup Poll*, 3, p. 1850; Thomas E. Cronin, *The State of the Presidency*, 2d ed. (Boston: Little, Brown, 1980), pp. 328–329.

27. Tom Wicker popularized this view in *JFK and LBJ: The Influence of Personality upon Politics* (New York: William Morrow, 1968).

28. James L. Sundquist, *Politics and Policy: The Eisenhower, Kennedy, and Johnson Years* (Washington, D.C.: Brookings Institution, 1968); Lawrence F. O'Brien, *No Final Victories: A Life in Politics from John F. Kennedy to Watergate* (Garden City, N.Y.: Doubleday, 1974), p. 104.

29. John M. Logsdon, *The Decision to Go to the Moon: Project Apollo and the National Interest* (Cambridge, Mass.: MIT Press, 1970), pp. 93–130; Sorensen, *Kennedy*, pp. 523–529; O'Donnell and Powers, *"Johnny,"* p. 410; Walter D. McDougall, *"The Heavens and the Earth": A Political History of the Space Age* (New York: Basic Books, 1985), pp. 302–324.

30. Kennedy is quoted in Council of Economic Advisers, Kennedy Library Oral History. This discussion of Kennedy's economic policy draws on that oral history; on the Walter Heller Papers, Kennedy Library; and on Herbert Stein, *The Fiscal Revolution in America* (Chicago: University of Chicago Press, 1969).

31. Quoted in Sorensen, *Kennedy*, p. 430.

32. For a detailed account of Kennedy and civil rights see Carl M. Brauer, *John F. Kennedy and the Second Reconstruction* (New York: Columbia University Press, 1977).

33. Esp. ibid., pp. 152–167. The tensions between civil rights activists and the Kennedy administration over the issue of federal protection have been extensively documented, as in the compelling and balanced television series *Eyes on the Prize*, which first aired on the Public Broadcasting System in 1987.

34. Quoted in Brauer, *Kennedy and the Second Reconstruction*, p. 204.

35. In his painstaking biography of Martin Luther King, Jr., David Garrow gives a careful account of the Birmingham crisis and much else; see David J. Garrow, *Bearing the Cross: Martin Luther King, Jr. and the*

Southern Christian Leadership Conference (New York: William Morrow, 1986), pp. 231–269.

36. Quoted in Brauer, *Kennedy and the Second Reconstruction*, p. 260.

37. Quoted in ibid., p. 246; see also Schlesinger, *Robert Kennedy*, pp. 327–348.

38. Quoted in Brauer, *Kennedy and the Second Reconstruction*, p. 261.

39. Ibid., pp. 263–320.

40. Peter Collier and David Horowitz, "Another 'Low Dishonest Decade' on the Left," *Commentary*, 83 (January 1987), 18–19.

41. Schlesinger, *Cycles of American History*, p. 414. The writings on American intervention in Vietnam are voluminous; probably the two best scholarly studies to date are George Herring, *America's Longest War: The United States and Vietnam, 1950–1975* (New York: Wiley, 1979); and George McT. Kahin, *Intervention: How America Became Involved in Vietnam* (New York: Knopf, 1986).

42. Quoted in Richard D. Mahoney, *JFK: Ordeal in Africa* (New York: Oxford University Press, 1983), p. 245.

43. Ibid., p. 248. See also Roger Hilsman, *To Move a Nation: The Politics of Foreign Policy in the Administration of John F. Kennedy* (Garden City, N.Y.: Doubleday, 1967).

44. Arthur M. Schlesinger, Jr., *A Thousand Days: John F. Kennedy in the White House* (Boston: Houghton Mifflin, 1965), pp. 186–205, 759–793; Jerome Levinson and Juan DeOnis, *The Alliance That Lost Its Way: A Critical Report on the Alliance for Progress* (Chicago: Quadrangle Books, 1970); Milton E. Eisenhower, *The Wine Is Bitter: The United States and Latin America* (Garden City, N.Y.: Doubleday, 1963).

45. Brauer, *Presidential Transitions*, pp. 112–116.

46. Quoted in Schlesinger, *Thousand Days*, p. 426.

47. Quoted in Brauer, *Presidential Transitions*, p. 116.

48. Robert Kennedy (by J. B. Martin), Kennedy Library Oral History.

49. Among the many fine works on military and strategic matters in the Kennedy years are John Lewis Gaddis, *Strategies of Containment: An Appraisal of Postwar American National Security Policy* (New York: Oxford University Press, 1982), pp. 198–273; Michael Mandelbaum, *The Nuclear Question: The United States and Nuclear Weapons, 1946–1976* (Cambridge: Cambridge University Press, 1979), pp. 69–189; Desmond Ball, *Politics and Force Levels: The Strategic Missile Program of the Kennedy Adminstration* (Berkeley and Los Angeles: University of California Press, 1980); Richard Aliano, *American Defense Policy from Eisenhower to Kennedy: The Politics of Changing Military Requirements* (Athens: Ohio University Press, 1975).

50. The Cuban missile crisis has also been the subject of much dis-

cussion, with no end in sight; see, for example, Elie Abel, *The Missile Crisis* (Philadelphia: J. B. Lippincott, 1966); Graham T. Allison, *Essence of Decision: Explaining the Cuban Missile Crisis* (Boston: Little, Brown, 1971); Schlesinger, *Robert Kennedy*, pp. 499–532; James A. Nathan, "The Missile Crisis: His Finest Hour Now," *World Politics*, 27 (January 1975), 265–281; Barton J. Bernstein, "The Cuban Missile Crisis: Trading the Jupiters in Turkey?" *Political Science Quarterly*, 95 (Spring 1980), 97–125; Richard Ned Lebow, "The Cuban Missile Crisis: Reading the Lessons Correctly," *Political Science Quarterly*, 98 (Fall 1983), 431–458; Thomas G. Paterson and William J. Brophy, "October Missiles and November Elections: The Cuban Missile Crisis and American Politics, 1962," *Journal of American History*, 73 (June 1986), 87–119.

51. *Public Papers of the Presidents: John F. Kennedy, 1963* (Washington, D.C.: Government Printing Office, 1964), p. 462.

52. Walter Isaacson and Even Thomas, *The Wise Men: Six Friends and the World They Made* (New York: Simon and Schuster, 1986), pp. 630–633; Glenn T. Seaborg, *Kennedy, Khrushchev, and the Test Ban* (Berkeley and Los Angeles: University of California Press, 1981); Robert S. McNamara, *Blundering into Disaster: Surviving the First Century of the Nuclear Age* (New York: Pantheon, 1986), pp. 63–64.

5. Lyndon B. Johnson

1. Lyndon Baines Johnson, *The Vantage Point: Perspectives on the Presidency 1963–1969* (New York: Popular Library, 1971), pp. 18–19.

2. Ibid., pp. 156–157.

3. Theodore H. White, *The Making of the President, 1964* (New York: Atheneum, 1965), pp. 324–326.

4. Johnson, *Vantage Point*, p. 10.

5. Harry McPherson, Oral history transcript, Lyndon Baines Johnson Presidential Library, Austin, Texas (hereafter cited as LBJ Library). See Harry McPherson, *A Political Education* (Boston: Little, Brown, 1972).

6. John Roche, "Analysis of U.S. Role in Vietnam on Target," *Detroit News*, September 22, 1982.

7. Ralph Huitt, "Democratic Party Leadership in the Senate," *American Political Science Review*, 55 (June 1961), 336–338.

8. Quoted in Kenneth W. Thompson, ed., *The Johnson Presidency* (Lanham, Md.: University Press of America, 1987), p. 11.

9. Quoted in Theodore H. White, *The Making of the President, 1968* (New York: Atheneum, 1969), p. 101.

10. Johnson, *Vantage Point*, pp. 432–433.

11. David Halberstam, *The Best and the Brightest* (New York: Random House, 1972), p. 432.

12. Robert Donovan, *Nemesis: Truman and Johnson in the Coils of*

War in Asia (New York: St. Martin's Press, 1984), pp. 10–11.

13. Robert Caro, *The Path to Power* (New York: Knopf, 1982), p. xii.

14. Doris Kearns, "The Art of Biography: The Power and Pathos of LBJ," *New Republic*, March 3, 1979.

15. Bill Gulley with Mary Ellen Reese, *Breaking Cover* (New York: Simon and Schuster, 1980), pp. 44–45.

16. George Reedy, *Lyndon Johnson: A Memoir* (New York: Andrews and McNeal, 1982), p. 157.

17. *New Republic*, November 14, 1964, p. 3.

18. Rowland Evans and Robert Novak, *Lyndon B. Johnson: The Exercise of Power* (New York: New American Library, 1966), pp. 115–117.

19. Memorandum, John Roche to the President, November 14, 1967, LBJ Library.

20. Meeting notes, November 15, 1967, Meeting Notes File, LBJ Library (cited hereafter as MNF).

21. Meeting notes, June 1, 1967, MNF.

22. Interview with Helen Thomas and Jack Horner, August 25, 1965, MNF.

23. Harry McPherson, Oral history transcript, LBJ Library.

24. Quoted in Thompson, *Johnson Presidency*, pp. 284–285.

25. See, for example, James David Barber, *The Presidential Character* (Englewood Cliffs, N.J.: Prentice-Hall, 1987), pp. 66–80; Alonzo Hamby, *Liberalism and Its Challengers* (New York: Oxford University Press, 1985), pp. 231–281.

26. Quoted in Thompson, *Johnson Presidency*, p. 258.

27. Quoted in ibid., pp. 89–90.

28. Quoted in ibid., p. 220.

29. Doris Kearns, *Lyndon Johnson and the American Dream*, pp. 360–361.

30. Johnson, Memorandum of meeting, September 15, 1967, MNF.

31. Cited by Robert Caro, Plenary address at Hofstra University Conference on the Johnson Presidency, April 22, 1986.

32. Quoted in White, *Making of the President, 1968*, p. 101.

33. Memorandum, John Roche to President Johnson, September 5, 1967, LBJ Library.

34. Meeting notes, February 13, 1968, MNF.

35. Memorandum, Walt Rostow to the President, September 22, 1966, LBJ Library.

36. Meeting notes, August 19, 1967, MNF.

37. Chalmers Roberts, *First Rough Draft: A Journalist's Journal of Our Times* (New York: Praeger, 1973), p. 233; Jim Heath, *Decade of Disillusionment: The Kennedy-Johnson Years* (Bloomington: Indiana University Press, 1975), pp. 248–249.

38. Memorandum, John Roche to President Johnson, February 7, 1967, LBJ Library.

39. Memorandum, Walt Rostow to President Johnson, September 15, 1967, LBJ Library.

40. Meeting notes, August 21, 1967, MNF.

41. Meeting notes, February 9, 1968, MNF.

42. Quoted in Roberts, *First Rough Draft*, p. 246.

43. Meeting notes, September 20, 1967, MNF.

44. For an extended discussion see Larry Berman, "Johnson and the White House Staff," in *Exploring the Johnson Years*, ed. Robert Divine (Lawrence: University of Kansas Press, 1987), pp. 183–187.

45. Memorandum, Tom Johnson to the President, December 9, 1966, FG1 File, LBJ Library.

46. On the effort to discredit Lippmann see Fred Panzer to the President, March 12, 1967–March 31, 1967, folder, FG1 [14] Executive File, White House Central File, LBJ Library; Kathleen J. Turner, *Lyndon Johnson's Dual War: Vietnam and the Press* (Chicago: University of Chicago Press, 1985); David Culbert, "Johnson and the Media," in Divine, *Exploring the Johnson Years*, p. 239.

47. Meeting notes, August 21, 1967, MNF.

48. Doris Kearns, *Lyndon Johnson and the American Dream*, p. 352.

49. General William Westmoreland, Deposition for CBS-Westmoreland trial in author's possession.

50. Walt Rostow, Deposition, ibid.

51. Robert Ginsburg, Deposition, ibid.

52. Gulley, *Breaking Cover*, pp. 77–79.

53. Quoted in Thompson, *Johnson Presidency*, p. 32.

54. Moyers to Johnson, May 11, 1967, LBJ Library.

55. Ginsburg to Rostow, November 18, 1967, LBJ Library.

56. Meeting notes, November 19, 1967, MNF.

57. Meeting notes, November 2, 1967, MNF.

58. George Herring, *America's Longest War: The United States and Vietnam 1950–1975*, 2d ed. (New York: Knopf, 1986), p. 178. For an extended analysis see Larry Berman, *Lyndon Johnson's War* (New York: Norton, in press).

59. Meeting notes, November 2, 1967, MNF. See Walter Isaacson and Evan Thomas, *The Wise Men*.

60. Meeting notes, August 9, 1967, MNF.

61. Meeting notes, April 15, 1967, MNF.

62. Memorandum, Nicholas Katzenbach to the President, November 16, 1967, LBJ Library.

63. Cable, Ambassador Bunker to Walt Rostow, August 29, 1967, LBJ Library. The dispute between the CIA and MACV receives detailed analysis in Renata Adler, *Reckless Disregard: Westmoreland v. CBS et al. Sharon v. Time* (New York: Knopf, 1986); Bob Berwin and Sydney Shaw, *Vietnam on Trial: Westmoreland v. CBS* (New York: Atheneum, 1987).

64. William Westmoreland, Deposition for CBS-Westmoreland trial.

65. Robert McNamara, Deposition, ibid.; see also Johnson, *Vantage Point*, pp. 372–373.

66. McNamara, Deposition for CBS-Westmoreland trial.

67. See Andrew Krepinevich, Jr., *The Army and Vietnam* (Baltimore: Johns Hopkins University Press, 1986).

68. Meeting notes, August 26, 1967, MNF.

69. Cable, Walt Rostow to Bunker, September 27, 1967, LBJ Library.

70. Memorandum, Rostow to McNamara, Rusk, Helms, and Leonhart, October 12, 1967, LBJ Library.

71. Quoted in Johnson, *Vantage Point*, p. 372.

72. Ibid.; see also Memorandum, Robert McNamara to the President, November 1, 1967, LBJ Library.

73. Memorandum, Abe Fortas to the President, November 5, 1967, LBJ Library.

74. Johnson, *Vantage Point*, pp. 380, 381.

75. Memorandum, McGeorge Bundy to the President, May 4, 1967, LBJ Library.

76. Quoted in Thompson, *Johnson Presidency*, pp. 285–286; see also Leonard Marks, Oral history transcript, p. 29, LBJ Library.

6. Richard M. Nixon

1. Lloyd C. Gardner, *The Great Nixon Turn Around: New Foreign Policy in the Post-Liberal Era* (New York: Viewpoints, 1973), pp. 25–28; Allen J. Matusow, *The Unraveling of America: A History of Liberalism in the 1960s* (New York: Harper & Row, 1984), pp. 376–439; Charles R. Morris, *A Time of Passion: America 1960–1980* (New York: Harper & Row, 1984), pp. 129–134; Richard P. Nathan, *The Plot That Failed: Nixon and the Administrative Presidency* (New York: Wiley, 1975), pp. 14–16; Nelson W. Polsby, *The Citizen's Choice: Humphrey or Nixon* (Washington, D.C.: Public Affairs Press, 1968), pp. 1–69; Richard Rose, *Managing Presidential Objectives* (New York: Free Press, 1976), pp. 48–49; Jonathan Schell, *The Time of Illusion* (New York: Knopf, 1976), pp. 5–14; Tom Shactman, *Decade of Shocks: Dallas to Watergate, 1968–1974* (New York: Poseidon Press, 1983), pp. 285–296.

2. All the presidents serving in these periods have been rated either "average" or "failures" by scholars. Those traditionally deemed absolute failures by historians are John Tyler, Zachary Taylor, Millard Fillmore, Franklin Pierce, James Buchanan, Andrew Johnson, Ulysses S. Grant, Warren G. Harding, and Calvin Coolidge. Until 1982, when Nixon and Carter were added to this list, all the "failed" presidencies were clustered in the 1840s through 1870s (the notable exception being Lincoln) and in the 1920s, between World War I and the Great Depression. Despite the negative treat-

ment accorded Herbert Hoover by his contemporaries, historians have since categorized him as average rather than a failure, *above* the "low" average presidencies of Gerald Ford and Jimmy Carter (whose failure ratings were only temporary). In the twentieth century only Hoover experienced a severe and irrevocable fall in popularity and a subsequent low ranking in scholarly polls. Since the late 1960s, however, Lyndon Johnson, Nixon, Ford, and Carter experienced extreme shifts in public approval that were ultimately reflected in the attitudes of experts on the presidency polled in 1981 and 1982; see Robert K. Murray and Tim H. Blessing, "The Presidential Performance Study: A Progress Report," *Journal of American History,* 70 (December 1983), 535–555.

    3. Lewis Chester, Godfrey Hodgson, and Bruce Page, *An American Melodrama: The Presidential Campaign of 1968* (New York: Viking, 1969), p. 236.

    4. Nixon interview with Stuart Alsop, *Saturday Evening Post,* July 12, 1958, p. 28. For the complete, unedited transcript of this interview, which I consider the most revealing of any conducted with Nixon, see Fawn M. Brodie Papers, box 42, Special Collections Department, Marriot Library, University of Utah, Salt Lake City (hereafter cited as Brodie Papers). The risk-taking aspects of Nixon's career are best discussed and analyzed by Leo Rangell in *The Mind of Watergate: An Exploration of the Compromise of Integrity* (New York: Norton, 1980). Although Stephen E. Ambrose relies on Rangell, the first volume of his biography of Nixon uses the term *risk taker* only once, and then it is to compare Truman and Nixon. Likewise, Ambrose asserts that Nixon "thrived on crisis," but again he makes the comparison with Truman and focuses primarily on the Hiss case. Since Ambrose does not detail the significance between real and false crises in Nixon's career up to 1962, his book does not go beyond Rangell's original thesis in helping us understand how his earlier career related to his ill-fated presidency. See *Nixon: The Education of a Politician 1913–1962* (New York: Simon and Schuster, 1987), pp. 195–196, 222, 637–642.

    5. Garry Wills, *Newsday,* June 13, 1982, p. 12. Along the same lines, A. James Reichley suggests that "the cynicism that has always pervaded a large sector of American politics" since World War II is in part the product of "prolonged acceptance of wartime standards of behavior [which] helped erode moral and ethical sensitivities"; see *Conservatives in an Age of Change: The Nixon and Ford Administrations* (Washington, D.C.: Brookings Institution, 1981), p. 256.

    6. Michael R. Belknap, "Vietnam and the Constitution: The War Power under Lyndon Johnson and Richard Nixon," *this Constitution,* no. 10 (Spring 1986), 19. Belknap argues that "Johnson and Nixon were merely following in the footsteps of Lincoln, Roosevelt, and Truman. They were implementing concepts accepted, and even applauded by most lawyers,

scholars, and politicians before the Vietnam debacle itself called them into question. Thus condemning Johnson and Nixon for unconstitutional conduct is scapegoating—it personalizes responsibility for a national mistake." For a similar but more partisan interpretation of the double standard used by critics of the war in judging Nixon, see Nicholas von Hoffman, "How Nixon Got Strung Up," *New Republic*, June 23, 1982, pp. 24–27.

7. One of the most unexpected references to Nixon as a peacetime president was made by Herbert Stein, chair of Nixon's Council of Economic Advisers (1972–1974), in *Presidential Economics: The Making of Economic Policy from Roosevelt to Reagan and Beyond* (New York: Simon and Schuster, 1984), p. 133. Stein describes Nixon's wage and price controls of 1971 as "an enormous peacetime intervention of the government in the American economy." The implication that Nixon was a peacetime president is often conveyed in standard textbooks, which to date have been largely critical of his administration because of Watergate. Perhaps this mistake is also made because in the minds of most people, including scholars, a war such as Vietnam does not automatically constitute a "wartime" period.

8. Arthur M. Schlesinger, Jr., *The Cycles of American History* (Boston: Houghton Mifflin, 1986), pp. 23–48. Unlike Schlesinger, however, I do not believe that a private interest era, that is, a conservative period, was initiated by the assassination of President Kennedy. This interpretation does a disservice to the reforms under Johnson and to the legitimate reform and some enlightened aspects of foreign policy during the first Nixon administration. Conservative periods simply follow wars. So the current one began in 1974 as a post-Vietnam phenomenon and had nothing to do with Kennedy's death.

9. For a discussion of the differences between generalists and specialists and Nixon's preference for the former which led him to appoint "politician managers," see Nathan, *Plot That Failed*, pp. 9–10, 25, 67; Stephen Hess, *Organizing the Presidency* (Washington, D.C.: Brookings Institution, 1976), pp. 113–115; Peri E. Arnold, *Making the Managerial Presidency: Comprehensive Reorganization Planning 1905–1980* (Princeton: Princeton University Press, 1986), pp. 274–277; John H. Kessel, *The Domestic Presidency: Decision-Making in the White House* (North Scituate, Mass.: Duxbury Press, 1975), pp. 18–20; Martha Derthick, *Uncontrollable Spending for Social Services Grants* (Washington, D.C.: Brookings Institution, 1975), pp. 106–115.

10. Reichley, *Conservatives in an Age of Change*, pp. 52–53, 105–107; Hess, *Organizing the Presidency*, pp. 112–113 (for Nixon's most complete May 1968 campaign remark about dispersing power; Nathan, *Plot That Failed*, pp. 13–15; Schell, *Time of Illusion*, pp. 19–21; Chester, Hodgson, and Page, *American Melodrama*, pp. 674–689. There are also many references to Nixon's attempts to disperse power in the unedited transcript of

Raymond Price's November 10, 1975, interview with H. R. Haldeman about
government reorganization under Nixon. Haldeman sent me this transcript
and granted permission to quote from it.

    11. Leonard Lurie, *The Running of Richard Nixon* (New York: McCann
& Geoghegan, 1972), pp. 301–303; Richard Nixon, "Asia After Vietnam,"
Foreign Affairs, 46 (October 1967), 121–124; idem, interview with author,
January 26, 1983, New York City. Raymond Price, a leading speechwriter
for Nixon beginning in 1967 and the man whom Nixon considered the
"ablest of his staff" both before and after his presidency, helped Nixon
articulate his views on China in the 1967 *Foreign Affairs* article. Price
accompanied Nixon on his round-the-world trip in 1967 and observed first-
hand his struggle to reevaluate the entire Asian question. See Raymond
Price, interview with author, January 26, 1983, New York City; idem, *With
Nixon* (New York: Viking, 1977), pp. 20–28; and William Safire, *Before the
Fall: An Inside View of the Pre-Watergate White House* (1975; reprint, New
York: Ballantine Books, 1977), pp. 474–493. Safire notes not only that Nixon
carefully weighed every word in his 1967 article, but also that it received
national distribution in condensed form in *Reader's Digest.* Theodore White
recalls that Nixon told him about his intentions to change relations with
China in March 1968; *The Making of the President, 1968* (New York: Atheneum, 1969), p. 148. According to C. L. Sulzberger, *The World and Richard
Nixon* (New York: Prentice-Hall, 1987), p. 77, Nixon had quietly discussed
China with foreign leaders when he was out of office in the 1960s. Another
correspondent, Henry Brandon, observes that as early as 1954 Nixon told a
group of reporters that "it was important to end the isolation of China
gradually and [recommended doing] this by reopening trade relations and
cultural exchanges"; *The Retreat of American Power* (Garden City, N.Y.:
Doubleday, 1973), pp. 181–182. In my interview with Nixon on January 26,
1983, he reminded me that he had also mentioned changing relations with
China in a 1956 LaFayette College speech. I have been unable to confirm
this claim.

    12. Matusow, *The Unraveling of America*, pp. 401–405, 429–432,
434–436; and Schell, *Time of Illusion*, pp. 17–22. Nixon denies that during
the 1968 campaign he implied he had a "secret plan" for ending the war in
Vietnam; *The Memoirs of Richard Nixon* (New York: Grosset & Dunlap,
1978), p. 298.

    13. For example, he approved reopening the Warsaw talks with China;
privately decided on a gradual, unilateral withdrawal of American troops
from Vietnam; made Henry Kissinger his national security adviser; approved
a plan for reorganizing the NSC system; and concluded that Roy Ash, president of Litton Industries, should initiate a massive reorganization of the
executive branch. But at the same time he also contacted Arthur Burns
about becoming his deputy for domestic affairs and decided to appoint Pat-

rick Moynihan head of a new Urban Affairs Council (UAC) to formulate domestic policy, although Burns and Moynihan were at opposite ends of the political and economic spectrum. In retrospect, these interregnum actions indicate that Nixon intended to restructure the office of the president in order to accomplish his domestic and foreign policy goals. See Nixon, *Memoirs*, pp. 335–362.

14. H. R. Haldeman, interview with Mike Wallace, March 30, 1975; tape and partial transcript in Brodie Papers, boxes 42, 53.

15. Nixon aides were particularly successful in convincing him that a "crisis" existed with respect to the environment and welfare. See note 91 below.

16. Theodore H. White, *The Making of the President, 1972* (New York: Atheneum, 1973), pp. 52–59, 353–358; I. M. Destler, "The Nixon System: A Further Look," *Foreign Service Journal*, February 1974, pp. 9–14, 28–29. White had significantly changed his formerly negative views on Nixon as early as 1968; see *Making of the President, 1968*, pp. 143–149.

17. Hess, *Organizing the Presidency*, p. 111; Richard Tanner Johnson, *Managing the White House: An Intimate Study of the Presidency* (New York: Harper & Row, 1974), p. 210.

18. Hess, *Organizing the Presidency*, p. 126; see also Richard P. Nathan, *The Administrative Presidency* (New York: Wiley, 1983), p. 38.

19. Hess, *Organizing the Presidency*, p. 126; Garry Wills, *Nixon Agonistes: The Crisis of the Self-Made Man* (Boston: Houghton Mifflin, 1969), p. 147.

20. In addition to the events leading up to his "Checkers" speech, Nixon discusses five other "crises" in *Six Crises:* the Hiss case in 1948, Eisenhower's heart attack in 1955, his visit to Caracas in 1958, his meeting with Khrushchev in 1959, and the 1960 presidential campaign. For Nixon's reactions to perceived crises see Rangell, *Mind of Watergate*, pp. 25–55.

21. The negative impact of Nixon's experience in the Office of Price Administration is corroborated in all the early biographies of him as well as in his 1958 interview with Stuart Alsop (cited above in note 4) and in Ambrose, *Nixon*, pp. 101–104, 137–138. See also Nixon, *Memoirs*, pp. 26–27.

22. Quoted in Earl Mazo and Stephen Hess, *Nixon: A Political Portrait* (New York: Popular Library, 1968), p. 32.

23. Safire, *Before the Fall*, p. 315.

24. Wills, *Nixon Agonistes*, pp. 90–138; Price interview with Haldeman; Anna Kasten Nelson, " 'On Top of Policy Hill': President Eisenhower and the National Security Council," *Diplomatic History*, 7 (Fall 1983), 307–326. Stephen E. Ambrose's biographies of Eisenhower and Nixon do not comment on or analyze in any detail Nixon's exclusion from the informal decision-making aspects of the NSC system in the 1950s.

25. Nixon, interview with author, January 26, 1983.

26. Richard M. Nixon, *Six Crises* (1962; reprint, New York: Warner Books, 1979), pp. xv, xii.

27. Haldeman, interview with Price, November 10, 1975. Although Haldeman claimed in this interview that "the basic idea [for reorganization] came as the President's," he strongly asserted in 1987, at the Princeton Conference on Leadership in the Modern Presidency, that Nixon "didn't give a darn about [governmental] operating procedures . . . or processes— just their results." In the 1975 interview Haldeman was primarily concerned with denying that government reorganizaion under Nixon was an attempt "to establish a fascist dictatorship," but in the process he attributed considerable interest, initiative, and determination to the president in planning to bring the bureaucracy under control. The question of Nixon's personal interest in and knowledge of the government reorganization that took place during his administration will probably not be answered until scholars have had time to analyze material in the papers of both Ehrlichman and Haldeman, which were opened in 1987 by the National Archives and Records Administration (NARA), especially the H. R. Haldeman Papers, Alpha Subject Files, boxes 144–145: Haldeman Reorganization/Ash (five folders, including one on the October 1969 report of the Ash Council), and boxes 172– 174: Reorganization/Departments and Agencies (four folders), Departmental Reorganization (three folders), Reorganization/Ambassadors (one folder), Reorganization/Cabinet (one folder), and Reorganization/EOP (one folder), all in Nixon Presidential Materials Project (NPMP), White House Special Files (WHSP), NARA.

28. Theodore H. White, *Breach of Faith: The Fall of Richard Nixon* (New York: Atheneum and Reader's Digest Press, 1975), p. 62; John Osborne, *The First Two Years of the Nixon Watch*, 2 vols. in 1 (New York: Liveright, 1971), 2: 28, 96. White also noted in an earlier book that Nixon's mind was "neat, disciplined, severely sequential, [and] compulsively orderly"; *Making of the President, 1972*, p. 52. My interview with John Ehrlichman on April 9, 1984, confirmed Nixon's interest in the details of complicated governmental operations—a characteristic exacerbated by anything smacking of intrigue, such as secret negotiations with foreign powers or the Watergate cover-up that ultimately led to his downfall.

29. John Connally was secretary of the treasury under Nixon from February 1971 to May 1972. Although he campaigned for Nixon's reelection, he did not formally announce that he had become a Republican until May 1, 1973. The working papers of the Ash Council were opened by NARA in December 1986. Those of greatest importance for government reorganization under Nixon can be found in PACEO, boxes 71–72, White House Central File (WHCF), NPMP, NARA. I have also used the 428-page bound in-house summary of all the recommendations made to Nixon by the Ash Council, "Memoranda of the President's Advisory Council on Executive

Organization." This document was given to me several years ago by John Whitaker.

30. Safire, *Before the Fall*, pp. 332, 333 (quotations), 334–335; Arnold, *Making the Managerial Presidency*, pp. 272–280.

31. In addition to White, *Breach of Faith*, and Osborne, *First Two Years of Nixon Watch*, the best analysis of the Ash Council's philosophy, work schedule, and recommendations is Arnold, *Making the Managerial Presidency*, pp. 280–302.

32. Nathan, *Plot That Failed*, pp. 37 (first quotation), 38–56; Nixon, *Memoirs*, p. 338 (second quotation).

33. Hugh Heclo, *Studying the Presidency: A Report to the Ford Foundation* (New York: Ford Foundation, 1977), pp. 33–37; Rose, *Managing Presidential Objectives*, p. 32; Kessel, *Domestic Presidency*, pp. 17–18.

34. John C. Whitaker, *Striking a Balance: Environment and Natural Resources Policy in the Nixon-Ford Years* (Washington, D.C.: American Enterprise Institute, 1976), pp. 43–47; Kessel, *Domestic Presidency*, pp. 19–23; Marian D. Irish, "The President's Foreign Policy Machine," in *The Future of the American Presidency*, ed. Charles W. Dunn (Morristown, N.J.: General Learning Press), p. 162; Arnold, *Making the Managerial Presidency*, pp. 282–292. On February 27, 1970, the *New York Times* reported that of fifty-seven actions taken by the president to reorganize government programs, forty-three were administrative and only fourteen required congressional approval (p. 14).

35. For example, the heads of Housing and Urban Development, HEW, and the Treasury and Agriculture Departments were to be given responsibility for community development, human resources, economic affairs, and natural resources, respectively. These supersecretaries were to have direct and frequent access to Nixon and his White House staff. In addition, four White House assistants—Haldeman, Ehrlichman, Ash, and Kissinger—were assigned the task of integrating policies and operations throughout the executive branch. See Arnold, *Making the Managerial Presidency*, pp. 294–301; Nathan, *Plot That Failed*, pp. 49–59; idem, *Administrative Presidency*, pp. 50–53; Whitaker, *Striking a Balance*, pp. 44–45.

36. Richard P. Nathan, "The 'Administrative Presidency,' " *The Public Interest*, 44 (Summer 1976), 41–44.

37. Haynes Johnson, *In the Absence of Power: Governing America* (New York: Viking, 1980), p. 58.

38. Destler, "Nixon System," p. 13.

39. David E. Wilson, *The National Planning Idea in U.S. Public Policy: Five Alternative Approaches* (Boulder, Colo.: Westview Press, 1980), p. 72; see also John Hart, "Executive Reorganization in the U.S.A. and the Growth of Presidential Power," *Public Administration*, 52 (Summer 1974), 179–208; Arnold, *Making the Managerial Presidency*, pp. 300–302.

40. James William Fulbright, *Old Myths and New Realities, and*

Other Commentaries (New York: Random House, 1964), p. 6.

41. Nathan, *Plot That Failed*, p. 19.

42. Michael D. Reagan and John G. Sanzone, *The New Federalism*, 2d ed. (New York: Oxford University Press, 1981), pp. 3–29.

43. Nathan, *Plot That Failed*, pp. 17–34; idem, *Administrative Presidency*, pp. 15–27; Safire, *Before the Fall*, pp. 275–295.

44. Otis L. Graham, Jr., *Toward a Planned Society: From Roosevelt to Nixon* (New York: Oxford University Press, 1976), pp. 187–263 (quotation p. 256). See also the sources cited in the previous note.

45. Reichley, *Conservatives in an Age of Change*, pp. 165–166 (quotation), 167–173. What Reichley calls "the felt loss of community" (p. 173) remains the driving force behind the strong emotional appeal of Reagan's New Federalism, although the latter's fiscal foundations are quite different: whereas Nixon's was grounded in expanding revenue sharing and block grants, Reagan's has been grounded in budget cuts and the elimination of such programs. See Nathan, *Administrative Presidency*, pp. 60–61; *New York Times*, January 31, 1987, p. 7 (evaluating the negative impact of the official end of the revenue-sharing program on September 30, 1987). The best private set of in-house memoranda on the origins of Nixon's revenue-sharing program (which ultimately affected more local governments than has any other federal program in history) is the Robert H. Finch Papers, Occidental College, Los Angeles, California. Because these papers remain unprocessed, no box numbers or folder titles are available for the copies now in my possession. Unfortunately, the revenue-sharing material opened by NARA in May 1987 does not contain as complete decision-making information about revenue-sharing policy as had been anticipated because of last-minute withdrawals of documents by representatives of the former president. This is particularly true of documents in the Ehrlichman papers. See Staff Members and Office Files (SMOF), Alphabetical Subject Files 1963[68]–1973, boxes 23–25, NPMP, WHSF, NARA. Less useful than they should be on the subject of revenue sharing, because his correspondence with Nixon is still classified, are the Arthur Burns Papers, Nixon White House Files (NWHF), 1969–70, box A19, Gerald R. Ford Library, Ann Arbor, Michigan. However, material in box A32 clearly shows the trade-off between revenue sharing and welfare that Burns helped to forge.

46. Nathan, *Plot That Failed*, pp. 70–76.

47. Hostility between the White House and the federal bureaucracy had already reached dangerous levels over Nixon's attempts to restructure the executive branch. The New Federalism simply exacerbated this hostility because certain aspects of it were inextricably involved with organizational reform. It is Haldeman's contention that reorganization in all its forms, including its New Federalist features, constitutes the "secret story of Watergate." As Nixon moved "to control the executive branch from the White House . . . the great power blocs in Washington" turned against him and

were ready to take advantage of Watergate in any way possible by the beginning of his second term; *The Ends of Power* (New York: Times Books, 1978), pp. 167–181; see also Nathan, *Plot That Failed*, pp. 81–89.

48. Reichley, *Conservatives in an Age of Change*, p. 259; Nixon, interview with author, January 26, 1983. In discussing this same paradox Nathan has noted that "the New Federalism called for decentralizing some governmental programs and at the same time for centralizing and reforming others where it was deemed appropriate for the national government to have principal responsibility . . . Functions to be decentralized were primarily those involving services provided in the community . . . [but] the administration over time developed an increasingly specific position on the appropriateness of national responsibility for income-transfer programs"; *Administrative Presidency*, pp. 19–21. From a slightly different perspective Peri Arnold concludes that one of the major aims of the Ash Council's recommendations on government reorganization "was to make federal activities at local and regional levels conform to national (read 'presidential') priorities. Thus decentralization was not meant to bring with it a devolution of [presidential] power"; *Making the Managerial Presidency*, pp. 291–293. Or, as David E. Wilson has said: "At the same time that Nixon moved to tighten his control of the government, he sought to loosen the basic social, administrative, and economic controls that government exercised over American society"; *National Planning Idea*, p. 162. Also see Dorothy Buckton James, "The Future of the Institutionalized Presidency," in Dunn, *Future of the American Presidency*, pp. 110–111.

49. White, *Making of the President, 1972*, p. 358; Safire, *Before the Fall*, p. 283. Safire created the term *national localism* in order to convey the New Federalist sense of national unity and local diversity. My term *regional globalism* is a shorthand way of describing an international economic phenomenon increasingly evident since the 1970s, namely, the significance of regional economic blocs. Nixon understood that "pragmatic regionalism rather than ideological or idealistic internationalism [was] the key to understanding geopolitical economic practices"; Joan Hoff-Wilson, "Economic Issues and Foreign Policy," in *Guide to American Foreign Relations since 1700*, ed. Richard Dean Burns (Santa Barbara Calif.: ABC-Clio, 1983), p. 1145. also see Hoff-Wilson, *Nixon without Watergate: A Presidency Reconsidered* (forthcoming), chap. 9; Robert S. Litwak, *Détente and the Nixon Doctrine: American Foreign Policy and the Pursuit of Stability, 1969–1976* (Cambridge: Cambridge University Press, 1984).

50. Rose, *Managing Presidential Objectives*, p. 50.

51. Rangell, *Mind of Watergate*, p. 35.

52. Alexander L. George, *Presidential Decisionmaking in Foreign Policy: The Effective Use of Information and Advice* (Boulder, Colo.: Westview Press, 1980), pp. 145–168. Roger B. Porter has used the terms *centralized management, multiple advocacy,* and *adhocracy* to describe roughly

the same three organizational approaches; *Presidential Decision Making: The Economic Policy Board* (Cambridge: Cambridge University Press, 1980), pp. 25–29, 229–252.

53. George, *Presidential Decisionmaking in Foreign Policy*, pp. 148 (quotation), 154–155; Johnson, *Managing the White House*, pp. 199–201, 209–210, 220, 227, 238. Both of these studies rely heavily on a psychological profile of Nixon as a "conflict avoider" that Nixon himself denies. "Those who have said I am not capable of confronting people one-on-one," he told me, "have not dealt with me one-on-one"; January 26, 1983, interview. In contrast, Porter views the NSC and Domestic Council systems under Nixon as a combination of centralized management *and* multiple advocacy; *Presidential Decision Making*, p. 237.

54. George, *Presidential Decisionmaking in Foreign Policy*, p. 152.

55. Hoff-Wilson, *Nixon without Watergate*, chap. 1; J. Anthony Lukas, *Nightmare: The Underside of the Nixon Years* (New York: Viking, 1976), passim; Rangell, *Mind of Watergate*, p. 22.

56. Heclo, *Studying the Presidency*, p. 32; Paul Johnson, *Modern Times: The World from the Twenties to the Eighties* (New York: Harper & Row, 1983), pp. 295–298, 709.

57. Paul J. Halpern, "Personality, Politics and the Presidency—The Strange Case of Richard Nixon," August 1, 1973, Brodie Papers, box 49.

58. Hoff-Wilson, *Nixon without Watergate*, chaps. 4, 5.

59. Dan Rather, interview with Fawn Brodie, August 3, 1975; John Lindsay, interview with Brodie, April 16, 1975, Brodie Papers, boxes 43 and 42, respectively. See also Wills, *Nixon Agonistes*, pp. 13–14.

60. Nixon, interview with author, January 26, 1983; Halpern, "Personality, Politics, and the Presidency."

61. Halpern, "Personality, Politics, and the Presidency."

62. Price interview with Haldeman, November 10, 1975. In this interview Haldeman defended the abruptness with which Nixon called for the resignation of his entire cabinet following his reelection on the grounds that this move had been discussed for some time, was well thought out, and was "even-handed" in that it displaced "everybody on an equal basis all at the same time." Later, however, Haldeman admitted that it angered "not only Democrats but our own people who served us loyally and honorably. But ruthless was the only attitude that would work, and because of it in January 1973 we were well on the way to the point where the Administration could, for the first time in decades, be controlled by a President. And that caused pure fright in Washington because this President was Richard M. Nixon"; *Ends of Power*, p. 167.

63. Osborne, *First Two Years of Nixon Watch*, 2:xi.

64. Reichley, *Conservatives in an Age of Change*, p. 257.

65. Schell, *Time of Illusion*, pp. 111–116. For a defense of the "Houston Plan," see Nixon, *Memoirs*, pp. 475–476. According to Nixon, "The

irony of the controversy over the Houston Plan did not become apparent until a 1975 investigation revealed that the investigative techniques it would have involved had not only been carried out long before I approved the plan but continued to be carried out after I had rescinded my approval of it" (p. 475).

66. Schell, *Time of Illusion*, pp. 59–74, 111–127; Shachtman, *Decade of Shocks*, pp. 259–284.

67. Safire, *Before the Fall*, p. 644; see Hoff-Wilson, *Nixon without Watergate*, chaps. 5, 6.

68. Hoff-Wilson, *Nixon without Watergate*, chaps. 4, 5.

69. Ibid., Introduction and chap. 4.

70. Nixon, interview with author, January 26, 1983.

71. Anna Kasten Nelson, "President Truman and the Evolution of the National Security Council," *Journal of American History*, 72 (September 1985), 360–378; idem, "President Eisenhower and the NSC," pp. 307–326. I. M. Destler has discussed the futile ways in which most administrations have dealt with the problem of separating foreign policy formulation from its implementaton. Like Nathan on domestic matters, Destler believes that " 'operational' decisions are what policy usually consists of," and that attempts to make hard and fast distinctions are largely a waste of time; "Nixon System," p. 10; see also idem, *Presidents, Bureaucrats, and Foreign Policy: The Politics of Organization Reform* (Princeton: Princeton University Press, 1972), pp. 18–22; Nathan, *Plot That Failed*, p. 62.

72. Roger Morris, *Uncertain Greatness: Henry Kissinger and American Foreign Policy* (New York: Harper & Row, 1977), pp. 77–90.

73. Leonard Hall, interview with Fawn Brodie, August 29, 1975, Brodie Papers, box 42.

74. After the Iran-Contra scandal became public at the end of 1986, Henry Kissinger insisted that Nixon's NSC staff engaged only in policy, not in operational, matters. This claim is contradicted by Kissinger's own descriptions of the NSC in his memoirs and, more important, by a full-scale investigation of the NSC in 1974 by the Murphy Commission, whose official name was the Commission on the Organization of the Government for the Conduct of Foreign Policy. Its working papers can be found in Record Group (RG) 220, boxes 1–77, NARA. Questions to Kissinger and his answers are in box 43 and do not always conform with his description of the NSC in Kissinger, *White House Years* (Boston: Little, Brown, 1979), pp. 38–48. Also see Destler, "Nixon System," pp. 10–11. Writing in 1974, Destler observed that Nixon and Kissinger's " 'two-man' system for conducting our foreign policy has come to rest not on the once-emphasized distinction between 'policy' and 'operations' " (p. 10). Moreover, he noted that Nixon and Kissinger assumed at the time that their "two-man system could dominate the operational decisions that count" (p. 11). And, for better and sometimes worse, they did. What Destler did not realize in 1974 was that Nixon and

Kissinger also intended to bypass the NSC entirely whenever they did not need bureaucratic support for their covert operational decisions.

75. For a detailed analysis of both events based on declassified information, see Hoff-Wilson, *Nixon without Watergate*, chap. 7.

76. Ibid.; Guenter Lewy, *American in Vietnam* (New York: Oxford University Press, 1978), pp. 418–441; General Bruce Palmer, Jr., *The 25-Year War: America's Military Role in Vietnam* (Lexington: University Press of Kentucky, 1984), pp. 122–151; Hersch, *Price of Power*, pp. 610–638; William Shawcross, *Sideshow: Kissinger, Nixon, and the Destruction of Cambodia* (New York: Simon and Schuster, 1979), pp. 259–279; Tad Szulc, *The Illusion of Peace: Foreign Policy in the Nixon Years* (New York: Viking, 1978), pp. 653–684.

77. Hoff-Wilson, *Nixon without Watergate*, chap. 7; Morris, *Uncertain Greatness*, pp. 91–92; Szulc, *Illusion of Peace*, p. 200.

78. Hoff-Wilson, *Nixon without Watergate*, chap. 7; Shawcross, *Sideshow*, pp. 19–30. The relevant declassified documents on which this interpretation is based are Joint Chiefs of Staff Memoranda 558–68 (December 13, 1968), 558–69 (February 29, 1969), and 207–69 (April 9, 1969)—all with enclosures, Department of Defense; and Melvin Laird, interview with author, October 15, 1984, Washington, D.C.

79. Haldeman, *Ends of Power*, pp. 82–83.

80. Nixon, interview with author, June 6, 1984, New York City.

81. Seymour M. Hersh, *The Price of Power: Kissinger in the Nixon White House* (New York: Summit Books, 1983), pp. 52–53 (quotation); Hoff-Wilson, *Nixon without Watergate*, chap. 7.

82. Raymond Price, interview with author, January 26, 1983; see also Hoff-Wilson, *Nixon without Watergate*, chap. 6.

83. Hoff-Wilson, *Nixon without Watergate*, chaps. 8, 9.

84. Ibid., chap. 8; Nixon, interview with author, January 26, 1983.

85. For the most recent defense of Nixon's foreign policy successes see Sulzberger, *World and Richard Nixon*. The best general evaluation of Nixon's and Kissinger's diplomacy remains Seyom Brown, *The Crisis of Power: Foreign Policy in the Kissinger Years* (New York: Columbia University Press, 1979).

86. Halpern, "Personality, Politics and the Presidency."

87. For Nixon's "decade of reform" statement see *Public Papers of the Presidents: Richard Nixon, 1969* (Washington, D.C.: Government Printing Office, 1970), p. 789. The refusal of liberals or radicals to give his domestic programs any credence at the time is best represented in Alan Gartner, Colin Greer, and Frank Riessman, eds., *What Nixon Is Doing to Us* (New York: Harper & Row, 1973).

88. In addition to the two interviews I have cited throughout this chapter, aspects of Nixon's "rehabilitation" are discussed in the following: *New York Times*, June 13, 1985, p. 14, and October 16, 1985, p. 24(N);

Christian Science Monitor, October 8, 1985, p. 16; *Wall Street Journal,* October 8, 1985, p. 30(E); *Washington Post,* February 24, 1983, p. A15, and October 14, 1985, p. A2; *Newsweek,* May 19, 1986, pp. 26–34; and *Los Angeles Times,* March 8, 1984, pp. 1, 14.

89. John Ehrlichman, interview with author, April 9, 1984, Santa Fe, N.M.; Raymond Price, interview with author, January 26, 1983. Price's earlier account essentially accords with Ehrlichman's; Price said that except for the parks issue, the "environment was not an emotional issue for Nixon," but because the "press was in bed with the environmental extremists . . . the President got a bad press" on environmental questions when in fact he "was ten years ahead of his time." Gallup and other pollsters did not think the environment important enough to include in their questionnaires until 1965. In the five years from 1965 to 1970 concern about water pollution rose from a little over one-third to almost two-thirds. See Hazel Erskine, "The Polls: Pollution and Its Cost," *Public Opinion Quarterly,* Spring 1972, p. 121.

90. Professor Sally Fairfax, interview with author, October 21, 1980, Environmental Studies Department, University of California, Berkeley.

91. Whitaker, *Striking a Balance,* pp. 27–31, 79–80; Raymond Price, interview with author, January 26, 1983. Ehrlichman's involvement in national growth and land use policies is well documented in the private papers of John Roy Price and in my interview with him on February 6, 1980. Price was a founder of the Ripon Society who became counsel for the UAC under Moynihan. Files under the names John Whitaker, Richard K. Fairbanks, and L. Edwin Coate, SMOF, WHCF, NPMP, NARA (hereafter cited as SMOF), opened in December 1986, now constitute the single best source of primary material on formulation of environmental policy during the Nixon years. For poll data gathered by White House aides on environmental issues in an effort to convince Nixon of its growing importance, see Coate to Whitaker, June 1, 1971, Coate, box 153; and Whitaker memoranda, May 12 and 26, June 21 and 29, 1971, and Thomas W. Benham (president of Opinion Research Corporation) to Whitaker, June 22, 1971—all in Whitaker, box 4, SMOF.

92. Ehrlichman, interview with author, April 9, 1984.

93. Details about how hard Nixon's staff worked to keep water pollution legislation within the spending ceilings they had set can be found in Whitaker, boxes 4, 113, 114, and 149, SMOF. Whitaker told Ehrlichman on October 5, 1971, that "the political fallout if the President ever vetoes a Water Bill will be disastrous for him." On October 9, 1972, Whitaker urged Nixon to sign the bill he and Ehrlichman had tried so hard to defeat on the grounds that, given the state of antipollution technology, the additional $18 billion it contained would only marginally improve water quality. These files indicate that Nixon had decided as early as July 24, 1972, to veto the legislation if it violated his spending ceiling, even though he knew that his

veto would not be sustained. When Congress overrode his veto Nixon refused to appropriate the full additional $18 billion Congress had authorized,
"impounding" half. In 1975 the Supreme Court finally ruled that the executive branch could not curtail use of these funds by reducing authorized
allotment to individual states. This ruling was the result of suits brought
against the head of EPA, Russell Train, who agreed with Nixon and his staff
that the additional spending would not improve overall water quality in
the United States. See also Whitaker, *Striking a Balance*, pp. 79–92.

94. For example, while still campaigning for the presidential nomination Nixon said on May 15: "at the present time, I do not see a reasonable
prospect that I will recommend . . . a guaranteed annual income or a negative income tax." Later, on October 25 and 28, he stated that welfare should
be based on "national standards," should preserve "the dignity of the individual and the integrity of the family," and should provide incentives for
moving people "onto private payrolls." Personally he was known to harbor
a distrust of social workers and to think that Johnson's "welfare system
was an 'utter disaster' and required fundamental change"; Kenneth H. Bowler, *The Nixon Guaranteed Income Proposal: Substance and Process in
Policy Change* (Cambridge, Mass.: Ballinger, 1974), p. 39; see also Daniel
P. Moynihan, *The Politics of a Guaranteed Annual Income: The Nixon
Administration and the Family Assistance Plan* (New York: Random House,
1973), pp. 67–68.

95. Vincent J. Burke and Vee Burke, *Nixon's Good Deed: Welfare
Reform* (New York: Columbia University Press, 1974), pp. 167–211; Reichley, *Conservatives in an Age of Change*, pp. 138–153; Bowler, *Nixon Guaranteed Income Proposal*, pp. 83–147.

96. Martha Derthick, *Policy Making for Social Security* (Washington,
D.C.: Brookings Institution, 1979), pp. 357–368.

97. Martha Derthick, *Uncontrollable Spending for Social Service
Grants* (Washington, D.C.: Brookings, Institution, 1975), pp. 35–42; Jodie
T. Allen, "Last of the Big Spenders: Richard Nixon and the Greater Society,"
Washington Post, February 24, 1983, p. A15. From 1969 to 1971 the per-
centage of federal budget outlays for defense dropped from 43 to 36 percent,
and by 1975 to 26 percent. In the same years human resource outlays (including payments to individuals) increased from 34 to 42 and then to 51
percent. Although some of this spending represented Social Security, Medicare, and Medicaid increases, which Nixon only reluctantly approved, it
also represented his initiatives in the area of food stamps, health insurance,
family assistance, and, of course, the COLAs. See Nathan, *Adminstrative
Presidency*, chart on p. 25.

98. Reichley, *Conservatives in an Age of Change*, pp. 174–176, 179–
180. Nixon told me on January 26, 1983, that he had always been for civil
rights for blacks and equal rights for women, not because it would "help"
members of either group but because "it is fair," and that it was good for
the nation because it prevented "wasted talent."

99. *Statistical Abstract of the United States* (Washington, D.C.: Government Printing Office, 1978), p. 151; *Washington Post*, July 4, 1972, pp. A11–12; Reichley, *Conservatives in an Age of Change*, pp. 176–178.

100. Hoff-Wilson, *Nixon without Watergate*, chap. 5.

101. *Congressional Quarterly*, February 14, 1969, pp. 255–261; *New York Post*, June 20, 1969, p. 14; *Public Papers of Nixon, 1969*, p. 3.

102. Hoff-Wilson, *Nixon without Watergate*, chap. 5.

103. Ibid.; Reichley, *Conservatives in an Age of Change*, pp. 185–199.

104. *Statistical Abstract of the United States*, p. 151.

105. "White House Fact Sheet," August 18, 1972, Finch Papers.

106. Stein, *Presidential Eonomics*, pp. 175–187; Safire, *Before the Fall*, pp. 659–686.

107. Nixon, interview with author, January 26, 1983. For a review of Nixon's domestic and foreign economic policies see Hoff-Wilson, *Nixon without Watergate*, chaps. 5, 10; Stein, *Presidential Economics*, pp. 133–207.

108. Peter G. Peterson, *A Foreign Economic Perspective* (Washington, D.C.: Government Printing Office, 1972), p. 2.

109. Peter M. Flannigan, CIEP executive director, testimony to Murphy Commission, RG 220, box 41, p. 209, NARA.

110. Ibid., pp. 212, 214.

111. For example, a 1982 poll of specialists in U.S. history and politics rated Nixon a failure as president, ranking him above only Grant and Harding; Murray and Blessing, "Presidential Performance Study," p. 540. Although the survey instrument employed in this poll is one of the most reliable and sophisticated, some of its analytical conclusions are contradicted by Nixon's failure rating. Perhaps the most glaring of these contradictions is a concluding one which suggests (citing another presidential poll) that "a president's prestige has its closest correlation with the accomplishments of his administration," and accomplishments in turn are related to his "activeness." In other words, if historians do indeed "rate presidents mainly on the basis of their *actual* presidential accomplishments" (p. 555), apparently, in responding to this latest poll in 1981 and 1982, they could not remember any accomplishments by Nixon or any positive actions during his six years in office. This evaluation was confirmed in a somewhat backhanded way in the May 19, 1986, issue of *Newsweek*, which, after proclaiming that Nixon had "rehabilitated himself," quoted scholars who denied that this was possible because of Watergate (p. 27).

112. Chester, Hodgson, and Page, *American Melodrama*, p. 224.

7. Gerald R. Ford

1. Henry Kissinger, "Special Introduction to *A Time to Heal*," in Gerald R. Ford, *A Time to Heal* (Norwalk, Conn.: Easton Press, 1987), p. 2. This chapter draws not only upon Ford's memoir and an interview with

the former president, but also upon the author's experience on the White House staff throughout the Ford administration.

2. Gerald R. Ford, *A Time to Heal* (New York: Harper & Row, 1979), p. 38.

3. For a reasonably complete and accurate account of the origins of the transition team, see James M. Naughton, "The Change in Presidents: Plans Began Months Ago," *New York Times*, August 26, 1974, pp. 1, 24. Other useful accounts of the transition team's work are David S. Broder, "Ford Team Seeks Small, Open Staff," *Washington Post*, August 17, 1974; Godfrey Sperling, Jr., "Ford Method: Quiet Transition," *Christian Science Monitor*, August 16, 1974. The actual transition team included several others who were not publicly announced on August 9: Senator Robert Griffin, Philip Buchen, former congressman John Byrnes, William Whyte, and L. William Seidman.

4. Ford, *A Time to Heal*, p. 146.

5. "Q. You have been accused of moving too slowly in putting your own stamp and personality on this Administration. You have talked about the standards by which you are going to judge members of the Cabinet. Do you plan, other than what you have mentioned before about the Cabinet, to move more quickly in making this a Ford Administration, rather than a Ford-Nixon Administration?

"A. I think that the most important job for me to do at the outset was to put a Ford Administration into the White House. That is about 99 percent achieved at the present time. Nobody in the old Administration who at the top level had any responsibility is still here"; "How It Looked to Ford," *Newsweek*, December 9, 1974.

6. Ford, *A Time to Heal*, p. 114.

7. Ibid., p. 185.

8. Ibid., p. 148.

9. Ibid., p. 241.

10. Gerald R. Ford, interview with author, December 4, 1986, Washington, D.C.

11. Ford, *A Time to Heal*, p. 136.

12. Ibid., p. 141.

13. Ibid., pp. 252–253.

14. The changes, which Ford announced at his November 3, 1975, press conference, included: Donald Rumsfeld, replacing James Schlesinger as secretary of defense; Brent Scowcroft replacing Henry Kissinger as assistant to the president for national security affairs (Kissinger remained as secretary of state); George Bush replacing William Colby as director of the Central Intelligence Agency; Richard Cheney replacing Donald Rumsfeld as assistant to the president with responsibility for coordinating the White House staff; and Elliot Richardson replacing Rogers Morton as secretary of commerce; *Public Papers of the Presidents: Gerald R. Ford, 1975, Book II*

(Washington, D.C.: Government Printing Office, 1977), pp. 1791–1804.

For the most thorough account of the events leading up to and following the November 3 announcement on personnel changes, see John Osborne, *White House Watch: The Ford Years* (Washington, D.C.: New Republic Books, 1977), pp. xxiv–xxxiii, 216–228. See also Robert T. Hartmann, *Palace Politics* (New York: McGraw-Hill, 1980), pp. 360–379.

15. Gerald R. Ford, interview with author, December 4, 1986.

16. Ford, *A Time to Heal*, p. 31.

17. Ibid., p. 126.

18. Hartmann, *Palace Politics*, pp. 180–181.

19. Ford, *A Time to Heal*, p. 127.

20. Roger B. Porter, *Presidential Decision Making: The Economic Policy Making Board* (New York: Cambridge University Press, 1980), p. 101. Sectoral meetings were held on finance; labor; agriculture and food; housing and construction; natural resources and recreation; health, education, income security, and social services; transportation; science and technology; and business and industry. Preparatory meetings were also held by representatives from state and local governments, along with two sessions by a nonpartisan group of economists; *The Conference on Inflation* (Washington, D.C.: Government Printing Office, 1974).

21. Ford, *A Time to Heal*, pp. 141–142, 181–182. That Ford attached great importance to his amnesty program is shown by the fact that it is one of the few issues he discusses twice in his memoir. The program permitted draft dodgers to escape punishment if they satisfied three conditions: presented themselves to a U.S. attorney before January 31, 1975; pledged allegiance to the United States and agreed to fulfill a two-year period of alternative service; and satisfactorily completed that two-year obligation. Deserters could escape punishment by pledging allegiance to the United States and spending two years in the branch of the service to which they had belonged.

22. Ibid., p. 178. For Ford's account of the entire pardon episode see pp. 157–181. The other most detailed insider account is Hartmann, *Palace Politics*, pp. 240–271.

23. Ford, *A Time to Heal*, p. 178.

24. Ibid., pp. 148, 152, 207, 257.

25. Ibid., pp. 34–35.

26. Ibid., p. 38.

27. Ibid., p. 147.

28. Ibid., pp. 185–186.

29. Gerald R. Ford, interview with author, December 4, 1986.

30. Ford claims that putting Robert Hartmann in charge of his vice-presidential staff was "a dreadful mistake." He invited Bill Seidman to organize his vice-presidential office because "I desperately needed a first-class manager." His assessment of Donald Rumsfeld echoes this priority:

"Above all, he was a superior administrator"; Ford, *A Time to Heal*, pp. 118, 130.

31. Ibid., p. 132.
32. Gerald R. Ford, interview with author, December 4, 1986.
33. Ibid.
34. *Public Papers of the Presidents: Gerald R. Ford, 1974* (Washington, D.C.: Government Printing Office, 1974), pp. 733–735.
35. Gerald R. Ford, interview with author, December 4, 1986.
36. Ford, *A Time to Heal*, p. 133.
37. Gerald R. Ford, interview with author, December 4, 1986.
38. Porter, *Presidential Decision Making*, pp. 68–69.
39. Ibid., p. 203.
40. For an illustration of the important role in shaping policy played by both the President's Labor-Management Committee and the transition team, see ibid., pp. 109–120.
41. These models are described and evaluated in ibid., pp. 229–252.
42. Ford, *A Time to Heal*, p. 129.
43. Ibid.
44. Ibid., p. 30.
45. Kissinger, "Special Introduction to *A Time to Heal*," p. 4.
46. Ford, *A Time to Heal*, p. 199.
47. Ibid., pp. 253–254.
48. Gerald R. Ford, interview with author, December 4, 1986.
49. Ibid.
50. Ibid.
51. Ford, *A Time to Heal*, pp. 234–235.
52. Porter, *Presidential Decision Making*, p. 178.
53. Ibid., p. 212.
54. Transition team briefing document for the President, August 15, 1974.
55. Haig Memorandum to the President, "Economic Organization," September 19, 1974.
56. Gerald R. Ford, interview with author, December 4, 1986.
57. Porter, *Presidential Decision Making*, p. 175.
58. Ibid.
59. Ibid., p. 176.
60. Ibid., p. 192.

8. Jimmy Carter

1. Richard E. Neustadt, *Presidential Power: The Politics of Leadership from FDR to Carter* (New York: Wiley, 1980).
2. Robert C. Tucker, *Politics as Leadership* (Columbia: University of Missouri Press, 1981), chap. 1; Erwin C. Hargrove and Michael Nelson,

Presidents, Politics, and Policy (Baltimore: Johns Hopkins University Press, 1984), chap. 4.

3. Ben W. Heineman, Jr., and Curtis A. Hessler, *Memorandum for the President: A Strategic Approach to Domestic Affairs in the 1980s* (New York: Random House, 1980), chap. 1.

4. Bert A. Rockman, *The Leadership Question, the Presidency, and the American System* (New York: Praeger, 1984), chaps. 5, 6.

5. Carter, Carter Presidency Project, 19: 6, 69, University of Virginia, Miller Center of Public Affairs (hereafter cited as CPP). The CPP volumes are transcripts of oral history interviews conducted by panels of scholars with each of the principal persons and staff groups in the Carter White House. These interviews, begun in 1981, are currently being used, with the permission of the respondents, as source material for a series of monographs on the Carter presidency sponsored by the Miller Center. Upon completion of this series the transcripts will be deposited in the Carter Presidential Library in Atlanta, where they will become available to other researchers in accordance with conditions stipulated by the respondents, the Miller Center, and the Carter Library. In the interests of confidentiality, the respondents are not cited by name in the following notes.

6. Jimmy Carter, *Why Not the Best?* (New York: Bantam Books, 1966), p. 101.

7. Ibid., pp. 105–106.

8. Ibid., p. 99.

9. CPP, 10: 85.

10. CPP, 16: 85.

11. Charles O. Jones, *The Trusteeship Presidency: Jimmy Carter and the United States Congress*, vol. 1 of *Retrospectives on the Carter Presidency*, ed. James Sterling Young (Baton Rouge: Louisiana State University Press, 1988).

12. Carter, CPP, 19: 70.

13. CPP, 13: 60.

14. CPP, 7: 14.

15. Rosalynn Carter, "Late Night America," August 27, 1984, Public Broadcasting System.

16. CPP, 11: 65; 20: 45; 18: 45.

17. CPP, 13: 51–53, 63.

18. Zbigniew Brzezinski, *Power and Principle: Memoirs of the National Security Adviser* (New York: Farrar, Straus and Giroux, 1983), p. 68; CPP, 7: 36, 53.

19. CPP, 14: 29.

20. Dewey W. Grantham, *Southern Progressivism: The Reconciliation of Progress and Tradition* (Knoxville: University of Tennessee Press, 1983), pp. xv, xviii, xxii, 413–442.

21. William C. Havard, Jr., "Southern Politics: Old and New Style,"

in *The American South, Portrait of a Culture,* ed. Louis D. Rubin, Jr. (Baton Rouge: Louisana State University Press, 1979), pp. 56–59.

22. Brzezinski, *Power and Principle,* pp. 30–31, 432.

23. James Fallows, "The Passionless Presidency," *Atlantic Monthly,* May 1979, p. 42.

24. "Jimmy Carter Talks about His Inner Life," interview with Bill Moyers, *Washington Post,* May 11, 1976, p. A-19.

25. CPP, 19: 16–17.

26. CPP, 20: 7.

27. CPP, 17: 38.

28. Richard E. Neustadt and Ernest R. May, *Thinking in Time: The Uses of History for Decision Makers* (New York: Free Press, 1986), chap. 7.

29. CPP, 19: 16–17.

30. CPP, 13: 58.

31. Jimmy Carter, *Keeping Faith: Memoirs of a President* (New York: Bantam Books, 1982), pp. 56–57; CPP, 19: 32–33.

32. Jules Witcover, *Marathon: The Pursuit of the Presidency* (New York: Viking, 1977), pp. 109–110.

33. Carter, *Why Not the Best?* p. 3.

34. Witcover, *Marathon,* p. 306.

35. CPP, 13: 10–11.

36. Heineman and Hessler, *Memorandum for the President,* p. 252.

37. Stanley Hoffman, "Détente," in *The Making of America's Soviet Policy,* ed. Joseph S. Nye, Jr. (New Haven: Yale University Press, 1984), pp. 238–239, 244, 248, 254–257.

38. Carter, *Keeping Faith,* p. 142; Hoffman, "Détente," pp. 257–259; William Schneider, "Public Opinions," in Nye, *Making of America's Soviet Policy,* pp. 20–21.

39. White House domestic policy assistant, Memorandum on development of the economic stimulus package, 1983, pp. 1–2, Carter Presidential Library, Atlanta.

40. CPP, 16: 18–19; Charles Schultze, "The Council of Economic Advisers Under Chairman Charles Schultze, 1977–1981, 'Summary History' and 'Oral History Interview,' " in *The President and the Council of Economic Advisers: Interviews with CEA Chairmen,* ed. Erwin C. Hargrove and Samuel A. Moreley (Boulder, Colo.: Westview Press, 1984), pp. 463, 476–478; White House domestic policy assistant, Memorandum on economic package, 1983, p. 11.

41. White House domestic policy assistant, Memorandum on economic package, 1983, p. 22; CPP, 11: 29; 19: 12.

42. Carter, *Keeping Faith,* pp. 77–78; CPP, 19: 68–69.

43. Walter W. Heller, "The Council of Economic Advisers under Chairman Walter W. Heller, 1961–1964, 'Summary History' and 'Oral His-

tory Interview,' " in Hargrove and Moreley, *President and Council of Economic Advisers*, pp. 200–202.

44. CPP, 11: 2–4.

45. Schultze, "CEA under Schultze," pp. 482, 487.

46. W. Bowman Cutter, "The Presidency and Economic Policy: A Tale of Two Budgets," in *The Presidency and the Political System*, ed. Michael Nelson (Washington, D.C.: Congressional Quarterly Press, 1984), pp. 482–483; CPP, 11: 43–44.

47. Schultze, "CEA under Schultze," pp. 493–495; CPP, 6: 114–115.

48. Schultze, "CEA under Schultze," p. 485; CPP, 13: 89; Heinemann and Hessler, *Memorandum for the President*, pp. 264–265.

49. Cutter, "Presidency and Economic Policy," p. 481.

50. CPP, 11: 2–4, 46–47, 78; Schultze, "CEA under Schultze," pp. 459–461.

51. CPP, 10: 91; 13: 63.

52. CPP, 19: 48.

53. Laurence E. Lynn, Jr., and David deF. Whitman, *The President as Policymaker: Jimmy Carter and Welfare Reform* (Philadelphia: Temple University Press, 1981), pp. 44, 88–89; Joseph A. Califano, Jr., *Governing America: An Insider's Report from the White House and the Cabinet* (New York: Simon and Schuster, 1981), pp. 329–334.

54. Lynn and Whitman, *President as Policymaker*, pp. 136, 192; Califano, *Governing America*, pp. 3–34.

55. Former Carter assistant, interview with author, August 24, 1983, Washington, D.C.

56. Heinemann and Hessler, *Memorandum for the President*, pp. 286–287; Lynn and Whitman, *President as Policymaker*, pp. 149–152, 250; Califano, *Governing America*, p. 361; CPP, 13: 33.

57. CPP, 13: 10.

58. Heinemann and Hessler, *Memorandum for the President*, pp. 278, 293.

59. Jones, *Trusteeship Presidency*, chap. 6.

60. CPP, 17: 54; *Congressional Quarterly Weekly*, April 23, 1977, pp. 735–755.

61. Jones, *Trusteeship Presidency*, chap. 6.

62. Ibid., chap. 7.

63. CPP, 13: 69–70; Harold L. Wolman and Astrid D. Merget, "The Presidency and Policy Formulation: President Carter and Urban Policy," *Presidential Studies Quarterly*, 10 (Summer 1980), 403; Robert Reinhold, "How Urban Policy Gets Made—Very Carefully," *New York Times*, April 2, 1978.

64. Willis D. Hawley and Beryl A. Radin, "The Presidency and Domestic Policy: Organizing the Department of Education," in Nelson, *Presidency and the Political System*, p. 459; Former PRP official, interview with

author, Washington, D.C., August 25, 1983; Carter White House assistant, interview with author, Washington, D.C., August 24, 1983.

65. Carter, *Why Not the Best?* pp. 177–178; idem, *Keeping Faith,* pp. 142–144; Brzezinski, *Power and Principle,* pp. 48–49, 520–521; Cyrus M. Vance, *Hard Choices: Critical Years in America's Foreign Policy* (New York: Simon and Schuster, 1983), p. 157.

66. William McKinley Runyon, *Life Histories and Psychobiography: Explanations in Theory and Method* (New York: Oxford University Press, 1984), p. 93. Runyon describes how individuals go through life creating situations that will evoke the actions they wish to take.

67. Rosalynn Carter, "Late Night America," August 27, 1984, Public Broadcasting System; Carter, *Keeping Faith,* pp. 315, 317; Vance, *Hard Choices,* pp. 78, 445–446.

68. Neustadt and May, *Thinking in Time,* chap. 7; William B. Quandt, *Camp David, Peacemaking and Policies* (Washington, D.C.: Brookings Institution, 1986), pp. 179, 207, 212–219, 235–239, 247.

69. Hoffmann, "Détente," pp. 253–259.

70. Schneider, "Public Opinions," pp. 20–21.

71. Hargrove and Morley, *President and Council of Economic Advisers,* pp. 1–44.

72. Lester M. Salamon and Alan J. Abramson, "Governance: The Politics of Retrenchment," in *The Reagan Record: An Assessment of America's Changing Domestic Priorities,* ed. John L. Palmer and Isabel V. Sawhill (Cambridge, Mass.: 1984), pp. 42–44.

73. Lynn and Whitman, *President as Policymaker,* p. 239.

74. Carter, *Keeping Faith,* pp. 53–55; Erwin C. Hargrove, *Jimmy Carter as President: A Study of Policy Leadership,* vol. 2 of *Retrospectives of the Carter Presidency,* ed. James Sterling Young (Baton Rouge: Louisiana State University Press, 1988), chap. 5.

75. Carter, *Keeping Faith,* p. 230.

76. Former Carter assistant, interview with author, Washington, D.C., April 5, 1983.

77. Jones, *Trusteeship Presidency,* chap. 8.

78. CPP, 13: 42–43, 50.

79. CPP, 7: 50–51, 53; Jones, *Trusteeship Presidency,* chap. 7.

80. Ibid.

81. Ibid.

82. Ibid. and fig. 7.1.

83. Conversation with the author, October 1976.

84. CPP, 8: 1–2, 8–9.

85. Carter OMB official, interview with author, Washington, D.C., April 4, 1983.

86. CPP, 13: 22.

87. CPP, 15: 51.

88. Hargrove, *Jimmy Carter as President*, chaps. 4 and 5.

89. CPP, 19: 67.

90. Vance, *Hard Choices*, p. 147.

91. Quandt, *Camp David*, pp. 218–219, 290–291.

92. Vance, *Hard Choices*, pp. 59–61.

93. Strode Talbott, *Endgame: The Inside Story of Salt II* (New York: Harper & Row, 1979), pp. 46–48, 54–55, 58–59; Brzezinski, *Power and Principle*, pp. 169–170.

94. Gaddis Smith, *Morality, Reason and Power: American Diplomacy in the Carter Years* (New York: Hill and Wang, 1986), chap. 8.

95. Heinemann, and Hessler, *Memorandum for the President*, chap. 1.

9. Ronald Reagan

1. Alexis de Tocqueville, *Democracy in America*, ed. Phillips Bradley, trans. Henry Reeve, rev. Francis Bowen, 2 vols. (New York: Random House/Vintage, 1954), 2: 21.

2. Consider the president's personal letter to James W. Baker on the latter's resignation as chief of staff: "You have mastered the art of Washington politics, but your roots are still deep in the soil of Texas, and it was there that you learned the fundamental values that you and I share. You know that life can be hard and unpredictable, but you also know that Americans are a people who look forward to the future with optimism. That sense of optimism is the most important thing we have tried to restore to America during the past four years, and it has helped me more than I can say to have someone by my side who understands that bedrock faith in our nation's future as well as you do"; Ronald Reagan to James W. Baker, Febrrurary 1, 1985, in *Weekly Compilation of Presidential Documents*, vol. 21 (Washington, D.C.: Government Printing Office, 1985), 118–119.

3. Unemployment and inflation were both high in 1980 (7.1 and 13.5 percent, respectively), a condition economists dubbed "stagflation"; *Statistical Abstract of the United States, 1987*, 107th ed. (Washington, D.C.: Department of Commerce, 1986), tables 665 and 764. In 1979 President Carter had described the economic uncertainty of the times as follows: "A majority of our people believe that the next five years will be worse than the past five years. The productivity of American workers is actually dropping. We remember when the phrase 'sound as a dollar' was an expression of absolute dependability, until inflation began to shrink our dollar and our savings. There is growing disrespect for government and for churches and for schools. [We have] a system of government that seems incapable of action. [All we see is] paralysis and stagnation and drift. It's a crisis of confidence . . . a growing doubt about the meaning of our own lives and in the loss of unity of purpose for our nation. The symptoms of this crisis are

all around us"; "Address to the Nation," July 15, 1979, in *Weekly Compilation of Presidential Documents*, vol. 15 (Washington, D.C.: Government Printing Office, 1979), 1237.

4. On reciprocity and its benign effects on political behavior, see William K. Muir, Jr., *Legislature: California's School for Politics* (Chicago: University of Chicago Press, 1982).

5. One example of the American capacity for empathy is the fact that in 1986 over 90 million Americans donated a record $87.2 billion to nonprofit charitable and educational organizations; Lawrence Clancy, ed., *Giving USA, 1986* (New York: AAFRC Trust for Philanthropy, 1987), p. 11.

6. Rushworth M. Kidder, "Soviets' Lesson at Andover," *Christian Science Monitor*, February 24, 1986, p. 21.

7. Tocqueville, on the basis of his observations of nineteenth-century America, credited democracy, and not technology, for the fact "that our sensibility is extended to many more objects"; *Democracy in America*, 2: 175.

8. Ibid., p. 115.

9. Joan Didion, *Slouching towards Bethlehem* (New York: Simon and Schuster/Touchstone, 1979), pp. 122–123.

10. Tocqueville, *Democracy in America*, 2: 21.

11. Presidential speechwriter Peggy Noonan, interview with author, December 7, 1984, Washington, D.C.

12. "Commencement at Howard University: 'To Fulfill These Rights,' " June 4, 1965, in *Public Papers of the Presidents of the United States: Lyndon B. Johnson, 1965* (Washington, D.C.: Government Printing Office, 1966), p. 636.

13. *Public Papers of Johnson, 1965*, p. 636.

14. The point is not that Lyndon Johnson thought American life was a civil war. Rather, this specific piece of his rhetoric—and it unquestionably was the single most memorable rhetorical image in his administration—created unconditioned notions implying that all individuals were isolated from one another, that their competition was hostile and antagonistic, and that their race was a struggle to the death. These implications resonated with the modern world's most powerful single testament to material equality ("equality as a fact and as a result"), *The Communist Manifesto*, which, after depicting "the more or less veiled civil war, raging within society," concludes: "The proletarians have nothing to lose but their chains. They have a world to win"; Karl Marx and Friedrich Engels, *The Communist Manifesto* (New York and London: Modern Reader Paperbacks, 1968), pp. 23, 62.

15. Garry Wills, *Nixon Agonistes: The Crisis of the Self-Made Man* (Boston: Houghton Mifflin, 1970), p. 238.

16. The partnership notion probably came from the language of national security (the NATO alliance was a partnership), but it was no doubt

peculiarly congenial to people from the American West. In talking about a speech he had just prepared for Secretary of the Interior Bill Clark, a longtime California friend of President Reagan, Interior Department speechwriter Bob Walker said, "But government has a partnership with [the ranching] business. We're beating on that approach of partnership because the Secretary likes it . . . It's gotten so I don't put a draft speech on the Secretary's desk without the word 'partnership' in it"; Bob Walker, interview with author, September 6, 1984, Washington, D.C.

17. "Proclamation 4881—National Farm-City Week," October 29, 1981, *Public Papers of the Presidents of the United States: Ronald Reagan, 1981* (Washington, D.C.: Government Printing Office, 1982), p. 999.

18. "Address before the Japanese Diet in Tokyo," November 11, 1983, *Public Papers of the Presidents of the United States: Ronald Reagan, 1983,* 2 vols. (Washington, D.C.: Government Printing Office, 1985), 2: 1578.

19. "Toasts of the President and Prime Minister Zenko Suzuki of Japan at the State Dinner," May 7, 1981, *Public Papers of Reagan, 1981*, p. 411.

20. Richard Reeves, *American Journey: Traveling with Tocqueville in Search of "Democracy in America"* (New York: Simon and Schuster, 1982), p. 197.

21. Ibid., p. 198.

22. Ibid., p. 199.

23. Sigmund Freud, *New Introductory Lectures on Psycho-Analysis* (1932), trans. W. J. H. Sprott, in *The Works of Sigmund Freud*, ed. Robert Maynard Hutchins (Chicago: Encyclopedia Britannica, 1952), pp. 875, 831, 837, 835.

24. Ibid., p. 875.

25. Ibid., p. 878.

26. "Remarks at the Annual Convention of the National Association of Evangelicals in Orlando, Florida," March 8, 1983, *Public Papers of Ronald Reagan, 1983,* 1: 362.

27. Ibid.

28. Ibid.

29. Ibid., p. 363.

30. Ibid.

31. Ibid., pp. 363–364.

32. Ibid., p. 364.

33. "Address at Commencement Exercises at Eureka College in Illinois," May 9, 1982, *Public Papers of the Presidents of the United States: Ronald Reagan, 1982* (Washington, D.C.: Government Printing Office, 1983), 1:582.

34. "Address to Members of the British Parliament," June 8, 1982, ibid., p. 744.

35. Presidential speechwriter Anthony R. Dolan, interview with au-

thor, December 3, 1984, Washington, D.C. All of the following quotations of Dolan are from this interview.

36. Tocqueville, *Democracy in America*, 2: 3.

37. However, Dewey's *Theory of Valuation* (Chicago: University of Chicago Press, 1939) is silent on the question of assigning ethical value to efforts that fail to produce results.

38. Tocqueville, *Democracy in America*, 2: 27.

39. Max Weber, "Politics as a Vocation," in *From Max Weber: Essays in Sociology*, ed. and trans. Hans Gerth and C. Wright Mills (New York: Oxford University Press, 1946), pp. 77–128.

40. Ibid., p. 123.

41. Arthur Miller, *Death of a Salesman*, in *Arthur Miller's Collected Plays* (New York: Viking, 1959), p. 212.

42. Presidential speechwriter Peter Robinson, interview with author, April 6, 1984, Washington, D.C.

43. April 13, 1984, *Weekly Compilation of Presidential Documents, 1984*, vol. 20 (Washington, D.C.: Government Printing Office), 550.

44. See Herbert Kaufman, *The Forest Ranger* (Baltimore: Johns Hopkins University Press, 1960), for a stimulating discussion of building identification.

45. As it was in Tocqueville's time; see *Democracy in America*, 1: 106–107 and 283–290.

46. *Steward Machine Co. v. Davis*, 301 U.S. 548, 590, 81 L. Ed. 1279, 1292 (1937).

47. The estimate for 1984 was 649,000 lawyers; Barbara A. Curran, "American Lawyers in the 1980s: A Profession in Transition," *Law & Society Review*, 20 (1986), 20.

48. Herbert McClosky and Alida Brill demonstrate and explain an astonishing consensus among lawyers with regard to free speech, religious liberty, due process, tolerance, and privacy in their *Dimensions of Tolerance: What Americans Believe about Civil Liberties* (New York: Russell Sage Foundation, 1983). Their table 6.2, p. 249, shows that 83 percent of the lawyers surveyed scored high on the civil liberties scale.

49. Tocqueville made this same observation throughout *Democracy in America*, but esp. in 1:310–326 and 2:21–29 and 133–135.

50. At last count there were 321,627 clergy with a congregation; *Statistical Abstract of the United States: 1987*, table 74.

51. Henry Adams, *The Education of Henry Adams* (New York: Modern Library, 1931), p. 211.

52 The professional business schools also avoid such moral and intellectual discipline. The School of Business Adminstration at the University of California, Berkeley, is typical. Although it offers more than 150 courses, none deals systematically with what Peter L. Berger calls "a theory of capitalism"—a comprehensive account of the connection between cap-

italism and morals, political structure, values, culture, and innovation; Berger, *The Capitalist Revolution: Fifty Propositions about Prosperity, Equality, and Liberty* (New York: Basic Books, 1986).

53. For example, Lincoln liked to speak to regiments that were being mustered out of service so that he could express the purposes of the war. In his talk to the 166th Ohio Regiment on August 22, 1864, he said: "I beg you to remember this, not merely for my sake, but for yours. I happen temporarily to occupy this big White House. I am a living witness that any one of your children may look to come here as my father's child has. It is in order that each of you may have through this free government which we have enjoyed, an open field and a fair chance for your industry, enterprise and intelligence; that you may all have equal privileges in the race of life, with all its desirable human aspirations. It is for this the struggle should be maintained, that we may not lose our birthright"; Abraham Lincoln, *Selected Speeches, Messages, and Letters*, ed. T. Harry Williams (New York: Holt, Rinehart and Winston, 1957), p. 271.

54. Peter Robinson, interview with author, August 27, 1984, Washington, D.C.

55. Ronald Reagan, "A Time for Choosing," October 27, 1964, in *Ronald Reagan Talks to America*, intro. Richard M. Scaife (Old Greenwich, Conn.: Devin Adair, 1983), pp. 3–18.

56. Presidential speechwriter Bentley Elliott, interview with author, June 10, 1985, Washington, D.C.

57. Presidential speechwriter Al Meyer, interview with author, November 30, 1984, Washington, D.C.

58. Richard F. Fenno, Jr., "President-Cabinet Relations: A Pattern and a Case Study," *American Political Science Review*, 52 (June 1958), 388–405.

59. The subject areas of the cabinet councils were economic affairs, natural resources and environment, commerce and trade, human resources, food and agriculture, legal policy, and management and administration.

60. HUD Public Affairs Officer Jayne Gallagher, interview with author, June 14, 1985, Washington, D.C. All of the following quotations of Gallagher are from this interview.

61. "The Times Turns 5, Defies Odds, Confounds Critics," *Washington Times*, May 18, 1987, p. 1A. The publication's stated objective was "to give the conservative option a clear and quality voice in the information mix" (p. 9B).

62. Tocqueville, *Democracy in America*, 1:56.

63. That the conventional language of self-interest may deprive Americans of a meaninfgul understanding of their better aspirations and actions is the theme of Robert N. Bellah, Richard Madsen, William M. Sullivan, Ann Swidler, and Steven M. Tipton, *Habits of the Heart: Individual and Commitment in American Life* (Berkeley and Los Angeles: Uni-

versity of California Press, 1985). The book raises sensible and profound issues about the moral sentiments of a free people: "Perhaps life is not a race whose only goal is being foremost . . . Perhaps enduring commitment to those we love and civil friendship toward our fellow citizens are preferable to restless competition and anxious self-defense" (p. 295). Ironically, although the authors assume that presidential rhetoric can make a difference in how Americans feel about themselves, they caricature and dismiss the Reagan rhetoric: "with Ronald Reagan's assertion that 'we the people' are 'a special interest group,' our concern for the economy being the only thing that holds us together, we have reached a kind of end of the line. The citizen has been swallowed up in 'economic man' " (p. 271).

64. Jack Citrin and Donald Philip Green use National Election Studies data to show an "impressive" surge in government and attribute it in large part to the people's perception of Reagan's "strong leadership"; "Presidential Leadership and the Resurgence of Trust in Government," *British Journal of Political Science,* 16 (October 1986), 431–453. The data did not allow them to inquire into the source of that perception, but in my opinion it was the president's rhetoric.

10. Nine Presidents in Search of a Modern Presidency

1. This section is adapted from my "Continuity and Change in the Modern Presidency," in *The New American Political System,* ed. Anthony King (Washington, D.C.: American Enterprise Institute, 1978), pp. 40–61.

2. William Hopkins, Kennedy Library Oral History, June 3, 1964, John F. Kennedy Library, Boston. I am indebted to Mr. Hopkins for expanding on his oral history in a personal interview.

3. For a discussion that treats the exigencies of international power politics and other aspects of the international and national environment of the modern presidency as centrally (but not exclusively) responsible for the rise of what I am here calling the modern presidency, see Franz Schurmann, *The Logic of World Power: An Inquiry into the Origins, Currents, and Contributions of World Politics* (New York: Random House, 1974).

4. Note, for example, Senator George Hoar's comment that in the mid-nineteenth century congressmen "would have considered as a personal affront a private message from the White House expressing a desire that they should adopt any course in the discharge of their legislative duties that they did not approve," and similar congressional assertions quoted in John T. Patterson, "The Rise of Presidential Power before World War II," *Law and Contemporary Problems,* 40 (Spring 1976), 39–57. The presidents from McKinley to Hoover were in general more disposed to take an interest in legislative outcomes than were their nineteenth-century predecessors and in this respect anticipated the great increase in sustained presidential involvement in the legislative process that began with Franklin Roosevelt;

Stephen Wayne, *The Legislative Presidency* (New York: Harper and Row, 1978), pp. 13–16.

5. Charles L. Black, Jr., "Some Thoughts on the Veto," *Law and Contemporary Problems*, 40 (Spring 1976), 87–101.

6. For general background on the initial months of Roosevelt's first term see Frank Freidel, *Franklin D. Roosevelt: Launching the New Deal* (Boston: Little, Brown, 1973); E. P. Herring, *Presidential Leadership: The Political Relations of Congress and the Chief Executive* (New York: Rinehart, 1940).

7. Hopkins, Kennedy Library Oral History. Also see L. A. Sussman, *Dear FDR: A Study in Political Letter Writing* (Totawa, N.J.: Bedminister Press, 1963).

8. Merlin Gustafson, "The President's Mail," *Presidential Studies Quarterly*, 8 (1978), 36.

9. Patrick Anderson, *The President's Men: White House Assistants of Franklin D. Roosevelt, Harry S. Truman, Dwight D. Eisenhower, John F. Kennedy, Lyndon B. Johnson* (Garden City, N.Y.: Doubleday, 1968); Stephen Hess, *Organizing the Presidency* (Washington, D.C.: Brookings Institution, 1976).

10. President's Committee on Administrative Management, *Report with Studies of Administrative Management in the Federal Government* (Washington, D.C., 1937); B. D. Karl, *Executive Reorganization and Reform on the New Deal: The Genesis of Administrative Management, 1900–1939* (Cambridge, Mass.: Harvard University Press, 1963); R. Polenberg, *Reorganizing Roosevelt's Government* (Cambridge, Mass.: Boston University Press, 1966); Peri E. Arnold, *Making the Managerial Presidency: Comprehensive Reorganization Planning, 1905–1980* (Princeton: Princeton University Press, 1986), chap. 4.

11. Hugh Heclo, *Studying the Presidency* (New York: Ford Foundation, 1977), p. 37; Wayne, *Legislative Presidency*, pp. 220–221.

12. Harold Smith, Diary, Franklin D. Roosevelt Library, Hyde Park, N.Y. Much of the discussion of the Bureau of the Budget and its successor agency, the Office of Management and Budget, in this chapter relies on the comprehensive archivally based discussion of Larry Berman, *The Office of Management and Budget and the Presidency* (Princeton: Princeton University Press, 1979).

13. Alonzo Hamby, *Beyond the New Deal: Harry S. Truman and American Liberalism* (New York: Columbia University Press, 1973).

14. Compare Hamby's exploration, in Chapter 2 of this volume, of the hypothesis that one source of Truman's adult political style was a reaction to his feelings as a child and young man that he was insufficiently masculine.

15. Harry S. Truman, PSF, Historical County Judge Address, 1929–33, box 239, HSTL. Here is Truman on the importance of constitutionalism

and leadership in the development of the Constitution: "From the Magna Carta to the Declaration of Independence and the American Constitution is a space of some 560 years, and every step forward was the result of the ideals and self-sacrifice of some great leader . . . We have an idealist in the White House now, the first we've had since Woodrow Wilson, and he's going to show us how to pull ourselves out of our present woes"; Camp Pike, Arkansas, August 1933 (on this occasion Truman was "commandant" of a patriotic gathering of youths, probably a regular program of a veterans' organization). Also see his undated Washington's Birthday remarks (c. 1932) to a Masonic group: George Washington "was a human, powerful, straightforward man. He liked horse races, liked to take a chance in friendly games, liked a good drink of liquor once in a while and when necessity called for it could swear as well and as effectively as Alexander, Caesar, Napoleon, or any other great commander of men. Men handled in the mass expect the boss to cuss them out when they need it and they like it."

16. Fred I. Greenstein, *The Hidden-Hand Presidency: Eisenhower as Leader* (New York: Basic Books, 1982). Also see Richard Immerman, "Eisenhower and Dulles: Who Made the Decisions?" *Political Psychology*, 1 (Autumn 1979), 21–38.

17. Ann Whitman to Milton Eisenhower, August 28, 1956, Name Series, box 13, DDEL.

18. Richard E. Neustadt, *Presidential Power: The Politics of Leadership* (New York: Wiley, 1960). Subsequent editions of this classic analysis include a postscript on Kennedy (undated) and additional chapters on later presidents (with the subtitles *The Politics of Leadership with Reflections on Johnson and Nixon*, 1976; and *The Politics of Leadership from FDR to Carter*, 1980). For a sympathetic clarification of an expansion on Neustadt's argument see Peter Sperlich, "Bargaining and Overload: An Essay on Presidential Power," in *The Presidency*, ed. Aaron Wildavsky (Boston: Little, Brown, 1969), pp. 168–192, and in *Perspectives on the Presidency*, ed. Aaron Wildavsky (Boston: Little, Brown, 1975), pp. 406–430.

19. For the hearings of the Jackson Committee see U.S. Senate, Subcommittee on National Policy Machinery of the Committee on Government Operations, *Organizing for National Security*, 3 vols. (Washington: Government Printing Office, 1961); Henry M. Jackson, ed., *The National Council: Jackson Subcommittee Papers on Policy Making at the Presidential Level* (New York: Praeger, 1965). Neustadt's "Memorandum on Staffing the President-Elect," October 30, 1960, is in Pre-Presidential Papers, President's Office Files, Staff Memoranda, box 1072, Kennedy Library.

20. For good discussions of trends in scholarly evaluation of the presidency see William G. Andrews, "The Presidency, Congress, and Constitutional Theory," in Wildavsky, *Perspectives on the Presidency*, pp. 24–44; Thomas Cronin, "The Textbook Presidency," in *Perspectives on the Pres-*

idency: A Collection, ed. Stanley Back and George T. Sulzner (Lexington, Mass.: D. C. Heath, 1974), pp. 54–74.

21. Quoted in Carl M. Brauer, "John F. Kennedy," in *The Presidents: A Reference History,* ed. Henry F. Graff (New York: Scribner's, 1984), p. 578.

22. Compare the view of discretionary presidential policy-making in Arthur M. Schlesinger, Jr., *The Imperial Presidency* (Boston: Houghton Mifflin, 1973), with that implicit in *The Age of Jackson* (Boston: Little, Brown, 1946); *The Age of Roosevelt,* 3 vols. (Boston: Houghton Mifflin, 1957, 1959, 1960); and *A Thousand Days: John F. Kennedy in the White House* (Boston: Houghton Mifflin, 1965).

In *The Imperial Presidency* Schlesinger rediscovers and pays homage to the main scholar of the presidency whose works focused on the chief executive's "aggrandizement of power," Edward Corwin. Given that Schlesinger and the many other liberal writers on the presidency became preoccupied with the dangers inherent in the institution only when they became distressed about particular policies pursued by Johnson and Nixon, it is instructive to note the development of Corwin's own thinking. Corwin was sufficiently enthusiastic about strong presidential leadership to be a chief academic supporter of Franklin Roosevelt's proposal to expand the size of the Supreme Court in order to reverse its proclivity to strike down New Deal legislation. The press of the day widely viewed Corwin as a major candidate for membership on the proposed "packed" Court.

In the event, "Court packing" never took place; Roosevelt soon had numerous openings to fill, and he never nominated Corwin. In 1940 the first edition of Corwin's textbook criticizing the rise of presidential power appeared. Without assuming a crass quid-pro-quo motivation on Corwin's part, one can reasonably surmise that his substantive evaluation of FDR had sharply altered after 1937 and that this change—like the changes in the 1960s liberals' views in response to presidential performance in office—was critical in reshaping his overall evaluation of the degree to which the institution itself was appropriately performing its constitutional responsibilities. Edward S. Corwin, *The President, Office and Powers, 1987–1957: History and Analysis of Practice and Opinion,* 4th ed. (New York: New York University Press, 1957). A posthumous fifth edition (1984) contains chapter postscripts by Randall W. Bland, Theodore T. Hindson, and Jack W. Peltason.

23. Gerald R. Ford, "Imperiled, Not Imperial," *Time,* November 10, 1980, pp. 30–31.

24. In August 1983 a Harris survey asked a cross section of Americans to name the president who inspired most confidence in the White House. The four presidents who received the highest ratings were Kennedy (40 percent), Franklin Roosevelt (23 percent), and Eisenhower and Truman (8 percent each); Hedley Donovan, *Roosevelt to Reagan: A Reporter's En-*

counters with Nine Presidents (New York: Harper and Row, 1985), p. 85.

25. For examples of revisionist critiques of Kennedy see Garry Wills, *The Kennedy Imprisonment: A Meditation on Power* (Boston: Little, Brown, 1982); Bruce Miroff, *Pragmatic Illusions: The Presidential Politics of John F. Kennedy* (New York: David McKay, 1976).

26. B. S. Greenberg and E. B. Parker, eds., *The Kennedy Assassination and the American Public: Social Communication in Crisis* (Stanford: Stanford University Press, 1965).

27. "Attitudes toward the Presidency: A National Opinion Summary," conducted by the Gallup Organization for PBS station WHYY's production "Every Four Years"; quoted in Hugh Heclo, "Introduction: The Presidential Illusion," *The Illusion of Presidential Government*, ed. Hugh Heclo and Lester M. Salamon (Boulder, Colo.: Westview Press, 1981), p. 5.

28. Austin Ranney, *Channels of Power: The Impact of Television on American Politics* (New York: Basic Books, 1983); Burns W. Roper, "Trends in Attitudes toward Television and Other Media: A Twenty-six Year Review," in *Public Attitudes toward Television and Other Media in a Time of Change* (New York: Television Information Office, n.d. [c. 1985]), pp. 1–5; David C. Hallin, "The Rise of the Ten-Second Sound Bite: Changing Conventions in Television Coverage of the Presidency, 1965–1985" (Paper delivered at the annual meeting of the Southern Political Science Association, November 1985).

29. For an instructive analysis of how Kennedy used live press conferences to win public support, and more generally of the consequences of grounding presidential leadership on appeals to the public rather than bargaining in the Washington community, see Samuel Kernell, *Going Public: New Strategies of Presidential Leadership* (Washington, D.C.: CQ Press, 1986).

30. Richard E. Neustadt, "Approaches to Staffing the Presidency: Notes on FDR and JFK," *American Science Review*, 59 (1963), 855–864. For scholarly efforts to classify types of presidential advising arrangements, see Richard Tanner Johnson, *Managing the White House* (New York: Harper and Row, 1974); Alexander L. George, *Presidential Decisionmaking in Foreign Policy* (Boulder, Colo.: Westview Press, 1980).

31. On the origins of project Apollo see Theodore Sorensen, Kennedy Library Oral History. When Kennedy announced the project, T. Keith Glennon, the first National Aeronautics and Space Administration head, wrote in his diary: "This single speech is likely to cost the people of this nation at least an extra 20 billion dollars and probably much more to race an uncertain opponent on an uncertain course toward an uncertain goal"; Glennon Diary, May 26, 1961, DDEL.

32. For a useful guide to the voluminous literature assessing Kennedy's missile crisis leadership, see Ned Lebow, "Cuban Missile Crisis: Reading the Lessons Correctly," *Political Science Quarterly*, 98 (1983), 431–458. For the first assessment of the secret tape recordings of the missile

crisis decision makers see Marc Trachtenberg's "The Influence of Nuclear Weapons in the Cuban Missile Crisis," *International Security*, 10 (Summer 1985), 137–163, and "White House Tapes and Minutes of the Cuban Missile Crisis," ibid., pp. 165–185. See also Thomas G. Paterson and William J. Brophy, "October Missiles and November Elections: The Cuban Missile Crisis and American Politics, 1962," *Journal of American History*, 73 (June 1986), 87–119.

33. Desmond Ball, *Politics and Force Levels: The Strategic Missile Program of the Kennedy Administration* (Berkeley and Los Angeles: University of California Press, 1980).

34. I. M. Destler, *Presidents, Bureaucrats, and Foreign Policy* (Princeton: Princeton University Press, 1972); idem, "National Security Management: What Have Presidents Wrought?" *Political Science Quarterly*, 95 (1980–81), 573–588; Bert A. Rockman, "America's Departments of State: Irregular and Regular Syndromes of Policy Making," *American Political Science Review*, 75 (December 1981), 911–927.

35. "LBJ Goes to War: 1964–65," part 4 of the documentary "Vietnam: A Television History."

36. Larry Berman, *Planning a Tragedy: The Americanization of the War in Vietnam* (New York: Norton, 1982).

37. Charles E. Lindblom, "The Science of Muddling Through," *Public Administration Review*, 19 (Spring 1959), 79–88; also David Braybrooke and Charles E. Lindblom, *A Strategy for Decision: Policy Evaluation as a Social Process* (New York: Free Press, 1963).

38. For a careful examination of whether the guns-and-butter policy stemmed from Johnson's blind spots as a policy analyst or from uncertainties inherent in the situation Johnson faced, see Ronald F. King, "The President and Fiscal Policy in 1966: The Year Taxes Were Not Raised," *Polity*, 17 (Summer 1985), 685–714.

39. On Johnson's use of task forces and related matters see W. D. Carey, "Presidential Staffing in the Sixties and Seventies," *Public Administration Review*, 29 (Fall 1969), 450–458.

40. Byron E. Shafer, *The Quiet Revolution: The Struggle for the Democratic Party and the Shaping of Post-Reform Politics* (New York: Russell Sage Foundation, 1983); Nelson W. Polsby, *Consequences of Party Reform* (New York: Oxford University Press, 1983). The post-1968 changes appear to have caught on because of a long-term decline in the strength of traditional state and local parties, and hence in grass-roots resistance to the national reforms. See David Truman, "Party Reform, Party Atrophy, and Constitutional Change: Some Reflections," *Political Science Quarterly*, 99 (1984–85), 637–655.

41. Joel D. Aberbach and Bert A. Rockman, "Clashing Beliefs within the Executive Branch," *American Political Science Review*, 70 (June 1976), 456–468.

42. On Nixon's effort to institute the supercabinet and otherwise concentrate presidential capacity to shape policy administratively, see Richard P. Nathan, *The Plot That Failed: Nixon and the Administrative Presidency* (New York: Wiley, 1975); see also Nathan's revised edition, with attention to administrative policy-making in the Reagan presidency, *The Adminstrative Presidency* (New York: Wiley, 1983).

43. John P. Leacocos, "Kissinger's Apparat," *Foreign Policy*, 5 (Winter 1971–72), 3–28; I. M. Destler, "The Nixon System: A Further Look," *Foreign Service Journal*, 51 (February 1974), 9–15, 28–29.

44. Hugh Heclo, "OMB and the Presidency: The Problem of Neutral Competence," *Public Interest*, 38 (Winter 1975), 80–98.

45. John Hebers, *New York Times*, March 4, 5, and 6, 1973. The gist of the series is captured in the headline and runover head of the March 4 article: "Nixon's Presidency: Expansion of Power . . . Likely to Transform the National Government."

46. For a good statement of the rationale for eschewing a chief of staff see Richard E. Neustadt, "The Constraining of the President: The Presidency after Watergate," *British Journal of Political Science*, 4 (October 1974), 383–397.

47. Thomas E. Cronin, "The Swelling of the Presidency," *Saturday Review*, Feburary 1973, pp. 30–36.

48. Neustadt, *Presidential Power*, chaps. 2, 3.

49. For a thorough discussion of current legislation and precedents bearing on the separation of powers, see Louis Fisher, *Constitutional Conflicts between Congress and the President* (Princeton: Princeton University Press, 1985).

50. *A Discussion with Gerald R. Ford: The American Presidency* (Washington, D.C.: American Enterprise Institute, 1977), p. 4.

51. Roger Porter, *Presidential Decision Making: The Economic Policy Board* (New York: Cambridge University Press, 1980).

52. For a valuable account of Carter in general and the media's portrayal of his victories and defeats in primaries as the triumphant procession of a front-runner, see Betty Glad, *Jimmy Carter in Search of the Great White House* (New York: Norton, 1980).

53. Aaron Wildavsky, *Speaking Truth to Power: The Art and Craft of Policy Analysis* (Boston: Little, Brown, 1979), pp. 235–251.

54. Lawrence E. Lynn, Jr., and David DeF. Whitman, *The President as Policymaker: Jimmy Carter and Welfare Reform* (Philadelphia: Temple University Press, 1981).

55. Though commendable in its aim to eliminate a legacy of American empire building in Latin America, the Panama Canal initative was, as has often been said, a second-term issue. Ronald Reagan was able to use the canal "giveaway" as a 1980 campaign issue, and treaty ratification politics preempted time, energy, and political capital that might have been

invested in enacting domestic legislation; George D. Moffett III, *The Limits of Victory: The Ratification of the Panama Canal Treaties* (Ithaca, N.Y.: Cornell University Press, 1978).

56. William B. Quandt, *Camp David: Peacemaking and Politics* (Washington, D.C.: Brookings Institution, 1986).

57. Compare Zbigniew Brzezinski, *Power and Principle* (New York: Farrar, Straus and Giroux, 1983), with Cyrus Vance, *Hard Choices* (New York: Simon and Schuster, 1983).

58. Rowland Evans and Robert Novak, *The Reagan Revolution* (New York: E.P. Dutton, 1981).

59. For an expansion on my assertions here about Reagan's political development and the 1980 election, see Fred I. Greenstein, ed., *The Reagan Presidency: An Early Appraisal* (Baltimore: Johns Hopkins University Press, 1983), chaps. 1, 6.

60. For a systematic analysis of the widespread tendency to misinterpret the 1980 findings as a reflection of strong approval of Reagan and his policies, see Stanley Kelley, Jr., *Interpreting Elections* (Princeton: Princeton University Press, 1983).

61. Edwin Meese III, remarks at the Conference on Leadership in the Modern Presidency, Woodrow Wilson School, Princeton University, April 3, 1987.

62. Hugh Heclo and Rudolph G. Penner, "Fiscal and Political Strategy in the Reagan Presidency," in Greenstein, *Reagan Presidency*, p. 39.

63. Alexander Haig, *Caveat: Realism, Reagan, and Foreign Policy* (New York: Macmillan, 1984); David A. Stockman, *The Triumph of Politics: Why the Reagan Revolution Failed* (New York: Harper & Row, 1986).

64. Report of the President's Special Review Board, February 26, 1987 (New Executive Office Building, Washington, D.C., February 26, 1987), app. B, p. 64; reprinted as *The Tower Commission Report* (New York: Bantam Books and Times Books, 1987), p. 267.

65. Stockman, *Triumph of Politics*; William Greider, *The Education of David Stockman and Other Americans* (New York: E.P. Dutton, 1983). On the absence of research evidence for the supply-side economic theories on which the Reagan tax cut was based, see Heclo and Penner, "Fiscal and Political Strategy," pp. 21–47. For a scholarly analysis of the effects of the Reagan policies, see Michael Comiskey, "Has Reaganomics Worked?" *Polity*, forthcoming.

66. Nathan, *Administrative Presidency*.

67. Richard Nathan, "The Reagan Presidency in Domestic Affairs," in Greenstein, *Reagan Presidency*, pp. 48–81; Michael E. Kraft and Norman J. Vig, "Environmental Policy in the Reagan Presidency," *Political Science Quarterly*, 99 (1984), 415–448.

68. John P. Burke, "Presidential Influence and the Budget Process: A Comparative Analysis," in *The President and Public Policy Making*, ed.

George Edwards, Steven Shul, and Norman Thomas (Pittsburgh: University of Pittsburgh Press, 1985), pp. 71–94.

69. David A. Stockman, Interview, Station WHYY, Philadelphia, November 12, 1986.

70. Jeffrey H. Birnbaum and Alan S. Murray, *Showdown at Gucci Gulch: Lawmakers, Lobbyists, and the Unlikely Triumph of Tax Reform* (New York: Random House, 1987).

71. Samuel Kernell, *Going Public: New Strategies of Presidential Leadership* (Washington, D.C.: Congressional Quarterly Press, 1987).

72. Telephone conversation between Dwight D. Eisenhower and Lyndon B. Johnson re Civil Rights Bill, August 22, 1957, DDE Diaries, DDEL.

73. *Toward a More Responsible Two-Party System: A Report of the Committee on Political Parties, American Political Science Association* (New York: Reinhart, 1950), p. 94.

74. Hugh Heclo, "Introduction: The Presidential Illusion," in *The Illusion of Presidential Government*, ed. Hugh Heclo and Lester M. Salamon (Boulder, Colo.: Westview Press, 1981), pp. 1–20.

75. George Reedy, *The Twilight of the Presidency* (New York: World, 1970).

76. Robert L. Gallucci, *Neither Peace nor Honor: The Politics of U.S. Military Policy in Vietnam* (Baltimore: Johns Hopkins University Press, 1975), p. 7.

77. The principal writings are Johnson, *Managing the White House*, and George, *Presidential Decisionmaking in Foreign Policy*.

78. David S. Broder, "Hail to the Chiefs," *Washington Post National Weekly Edition*, February 3, 1986, p. 4. The proceedings of this conference appear in Samuel Kernell and Samuel Popkin, eds., *Chief of Staff: Twenty-five Years of Managing the Presidency* (Berkeley and Los Angeles: University of California Press, 1986).

Acknowledgments

This book incorporates, in revised form, papers presented and discussed at a symposium supported by the Henry Luce Foundation, the Conference on Leadership in the Modern Presidency, held at the Woodrow Wilson School, Princeton University, April 3, 1987. The formal commentators on the papers were associates of the nine modern presidents from Franklin D. Roosevelt to Ronald Reagan: Wilbur J. Cohen, Roosevelt; Ken Hechler, Truman; Andrew J. Goodpaster, Eisenhower; Nicholas DeB. Katzenbach, Kennedy; John P. Roche, Johnson; H. R. Haldeman, Nixon; Richard B. Cheney, Ford; Jack H. Watson, Carter; and Richard Wirthlin and Edwin Meese III, Reagan. Vice-President George Bush presented general remarks on leadership in the modern presidency.

Other participants in the conference included R. Douglas Arnold, Dom Bonafede, William P. Bundy, John Burke, Thomas Cronin, Jameson Doig, George Edwards, Jeffrey Fishel, Irwin Gertzog, Betty Glad, Michael Grossman, Mary Jane Hickey, Charles Jacob, John Kessel, Dick Kirschten, Martha Kumar, Deborah Larson, Henry Luce III, Annabel McHugh, Jerome P. McHugh, Andrea Mitchell, Diane Monson, Richard Nathan, Michael Nelson, Richard E. Neustadt, Bradley H. Patterson, Jr., Joseph A. Pika III, Richard Pious, Harry Sayen, Robert Shogan, Charles Tidmarch, Jeffrey Tulis, and Stephen J. Wayne.

Dean Donald E. Stokes of the Woodrow Wilson School provided unflagging support for the conference and symposium and for leadership and presidency studies at Princeton in general. Amanda Thornton was tireless, efficient, and sensitive in organizing the conference and coordinating the editorial aspects of this volume.

Index